Risk Analysis and Management of Petroleum Exploration Ventures

by Peter R. Rose
Managing Partner
Rose & Associates, LLP
Austin, Texas, U.S.A.

AAPG Methods in Exploration Series, No. 12

Published by
The American Association of Petroleum Geologists
Tulsa, Oklahoma, U.S.A.
Printed in the U.S.A.

Copyright © 2001 by
The American Association of Petroleum Geologists
All Rights Reserved
Printed in the U.S.A.
Published May 2001; second printing, March 2002; third printing, January 2003; fourth printing, January 2004

ISBN: 0-89181-662-3 hardbound; 0-89181-663-1 softbound

AAPG grants permission for a single photocopy of an item from this publication for personal use. Authorization for additional copies of items from this publication for personal or internal use is granted by AAPG provided that the base fee of $3.50 per copy and $.50 per page is paid directly to the Copyright Clearance Center, 222 Rosewood Drive, Danvers, Massachusetts 01923 (phone: 978/750-8400). Fees are subject to change. Any form of electronic or digital scanning or other digital transformation of portions of this publication into computer-readable and/or transmittable form for personal or corporate use requires special permission from, and is subject to fee charges by, the AAPG.

Association Editor: Neil F. Hurley
Geoscience Director: Robert C. Millspaugh
Publications Manager: Kenneth M. Wolgemuth
Managing Editor, Publications: Anne H. Thomas
Special Publications Editor: Hazel Rowena Mills
Cover Design: Carl Brune
Cover Illustration: Glenn Godsey
Oil-rig Image: Helmerich & Payne, Inc.
Production: Custom Editorial Productions, Inc., Cincinnati, Ohio

THE AMERICAN ASSOCIATION OF PETROLEUM GEOLOGISTS (AAPG) DOES NOT ENDORSE OR RECOMMEND ANY PRODUCTS OR SERVICES THAT MAY BE CITED, USED, OR DISCUSSED IN AAPG PUBLICATIONS OR IN PRESENTATIONS AT EVENTS ASSOCIATED WITH THE AAPG.

This and other AAPG publications are available from:

The AAPG Bookstore
P.O. Box 979
Tulsa, OK 74101-0979
Telephone: 1-918-584-2555 or 1-800-364-AAPG (USA)
Fax: 1-918-560-2652 or 1-800-898-2274 (USA)
www.aapg.org

Geological Society Publishing House
Unit 7, Brassmill Enterprise Centre
Brassmill Lane, Bath, U.K.
BA1 3JN
Tel +44-1225-445046
Fax +44-1225-442836
www.geolsoc.org.uk

Canadian Society of Petroleum Geologists
No. 160, 540 Fifth Avenue S.W.
Calgary, Alberta T2P 0M2
Canada
Tel. 1-403-264-5610
Fax 1-403-264-5898
www.cspg.org

Affiliated East-West Press Private Ltd.
G-1/16 Ansari Road   Darya Ganj
New Delhi 110 002
India
Tel +91 11 3279113
Fax +91 11 3260538
e-mail: affiliat@nda.vsnl.n

AAPG

wishes to thank

Japan National Oil Corporation

for graciously allowing the publication in this book

of material that Dr. Peter R. Rose

originally presented in two reports

to JNOC

Preface

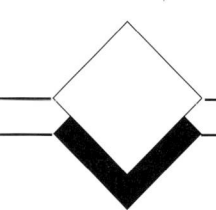

In the summer of 1996, I was invited by Japan National Oil Company (JNOC) to prepare a report summarizing the current status of exploration risk analysis as practiced by modern international oil and gas companies—the main concepts, procedures, and problems as I had observed them during my deep involvement in that area during the late 1980s and 1990s. Following the presentation and acceptance of that report in March 1997, JNOC asked me to prepare a companion report covering risk analysis of exploration plays, which was presented in Tokyo in March 1998. Later that year, encouraged by the American Association of Petroleum Geologists' (AAPG) Publications Department, I asked JNOC whether they would be willing to release the two reports, which would be merged into a single AAPG publication. JNOC gave their official blessing in August 1999, and this book is the result. I wish to thank JNOC for their far-sighted and generous spirit in sharing this material with the international E&P community, JNOC's Mr. Yasuhisa Kanehara, Director of Exploration, for his interest and support, and Mr. Masami Ishizaka, JNOC Executive Vice President, for formal release of English-language rights to the AAPG.

I have consulted and taught in the field of exploration risk analysis for more than 15 years. After being indoctrinated in the 1970s through courses taught by Paul Newendorp and John Cozzolino, as well as through their articles, I began to apply rudimentary risk analysis principles to exploration projects and to measure the predictive accuracy of prospectors with whom I was working during 1976–1980. In 1984, I began team-teaching an annual AAPG school on the topic with Bob Megill (ex-Exxon) and Ed Capen (ARCO). Starting in 1990, I began to devote the bulk of my professional practice to the now rapidly expanding risk analysis specialty, including extensive team-teaching with Ed Capen and Bob Clapp from 1992 to 1998.

The following volume is an overview of this important aspect of petroleum exploration and development. Many of the concepts and techniques were originated by professional colleagues in other companies and shared through many conferences and publications (most sponsored by the AAPG) as well as consulting assignments. The following people deserve special mention as significant contributors to risk analysis as practiced in the late 1990s:

Jeff Brown, David Cook, Eric Dion, Mike Effler (Mobil)
Laurens Garenstroom, Rien Nederlof, the late Dieter Schluijk, Harry Thomsen, Daniel Zweidler (Shell)
Bob Baker, the late Harry Gehman, Bill James, Bob Megill, David White (Exxon)
Richard Campbell, Ed Capen, Bob Clapp, Marlan Downey (ARCO)
Tom Burnett, Jim MacKay (Texaco)
Bill Haskett, Ace Alexander, Jerry Lohr, Bob Merrill, Jack Schanck (Unocal)
Andrew Conway, Julia Ericsson, Greg Leveille, Jim McColgin (Conoco)
Gerard Demaison, Bob Otis, Nahum Schneidermann (Chevron)
Peter Carragher, Gary Citron, Glenn McMaster, Richard Steinmetz (Amoco)
Francis Harper, David Roberts (British Petroleum)
Roger Holeywell (Marathon)
Richard McCrossan, Ken Roy (Geological Survey of Canada)
Gordon Kaufmann (M.I.T.)
Brett Edwards, Phil Jefferies, Steve McIntyre (Ampolex Ltd.)
Andrew Freeman, Barry Goldstein, Rhodri Johns, Lloyd Taylor (SANTOS)
Mark McLane, David Sanders (Pioneer)
Mike Andersen, Henry Pettingill, Ricardo Vines (YPF-Repsol)
John Campbell, Chap Cronquist, John Howell (Consultants)

However, most of the present publication draws on concepts and procedures that emerged and evolved during the AAPG school, "Managing and Assessing Exploration Risk," team-taught from 1984 until 1998 by Ed Capen, Bob Clapp, Bob Megill, and myself. I acknowledge their substantial contributions to this volume with admiration, gratitude, and many pleasant recollections.

Roger Holeywell, Daniel Zweidler, and Chap Cronquist reviewed the manuscript, to its great benefit. My colleagues at R&A, Jeff Brown, Gary Citron, and Mark McLane, improved the book through their encouragement, critical review, and suggestions. Any errors of commission or omission, however, are entirely my own. My profound thanks go to Ms. Elizabeth Ethridge for her usual excellence and cheerfulness in preparing the original reports for JNOC, as well as the merged final manuscript for publication. Ms. Anne Thomas and Ms. Rowena Mills provided expert editing assistance through the AAPG's Publications Department. Finally, I thank my wife, Alice, and our family for their encouragement and patience during the production of this book.

Peter R. Rose
Rose & Associates, LLP
Austin, Texas
December 5, 2000

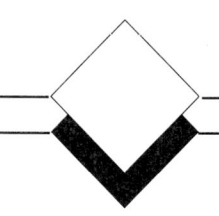

List of Abbreviations

BCFG = billion cubic feet gas
BOE = barrels oil equivalent
COF = cost of finding
DCF = discounted cash flow
DCFROR = discounted cash-flow rate of return
DHC = dry-hole cost
DHI = direct HC indicator
DST = drill-stem test
EMV = expected monetary value
ENPV = estimated net present value
EOR = enhanced oil recovery
EUR = estimated ultimate recovery
EV = expected value
F/O = farm-out
FSD = field-size distribution
FVF = formation volume factor
G&G = geology and geophysics
GRR = growth rate of return
GRV = gross rock volume
HC = hydrocarbon
IE = investment efficiency
IP = initial production
mcf = thousand cubic feet
MCFG = thousand cubic feet gas

MCFS = minimum commercial field size
MEFS = minimum economic field size
MMBO = million barrels oil
MNCF = maximum negative cash flow
NRI = net revenue interest
NFW = new-field wildcat
NPV = net present value
OWI = optimum working interest
PV = present value
P_c = probability of commercial success
P_e = probability of economic success
P_f = probability of failure
P_g = probability of geologic success
r = risk quotient (unique to each company)
RAV = risk-adjusted value
ROR = rate of return
RT = risk tolerance
SPI = source potential index
SR = source rocks
TAI = thermal alteration index
TOC = total organic carbon
TTI = time-temperature index
VR = vitrinite reflectance

Dedication

This book is dedicated to the more than 8,000 professional geoscientists and engineers who participated in my short courses during 1984–2000. Motivated by a sincere desire to improve the efficiency and economic performance of the E&P business, they received and utilized risk analysis concepts eagerly and responded with thousands of thoughtful and generous observations and suggestions, which led to an open sharing of ideas and continuous, rapid progress in this emerging specialty.

AAPG
wishes to thank the following
for their generous contributions
to

*Risk Analysis and Management of
Petroleum Exploration Ventures*

AEC International
Forest Oil Corporation
Gulf Canada Resources Ltd.
Ocean Energy, Inc.
Phillips Petroleum Company
Pioneer Natural Resources USA, Inc.
Pluspetrol E&P SA
Samson
Texaco Inc.

Contributions are applied toward the production
cost of publication, thus directly reducing the book's
purchase price and making the volume
available to a larger readership.

Table of Contents

Chapter 1: Introduction 1
Casino Analog for Exploration Portfolio 1
Exploration Tasks and Risk Analysis 2
Background of Risk Analysis 2
Risk Analysis and Petroleum Exploration 3
Purposes and Organization of this Volume 4
Differing Definitions of Reserves 4

Chapter 2: Geotechnical Estimates under Uncertainty 5
Risk, Uncertainty, and Estimating 5
Magnitude of Geotechnical Uncertainty 6
Lognormality 9
Calculating the Mean of Lognormal Distributions 12
Techniques for Improving Geotechnical Estimates 13

Chapter 3: Risk Analysis of Exploration Prospects 17
Estimating Prospect Reserves 17
    Constituent Parameters 17
    Generation of the Prospect-reserves Distribution 24
    Economic Translation of the Prospect-reserves Distribution 24
    Monitoring and Improving Predictive Performance 26
    Industry Experience 28
Chance of Prospect Success 31
    The Expected Value Concept 31
    Requirements for a Corporate System to Estimate Geologic Chance 31
    Recorded Success Rates versus Geologic Success Estimates 32
    Geologic Components of Prospect Chance of Success 34
    Subjective Probability Estimates in Exploration 36
    Practical Aspects of Implementation 36
    Geologic, Commercial, and Economic Chances of Success 38
    Independent versus Dependent Chance Factors 41
    Nongeologic Aspects of Success and Failure 42
    Monitoring and Improving Predictive Performance 43
    Industry Experience in Estimating Prospect Chance of Success 43

Chapter 4: Economic Analysis of Exploration Ventures 49
Introduction 49
Time Value of Money and Discount Rates 49
Exploration Cash-flow Models and Discounted Cash-flow Analysis 49
Problems with DCF Valuation of Exploratory Ventures 50
Option-pricing Theory and Valuation of Exploration Ventures 52
Recommended Economic Measures 53

Chapter 5: Exploration Plays—Risk Analysis and Economic Assessment 57

Introduction 57
    The Problem with Most Exploration Contracts 57
    History and Development of the Play Concept 57
    Plays and Petroleum Systems 58
    Play Selection as the Critical Exploration Decision 60
    Risk Analysis of Prospects and Plays Compared 61
    Integration of Geotechnology, Economics, and Management in Play Analysis 62
Important Geologic Concepts for Play Analysis 62
    Stratigraphic Sequences in Play Analysis 63
    Worldwide versus Provincial Petroleum Source Rocks 64
    The Kitchen—Geochemical Modeling 64
    Total Geology and Geologic Play Maps 64
    Use of Analogs in Play Analysis 65
Key Concepts and Techniques for Risk Analysis of Exploration Plays 67
    Field-size Distributions 67
    Estimating Field Numbers 69
    Use of Field-size Distributions in Play Analysis 70
    Minimum Economic Field Size 77
    Economic Truncation of Field-size Distributions 78
Chance of Play Success 80
    Geologic Chance Factors 80
    Integration: Calculating the Chance of Economic Play Success 82
Summary of Geotechnical Data Required for Play Risk Analysis 84
    Primary Parameters 84
    Secondary (Derived) Parameters 86
Process for Systematic Risk Analysis of Exploration Plays 87
    Recommended Procedure 87

Chapter 6: Management of Exploration Projects as Business Ventures 91

Introduction 91
Dealing with Risk and Risk Aversion 91
    Practical Expressions and Applications 91
    Common Business Conventions for Mitigating Risk 93
Common Methods for Acquiring Petroleum Rights 93
    Staged Exploration 93
    Conditions of Acquisition 94
    Sealed Bonus Bidding 94
    Serial, Time-constrained Auctions 98
    Oral Auctions 98
    Performance Contracts 98
    Private Treaties 98
    Corporate Acquisitions 99
    Sanctity of Contracts versus Subsequent Renegotiations 99
    Conclusion 99
Prospect and Play Portfolios 99
    Requirements 99
    Benefits 99
    Lognormality and Performance of Prospect Portfolios 100
    Predictability versus Portfolio Size 102
    Principles of Exploration Portfolio Management 104
    Problems with Exploration Portfolios 105
Managing Exploration Plays 107
    Matching Play Attributes to Business Strategies 107
    Comparing Plays and Planning Exploration Campaigns 111
    Assessment of Exploration Performance 113
    Play Analysis: Organizational Patterns and Principles 115

Chapter 7: Petroleum Industry Practices of Exploration Risk Analysis 117

The "Prospector Myth" versus Systematic Exploration: Dealing with the Dilemma 117
Characteristic Corporate Process for Exploration Risk Analysis 120

Play Analysis 120
Implementation of Risk Analysis in Exploration Organizations 121

Appendix A: Methods for Calculating the Mean of a Lognormal Distribution 125

Appendix B: Graphical Method for Combining Probabilistic Distributions by Multiplication 127

Appendix C: A Recurring Problem in Estimating Prospect Reserves—Determining Reasonable "Low-side" Values (P99% and P90%) 131

Appendix D: Evaluating and Combining Multiple-objective Ventures 137
Part 1: Multiple-zone Prospect Example: Geologic and Economic Assumptions 138
Part 2: Combining Multiple Types of Ventures 140

Appendix E: Steps in Geotechnical Procedure for Prioritizing Petroleum Prospectivity in New Exploration Areas 147

Appendix F: Reconstructing Parent Field-size Distributions from Offshore FSDs 149

Appendix G: Matrix for Comparing, Ranking, and Planning New Exploration Plays 153

References Cited 155

Index 159

FIGURES

1.	Global large field discoveries	2
2.	(a, b, c, d) Geotechnical estimates of prospect reserves	7
3.	(a, b, c, d, e) Forms of statistical distributions	9
4.	a) Cumulative probability graph; b) Cumulative log probability graph	10
5.	a) Field-size distributions change as play matures	11
	b) Economic truncation causes convex curve at lower end of FSDs	12
6.	Reserves parameters for exploration prospect (deterministic)	18
7.	Area, average net pay, and HC-recovery factor are lognormal	19
8.	(a, b, c, d) Distributions of estimated parameters for prospect reserves	21
9.	Productive field areas, East Texas	22
10.	Graphs to derive geometry factor adjustment	22
11.	Area versus depth plot	23
12.	Graphical method for analytical solution for combining three lognormal distributions by multiplication	25
13.	(a, b, c, d) Comparison of predictions versus outcomes	27
14.	(a, b, c, d) Continuous tracking of organizational predictive performance	28
15.	Pre- and postdrill discovery sizes	29
16.	Volume accuracy	29
17.	Exploration failure and exploration success (economic, commercial, and geologic)	32
18.	Subjective expressions of confidence	37
19.	Chance adequacy matrix	38
20.	Calculating chance of commercial success and economic success	39
21.	Relative frequency of four geologic chance factors causing dry holes	44
22.	Global discovery percentages through time	45
23.	Annual and cumulative success rates compared with annual drilling	46
24.	Option concept applied to E&P projects	53
25.	Cumulative net present value and maximum negative net cash flow	55
26.	Hypothetical geologic cross section of a basin showing the essential elements of a petroleum system	59
27.	Map of the hypothetical basin showing areal extent of the petroleum system	59
28.	Relationship between essential elements and processes as well as preservation time and critical moment	60
29.	Four levels of petroleum investigation	61
30.	a) Traditional facies interpretation; b) Depositional topography interpretation	63
31.	Hydrocarbon charge model	65

32.	Integrated methods produce more efficient exploration results	66
33.	Creaming curves	68
34.	Global field-size distribution	72
35.	(a, b, c) Use of analog FSDs in forecasting actual FSDs	73
36.	(a, b) Use of analog FSDs in forecasting actual FSDs: second stage	75
37.	(a, b, c, d) Downward shifts in FSDs in area Y between first cycle of exploration and second cycle	76–77
38.	(a, b) Offshore FSDs are truncated by platform cost	79
39.	Effects of operative geologic chance factors must coincide in the prospective area	81
40.	Staged exploration	94
41.	Sealed bidding for uncertain reserves leads to the winner's curse	95
42.	Net purchases by company: Gulf of Mexico sales	96
43.	Gulf of Mexico bidding efficiency	96
44.	High bids and second bids: area-wide GOM lease overbids averaged 50%	97
45.	High bids and second bids: area-wide GOM lease overbids averaged 75%	97
46.	Spinner for simulating chance of success and reserves discovered	103
47.	Predictive accuracy of portfolio performance improves with the number of wells in the portfolio	104
48.	The efficient frontier	105
49.	a) Post-1900 BBOE discovered by year; b) Discovery data, 1990–1999	108
50.	Six generalized planning steps	112
51.	Lognormality—two modes of portrayal	118
52.	Exploration reality	119

TABLES

1.	Estimated geotechnical parameters	5
2.	Biases affecting judgments under uncertainty	8
3.	Ways to improve accuracy and build confidence in estimating	13
4.	Reality checks (1): Characteristics of the endpoints of the reserves distribution	20
5.	Getting a sense of scale about HC-recovery factor	24
6.	Reality checks (2): Characteristic ranges associated with oil and gas ventures having different magnitudes of uncertainty	26
7.	Expected value examples (coin toss)	31
8.	Example calculation of simplistic probability of geologic success and failure using three geologic chance factors	34
9.	Generalized success rates of various well classes drilled in the 1980s	45
10.	Present value factors	51
11.	Factor comparison in the four levels of petroleum investigation	60
12.	Exploration risk analysis—prospects versus plays	61
13.	System of graduated size classes used currently by the U.S. Geological Survey	70
14.	Comparison of analog, predicted, and actual FSDs	74
15.	Geologic chance factors required for play and prospect success	81
16.	Geotechnical parameters required for play analysis	84
17.	Form: flow sheet for play risk analysis	85
18.	Biases affecting risk decisions	92
19.	EV implies "risk-neutral"	92
20.	A model prospect portfolio	101
21.	Simulation of results for a prospect portfolio	102
22.	Uncertainty leads to common underperformance of exploration portfolios	106

EQUATIONS

1.	Generic expected value	1
2.	Expected net present value of an exploratory prospect	5
3.	Expected net present value of mean commercial reserves case	54
4.	Investment efficiency	54
5.	Risked investment efficiency	54
6.	Risk-adjusted value	55
7.	Optimum working interest	55
8.	Discovery process model	67
9.	Calculating minimum economic field size	78
10.	Calculating estimated chance of economic play success	83
11.	Prospect grading procedure	88
12.	Application of OWI to a prospect	92

About the Author

Peter R. Rose is the managing partner in a newly established consulting firm, Rose & Associates, LLP (R&A).

He earned a B.S., M.A., and Ph.D. in geology at the University of Texas at Austin and is a certified petroleum geologist. Rose was staff geologist with Shell Oil Company; chief of the Oil and Gas Branch of the United States Geological Survey; and chief geologist and director of frontier exploration for Energy Reserves Group, Inc. (now BHP Petroleum [Americas], Inc). In 1980, he established his own independent oil and gas consulting firm, Telegraph Exploration, Inc. His clients include most major U.S. companies and many prominent independents as well as many international firms and state oil companies.

Rose has explored for oil and gas in most North American geologic provinces and has published and lectured widely on U.S. resource assessment, basin analysis, play development, prospect evaluation, and risk and uncertainty in exploration. He has taught extensively at the professional level and was a distinguished lecturer for the American Association of Petroleum Geologists (AAPG) in 1985–1986. Since 1989, he has been deeply involved in design and implementation of comprehensive exploration risk-analysis systems for executive management of many major and independent oil companies, operating in domestic and international theaters. His courses emphasize the link between geoscience and moneymaking in the petroleum-exploration business.

Rose was president of AAPG's Division of Professional Affairs in 1996–1997. He received the coveted Parker Memorial Medal from the American Institute of Professional Geologists in 1998.

Chapter 1

Introduction

During the 1990s, many international petroleum companies improved their exploration performance significantly by using principles of risk analysis and portfolio management, in combination with new geotechnologies. While exploration risk cannot be eliminated, it can certainly be reduced substantially, on a portfolio scale. And the widespread adoption of standardized risk analysis methods during the 1990s brought badly needed discipline to petroleum exploration.

By the mid-1980s, most well-informed major international petroleum firms that were engaged in exploration recognized that, globally, the average size of new discoveries was diminishing **(Figure 1)**. Not coincidentally, the class of exploratory prospects categorized as "high-risk/high-potential" was showing marked signs of underperformance. For major companies such as Shell, Mobil, and Amoco, when all such ventures—which averaged around a 10% perceived probability of success—were considered, less than 1% actually discovered profitable oil and gas reserves, and the sizes of these discoveries were generally far smaller than predicted. All in all, such exploration for new giant fields *destroyed value*, rather than *creating it*, in the 1980s and early 1990s.

Consequently, exploration, as a corporate function, lost credibility. It badly needed to begin delivering on its corporate promises. It needed to become more efficient, and thereby more profitable. At the same time, as superior new technologies were introduced, and exploration came to be a global effort under more centralized coordination, corporations realized that they needed to adopt systematic procedures to better manage the exploration function. To optimize the allocation of exploration capital, concepts of portfolio management began to be considered.

Casino Analog for Exploration Portfolio

Consider the operator of a casino containing a certain number of gaming devices and tables: the odds on each game are well known to the owner, and they are set to be slightly in his favor. He is playing a repeated-trials game in which the expected value (EV) of each trial, for him, is positive. Please note here the definition of expected value: The chance of success times the value of success, minus the chance of failure times the cost of failure **(Equation 1)**. When EV is positive, you're investing; when it's negative, you're gambling. If the casino operator knows the number of tables, the number of players in an evening, and the house rules, he can predict with considerable precision what his profit will be. He is not a gambler, any more than a life insurance company is. He is an investor. And he knows what the odds are.

$$\text{EXPECTED VALUE:} \quad (1)$$
$$(\text{Chance of Success} \times \text{Value of Success}) -$$
$$(\text{Chance of Failure} \times \text{Cost of Failure})$$
$$(+) \text{ EV} = \text{Investing}$$
$$(-) \text{ EV} = \text{Gambling}$$

The casino analogy may be distasteful to petroleum geoscientists and corporate managers, but it is actually a pretty fair analog to the centralized drilling portfolio:

- The diversity of investment opportunities, such as new-field wildcats, step-outs, development wells, enhanced-recovery projects, and property acquisitions, could be likened to the various types of games in the casino, such as roulette, blackjack, craps, and keno.
- Repeated trials at the roulette wheel (which is set to favor the house) are analogous to the prospects in the annual exploration portfolio: all represent positive expected value and are selected to maximize value and be consistent with acceptable risk.
- The casino operator cannot predict which spin of the wheel will produce a "win" for the house (any more than the Exploration vice president can scan the annual portfolio and predict which prospect will be a discovery), but he knows that at the end of the evening the house will be ahead.

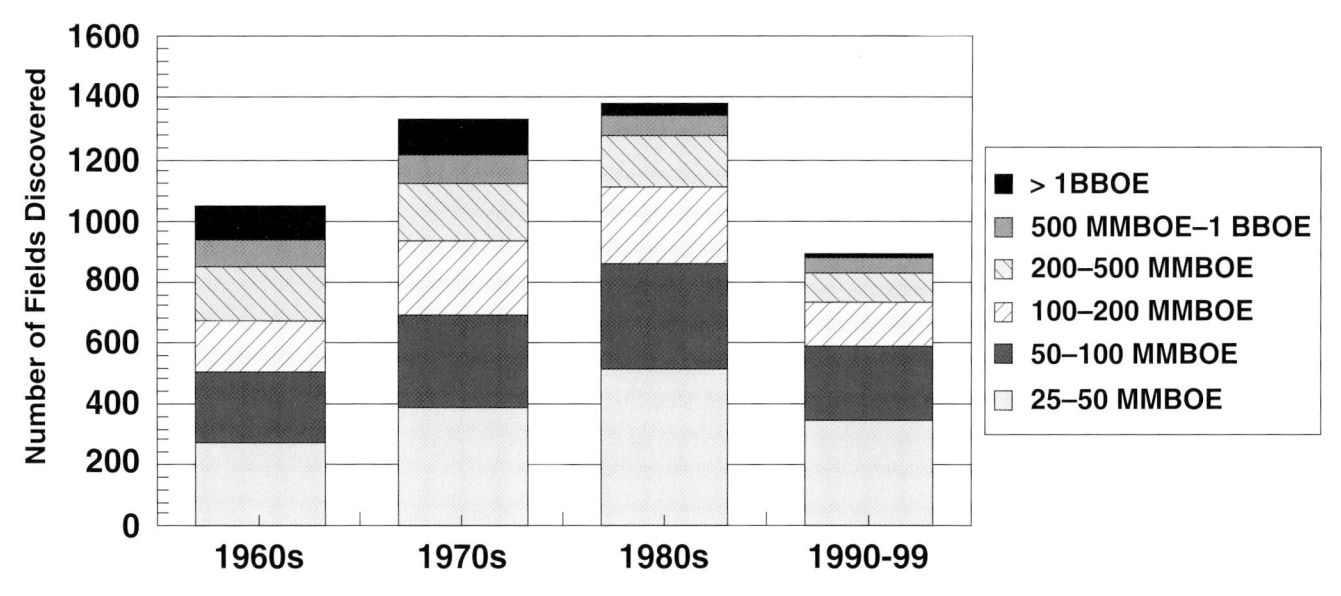

Figure 1 Global large field discoveries, 1960–1999. While the rate of global scale (>1 BBOE, or billion barrels of oil equivalent) discoveries has decreased since 1980, opportunities for smaller, but significant, fields have remained high. MMBOE = million barrels of oil equivalent. Source: Petroconsultants; reprinted with permission.

However, there are some significant differences between operating a casino and an annual exploration portfolio:

- The actual odds on every drilling venture can't be certainly known; they can only be estimated. However, the ability of the firm's geoscientists to estimate chance correctly can be measured and calibrated by reviewing the performance of past portfolios, and can be thus improved. The basic problem is that different geoscientists, in different geologic areas, are estimating prospect reserves, profitability, and chance of success; this calls for the adoption of consistent methods throughout the company. Also, all prospectors are competing for advancement, which promotes optimistic bias.
- Greater uncertainty attends prospect reserves, and thus profitability, than attends the payoff for each spin of the roulette wheel. The magnitude of exploration uncertainty, and geoscience's limited ability to reduce it, are widely unappreciated by managers and directors.
- Usually, there are fewer wells in the drilling portfolio than there are spins of the roulette wheel in any evening. Most exploration portfolios contain only about 10 to 100 exploration wells.
- The payoff at the gaming table is immediate; the payoff at the wellhead is long-term and subject to fluctuations in price and politics.

Exploration Tasks and Risk Analysis

Beginning in the late 1980s and early 1990s, most exploration organizations began to (1) adopt various methods of risk analysis, (2) bring objectivity and consistency to the valuation of the ventures in their prospect inventories, and (3) adopt more discriminating economic yardsticks and risk/reward definitions in selecting their annual exploration portfolios. By 1999, most prospectors had begun to accept three main professional responsibilities:

1. To identify geologic anomalies that have an enhanced likelihood of containing commercial hydrocarbons;
2. To measure them, by estimating chance of success and reserves (translated into profitability), if successful;
3. To be professionally objective—to recognize that if the estimates are biased, portfolio value is not optimized, and the firm (as well as the stockholder), is damaged.

Background of Risk Analysis

Modern risk analysis, as it is now applied in international petroleum exploration, utilizes principles of *statistics, probability theory,* and *utility theory,* which began to be recognized as significant subdisciplines of mathematics and philosophy during the 16th, 17th, and 18th centuries (Bernstein, 1996) through published and unpublished works by Cardono (1545), Pascal and Fermat (1654, unpub., cited by Bernstein, 1996), Graunt and Petty (1662), Halley (1693), Jacob Bernoulli (1713, posthumously), De Moivre (1733), Daniel Bernoulli (1738), and Bayes (1764, posthumously). The impetus and applications for the early studies concerned games and gambling; subsequent applications had to do with actuarial and insurance matters.

Petroleum exploration—like many serial business ventures—is clearly a process of repeated trials under conditions of uncertainty, each trial requiring a substantial commitment of investment capital. As such, the casino analog is apt, but because we do not know certainly what the odds are, or the size of the prize, we have learned to employ modern science and technology to refine our "bets." For example:

- *Stratigraphy* may help us predict the presence and quality of reservoir rocks;
- *Geochemistry* may give us a better idea whether or not oil or natural gas has migrated into the area of our prospect, thus allowing better estimates of the chance of hydrocarbon presence;
- *Geophysics* may help refine our estimates as to how large an accumulation may be contained in the trap, thus the "size of the prize," as well as the likelihood that the trap indeed contains reservoired oil or gas;
- *Drilling technology* may let us reduce our investment by testing the prospect at lower cost; and
- *Reservoir technology* may allow us to develop and produce the successful prospect (= discovery) more efficiently, thus increasing our profit.

The success of exploration science and technology during the 1945–1995 period helped advance the myth that petroleum exploration was "driven by science" and obscure its analogy to the casino example, which was distasteful to many businessmen and scientists. Pioneering publications by Grayson (1960) on decision analysis in petroleum exploration, and by Kaufman (1962) on lognormality, provided the basis for practical applications in valuing exploration ventures. However, the systematic employment of statistics and probability theory in exploration did not begin until the mid-1960s, led by Exxon, Shell, Arco, and Cities Service (Newendorp, 1975). By the late 1970s, companies like Chevron, BP, and ELF, as well as some governmental agencies (G.S.C., I.F.P., and U.S.G.S.) were also beginning to employ risk analysis routinely in their exploration evaluations and ventures. But in the late 1980s and early 1990s, a technological explosion in risk analysis took place because most modern oil and gas companies saw the need for systematic management of their exploration portfolios on a worldwide basis.

Today, the concepts and methodologies of exploration risk analysis used by most large oil companies and state petroleum agencies have converged to the status of "a generally accepted technology" (MacKay, 1996), and many smaller firms are now adopting this technology.

Risk Analysis and Petroleum Exploration

The most critical decision in petroleum exploration is not which prospect to drill—it is which basin or trend ("play") to explore (Rose, 1996a, 1996b; Brown and Rose, 2000). A play is a family of geologically similar fields, discoveries, prospects, and leads (McCrossan, 1973; Roy, 1975; Baker et al., 1986; Miller, 1986; White, 1992). Because of the similarity of reservoir type and trap geometry, commonality of hydrocarbon charge, and consistent exploration and development methods, it is possible to carry out economic evaluations of plays as full-cycle economic ventures. Such evaluations utilize regional geologic, geochemical, and geophysical studies (see Appendix E and Appendix G), and they are conducted by applying basic principles of prospect risk analysis, as outlined in the first part of this volume. However, in order to understand the principles of play analysis, we must first understand the risk analysis of prospects, simply because plays are aggregates of geologically similar prospects.

Accordingly, we begin with the assumption that the company has already committed to explore in several different basins and trends (i.e., the process of play selection has already occurred), and drilling prospects are now being searched for, identified, and evaluated. Later, in Chapter 5, we return to play analysis.

Step one in petroleum exploration, once the exploration trend has been selected, is *identification of the drilling prospect* by geoscientists. This is the basic value-creating act. It requires geotechnical skill and creative imagination.

After the exploration prospect has been identified, there are key tasks involved throughout the life cycle of petroleum exploration and development. The first three tasks deal with measuring the prospect's value.

Step two in petroleum exploration is *measuring value*:

1. *Estimating how large the producible reserves are* likely to be (assuming that a hydrocarbon accumulation is indeed present);
2. *Estimating the chance* that a producible hydrocarbon accumulation is present; and
3. *Estimating the profitability* of the entire project, given that producible hydrocarbons are present.

Step three consists of *implementation and management of exploration projects as business ventures,* and includes three additional tasks:

4. *Acquisition strategies*—determining the terms under which the company would commit to explore and develop the prospect, whether acquisition is by sealed bonus-bidding, oral auction, performance contract, serial contract negotiations, private treaty, contract renegotiations, or the like. Note: acquisition strategies often apply to properties much larger than individual prospects, such as plays and contract areas.
5. *Inventory and portfolio management*—choosing which prospects should be included in the annual drilling program to maximize economic return, consistent with the company's risk tolerance. This topic may also include considerations of risk aversion or utility theory.
6. *Operations*—carrying out the various business operations that result in leasing, data acquisition, drilling, completion, and delineation of new discoveries. The cost-effectiveness of data acquisition for emerging prospects may be addressed operationally, using principles of *Valuation of Information.*

Tasks (1) through (5) are ordinarily included in the overall subject of exploration risk analysis, which may also include considerations such as the value of information.

Purposes and Organization of this Volume

The purposes of this book are to review the main principles and procedures of exploration risk analysis, and to discuss industry patterns of implementation, experience, and general results. The book follows the general sequence outlined above. Following this introduction, Chapter 2 addresses theory, procedures, and problems in making geotechnical estimates under uncertainty, and techniques for improving staff performance in estimating.

Chapter 3 reviews the key aspects of risk analysis of the prospect as the economic unit of exploration. The key aspects include (1) estimation of the range of potential recoverable reserves, (2) chances of geologic and commercial success, and (3) combination of reserves and chance leading to expected monetary value (EMV). Chapter 4 covers the topic of project profitability, given success, and reviews considerations of both reserves as well as chance of success.

With the principles of prospect risk analysis set out, we proceed to Chapter 5, which covers the key aspects of analysis of the exploration play, which is the operational unit of exploration. This distinction acknowledges that companies usually explore on the basis of regional trends and seismic programs, hoping to make multiple discoveries—given successful exploration—even though individual prospects constitute the economic "building blocks" in the overall evaluations of the trend.

Chapter 6 concerns effective practices by which successful companies make and implement sound business decisions based on proper risk analysis of prospects as well as plays. It deals with topics such as risk-reduction techniques, acquisition strategies, inventory and portfolio management, and management of exploration plays. Chapter 7 reviews current organizational practices commonly used by industry in carrying out exploration risk analysis.

Seven appendices cover various aspects of risk analysis concepts and procedures, which are too detailed to be included in the text.

Differing Definitions of Reserves

Much confusion attends the use of the term "reserves." The term is commonly used in both formal and casual ways. It is important to understand that there are two primary definitions of reserves in petroleum exploration and production.

The term "reserves" has measured, fiduciary implications to the engineer, chief financial officer, banker, or financial analyst. Terms such as "proved," "probable," "possible," "developed," and "undeveloped" connote varying levels of confidence in the existence of the different categories. A fundamental problem with such terms is that no consistent definition for such categories can exist, beyond nebulous guidelines like "reasonable certainty." The engineering profession appears to be evolving toward the more preferable probabilistic expression of such confidence (Cronquist, 1997).

The term "reserves" used by the explorationist usually means the projected ultimate recovery of hydrocarbons from a given field or drilling prospect; general synonyms are "geologic reserves," "volumetric reserves," "potential reserves," or "estimated ultimate recovery "(EUR). Thus, "field size," as used in a field-size distribution, represents the projected final cumulative production from a given field—cumulative production, plus proved reserves, plus projected future reserves additions (i.e., anticipated reserves appreciation). This same concept is used when explorationists talk about "prospect reserves" or "potential reserves." This usage naturally lends itself to the probabilistic expression of confidence in the existence (and eventual recovery) of such hydrocarbons under the economic and technologic conditions currently prevailing.

In most places in this book, the intended meaning should be clear. Where any doubt may exist, I have attempted to specify the meaning intended.

Chapter 2

Geotechnical Estimates under Uncertainty

Risk, Uncertainty, and Estimating

Risk and uncertainty are not synonymous (Megill, 1984; Rose, 1987). Risk connotes the threat of loss. Risk decisions weigh the level of investment against four considerations: net financial assets, chance of success/failure, potential gain, and potential loss. The last three considerations must rely on estimates, made under uncertainty, of the range of probabilities that some condition may exist or occur.

Every exploration decision involves considerations of both risk and uncertainty. Risk comes into play in deciding how much we are willing to pay for additional data or mineral interests, considering the high impact of front-end costs on project profitability. Uncertainty is intrinsically involved in all geotechnical predictions about the range of magnitude of the inferred mineral deposit, the chance of discovery, and the cost of finding and developing it. Therefore, once prospects have been identified, the problem in serial exploration decision making is twofold:

- to be consistent in the way we deal with risk and uncertainty, and
- to perceive uncertainty accurately and reduce it where possible.

Although extensive scientific and geotechnical work is indeed essential to successful modern petroleum exploration, we must also recognize that nearly all of the parameters required to assign expected monetary value to the exploratory prospect can only be estimates made under substantial uncertainty. **Table 1** lists the most significant ones.

Given the importance of responsible estimating, it is quite remarkable that until recently so little effort has been made by most modern oil companies to monitor and improve their geotechnical staff's estimating performance. Many organizations, even today, persist in utilizing deterministic estimates—"single-value forecasts." These are hopelessly inadequate given the wide uncertainties that usually exist and the multiplicity of interactive parameters involved in calculating the chance-weighted after-tax net present worth [Expected Net Present Value (After Tax) = ENPV(AT)] of a typical exploration prospect **(Equation 2)**:

(2)

$$\text{ENPV}_{(AT)} = \begin{array}{l} \text{Chance of Success [(Net Revenue Interest} \times \text{Reserves} \times \text{Wellhead Prices) minus} \\ \text{(Investments + Operating Costs + Wellhead Taxes + Income Taxes)] minus} \\ \text{Chance of Failure [After-tax dry-hole costs + geotechnical and lease costs]} \end{array}$$

Table 1 Estimated geotechnical parameters.

Dimensional	thickness, area, volume, depth
Reservoir	net/gross, ϕ (porosity), K (permeability), HC-rec %, GOR, S_W, etc.
Well Performance	IP, % decline, etc.
Geochemical Values	SR-type, TOC, maturity, composition
Migration	impedance, dispersal, routes
Trap Integrity	seal effectiveness, leakage, flushing, etc.
Timing	migration vs. trap creation
Front-end Costs	land, drilling, completion, geotechnical data acquisition, overhead
Discovery Probability	geologic chance factors, commercial and economic reserve thresholds
Wellhead Price	local vs. international influences, envelope of historical real oil prices

There are several important observations to be made about this equation. First, in an American-style tax and royalty license, the owners of the producing property usually pay 100% of the costs but receive a reduced proportion—ordinarily from about 70% to 87.5%—of the revenues from production. This reduced proportion is the net revenue interest (NRI); the remainder goes to the royalty owner(s)—generally the landowner. In production-sharing contracts the formula is different, although the general principle still prevails that the operator provides most or all of the capital, especially the exploration investment, but receives only a part of the production revenues. Second, the equation expresses the profit or (loss) as if it were a "lump-sum" payment, whereas it is actually received over a long period of time: a complex net cash-flow stream combining investments, production decline, price fluctuations, expenses (including taxes), and inflation. Third, in order to consider the time value of money, the net cash flows are expressed as a *discounted* cash-flow stream so the entire venture can be compared with current alternative investments. Wherever a dollar value is expressed as Present Value (PV), it means that the value has been discounted to reflect the time value of money.

Uncertainty attends every item in this ENPV equation except the net revenue interest. These uncertainties are diverse, relating to geology, engineering, law, politics, economics, and acts of God. It is the special professional responsibility of geotechnical staff to estimate the magnitude of reserves, production rates, and costs; to reduce the level of uncertainty as much as possible through sound scientific and technological judgment (and additional investigation, where warranted); and to accurately and consistently convey estimates—as well as uncertainty levels—to management. Otherwise management's investment decisions may be misguided and imprudent. Thus the financial consequences of their geotechnical predictions and estimates constitute a weighty professional responsibility of the geotechnical staff.

Magnitude of Geotechnical Uncertainty

The earth is a coarse filter. Even though petroleum explorationists employ increasingly sophisticated and discriminating technology, our precision in measuring most of the important geotechnical factors and parameters bearing on prospect value is much more limited than many of us care to admit. Technology can reduce, but not eliminate, uncertainty. Moreover, exploration always operates at the cutting edge—the threshold of resolution—so that the potential effectiveness of new tools and concepts is constantly and aggressively being evaluated by applications in new and old exploration theaters. Accordingly, explorationists will always have to deal with uncomfortably large uncertainties. **Figure 2** shows, by cross-plot, four actual experiences of modern oil companies in attempting to estimate reserves contained in prospects that turned out to be discoveries (Capen, 1992). Figure 15 shows similarly wide uncertainties by a large number of companies exploring in the Norwegian North Sea over an extended period of time.

The cross-plots in **Figure 2** express two important attributes of prospect reserves forecasting:

1. *Prevalent optimistic bias* of estimates vs. actual outcomes—in cross-plots B, C, and D, most of the outcomes are overestimates (cross-plot A is an unbiased data set). We will address bias later.
2. *Substantial uncertainty*, expressed as a characteristic, wide "scatter" of estimates. Given a continuing and substantial number of exploration ventures (repeated trials), statistics offers a practical way to deal with the prevailing large uncertainties that characterize petroleum exploration.

This characteristic, wide "scatter" conveys a profound (if disagreeable) message that petroleum prospectors would do well to absorb: *Explorationists cannot predict very well how much oil or gas their successful prospects (= discoveries) will contain. We can generally identify those closures that are too small to contain large volumes, but we cannot forecast how much oil or gas the large closures may contain, often because of unanticipated variations in trap fill-up, reservoir quality, and dip rate.*

Stated more pragmatically, we can usually distinguish between a 5-million-barrel (MM bbl) closure and a 50-million-barrel closure, but we cannot distinguish between 3-million and 5-million-barrel closures, or 30-million and 50-million-barrel closures. Moreover, we often cannot tell how much oil may be present in a closure having 50-million-barrel capacity—1 million, 5 million, 20 million, or even 50 million. This basic "fact of life" has profound (and often ignored) implications for explorationists.

Ranges and Probabilities

The problem is how to express our technical uncertainties realistically, and in a form by which they can be utilized in economic equations and formulae and subjected to subsequent evaluation. The most common convention in use today by modern petroleum corporations involves the formulation of a range of anticipated values for a given parameter, with probabilities—ordinarily 90%, 50%, and 10%—assigned to the values that constitute the range. For example, the geologist may believe there is a 90% chance that the anticipated pay-zone will be more than 10 feet thick, and she may

ESTIMATES VS. ACTUALS
GULF OF MEXICO
Company V

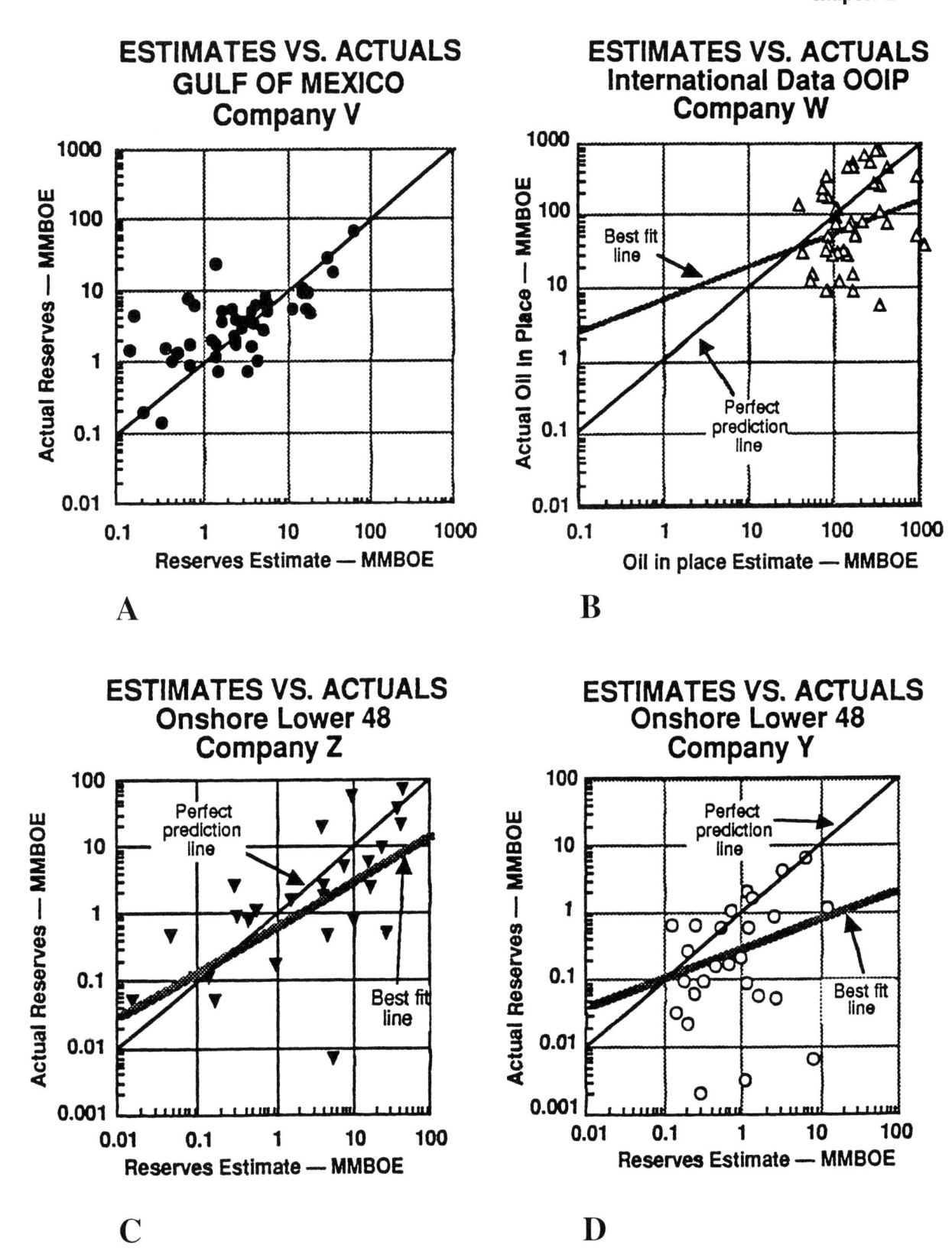

ESTIMATES VS. ACTUALS
International Data OOIP
Company W

A

B

ESTIMATES VS. ACTUALS
Onshore Lower 48
Company Z

ESTIMATES VS. ACTUALS
Onshore Lower 48
Company Y

C

D

Figure 2 *Geotechnical estimates of prospect reserves; modified after Capen, 1992.*

be 50% confident that it will be more than 20 feet thick, but she is only 10% sure that it could be more than 40 feet thick. The same procedure may be applied to any parameter—productive area, reservoir-yield, initial production rate, decline-rate, wellhead price, drilling costs, and the like.

However, such estimates cannot be pulled out of the air! They must rely on objective considerations of

Table 2 *Biases affecting judgments under uncertainty (modified after Rose, 1987).*

Type of Bias	Common Example
Overconfidence	Predictive ranges are too narrow, indicating that estimators are much less accurate than they think they are. Symptom: frequent surprises about exploration results.
Representativeness	Analog based on small sample size may not be statistically significant; chosen analog may not be analogous.
Availability	Recent or spectacular examples are more prone to be cited, regardless of their real frequency in nature; limited imagination limits number of possible interpretations.
Anchoring	In estimating, the desired iterative-reiterative process is attenuated, so a low starting point leads to a lower final estimate, and a high starting point leads to a higher final estimate. Conservative estimators find difficulty in accepting the possibility of a large outcome.
Unrecognized limits	Geologists forecasting future discoveries may disregard nongeologic factors that affect such discoveries.
Overoptimism	Prospectors exaggerate magnitude of reserves or chance of success in order to sell the deal.
Conservatism	Technical staff may think that overestimating a project is worse than underestimating it, and therefore err on the safe side.

all relevant data, especially maps, cross sections, geophysical data, borehole log interpretations, analogous production records, and the like. Moreover, geotechnical professionals must arrive at a final distribution for each parameter by repeated iterations—making trial estimates, examining the implications of various values in the distribution, determining through credibility checks and reality checks that the distribution makes sense, comparing it with analog data, considering the independently derived opinions of other professionals, and adjusting it repeatedly until finally becoming comfortable with all the estimates in the distribution, as constituting a "best fit" to the facts.

Biases in Estimating under Uncertainty

Bias is a more serious problem in geotechnical forecasting than is the characteristic wide uncertainty. If the exploration company's decisionmakers consistently receive biased estimates concerning prospect value, their investment decisions will be correspondingly flawed, leading to suboptimal economic performance of the company's exploration portfolio. The stockholder will suffer. **Table 2** lists the most significant biases observed in modern exploration companies (Rose, 1987).

For the exploration company, three of these biases are especially dangerous.

Overconfidence

This bias typically leads to excessively narrow ranges: Technical specialists think they know more than they really do, so they tend naturally to set predictive ranges that correspond to a confidence significantly less than the ranges they think they are setting. A common result is that, for prospect reserves forecasts, the anticipated "low-side" reserves prediction is too large and the projected "high-side" prediction is too small. The common operational symptom of the problem is that prospectors experience frequent surprises on reserve sizes of discoveries (Capen, 1976), as well as many other geotechnical parameters. **Figure 2** indicates that the real ranges of new-field wildcat prospect reserves uncertainties are commonly about two orders of magnitude (powers of 10) at about the 90% confidence level.

Conservatism

This bias commonly leads to underestimates because professionals, fearing criticism if results are disappointing, may think it is worse to overestimate a project than to underestimate it. The psychology of an unexpected upward revision in project profitability is much more pleasant than a disappointing downward revision. In fact, however, either error may result in a loss to the investor (Rose, 1987). Overestimates result in overinvesting in projects, whereas underestimating may cause the firm to invest too little, or even decline to invest. Either result is a loss.

Overoptimism

This form of motivational bias leads to overestimates because of perceived career or economic self-interest on the part of the professional. The most common example in exploration is prospectors inflating estimates of prospect reserves or probability of success in order to "sell the deal" and get the prospect drilled (Rose, 1987).

Lognormality

Basis

Statistics is routinely taught to students by employing the "normal" distribution—the well-known symmetrical "bell-shaped" curve. Even though students of mathematical statistics have long known the significance of the Central Limit Theorem, the lognormal distribution in petroleum science has only gained wide acceptance—and more importantly, routine analytical application—during the past decade.

The Central Limit Theorem states that distributions resulting from the natural *addition* of independent random variables will be "normal"—that is, a *frequency distribution* will tend to take the form of the familiar "bell-shaped" curve, in which the vertical axis is ordinarily expressed as a percent of the total, and the horizontal axis is an arithmetic scale expressing some variable such as dimension or value **(Figure 3a)**. Another convention for presenting the same data is the *cumulative probability distribution*, in which the vertical axis is 0–100% and the horizontal axis displays a dimensional variable, using an arithmetic scale **(Figure 3b)**. The power of the cumulative probability distribution is that, conceptually at least, it represents the full universe of all possible outcomes—100%—and probability is expressed as a cumulative percent of some outcome "equal to or less than" or "equal to or more than" a particular value.[1] Thus the cumulative probability distribution is especially useful as a predictive tool.

A special type of cumulative probability graph paper has been developed on which the vertical probability

---

[1] Statisticians seem to prefer the "equal to or less than" convention, arguing that it honors statistical notation, and it seems to be easier for people to associate large probabilities with large values, and small probabilities with small values. However, it is not incorrect to express cumulative probabilities as "equal to or greater than." The writer, after initially being influenced by the statisticians, has come to strongly prefer the "greater than" convention, which is used in this book. Most oil companies have increasingly come to use the "greater than" convention, recognizing four compelling reasons:

• The exploration expression of reserves is thereby made compatible with the traditional expression of "proved reserves," as an expression of high confidence in the presence of some specified conservative reserves value, or more;

• Explorationists, being keenly aware that oil companies are particularly interested in large discoveries, naturally prefer to focus on the potential for large reserves—thus the "or more" expression is more natural and appropriate;

• It eliminates the disturbing possibility that statistically naïve decisionmakers may be seduced into believing there is a 90% probability of finding the high-side (P90%) outcome or more, rather than only a 10% chance; and

• Commercial truncation is directly expressed as the proportion of the reserves distribution that is of commercial size or larger, rather than as the (1-Pc [probability of commercial success]) expression required by the ≤ convention.

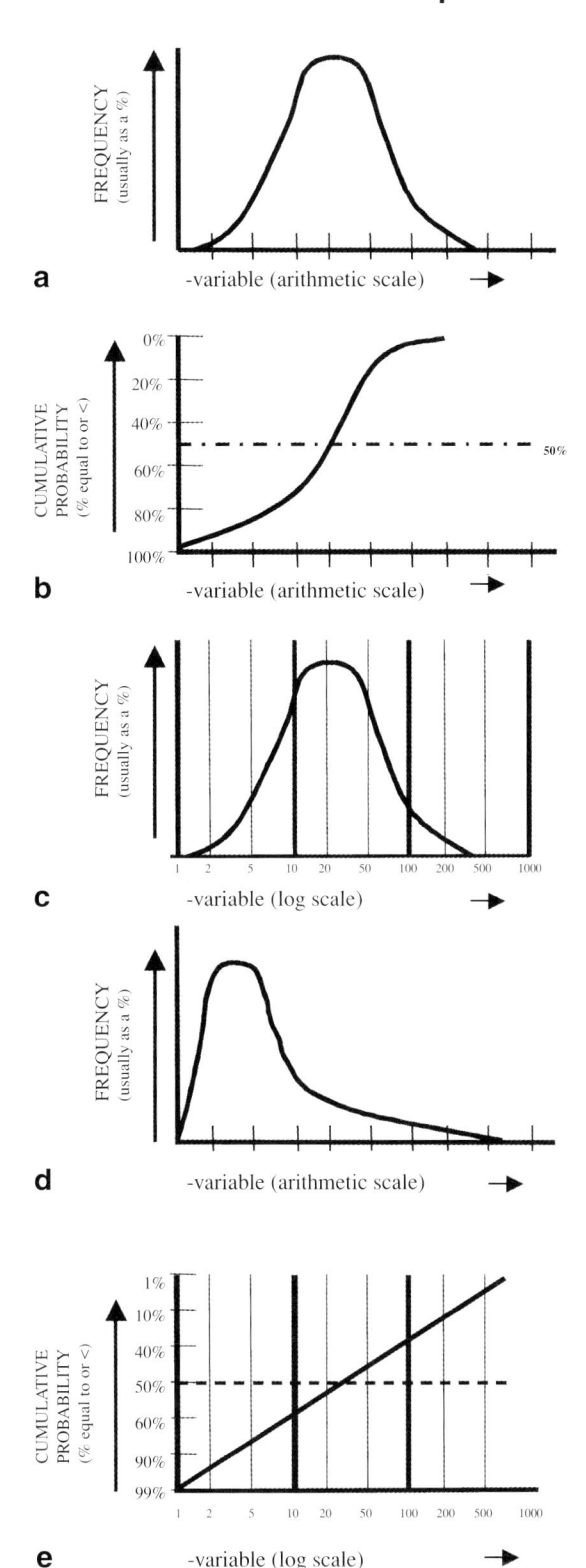

Figure 3 (a) *A symmetrical (normal, bell-shaped) frequency distribution on a regular coordinate graph.* (b) *A cumulative probability distribution on a regular coordinate graph.* (c) *A lognormal frequency distribution on a semi-log graph.* (d) *A lognormal frequency distribution on a regular coordinate graph.* (e) *A lognormal cumulative probability distribution on a log probability graph.*

axis is symmetrical around the 50% probability, with complementary probability intervals (40–50% and 50–60%; 30–40% and 60–70%, etc.) that are equal but of increasing spans upward and downward **(Figure 4a)**. Maximum and minimum probabilities are 1% and 99%, rather than 0% and 100%. The horizontal axis is arithmetic. The special property of the cumulative probability graph is that a cumulative probability distribution that is perfectly *normal* will plot as a straight, sloping line.

The Central Limit Theorem also provides that distributions resulting from the natural *multiplication* of independent random variables will be "lognormal"—that is, the *frequency distribution* will tend to form a symmetrical "bell-shaped" curve where the horizontal

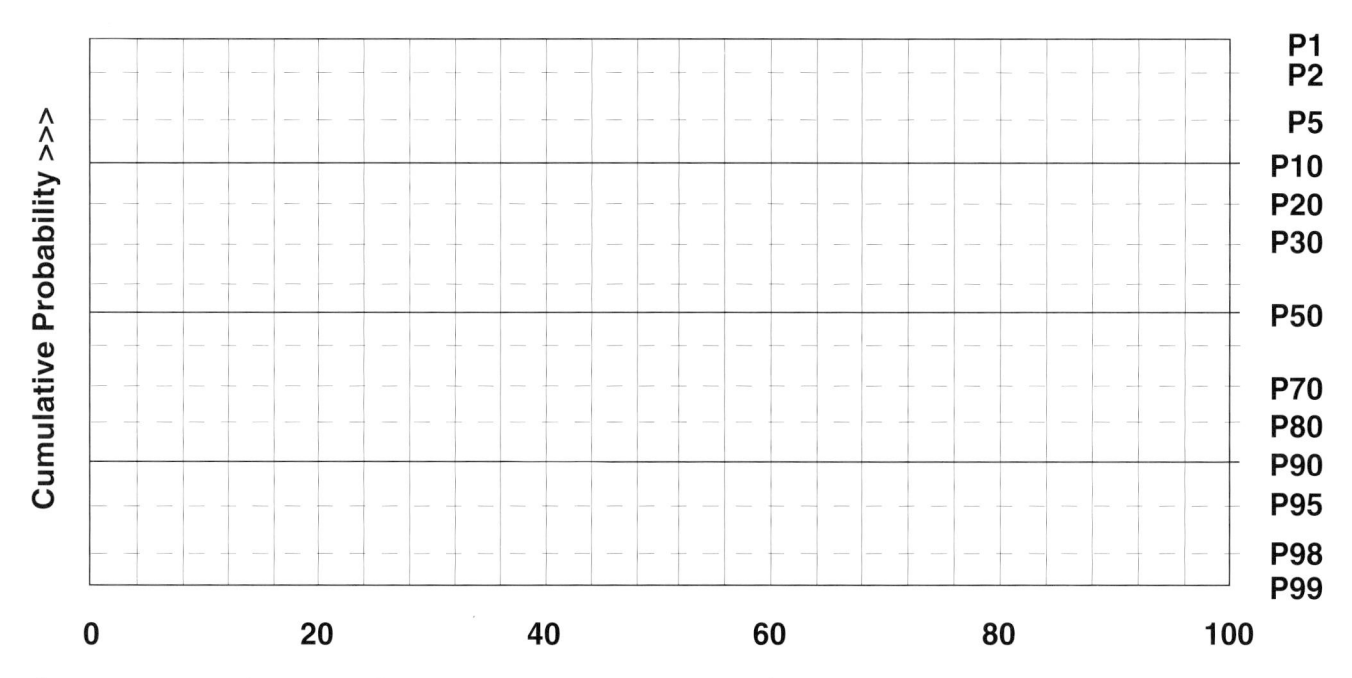

Figure 4a *Cumulative probability graph; note vertical axis is nonlinear probability scale, whereas horizontal axis is arithmetic scale.*

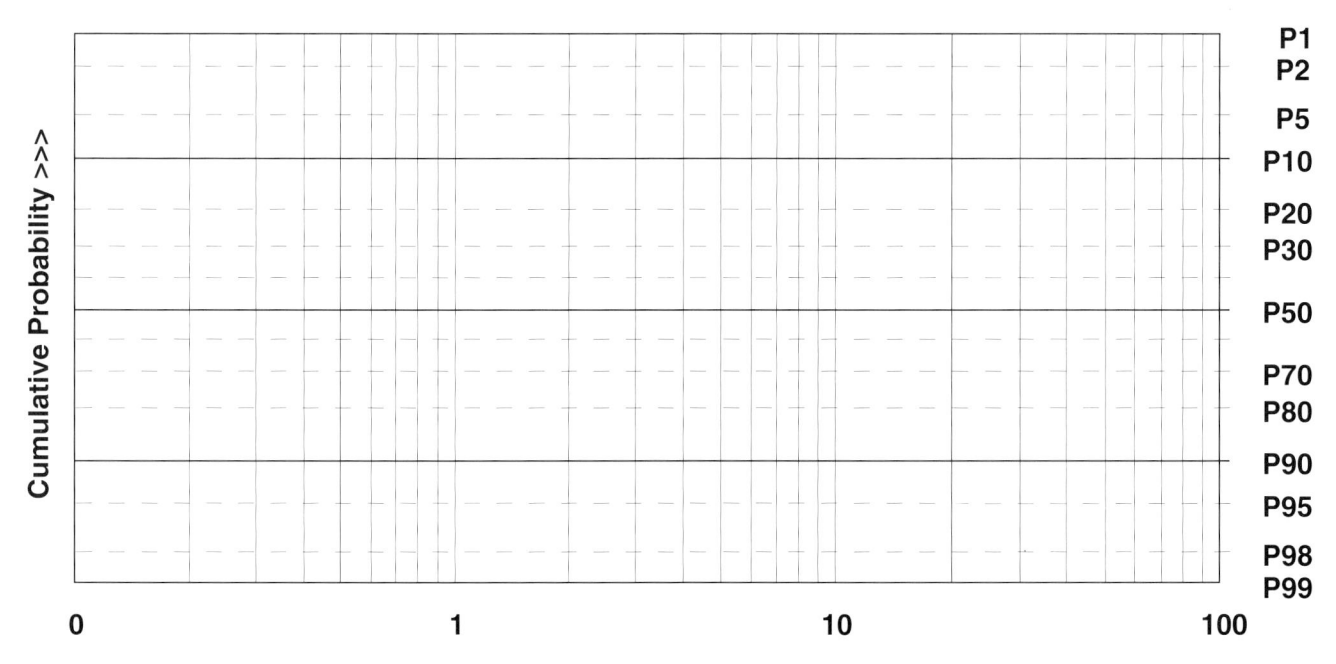

Figure 4b *Cumulative log probability graph; note vertical axis is nonlinear probability scale, whereas horizontal axis is logarithmic scale.*

axis is *logarithmic* **(Figure 3c)**. When a lognormal distribution is plotted as a frequency curve on a regular coordinate graph (i.e., arithmetic scale), it takes the form of a severely right-skewed frequency curve **(Figure 3d)**. Another special type of graph paper has also been developed for plotting *"cumulative log probability,"* in which the vertical axis is the cumulative probability scale, as described in the preceding paragraph, whereas the horizontal axis is a logarithmic scale. A cumulative probability distribution that is perfectly *lognormal* will appear as a straight, sloping line **(Figure 3e)**. **Figure 4b** shows a cumulative log probability graph; note that maximum and minimum values on the vertical probability scale are 1% and 99%, and the horizontal axis is a log scale.

So natural multiplication of independent, random variables yields lognormal distributions. Most important geotechnical parameters involved with oil and gas occurrence are lognormal (Megill, 1984; Capen, 1984, 1992). Geoscientists who are aware of the prevalence of lognormality (and who constrain their estimates in the expectation of lognormality) will tend to make better predictions of most parameters having to do with oil and gas reserves (Rose, 1996c). A few petroleum parameters are exponential; fewer still are normal. Predictions of all such parameters should be constrained by the expected form of the distribution.

Field-size Distributions

Distributions of reserve sizes (projected ultimate recoveries) in fields in a given trend, play, or basin show a pronounced tendency to follow a conventional lognormal pattern:

- just a few very small fields,
- a great many small fields,
- a handful of medium-size fields, and
- a very few very large fields

The reason, of course, why field-size distributions (FSDs) are lognormal is that the parameters controlling field size are multiplicative: Field Area × Average Net Pay Thickness × Hydrocarbon Recovery Factor = Field Reserves. Several attributes of FSDs are noteworthy. First, they typically shift toward smaller sizes as exploration progresses **(Figure 5a)**. Second, where many small fields (1,000 to 100,000 BOE [barrels of oil equivalent]) are included, the FSD may depart from a straight line on a cumulative log probability graph, taking a concave form at the lower end **(Figure 5a)**,

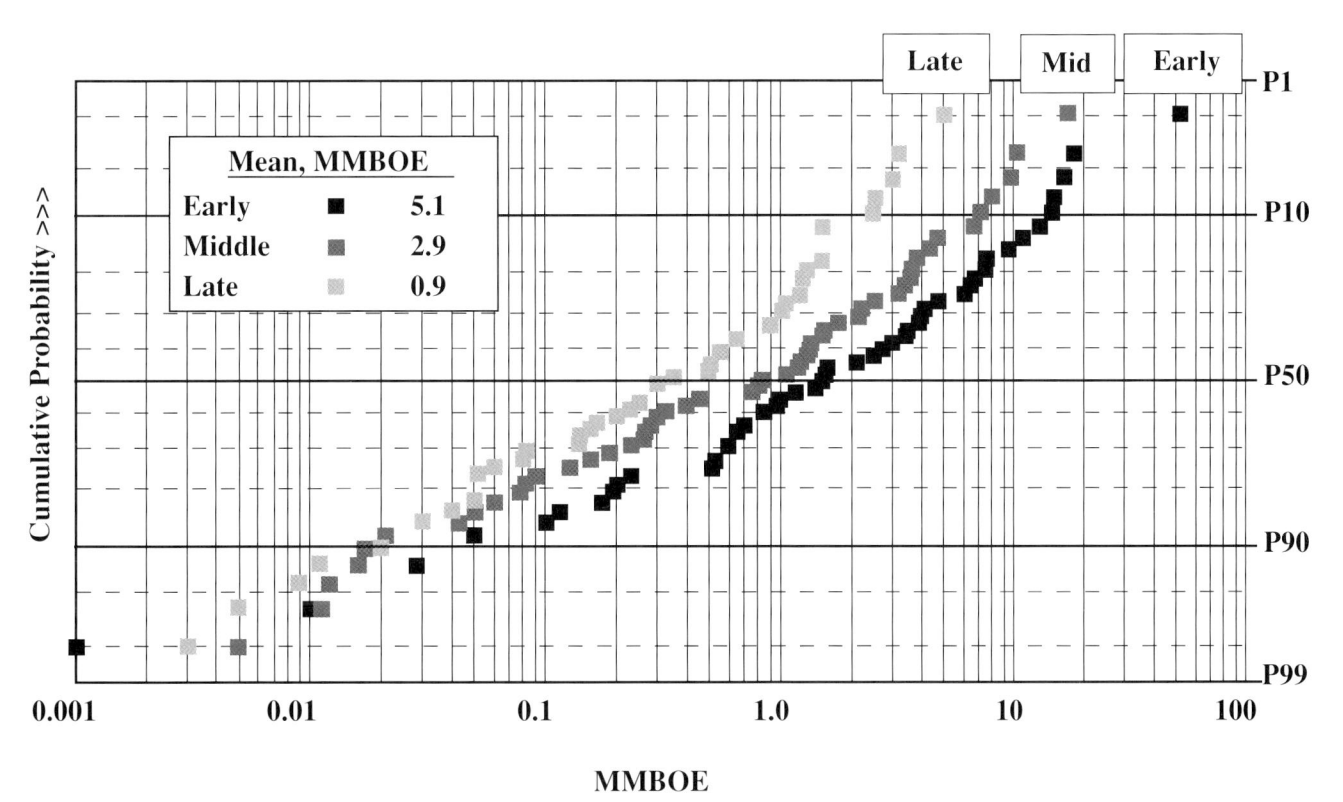

Figure 5a *Field-size distributions change as play matures.*

12   Geotechnical Estimates under Uncertainty

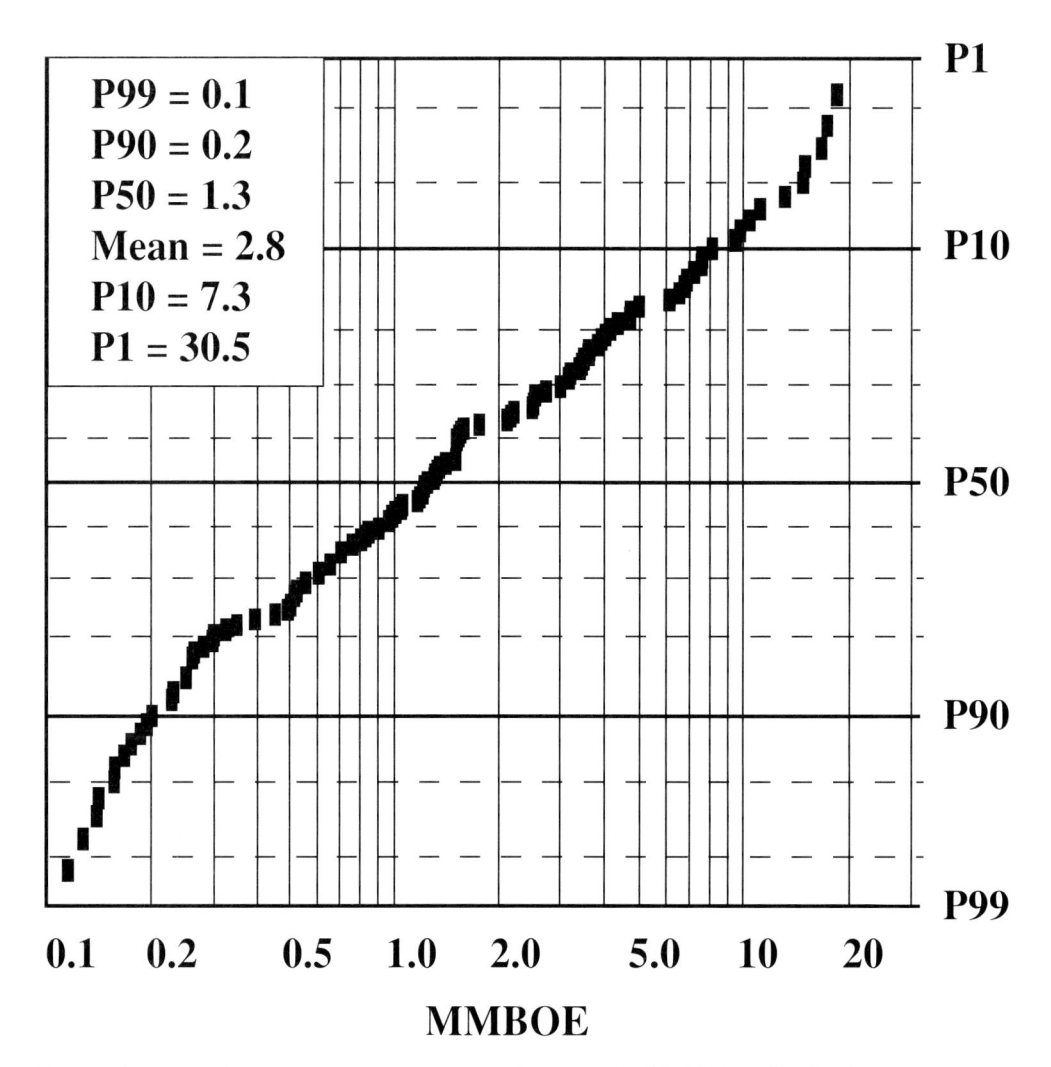

P99 = 0.1
P90 = 0.2
P50 = 1.3
Mean = 2.8
P10 = 7.3
P1 = 30.5

MMBOE

Figure 5b *Economic truncation causes convex curve at lower end of field-size distributions.*

because of incomplete sampling of smaller fields. Such smaller accumulations may be incompletely represented in the population of discovered fields because of economic and technological censoring:

1. anomalies recognized to be small may therefore not be drilled;
2. discoveries recognized to be very small by testing may not be completed for production; and
3. small anomalies may not be visible geotechnically, and therefore never drilled.

When FSDs are truncated at the low end to eliminate fields that are noncommercial, the resulting distribution typically fits a straight, sloping line, but in the lower part (the P99%–P80% sector), the FSD has a characteristic convex shape at the lower end as a consequence of the arbitrary elimination of the small part of the sample **(Figure 5b)**. FSDs of trends in economically demanding regions, such as the North Sea or deep Gulf of Mexico, where only larger discoveries qualify for platform installation, have already been severely truncated at the lower end by such minimum economic requirements. Parent distributions in such areas contain very many uncompleted accumulations, ordinarily reported as "shows," many of which were not even tested. If such a trend were located onshore, however, many such "shows" would have been completed as small fields. This point is elaborated further on page 80 and in Appendix F.

Construction of FSDs sheds great light on exploration of most trends and basins. They are recognized as an indispensable tool by most modern companies, serving as "reality checks" and giving essential perspective on proposed exploration ventures.

Calculating the Mean of Lognormal Distributions

Statistically, the best single representation of a lognormal distribution is the mean, or average. Because events in the low-probability end of the distribution have disproportionately much greater "weight" than in the high-probability part, the arithmetic mean of a lognormal distribution typically increases as sample size (n) increases. The **statistical mean** assumes a continuous distribution; that is, that $n = \infty$ and characteristically represents the largest possible mean value. On the other hand, if we simply calculate the arithmetic average of a lognormal distribution composed of a small number of values (say $n = 6$, or $n = 10$), that mean will be smaller than the statistical mean.

A practical problem with use of the statistical mean in exploration forecasting is that extremely low-probability events (less than P1%), which have extremely large values, contribute to the mean. But such events are sufficiently unlikely that we are justified in treating them as "geologically impossible." By truncating such distributions above P1%, the resulting mean values are more realistic.

A widely used alternative is **Swanson's Mean** (Megill, 1984), which works well for (1) n values consistent with exploration experience (i.e., most trends do not contain an infinite number of fields), (2) distributions truncated at the upper end, beyond P1%, and (3) distributions of low to moderate variance, including distributions truncated toward the low end by economic threshold requirements. Appendix A illustrates and reviews various techniques for calculating the mean of a lognormal distribution.

Techniques for Improving Geotechnical Estimates

Exploration staffs can learn to improve their geotechnical estimating performance by using at least seven techniques **(Table 3)**.

Geotechnical Analog Models

Since about 1950, geoscientists have increasingly developed and used "analog models"—exceptionally well-documented and well-understood examples of various "type" geologic situations—to anticipate dimensions, patterns, and associations of newly encountered (and therefore poorly documented) counterpart geologic phenomena. The first such models were stratigraphic. One example is the very well-known carbonate facies-complex of the middle Permian Guadalupean shelf-margin of west Texas and New Mexico (Newell et al., 1953; Pray, 1988). Another is the modern delta of the Mississippi River feeding into the Gulf of Mexico (Fisk, 1954; Coleman and Prior, 1982). Stratigraphers familiar with such models can often make far-reaching and insightful forecasts about newly encountered geologic situations, even though very little prospect-specific data exist. Now we also have structural models, such as the balanced structural models used to resolve and interpret seismic lines in complex thrusted terranes. Engineers routinely set up models of reservoir behavior. Economic models predict economic trends, given certain technologic and market developments. Such models effectively widen our conceptual and predictive ranges by providing flexible templates and characteristic associations that would never have been available to someone using only traditional geologic or economic principles. However, experienced geoscientists and engineers have learned that utilizing models too literally can lead to predictive errors; the lesson is to maintain flexibility in interpreting new geology based on analog models.

Multiple Working Hypotheses and Maps

T.C. Chamberlin's (1931) classic paper emphasizes the importance in scientific investigations of the conscious identification and evaluation of independent, multiple working hypotheses. To the exploration mind, it offers a disciplined method to widen predictive ranges because it forces the investigator to systematically construct and evaluate alternative interpretations of incomplete data sets. In its simplest practical form, it requires the prospector to make several possible maps of various prospect parameters, showing optimistic, intermediate, and pessimistic possible cases, or various possible structural or depositional interpretations of the geotechnical data.

Table 3 *Ways to improve accuracy and build confidence in estimating.*

1. USE OF GEOTECHNICAL MODELS AS ANALOGS
2. USE OF MULTIPLE WORKING HYPOTHESES AND MAPS
3. INDEPENDENT MULTIPLE ESTIMATES
   "Delphi Rounds"
   Team Exploration
   Peer and Committee Reviews
   Technical Subcommittees in Joint Ventures
4. "NATURE'S ENVELOPES"
   Lognormality
   Known Ranges of Parameters
   Plausibility Checks
5. "REALITY CHECKS"
   Field-size Distributions
   Historical Record
   Comparisons with Worldwide Databases
   Iteration and Tests for Reasonableness
6. PROPER STATISTICAL PROCEDURES
7. PRACTICE AND COMPARISON OF PRIOR PREDICTIONS WITH OUTCOMES

Independent Multiple Estimates

When we are estimating under uncertainty, the consideration and reconciliation of independent multiple estimates of the parameter yields forecasts that are generally less biased and closer to reality than the more orthodox procedure of devoting more time, money, and technology to additional study by a single investigator. Modern exploration firms accomplish this by organizational means, such as multidisciplinary exploration teams, peer reviews of emerging projects, formal prospect review by a centralized exploration risk committee, or structured iterative estimating procedures called "Delphi Rounds." Exploration joint ventures provide a practical way to achieve similar balance among participating partners who interact through technical subcommittees.

Nature's Envelopes

Most geologic and engineering variables involved in petroleum occurrence and production are distributed lognormally; similarly, our estimates of such parameters are also distributed lognormally. A few are distributed exponentially; fewer still are distributed normally. By understanding the probable distribution of a given parameter, we can make estimates that honor and are constrained by the expected distribution. Such "natural envelopes" lead to reduced bias and more realistic predictive ranges. Another natural envelope is provided by the known natural ranges of parameters. For example, we know that the largest known hydrocarbon recovery factor is about 1200 barrels per acre-foot (bbl/af); also, any oil reservoir yielding less than about 50 bbl/af is likely to be physically unresponsive. All geotechnical predictions should be made in observance of such natural envelopes. By projecting distributions out to the extremes, provisional P1% and P99% values may be checked to see if such large or small values are plausible; that is, do they constitute values that, when honoring available data, represent credible extreme high-side and low-side values?[2] If such extreme values are not plausible, the distribution must be shifted until they are.

Reality Checks

Once a preliminary estimate has been made, it should be tested repeatedly against known examples to ensure reasonability and obtain a best-fit. FSDs provide such a "reality check" against which prospect reserves estimates can be compared. The historical drilling record can provide a basis for evaluating estimates of discovery probability. Comparison of predicted prospect parameters against parameters measured in fields of similar type in the trend or basin, or against worldwide databases, can help evaluate those predictions. Comparison of the prospect's reserves variance against observed variance of analogous prospect types also provides useful reality checks (see p. 26).

Proper Statistical Procedures

Predictions of prospect parameters should be made using 80% confidence ranges, which calls for estimating high-side (P10%) and low-side (P90%) cases. Special attention should be given to the mean and median values in all parameter distributions. Because the mean reserves case is the expected outcome of every prospect, the economic viability of the mean must be assessed, so the key cash-flow model required is ordinarily based on the mean reserves case. Nevertheless, it may also be important to carry out discounted cash-flow (DCF) analyses on the P90%, P50%, and P10% reserves cases, especially for large-potential, costly exploration prospects. This is especially true where the relationship between project reserves and project net present value (NPV) is not constant, such as with production-sharing contracts where the host country takes an increasing percent as field reserve-size increases, or in offshore projects where "step-functions" may be introduced because of varying costs for offshore production facilities. For such situations, what is needed is the mean of NPVs of all reserves outcomes, rather than the NPV of only the mean reserves case. Mode, or "most likely," is a widely misunderstood statistical term that commonly leads to overoptimistic reserves forecasts, and its use by geotechnical and economic staff should be discouraged. Many explorationists *say* "most likely" when they are really *thinking* about an average, median, or "best guess" value. Accordingly, I recommend that "most likely" be expunged from use in forecasting or estimating.

Practice and Comparison of Prior Predictions with Outcomes

Discussion, justification, and refinement of geotechnical estimates among professional staff provides an excellent way to clarify, standardize, and improve their ability to make sound and consistent estimates of prospect parameters. In addition, disciplined comparison of predictions with actual outcomes provides objective feedback as to individual, team, and organizational performance in predicting prospect parameters. This

---

[2]Although a few international companies have adapted P5%–P50%–P95% as consistently used parameters, most utilize P10% and P90%, primarily because of early published work by Megill involving applications of Swanson's Rule (see Appendix A), and because estimators seem to be more comfortable with a generally used convention such as a 10% confidence than with a smaller confidence such as 5%. Experience suggests that subjective probability estimates become increasingly tenuous at extreme probability levels (Boccia, 1996).

requires systematic recording of predictions and periodic review of actual outcomes over a year or more in order to acquire an adequate sample and to observe the result of learning as expressed by continual improvement in predictive performance. Commonly, this requires persistence, strong management encouragement, and monitoring, if it is to produce a permanent change in organizational values and professional behavior (Rose, 1987). Companies such as Chevron (Otis and Schneidermann, 1997), Amoco (McMaster and Carragher, 1996), Unocal (Alexander and Lohr, 1998), and Santos (Johns et al., 1998), have published compelling accounts about the improvement of exploration performance through such methods.

Chapter 3

Risk Analysis of Exploration Prospects

Estimating Prospect Reserves

Constituent Parameters

The prospect reserves distribution is really an estimate of the range of ultimate volumes of oil and natural gas that may be recovered if the prospect discovers a producible hydrocarbon accumulation, which may become an oil or gas field. As discussed earlier, this value does not equate to "proved," "probable," or "possible" reserves, as formally defined engineering parameters (Capen, 1996; Cronquist, 1997). Those engineering definitions arose out of fiduciary needs and are subject to continual revision throughout the life of the field. They involve considerations of reservoir volume as well as detailed reservoir parameters, flow rates and decline curves, and multiple economic assumptions. Obviously, such details are usually not available for exploration ventures.

Accordingly, many companies employ a simpler set of parameters (Figure 6) that are more consistent with the high degree of uncertainty that attends exploratory prospects: Prospect Reserves = Productive Area (in acres, hectares, or kilometers^2) × Average Net Pay Thickness (in feet or meters) × Hydrocarbon-Recovery Factor (in bbl or mcf [thousand cubic feet] per net acre-foot, bbl per net m^3/hectare-meter, or m^3 per net km^2–m). The parameters shown in **Figure 6** are deterministic; that is, single-value estimates for each parameter, all of which, because of substantial geotechnical uncertainty, are much better forecast as a probabilistic range of possible outcomes. Deterministic predictions are generally unreliable; fortunately, their use in the modern exploration industry is diminishing.

Productive Area

Utilizing geologic and geophysical data in the prospect area, professional staff are asked to make maps showing a reasonable high-side productive area, given optimistic geologic conditions such as seismic velocities, dip rates, contour configurations, fault extents, trap fill-up, and the like. They also construct maps showing a low-side area, assuming pessimistic geologic conditions, and an intermediate area using best-guess conditions. Values derived from such geologic cases are plotted on a cumulative log probability graph **(Figure 7),** equating to a reasonable, optimistic case (P10%) and a reasonable, pessimistic case (P90%), and a straight, sloping line is "best-fitted" to the data, forcing the distribution to be lognormal. The P50% case is consequential, derived from the intersection of the P50% horizontal line and the sloping line. Next, the provisional distribution is projected out to the low (P99%) and high (P1%) extremes, which are assessed for their plausibility as being highly unlikely but possible outcomes. The P1% value should be so large that it is barely possible, honoring the data; similarly, the P99% value should be just large enough to be consistent with a very small detectable reservoired accumulation. A "final" distribution should be developed, following several iterations and adjustments, utilizing given plausibility checks and reality checks such as those shown on **Table 4**. There is no "formula" for deriving the P90% area. It must be prospect-specific and consistent with anticipated structural configuration of the closure and stratigraphy of the reservoir section.[3] In general, however, the P90% area should be small, corresponding very roughly to an onshore, marginally economic area of drainage (assuming pay thickness and hydrocarbon [HC] recovery are sufficient to warrant completion)—a one- or two-well field. Based on theoretical grounds, empirical observations **(Figure 8)**, plots of actual fields in real basins **(Figure 9)**, and detailed analyses (Squire, 1996), the distribution of area forecasts is lognormal in form.

In practice, geoscientists seem to be able to arrive at high-side estimates for prospect area (P1% and P10%) fairly readily. However, settling on appropriate

---
[3]Elongated trap areas and reservoirs having low net-to-gross ratios will tend to be associated, of necessity, with larger P90% areas than equidimensional closures and high net-to-gross ratios, as described in Appendix C.

Estimating Prospect Reserves

Area
(1200 ac)

X

Average Net Pay
(75 ft)

X

HC-Recovery Factor
(200 bbl/af)

200 bbl/acre-foot

= Prospect Reserves
(18,000,000 bbl)

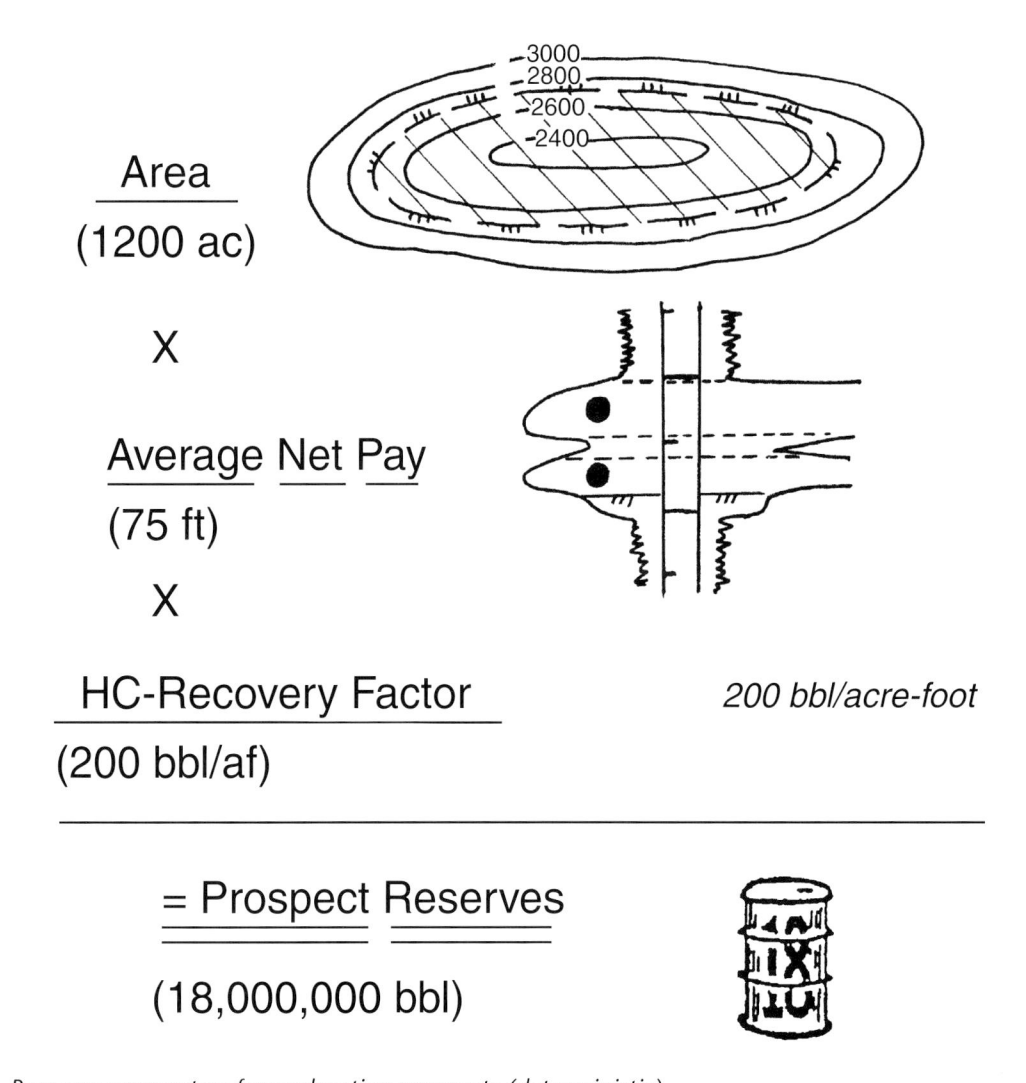

Figure 6 *Reserves parameters for exploration prospects (deterministic).*

low-side values seems to be more problematic. The most common error is that estimates of P90% and P99% areas are too large, leading to frequent overestimates of mean area and thus mean reserves. But the determination of the area distribution cannot be "formulaic"—it must be consistent with the data bearing on prospect geometry, and it must be prospect-specific. This is discussed in detail in Appendix C.

Two general estimating approaches seem to dominate:

1. Estimates are made of optimistic (P10%) and pessimistic (P90%) cases, which are then plotted on a log probability graph, and a straight, sloping line is drawn between the two points. This line is then extended out to the P1% and P99% extremes, which are evaluated for plausibility. If any of the derived values are implausible, the line is adjusted until a credible best fit is achieved. This approach is preferred, especially for less experienced prospectors.

2. Assuming all plausible conditions maximizing productive area are operative (velocities as they affect dip rates, contouring, trap fill-up), the resulting maximum outline of that area is mapped and measured; this "max area" is provisionally assigned to P1%. Next, the smallest possible area is assumed (consistent with the geologic attributes of the prospect) that would be consistent with a reservoired small HC-accumulation just large enough to sustain flow. This area is assigned a provisional P99% value. Both values are plotted on a log probability graph. From the

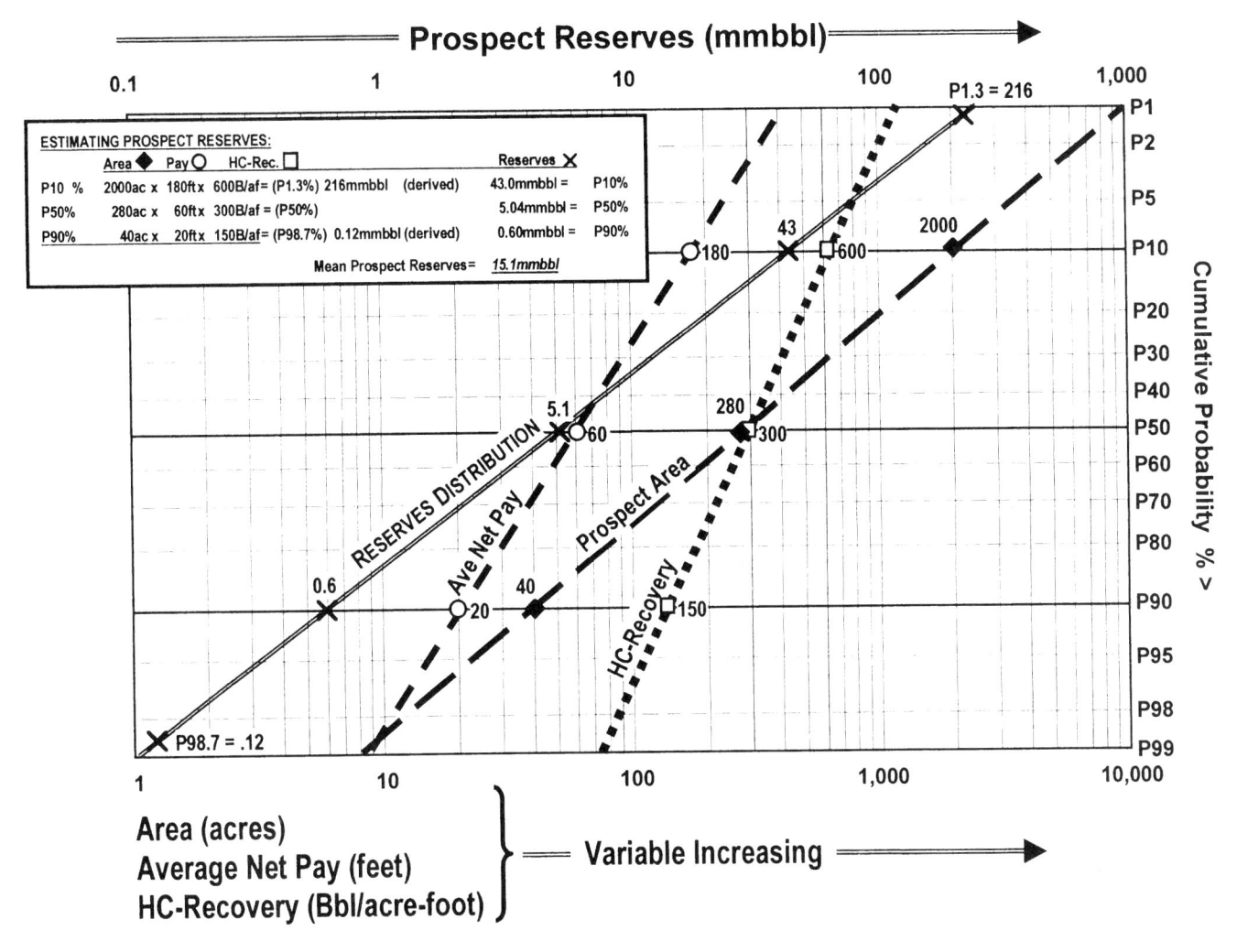

Figure 7 *Area, average net pay, and HC-recovery factor are lognormal.*

distribution line, the consequent P90%, P50%, and P10% values are derived and checked for credibility. Again, the line is adjusted as necessary to produce a plausible best-fit distribution.

It should be recognized that, following these methods, any outcome larger than the P1% forecast is treated as impossible, which is not strictly true but pragmatically can be dismissed as such. Thus no value larger than the P1% value can contribute to the mean of the distribution.

Average Net Pay Thickness

Using lithofacies, isopach, porosity and net-to-gross maps, geologic studies of pertinent depositional models, and analog field studies, and considering the interactive effects of the oil/water contact, geologic structure, and reservoir distribution, the exploration team generates a probabilistic distribution of estimated average net pay throughout the area of the accumulation based on P1%, P10%, P50%, P90%, and P99% confidence levels plotted on log probability graphs **(Figure 7)**. Such estimates should be derived in an analogous manner to the area estimates previously described and employing similar reality checks **(Table 4)**. This parameter also typically follows a lognormal distribution **(Figure 8)**, but one ordinarily having less variance than the area distribution. In order to consider porous and tight intervals, reservoir net-to-gross ratio must be considered. Also, a geometric adjustment will need to be made to take into account the geometry of the oil/water contact in relation to the reservoir geometry **(Figure 10)**. For most new-field wildcat (NFW) prospects, a distribution of estimated average net pay thickness (determined as described earlier), throughout the productive area will suffice. It is essential to understand that the "average net pay thickness" estimate integrates internal reservoir distribution, porosity cutoffs, trap fill-up, net-to-gross ratio, and the geometry of the "top-reservoir/oil-water contact" couplet.

Gross Rock Volume

A useful alternative to the Area × Average Net Pay approach outlined previously is to estimate the probabilistic range in Gross Rock Volume (GRV). There are

20 **Risk Analysis of Exploration Prospects**

Table 4 Reality checks (1): characteristics of the endpoints of the reserves distribution.*

	"Low End"			"High End"	
	Absolute Minimum (P99%)	**Reasonable Minimum (P90%)**	**Onshore Development Well**	**Absolute Maximum (P1%)**	**Known Max Values for N American Fields**
AREA	Area too small to be economic anywhere; roughly the area of a very small one-well field. Must be consistent with expected trap geometry.	Approximately the area of an onshore field that is economically marginal; typically about 1–3 onshore production spacing units. May vary according to structural configuration. Could be larger in a frontier play area.	Onshore production spacing units: 10–60 acres (oil) 160–640 acres (gas)	Honoring the data, the maximum area possible if all relevant geologic and geophysical factors are most favorable; area so large as to be barely possible.	500,000 acres (oil) 5,000,000 acres (gas)
AVERAGE NET PAY	Pay zone just thick enough to sustain flow of mobile HCs sufficient to sense in mudstream or logs, and sustain on a DST.	Roughly the minimum thickness you would consider completing in an onshore field. Could be thicker in a frontier play area.	More than 3 feet (= 1 meter)	Maximum average net pay thickness possible based on regional isopach and net/gross maps, and considering geometric factor. Thickness so large as to be barely possible.	1,000′ oil
HC-RECOVERY FACTOR	Ordinarily less than 100 bbl/af; too tight for an economic reservoir, even onshore; sufficient permeability to barely flow. Must be consistent with known reservoir properties in trend.	Minimum porosity and permeability to sustain flow, or to be commercial onshore, consistent with pertinent data in trend. Pay attention to values in analog fields.	More than 100 bbl/af (oil) More than 125 mcf/af (gas)	Compare critically with highest projected; HC-recovery factor known (or analogous) for trend. Also justify against high-side estimates of Ø, S_o, % Rec., and FVF.	1,200 bbl/af (oil) 2,000 mcf/af (gas)
ULTIMATE RECOVERY BOE	A small, noneconomic accumulation with only enough reserves to barely flow; comparable with a mediocre onshore one-well field.	A modest onshore field of about 1–3 wells; could be larger in a frontier play area.	More than ~40,000 bbl oil More than 250,000 MCFG	Compare critically with the largest existing field in the trend, or reasonable analog; check against trend FSD; must be prospect-specific.	16,000 BOE (Prudhoe) 6,000 MMBOE (E. Texas) 70,000 BCFG (Hugoton)

*originally developed by the writer, and vetted by geotechnical staff from Conoco, Marathon, and Mobil.

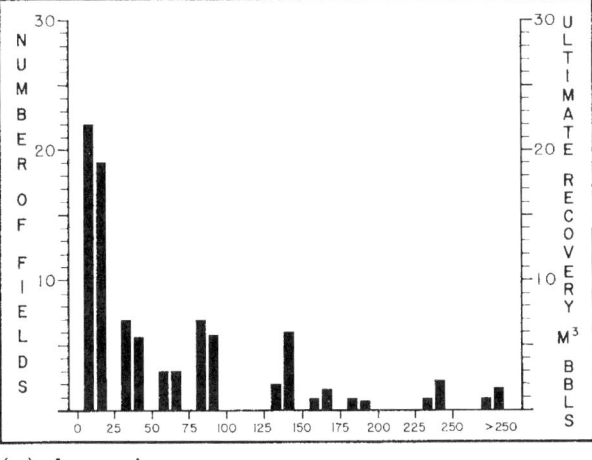

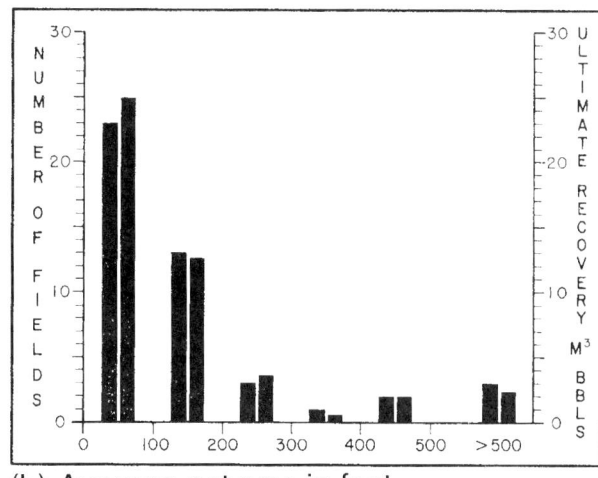

(a) Area, in acres

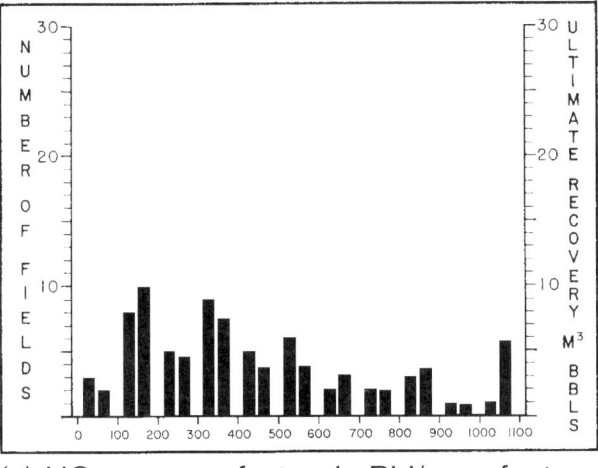

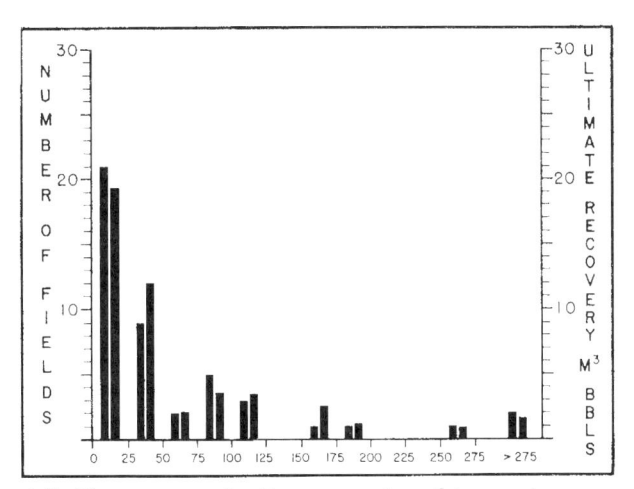

(b) Average net pay, in feet

(c) HC-recovery factor, in Bbl/acre-foot

(d) Recovery, in thousands of barrels per acre

Figure 8 *Distributions of estimated parameters for prospect reserves.*

both advantages and disadvantages to this alternative. The advantages are:

1. It eliminates minor problems caused by the common partial dependency of average net pay thickness on productive area;
2. Calculation of the geometry factor required for correct expressions of average net pay can be dispensed with;
3. Integration of maximum (P1%) area with associated vertical column height and gross reservoir thickness ("area vs. depth plots") will generate a maximum gross rock volume that represents a reality check on the upper limit for GRV **(Figure 11)**;
4. Consideration of minimum pay zone thickness (taking into account expected net/gross reservoir ratios and required HC column heights), together with the resulting associated area of accumulation that would be required to provide a reservoired accumulation of sufficient volume to support sustained flow, provides a reality check consistent with P99% for GRV; and
5. Plotting these upper and lower values as P1% and P99% on log probability graph paper allows derivation of P10%, P50%, and P90% values for GRV.

The disadvantages, however, are more compelling: GRV is a complex number combining area, thickness, and reservoir/water-level geometry considerations. Accordingly, geoscientists find it quite difficult to relate GRV intuitively to maps or cross sections and, therefore, often don't recognize whether their probabilistic estimates of GRV may be implausible. Moreover, when GRV estimates are checked in post-audit drilling reviews, it is not immediately apparent whether errors were related to area, thickness, or geometric misjudgments. The fundamental problem here is that explorationists conceptualize prospects in relation to maps (area) and logs and cross sections (thickness), and

22 Risk Analysis of Exploration Prospects

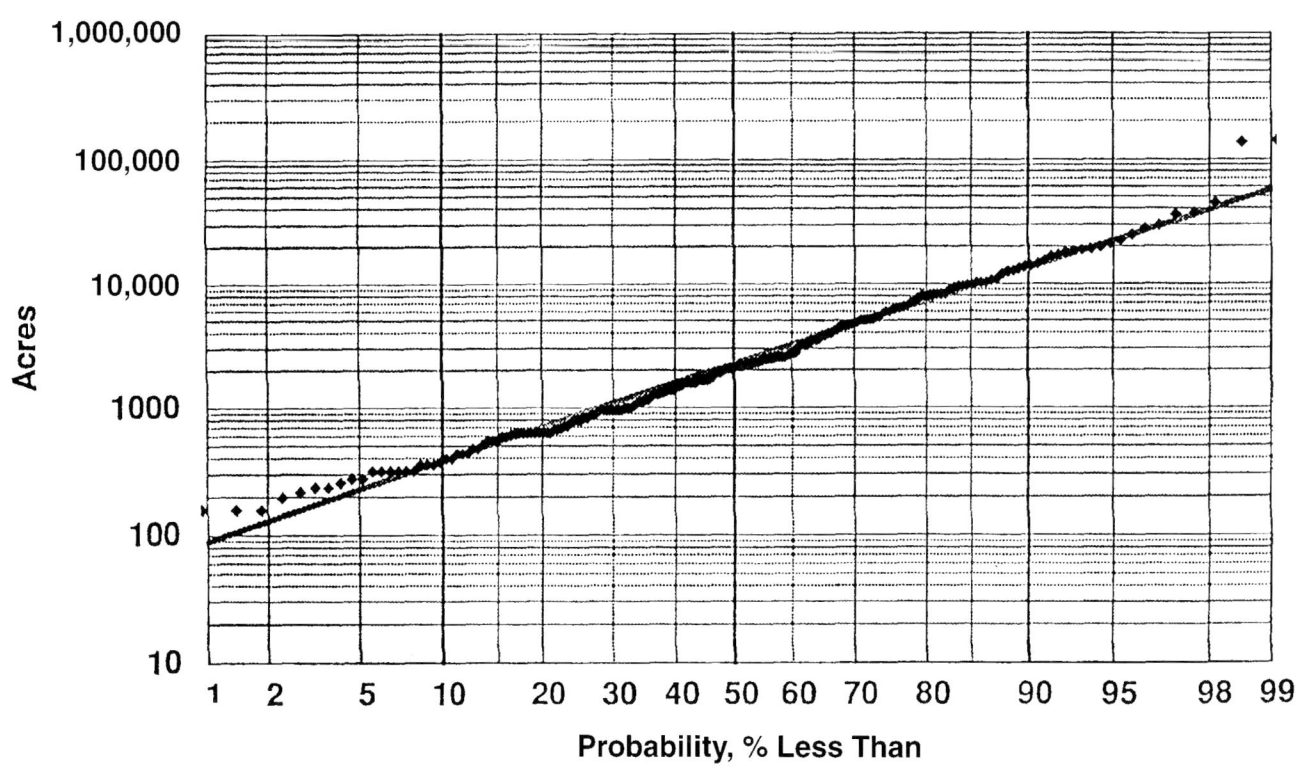

Figure 9 *Productive field areas, East Texas, Capen.*

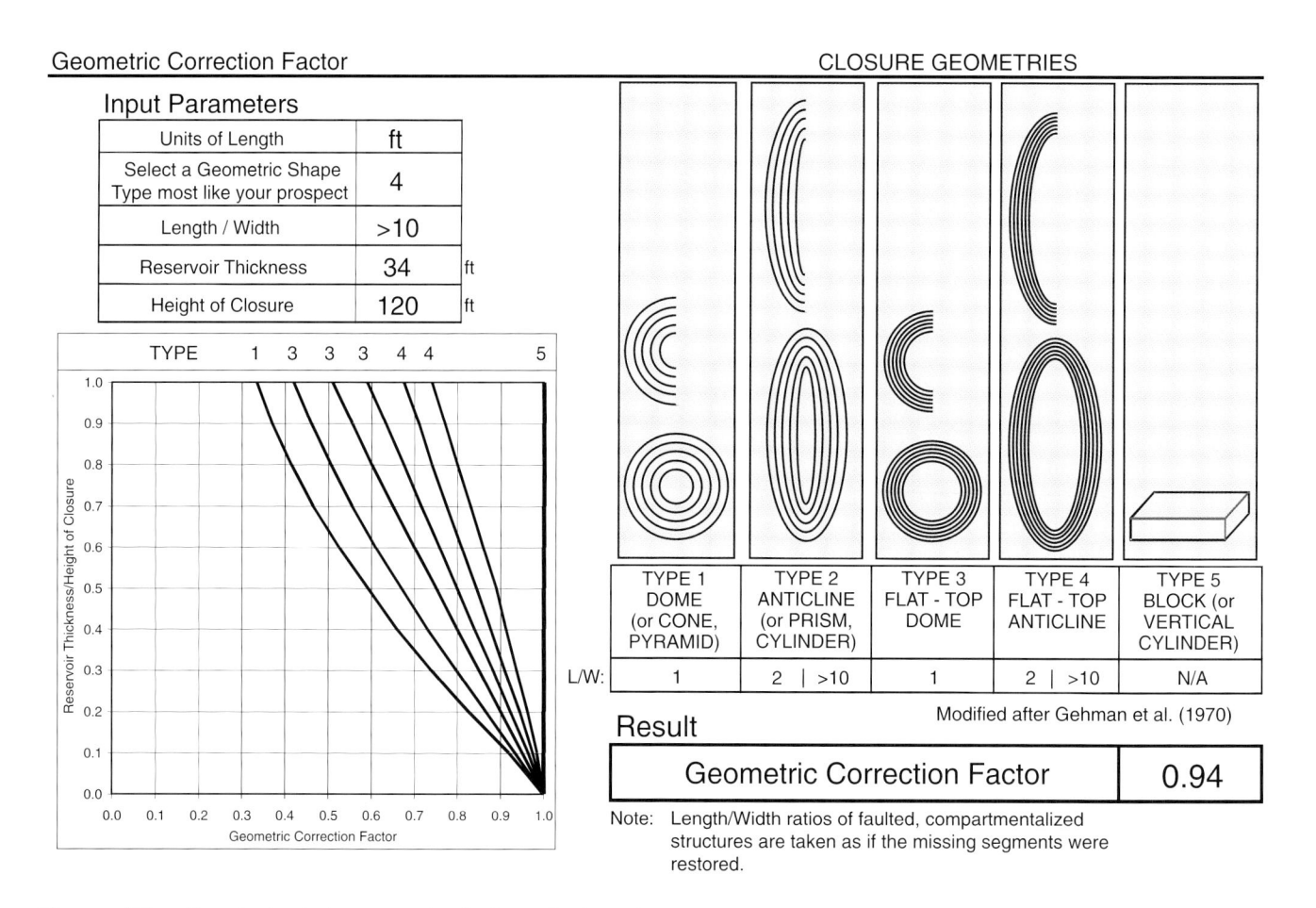

Figure 10 *Graphs to derive geometry factor adjustment.*

AREA, ACRES, OR AC-FT X 100

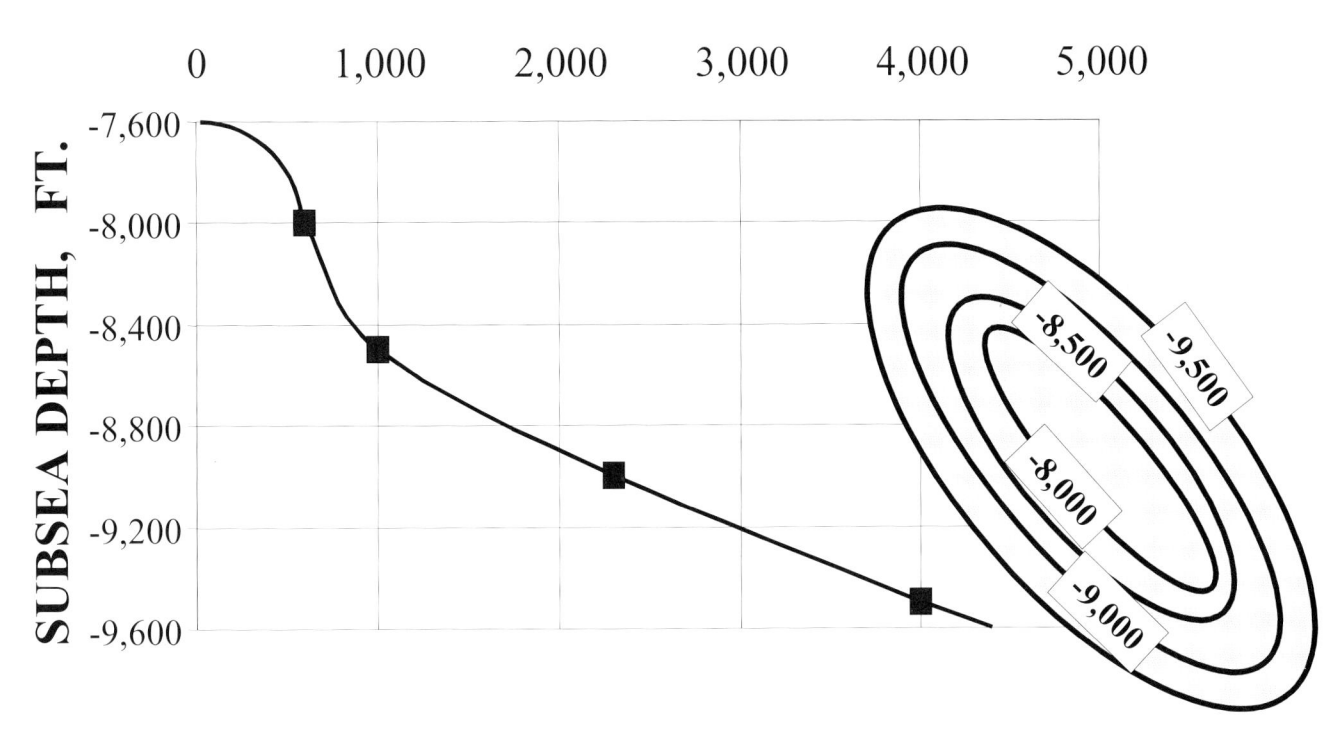

Figure 11 *Area versus depth plot.*

therefore they have a much better subjective appreciation of the credibility of such estimates than of their combination as GRV, which is a parameter having three variables (area, thickness, and geometry), and thus having a wide range of possible combinations capable of giving the same product.

In fact, utilization of both approaches often provides valuable cross-checks for consistency, and usually leads to better estimates of prospect reserves. That's why use of both procedures is recommended.

In any case, however, GRV, combined probabilistically with estimates of reservoir net/gross and HC-recovery factor, yields a lognormal probabilistic reserves distribution that should be compatible with the reserves distribution derived via the "Area × Average Net Pay × HC-recovery Factor" method.

Estimation of both the P1% and P99% cases will require construction of an "Area vs. Depth" plot, as shown in **Figure 11**. Such plots are readily constructed by measuring the areas enclosed by successive contours. "Depth" is understood to indicate the vertical difference from the crest of the feature to the projected oil/water contact (or gas/water or gas/oil contact where appropriate).

Hydrocarbon-recovery Factor

This parameter expresses "reservoir yield" as barrels (bbl) of oil or mcf (thousand cubic feet) of natural gas per acre-foot of reservoir. It is readily adaptable to the metric system, or to expressing oil in metric tons. Some companies choose to break this parameter down into its four constituent components: porosity, HC-saturation, percent recovery, and formation volume factor. This is not wrong, but for most exploratory ventures, it represents false precision and inefficient use of geotechnical effort: HC-recovery factor is entirely adequate given the high level of uncertainty that attends most exploratory prospects. However, many companies choose to estimate the four constituent components as reasonable P10%–P50%–P90% ranges, and combine them, via Monte Carlo simulation, as a reality check to ensure that HC-recovery factor estimates are indeed credible values consistent with known or postulated reservoir parameters. Also, expressing yield as bbls or mcf per acre-foot is compatible with the widespread use of analog field models in modern exploration. Again, a range of rational probabilistic estimates is generated by the exploration team, analogous to the process described previously **(Figure 7)**, and plotted on a cumulative log probability graph, then iterated and adjusted until a best-fit is reached. This parameter also takes a lognormal form **(Figure 8)**. The components of HC-recovery factor and metric equivalencies are shown on **Table 5**. All estimates should be reality-checked **(Table 4)**.

Table 5 *Getting a sense of scale about HC-recovery factor.**

	φ	S$_w$	FVF	% REC
100 BAF	15%	39%	1.4	20%
300 BAF	20%	32%	1.2	35%
460 BAF	25%	25%	1.4	45%

METRIC EQUIVALENTS: 100 bbl/af = 13,000 m^3/km^2–m = 130 m^3/hectare-m

1 acre = .004 km^2

1 km^2 = 247 acres

1 hectare = 2.47 acres

*S$_w$=water saturation; FVF=formation volume factor; % REC=percent recoverable; BAF=barrels per acre-foot

Generation of the Prospect-reserves Distribution

When probabilistic estimates of prospect area, average net pay, and HC-recovery have been posted on a log probability graph (**Figure 7**), reconciled with available reality checks (**Table 4**), and accepted by a consensus of concerned geotechnical staff, the three distributions should then be combined by multiplication into the prospect-reserves distribution. Ordinarily this combination is accomplished through reiterative computer procedures. The two most widely used procedures are Monte Carlo simulation and Latin Hypercube simulation. Through their AAPG school on risk analysis, Capen, Megill, and Rose developed an analytic method that graphically performs the combination on cumulative log probability paper, assuming the three component distributions are lognormal and have variances that are not drastically different (Appendix C). This method was described by Capen (1992), Megill (1992), and Rose and Thompson (1991). **Figure 12** illustrates this graphical procedure.

The resultant prospect-reserves distribution (**Figures 7 and 12**), because it involves the multiplication of three constituent independent variables, is expected to take a lognormal form. The mean represents the single best expression of the distribution's value. **Table 6** provides very useful reality checks of the prospect-reserves distribution, relating its variance to the category of exploratory venture, as well as modifying data, such as three-dimensional (3-D) seismic data, and positive indications of direct hydrocarbon indicators (DHIs).

Finally, it should be emphasized that most prospect-reserves overestimates do not arise because the high-side estimates are too high, but rather because the low-side estimates are too high. Accordingly, when reviewing any prospects, all prospectors (as well as their managers) should unfailingly ask the following question: Is there any chance this prospect could turn out to be a mediocre little one-well field? If the honest answer is yes, then the P99% value must reflect such an unfortunate outcome, and the consequential P90% value must also be compatible. Appendix B is an essay that covers this issue in detail, and all prospectors should read it carefully. **Table 6** is also useful in addressing such issues.

Note that multiplication of the three 90% values yields a value corresponding to the P98.7% reserves product, and the three P10% values multiply to give a P1.3% product. This pattern, explained in more detail in Appendix C, is important in considering what low-side geologic values are being risked when estimating the chance of geologic success (see pp. 35–36).

Economic Translation of the Prospect-reserves Distribution

Because the mean is the best single expression of the total prospect-reserves distribution, many companies perform an economic analysis on only the mean reserves case of prospects. This is adequate in many cases. For important projects, however, discounted cash-flow (DCF) analyses should be performed on all four key reserve parameters (P10%, P50%, Mean, P90%), in order to understand the relative profitabilities of a full range of prospect outcomes. This can then lead to a *profitability distribution* for the key prospect, given success. In other words, what we are really after is not the net present value (NPV) of the mean reserves case, but rather, the mean of the NPVs of all four reserves cases. This is especially important in production-sharing contracts and in expensive offshore projects where step-functions create a nonlinear reserves/PV ratio having multiple inflections in the curve.

If project managers can estimate the approximate reserves required for *completion* of the exploratory well as a commercial venture, on a cost-forward basis, or reserves required for *economic profitability* on a full-cycle economic basis, the prospect-reserves distribution can then be used to estimate the *chance of commercial success*,

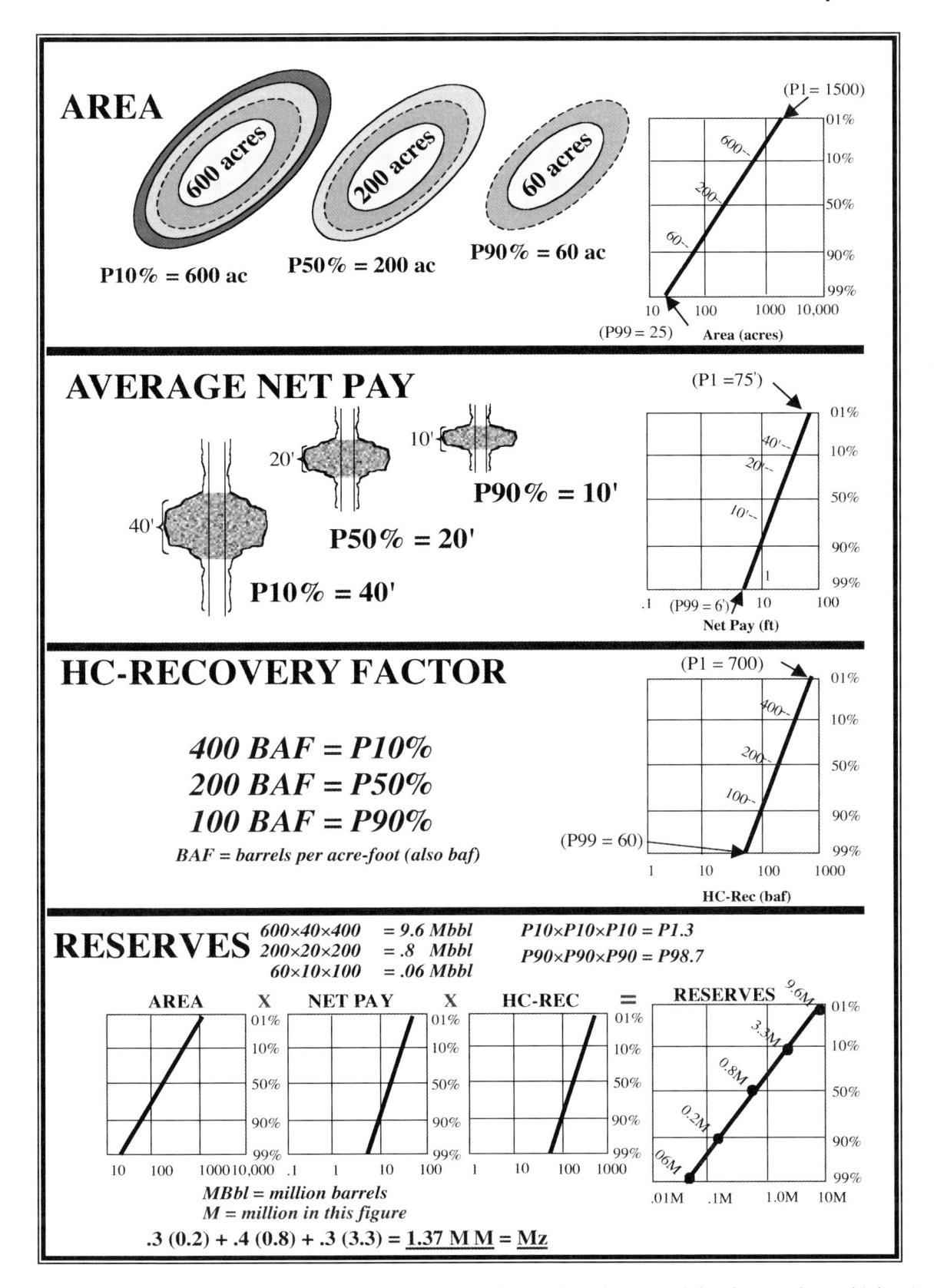

Figure 12 *Graphical method for analytical solution for combining three lognormal distributions by multiplication.*

and the *chance of economic success*, given that flowing hydrocarbons are discovered. The proportion, as a percent, of the reserves distribution that is larger than the minimum reserve amount needed to justify *commercial* and *economic* success, respectively, represents the chance of finding those volumes of reserves (or more), *given that reservoired mobile hydrocarbons are found at all*. This concept is discussed in further detail on pages 39–41.

Table 6 Reality checks (2): characteristic ranges associated with oil and gas ventures having different magnitudes of uncertainty.*

Statistical Parameters	Development Well	Step-out/ Extension	Wildcat in Known Productive Trend	Rank Wildcat in Proven Trend	Rank Wildcat in New Play or New Basin
P10%/P90%	2.2 → 7.0	5 → 25	10 → 120	55 → 220	120 → 650
Probability range in which Mean typically occurs	P44%–P33%	P38%–P26%	P33%–P17%	P22%–P14%	P17%–P10%
Variance (σ^2)	.09–.58	.40–1.58	.81–3.50	2.45–4.02	3.50–6.40

*This table was first developed by Julia B. Ericsson (Conoco) and subsequently vetted by geotechnical staff from Marathon, Mobil, and other companies.

Field-size distributions (FSDs) for the basin or play (see p. 11) provide effective reality checks against which the prospect-reserves distribution should be compared. Also, the variance of the prospect-reserves distribution should be compatible with the exploration well class, as shown in **Table 6**. But the variance of the prospect-reserves distribution is also a function of the quantity and quality of pertinent information, as well as of the geotechnical skill of the professional staff evaluating it, and all such factors must be considered. For all these reasons, the prospect-reserves distribution need not have the same variance as the parent FSD. In fact, prospect-reserves distributions commonly (but not always) show variances *smaller* than their parent FSD. Because FSDs tend to get smaller as exploration progresses **(Figure 5a)**, prospect-reserves distributions should be compared with fields that have been recently discovered, using compatible exploration concepts and technologies.

Monitoring and Improving Predictive Performance

Until recently, the systematic preservation of reserve predictions and their comparison with prospect outcomes has not been part of the corporate culture of most oil companies. Management often did not know how inaccurate reserve predictions were, whether there were any repetitive patterns of estimation errors, or what the specific causes for persistent errors might be.

From an organizational perspective, it is easy to understand the reluctance of geotechnical staffs to preserve their forecasts and compare against outcomes. But it is difficult to understand why higher management has not insisted on systematic monitoring of predictive performance by geotechnical staff and continuous efforts to improve such forecasts because of their profound impact on project profitability.

Two methods are currently in use. The first (Rose, 1987) employs simple log-log cross-plots **(Figure 13)** of prospect parameters such as:

- prospect area
- average net pay thickness
- HC-recovery factor (or its constituents—porosity, oil saturation, percent recovery, and formation volume factor)
- initial production rate
- percentage decline
- prospect reserves (= EUR)

By plotting the median of predicted parameter distributions against the actual outcomes, we can, with a relatively small number of trials, gain insight into the variance (scatter) as well as any existing bias. If staff are unbiased, we should have about the same number of overestimates as underestimates. About 10% of outcomes should be larger than their P10% estimate, and about 10% should fall below their P90% estimates. About 80% of outcomes should fall within their P10%–P90% ranges. Causes of undesirable performance patterns can be investigated by going back to individual prospect cases. This method is especially useful to individuals and smaller organizations who may drill only a few wells per year. The method can also be applied to geotechnical predictions made on competitor wells. Additional information can be gleaned by plotting the predicted P10%–P90% range on the horizontal axis and the actual outcome on the vertical axis.

The second method (Clapp and Stibolt, 1991) for monitoring and improving reserves forecasting **(Figure 14)** employs continuous "tracking" of an ongoing exploration program, comparing actual geologic

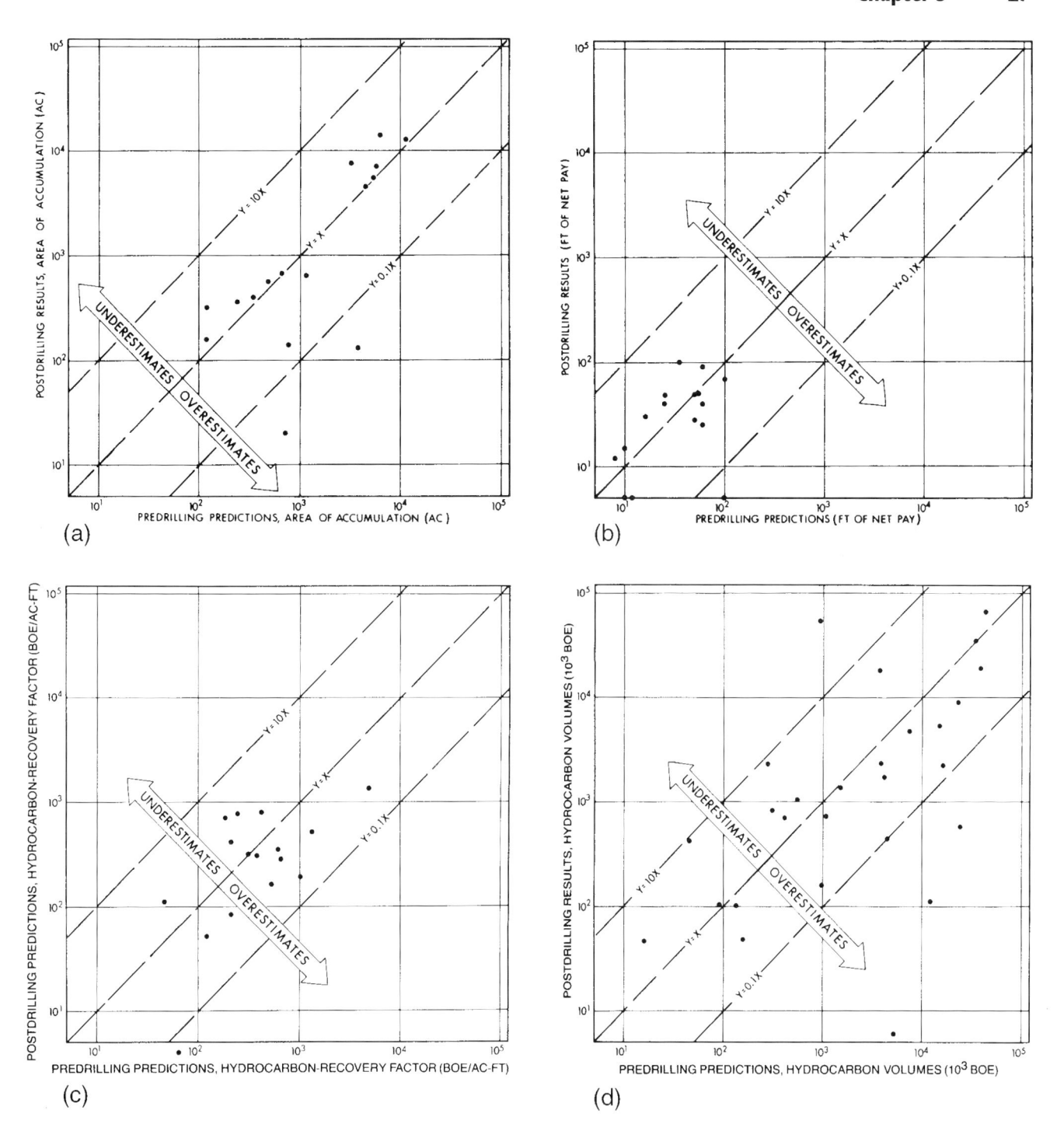

Figure 13 *Comparison of predictions versus outcomes (from Rose, 1987).*

reserves-added against chance-weighted mean reserves of all prospects in the program. A cumulative "actual reserves-added" curve is plotted in relation to an "envelope" bounded by the cumulative P10% and P90% predictions as well as the "expected" (= mean) curves. A predictive envelope for numbers of new discoveries can similarly be constructed, which can reveal bias in "chance of success" forecasts. Any time the actual performance goes outside the forecast P10%–P90% envelope, management legitimately can suspect that there are serious problems with reserves or chance predictions by geotechnical staff,[4] and corrective measures must be instituted. This second method requires Monte Carlo (or Latin Hypercube) simulation to *add* (rather than *multiply*) prospect reserves parameters of serial exploration ventures. The

---
[4] A series of outcomes that collectively fall below the P90% boundary would have less than a 10% chance of being the result of random chance alone.

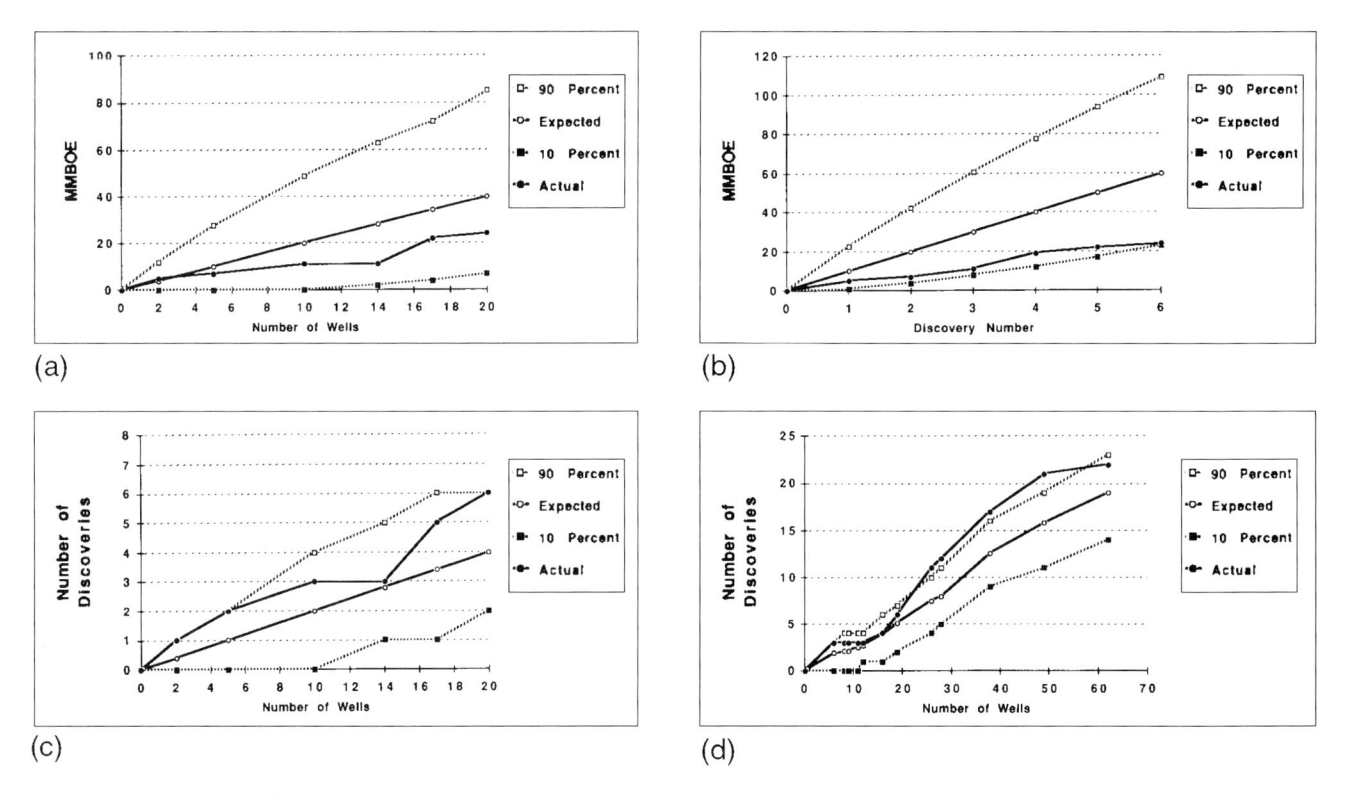

Figure 14 (a, b, c, d) *Continuous tracking of organizational predictive performance (Copyright SPE #22038. From Clapp & Stibolt, 1991, reprinted with permission.)*

only limitation to this method is that additional analysis, such as cross-plots as described earlier, are necessary to isolate and identify the specific causes of estimation bias because the method reveals only bias, not its root causes.

Such routine monitoring of actual performance can be instituted in exploration organizations if (1) management insists on such activity being carried out, (2) results are circulated openly within the organization, (3) geotechnical staff accept unbiased predictive performance as part of their professional obligations, and (4) results are used *constructively*, to improve staff performance, rather than *punitively*.

Industry Experience

Persistent Overestimation of Prospect Reserves

Since 1993, most oil companies have acknowledged that their geotechnical staffs persistently overestimate prospect reserves, commonly by about 30% to 80%. Three of the four cross-plots on **Figure 2 (b, c,** and **d)** document such overoptimistic bias as expressed by individual companies. But overoptimism is not limited to certain companies—it appears to be a chronic industry shortcoming that has proved to be difficult to correct. **Figure 15** records the predictive performance of all companies that made discoveries in the Norwegian North Sea during the 8th to 14th rounds, resulting in only 38% of the new reserves predicted. Moreover, this bias is not improved by modern technology: as an example, BP-Amoco (Harper, 1999) reports persistent overoptimistic bias in their deep-water exploration program, which employs state-of-the-art seismic technology, since the early 1990s **(Figure 16)**. BP-Amoco's successful deep-water ventures found only 45% of the reserves predicted. Before addressing the real causes of reserves overestimation, it is important to emphasize that the problem is *not* caused by comparison of "before-discovery EURs" with "after-discovery booked (or fiduciary) reserves." Exploration estimates of reserves before drilling and after discovery relate to the same parameter: EUR. At least six real causes are responsible for this bias.

Motivational Bias

Individual prospectors, *as well as their managers,* appear to allow their enthusiasm for drilling the exploratory well to overcome their objective estimates of prospect-reserve parameters. This can be overcome by emphasizing the correct criterion for company success: *adding value, not drilling wells.* Sometimes the operative motivation seems to be: "I cannot get promoted unless I find oil, and I cannot find oil unless I get my wells drilled," so prospect parameters are enhanced in order to encourage management to drill inferior prospects. Also, upper management's desire to find large new fields may tend to encourage the entire staff to expect such large discoveries (Boccia, 1996).

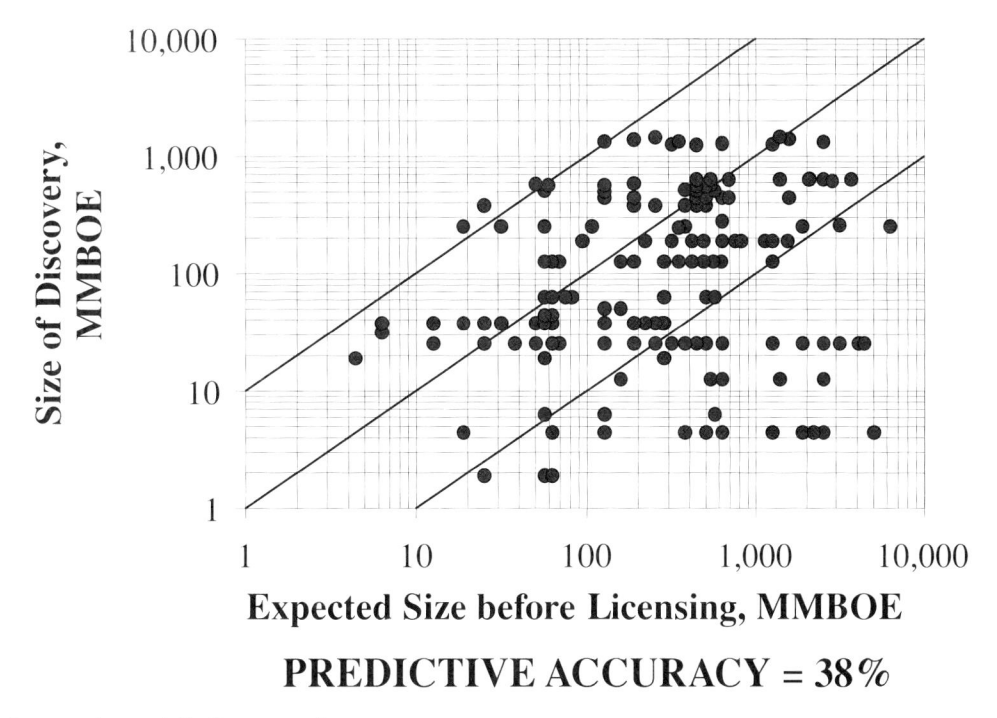

Figure 15 *Pre- and postdrill discovery sizes.*

Volume Accuracy - Deep-water Targets = 45%

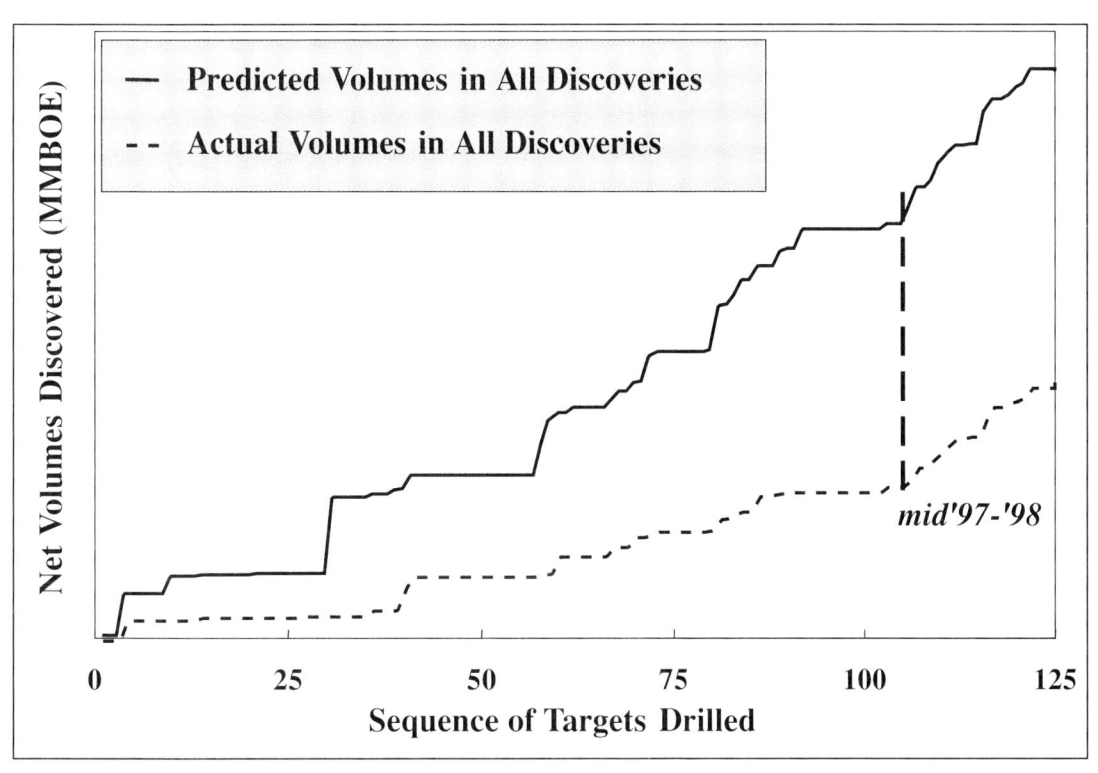

Harper, 1999, reprinted with permission

Figure 16 *Volume accuracy.*

Low-side Estimates Too Large

Large-company employees who have not worked extensively in mature, onshore provinces are simply unaware of how very many small fields can be present in a given basin or trend. Accordingly, they do not set their P90% estimates for prospect area, pay, and recovery factor small enough, so their resulting P99% reserves estimates are too large. Clear evidence of this problem is that the P10%/P90% ratios of prospect reserves for such prospects are too small (i.e. characteristic of development or extension wells rather than exploratory wells). Here are two useful paradigms that help convey reality: (1) The most common field size in the Permian Basin of west Texas is 10,000–20,000 barrels; (2) The P99% field size in most mature provinces is 1,000 to 10,000 barrels. Accordingly, this question should be addressed to every considered prospect: "Could this prospect turn out to be a mediocre little one-well field?" In most cases, the honest answer must be yes. The P99% reserve value should reflect this.

Overconfidence in Geotechnical Discrimination

Another key insight derived from examination of **Figure 2** is that geoscientists are not capable of effectively discriminating between prospects that contain large volumes of oil and prospects that contain small volumes of oil (see p. 6). Petroleum prospectors can identify anomalies (called "prospects") that have an enhanced likelihood of containing oil and gas accumulations. And they can also distinguish, to some degree, those prospects that are large enough to contain large reserves from those prospects that are not. But they usually cannot identify large prospects that are significantly underfilled, thus containing small-volume reserves. Furthermore, other parameters such as average net pay and HC-recovery have such a large impact on reserves and are so variable that our ability to predict them with precision is limited.

Deterministic Estimates Rather than Probabilistic Ranges

Single-value estimates of uncertain parameters predict an outcome that is possible, usually optimistic, and nearly always wrong.

Using Triangular Distributions Rather than Lognormal Distributions

Triangular distributions are a very poor proxy for the prevailing lognormal distribution and usually lead to substantial overestimation.

Nonrepresentative Analog Field-size Distributions

FSDs are very useful as reality checks, indicating the characteristic sizes of fields that exist in a basin or trend. However, it is important that the FSD employed as analog is in fact a valid example: it must comprise fields that have been discovered in current or recent exploration campaigns, using technology consistent with your prospect. It is incorrect and misleading to include in a "current" (2000) FSD, discoveries that were made 40 years ago, during the "flush" period of exploration.

Failure to Monitor Long-term Field Growth

Another factor may actually work the other way: work by Wood et al. (1990) and Attanasi and Root (1994) has emphasized that long after their discovery, oil and gas fields continue to grow. Such reserve appreciation goes on for 50 years or more in large fields, and it is surprisingly substantial: reserve appreciation of booked reserves is nearly 10 times the initial reserve estimate of U.S. oil and gas fields and more than 8 times the initial estimate for U.S. gas fields. When such subsequent field growth is not monitored and periodically compared against initial prospect reserve predictions, some prospect-reserve predictions may erroneously appear to have been more overoptimistic than they really were. However, unpublished data by Mobil Oil Corporation demonstrate that no bias exists in forecasts of field EURs made immediately after discovery, compared with field-reserve projections made after extensive drilling and production data were available: there is great uncertainty in such estimates, but little or no apparent bias (Dave Cook, personal communication, 1997). Unpublished data from BP-Amoco show a similar lack of bias.

Remedies

The few oil companies that can report unbiased reserves estimations (McMaster, 1998) are organizations whose staff professionals know that management desires their objective geotechnical estimates, that management is monitoring staff predictive performance, and that unbiased predictive performance will be recognized and rewarded. Such staffs have received and utilized training in estimating proposed parameters, and they know the patterns leading to bias. They typically accept professional accountability for objective estimating. Nevertheless, it must be acknowledged that overestimation of prospect reserves is a widespread industry bias that has proved difficult to eliminate (Johns et al., 1998; Alexander and Lohr, 1998; Harper, 1999). The single most effective remedy is to ensure that the P99% values reasonably represent a very small reservoired accumulation that would be flowable.

Reducing Uncertainty—What Is Possible?

With regard to reducing uncertainty, companies that rigorously employ methods like those described earlier report that they can consistently reduce predictive ranges of reserves from 2 to 3 orders of magnitude at 90% confidence, to 1.0 to 1.5 orders of magnitude at 80% confidence. Obviously, data quality

Table 7 *Expected value examples (coin toss).*

Trial	Outcome	Consequence − Cost	Profit/Loss × Probability =	Risked Result
Free trial	Correct call	+$20,000 − 0 =	+$20,000 × 0.5 =	+$10,000
	Incorrect call	0 − 0 =	0 × 0.5 =	0
				+$10,000 = EV
$10,000 trial	Correct call	+$20,000 − $10,000 =	+$10,000 × 0.5 =	+$5,000
	Incorrect call	0 − $10,000 =	−$10,000 × 0.5 =	−$5,000
				0 = EV
$4,000 trial	Correct call	+$20,000 − $4,000 =	+$16,000 × 0.5 =	+$8,000
	Incorrect call	0 − $4,000 =	−$4,000 × 0.5 =	−$2,000
				+$6,000 = EV

and quantity have substantial influence here. For the components of prospect reserves (area, average net pay, and HC-recovery), capable geotechnical professionals should expect consistent predictions within about 1 order of magnitude at 80% confidence, and they should strive for accuracy of 0.5X to 2X at 80% confidence. However, consistently achieving such levels of predictive performance is, realistically, unlikely, using conventional exploration methods. However, where geologic conditions render application of 3-D seismic data feasible and economic, reserve forecasting at such levels may be achieved, especially if amplitude anomalies and other DHIs reduce the likelihood of very large and very small reserves outcomes.

Chance of Prospect Success

The Expected Value Concept

Imagine that you have the opportunity to participate in a simple game in which you are asked to correctly call the fair toss of a coin. If your call is correct, you will win $20,000; if it is incorrect, you will win nothing.

If you were able to play such a game free of charge, the Expected Value (EV) of each trial would be (+)$10,000 **(Table 7)**. If you had to pay $10,000 each time you played, the EV would be zero, so that, statistically, you then would be "trading dollars." If you were willing to invest $4,000 in one trial of this game, the EV would be (+)$6,000. In this example, there are only two possible outcomes, and you are restricted to one trial. The chances of either outcome, as provided by our knowledge about coin-tossing, are essential to calculating the EV of the venture.

In order to calculate the EV for an exploratory well, we will use our knowledge about petroleum geology to estimate the chance (= our confidence) that a reservoired petroleum accumulation is in fact present and will be encountered by the drill bit. It is important to emphasize that for most companies involved in oil and gas exploration there are many ventures, each with an uncertain outcome. Furthermore, the employment of EV as a decision criterion encourages repeated trials, so that EV is the *average profit per decision*, assuming repeated trials are made. The power of the EV concept is that it allows (1) a high-risk prospect with large reserves potential to be compared with a low-risk prospect having small reserves potential; and (2) an excessively risky prospect (one with a negative EV) to be identified and avoided.

Faced with choosing among several options, the decision rule is to select the option having the highest EV. Obviously, when operators choose to participate in ventures having negative expected values, they are gambling—"in effect, betting against the house."

In exploratory ventures, the cost of failure usually includes dry-hole cost, cost for lease bonuses of the condemned leases, and some geological and geophysical (G&G) costs. For development ventures, there may also be substantial additional capital investments plus expense items that will have to be written off—expenditures that were needed in order to determine the viability of the project, such as several confirmation or delineation wells, equipment, materials, and supplies. Newendorp (1975) presents the subject of expected value very thoroughly for the reader who wishes additional background.

Requirements for a Corporate System to Estimate Geologic Chance

In order to calculate a prospect's expected value, we must have a basis for estimating the chance that nature has provided a detectable HC-accumulation in the objective section under the drilling location. Geology and geophysics provide that basis. Moreover, for most companies, many such prospects will be proposed annually, from many different basins, each competing for precious corporate capital. In order to construct a

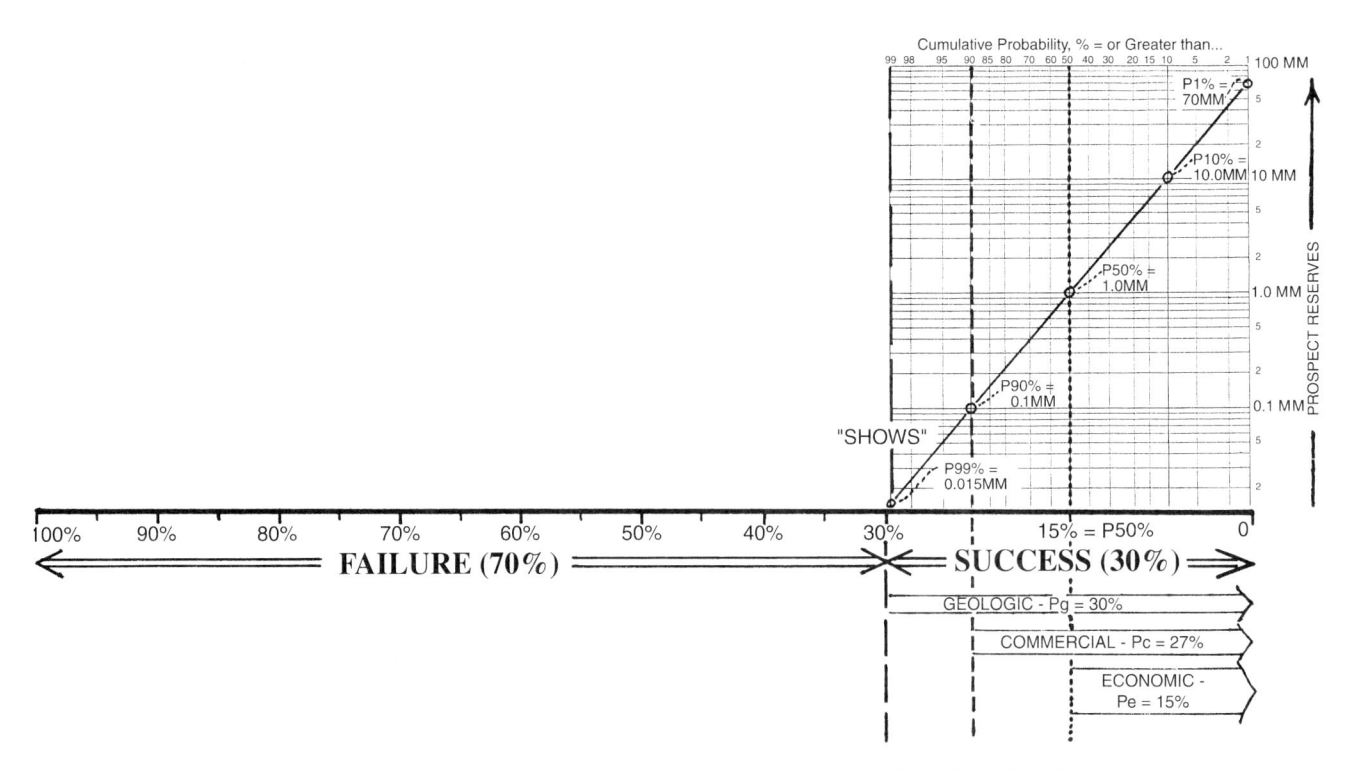

Figure 17 *Exploration failure and exploration success (economic, commercial, and geologic).*

consistent system for evaluating all prospects equitably, 10 requirements must be met:

1. The system must be geologically sound, so that all geologic aspects of oil generation, migration, reservoir emplacement, containment, preservation, and geotechnical detection are considered;
2. The system must be readily usable by many different geotechnical professionals;
3. The system must apply equally well in all geologic provinces;
4. The system must apply equally well to all types of petroleum traps—structural, stratigraphic, combination, basin-centered (generational), hydrodynamic, etc.;
5. The system must apply just as well to exploration plays as it does to the individual prospects that constitute the play;
6. Chance, expressed probabilistically as geologic confidence, must be expressed numerically, not subjectively;
7. The system must relate to reality (i.e., calibration) by periodic comparisons of portfolio outcomes (actual success-ratio) against forecasts (predicted success ratio);
8. The geologic components of chance must be independent of one another, or, if dependency is suspected, its influence must be understood and estimated;
9. The system must be independent of economic requirements such as minimum required reserves and flow rates—that is, the system must work just as well in a mature onshore province, such as the Permian Basin of west Texas, as it does in an economically demanding province such as the North Sea; and
10. All prospectors utilizing the system must be trained so they understand its basis and application.

Recorded Success Rates versus Geologic Success Estimates

Geologic success (Pg) is not necessarily the same as commercial success (Pc) or even economic success (Pe). The well-known phrase "geologic success but economic failure" refers to this issue—there are different definitions of success. According to official exploration drilling statistics, such as those reported annually by state and national petroleum agencies, the conventional definition of "success" means simply that the subject well was completed and did produce some hydrocarbons. This does not mean that the venture made a profit! In fact, such standard definitions of "success" contain five possible "successful" outcomes **(Figure 17)**:

- The well was completed as the discovery well for a field in which average wells will generate sufficient production revenues to recover the cost to drill, complete, and operate them (as well as the sunk costs to find the field), plus a reasonable profit.

This is an *economic success*, on a full-cycle basis, represented as PV > 0 at the firm's discount rate.

There are three possible outcomes comprising *commercial success* or *completion success*, wherein the exploratory well was completed but was not profitable on a full-cycle economic basis:

- The well was completed because anticipated future production revenues will return a profit on the cost of completing and operating it, but not on the costs of exploratory drilling, leasing, and seismic, which are thus viewed as sunk and not recoverable (Capen, 1991). Such a well is an *incremental success*. Ordinarily, no more wells would be drilled on such a prospect by the investor, assuming that subsequent events do not provide new encouragement to drill again.
- The well was completed as either an incremental success or an apparent economic success, but subsequent performance was inadequate even to recover completion and operating costs, resulting in early abandonment; completion of such a well was clearly a mistake.
- The well was completed only for business reasons; that is, to hold a lease position or to satisfy a contractual or regulatory obligation. Some production revenues will be recovered, but perhaps not even enough to cover completion and operating costs.
- The fifth outcome we call *geologic success*, meaning that a reservoired accumulation was found that was at least large enough to support a flowing test. For most onshore provinces any well that flows is likely to be completed, but many such small reservoirs encountered offshore are often reported only as shows.

The geologic chance factors (Rose, 1992a, 1995) are defined (pp. 34–36, 38) so as to exclude an onshore well that discovers a petroleum accumulation too small to warrant the expense of completing and operating it **(Figure 17)**. Such very small accumulations are commonly recognized only as *shows*. Practically speaking, we have eliminated this class by introducing concepts of minimum dimensionality or volumetrics into the definitions of the geologic chance factors, using the U.S. onshore as an effective minimum standard. This accomplishes three important purposes:

1. It allows the geologic chance factors to yield a product that corresponds effectively with the world's most liberal definition of chance of completion success, thus permitting the comparison of conventional reporting standards of success with independently derived geologic estimates of probability of success;
2. It provides a general and basic standard against which subsequent adjustments can be made for exploration projects having more demanding economic requirements, such as deep overpressured tests, offshore prospects, remote frontier ventures, or international contract areas with severe financial obligations; and
3. It ensures approximate compatibility between onshore completion success and minimum detectable reserves volumes, assuming that minimum but finite dimensions are required for area of accumulation, average net pay, and HC-recovery factor. The concept here is that some small but finite volume and minimum reservoir quality must exist for an accumulation even to be detected by an operator. In other words, the lower limit of an accumulation, thus defined, is substantially larger than one barrel of oil! Two independent lines of evidence suggest that appropriate minimum reserves values are generally quite small (consistent with trap geometry): Drilling experience indicates that reserves volumes in the range of perhaps 1,000 to 20,000 BOE are generally capable of being detected and sustaining flow into the borehole, at least for a few hours. Also, P99% values in FSDs in mature onshore trends and basins are commonly around 1,000 to 10,000 BOE (see p. 30 and Appendix C).

Chance of Success Equals "Flowability"

As previously stated, it is important to recognize that the conventional reporting standard for exploratory success in most petroleum-producing nations is not whether the exploratory well discovered a commercial new field—rather, it is simply whether the exploratory well was completed for production. The beauty of such a reporting standard is that it is unequivocal, and results of all wells ordinarily become matters of public record. In the case of expendable exploratory wells, most governmental agencies require the operator, within a reasonable time, to declare whether or not the well encountered commercial hydrocarbons.

Moreover, different companies have different criteria for commercial success, thus rendering profitability to be an inconsistent criterion among exploratory wells drilled by many different operators. So, in order to compare geologic chance of success estimates with actual outcomes by all companies, we have set up the geologic chance system to be consistent with the chance of discovering enough oil or gas to complete the well for production in the case of an onshore, mature petroleum province (Rose, 1992a). A practical proxy for this case is "encountering enough reservoired oil or gas to sustain flow." This criterion is widely used by most exploration firms as the basis for exploration success because it is independent of variable economic requirements of different trends or basins.

Geologic Components of Prospect Chance of Success
Requirements for a Hydrocarbon Accumulation

Petroleum geologists generally agree that for a subsurface accumulation of HCs to exist, there must be porous and permeable reservoir rock, HCs that have moved from a petroleum source rock to the reservoir rock, and a sealed closure or trap capable of containing the HCs (Landes, 1951; Dott and Reynolds, 1969). All three of these general requirements must be met for a HC accumulation to form; if any one of these requirements fail, no accumulation will be present. This paradigm becomes the fundamental basis for employing geologic chance factors in estimating probability of geologic success (Table 8). In its simplest form, each of the three geologic chance factors is treated as an independent variable having a probability ranging from 0 to 1.0.

Serial multiplication of all three factors produces a decimal fraction equivalent to the probability that a Hc-accumulation is present, which is the probability of geologic success, or Pg, 0.28 in this example. By subtracting Pg from 1.0, we get its derived counterpart, the probability of geologic failure, or Pf. These expressions, along with estimates of prospect value and failure cost, are needed to calculate the expected value of the venture.

Explorationists commonly ask whether one geologic chance factor is more important than another, thereby deserving more weight. The answer is definitely *no*. The chance factors should be thought of as links in a chain: if any link breaks, the chain fails (p. 62). By analogy, if any one of the geologic factors is zero, the prospect will be dry! In other words, all of the essential geologic chance factors must *coincide* in space and time if one or more reservoired HC-accumulations can occur. Coincidence is discussed further on pages 48 and 80.

Many different schemes and combinations of geologic chance factors have been proposed and utilized by petroleum explorationists, involving as many as 14 different geologic chance factors. Most companies today employ four or five critical chance factors, sometimes with subfactors assigned to each main chance factor. In most systems, however, the principle is the same: based on the geologic evidence, geoscientists are asked to estimate their confidence, expressed as decimal fractions or percentages, in the existence of specific geologic conditions in the subsurface under the prospect area. Serial multiplication of the chance factors then yields the geologic chance of success for the prospect.

A few companies have used geotechnical chance factors to focus on the chance of failure, believing that better results may be obtained by focusing on the specific geologic conditions that could cause project failure.

Expressions of geologic confidence are subjective probability estimates, and they depend on three factors:

1. reliability of evidence (direct, intermediate, indirect);
2. judgment about adequacy relative to the P99% reserves case, and to the P90% cases for area, average net pay thickness, and HC-recovery factor (more than adequate, adequate, less than adequate, inadequate); and
3. professional experience in estimating chance factors.

Geologic Chance Factors— Recommended System

For all exploratory prospects, including extensions (= step-outs), deeper-pool or shallower-pool tests, and NFWs, explorationists should independently express their confidence, as probability, in five critical geologic attributes of the prospect. Each of the five geologic chance factors has several subcomponents that must be considered in arriving at a confidence estimate for the chance factor. Because most of the subcomponents are partially dependent, we recommend use of the "weak link" approach, in which the lowest probability assigned to the several subcomponents within one chance factor is used as the probability for the parent chance factor (Rose, 1996a).

Table 8 *Example calculation of simplistic probability of geologic success and failure using three geologic chance factors.*

Geologic Chance Factor	Probability
Reservoir Rock	0.7
	X
Hydrocarbon Charge	0.8
	X
Sealed Closure	0.5
Product = Probability of Geologic Success—Pg	0.28
Probability of Geologic Failure—Pf = (1 – 0.28)	0.72

Hydrocarbon Source Rocks

First, we assess the probability (= confidence) that thermally mature HC source rocks are present in adequate thickness, extent, organic richness, and type to provide at least a modicum of HC-charge to the prospect area. Components that must be considered are:

- quantity (thickness, extent, organic richness),
- HC type (oil, natural gas, mixed), and
- thermal maturity.

Discussion In many frontier basins, confidence in HC generation may be relatively low, and therefore it is often one of the most important requirements that must be met if exploration is to proceed. In productive basins and established trends, however, confidence in this chance factor tends to be considerably higher. HC volumes generated must be at least large enough to satisfy the P99% reserves value of the prospect. For confirmation wells, step-outs, and development wells, this requirement has ordinarily been met.

Migration

Second, we evaluate the probability (= confidence) that HCs have migrated, utilizing conduits, carrier beds, fractures and/or faults, following migration pathways into the location of the existing closure(s), in volumes of oil and/or natural gas sufficient to charge such closure(s). Components to consider are:

- conduits (carrier beds or zones, fractures or faults),
- migration routes from "kitchen" to prospect area,
- efficiency (concentration during transmission vs. dispersal), and
- timing (sealed closures existed when migration occurred).

Discussion Again, this chance factor may be an important uncertainty in frontier exploration, but it is of much less concern in known productive basins and trends, and it may be entirely satisfied in cases of confirmation wells, step-outs, and development wells. For NFWs, explorationists should consider whether migration was dispersed, or concentrated by "structural focus," whether it was primarily vertical or lateral, and the degree to which migration has been impeded by subsurface geologic barriers (Demaison and Huizinga, 1994). Efficiency of migration must be at least adequate to provide the P99% reserves volume required for the prospect. Finally, was timing correct; that is, did sealed closures (= traps) exist at the time migration occurred ("critical moment" of Magoon and Dow, 1994)?

Reservoir Rock

The third geologic chance factor is the probability (= confidence) that reservoir rock is present in the prospect area in sufficient volume, porosity, and deliverability to support one or more flowing wells. Reservoir thickness and quality in the exploratory well bore must be consistent with the P90% forecast for prospect average net pay and HC-recovery factor. Essential considerations are:

- volume (thickness, extent),
- porosity, and
- reservoir performance (permeability, drive mechanism).

Discussion Note that the reservoir chance components are set up such that some minimum threshold standards of volume, porosity, and deliverability must be met or exceeded—specifically these reservoir components must be adequate, on an independent basis, to allow detectable, sustained flow of reservoired HCs into the borehole. Under this approach, encountering a water-bearing, reservoir-quality sandstone would not be a failure in the reservoir category, but rather, a failure in one of the other four categories, such as an unexpected structural low, an absence of HC-charge, or a leaky trap. However, the presence of a 1-ft tight siltstone where a 10-ft porous sandstone objective was forecast would constitute a failure in reservoir prediction. Reservoir thickness must be compatible with at least the P90% average net pay forecast for the prospect, and porosity and reservoir performance with the P90% HC-recovery factor forecast (pp. 24–25).

Closure

Fourth, we assess the probability (= confidence) that a structural and/or stratigraphic closure involving the reservoir objective, and of minimally adequate area (consistent with the P90% area forecast) and vertical relief, is present in the prospect area, and can be detected using current geotechnical means. Components to be considered are:

- Closure exists and is of adequate area and vertical relief to contain a volume of reservoired HCs sufficient to support flow (given that reservoir rock is present), and
- We have confidence in our ability to detect and delineate them using available geotechnological methods.

Discussion Closures can be of any type—structural, stratigraphic, diagenetic, hydrodynamic, or basin-centered. Additionally, the geoscientist is asked to estimate his or her confidence that such target closures can be detected and delineated using whatever technology is being applied. Seismic resolution, velocity conditions, and statics, as well as data quality, density, and reliability, all must be considered, for prospects relying on seismic mapping. Closure confidence must be compatible with at least the P90% area estimate (pp. 24–25).

The closure chance factor is formulated to apply equally well to stratigraphic as well as to structural traps. In combination with the reservoir chance factor, it focuses on the geometry of the envisioned oil or gas accumulation and on the volumes of fluids necessary to sustain a production test or prudent drillstem test. Stated in this way, the scheme can apply to all types of traps.

Containment

The fifth geologic chance factor is the probability (= confidence) that containment has occurred—that effective sealing rocks are present adjacent to the reservoir, and that emplaced hydrocarbons have been preserved. Essential considerations are:

- seal effectiveness (differential permeability, seal thickness, absence of open fractures),
- preservation from subsequent spillage (fault leakage, later fracturing, breaching, tilt-and-spill, etc.), and
- preservation from hydrocarbon degradation (biologic degradation, oxidation, thermal destruction).

Discussion Three issues are addressed here—first, the question of sealing capability between reservoir and top seals, seat seals, and lateral seals, whether formed by stratigraphic contrasts, diagenesis, or fault-gouge, and compatible with at least the P99% reserves forecast (pp. 24–25). The second issue concerns later geologic events that may have resulted in leakage and/or flushing of HCs from the trap. The third issue deals with degradation of reservoired HCs by biologic, chemical, or thermal agents. For most (but not all) confirmation wells and step-outs, most of the "containment" requirements have been met; for development wells, all have been met—otherwise there would not be a field to develop!

Subjective Probability Estimates in Exploration

Expert judgments about the probability of discovery of any drilling prospect are classic examples of subjective probability estimates, which some geoscientists resist or even reject (Rose, 1992a); they claim it is just guessing. The record argues otherwise. Given a logical procedure, knowledgeable explorationists can generate such estimates with surprising consistency, agreeing not only on discovery probability but also on the relative certainty or uncertainty of the several geologic chance factors in a given prospect.

Geoscientists have many reasons for their reluctance to estimate the chance of success. One has to do with the traditions of geology as an observational and descriptive natural science, not a predictive and quantified one. A second reason is that many professionals have never been trained in techniques of subjective probability estimating, nor have they been encouraged to examine the accuracy of their prior predictions. Third, a significant chance always exists that such predictions may turn out to be wrong, and our cultural and corporate values often associate scientific error with mediocrity or even moral turpitude, thus generating criticism, guilt, and loss of status. Yet a fourth reason is that geoscientists may not wish to acknowledge the high degree of uncertainty involved in petroleum exploration, still preferring to believe that the secret to exploration success lies almost entirely in geotechnical skill and effort. Finally, we hear the very common excuse: "We don't have enough data to make an estimate." Unfortunately, explorationists *never* have "enough" information—this is inherent in the business! Moreover, the more uncertainty that attends a given prospect, the more a systematic expression of subjective probability is needed—not less! All that can be reasonably requested is the best objective estimates possible, given the time, skill, and budget available. This is indeed the professional explorationist's responsibility.

Practical Aspects of Implementation

No substitute exists for actual experience in assessing and estimating confidence (= probability) in the various geologic chance factors, and comparing forecasts with outcomes. **Figure 18** relates various subjective phrases used by the writer in relation to a complete probability scale, which may help the novice get started. One point should be emphasized here: the use of probabilities of 1.0 for any geologic chance factor involving a NFW prospect in new trends or basins should be reserved for those cases where the positive evidence is overwhelming. Often the focused question—"What could hurt me regarding this chance factor?"—can illuminate problems that otherwise might be overlooked.

Figure 19 is a matrix widely used among many companies, whose origin is not known to the writer. Assuming that a geological model, or concept, is recognized, it compares (1) quantity and quality of information against (2) what the information is signifying with respect to at least minimal adequacy about the particular geologic chance factor. A partial consequence of **Figure 19** is that in order for us to render judgments of high confidence, either encouraging or discouraging, we require considerable data of good quality. Conversely, sparse or poor-quality data frequently allow only intermediate confidence statements. Many exploration teams find this matrix to be quite helpful in consistently assigning confidence values to various geologic components of chance pertaining to their prospects. Above all, geoscientists should recognize that the absence of information does not, by itself, imply a negative outcome—only that there are no data.

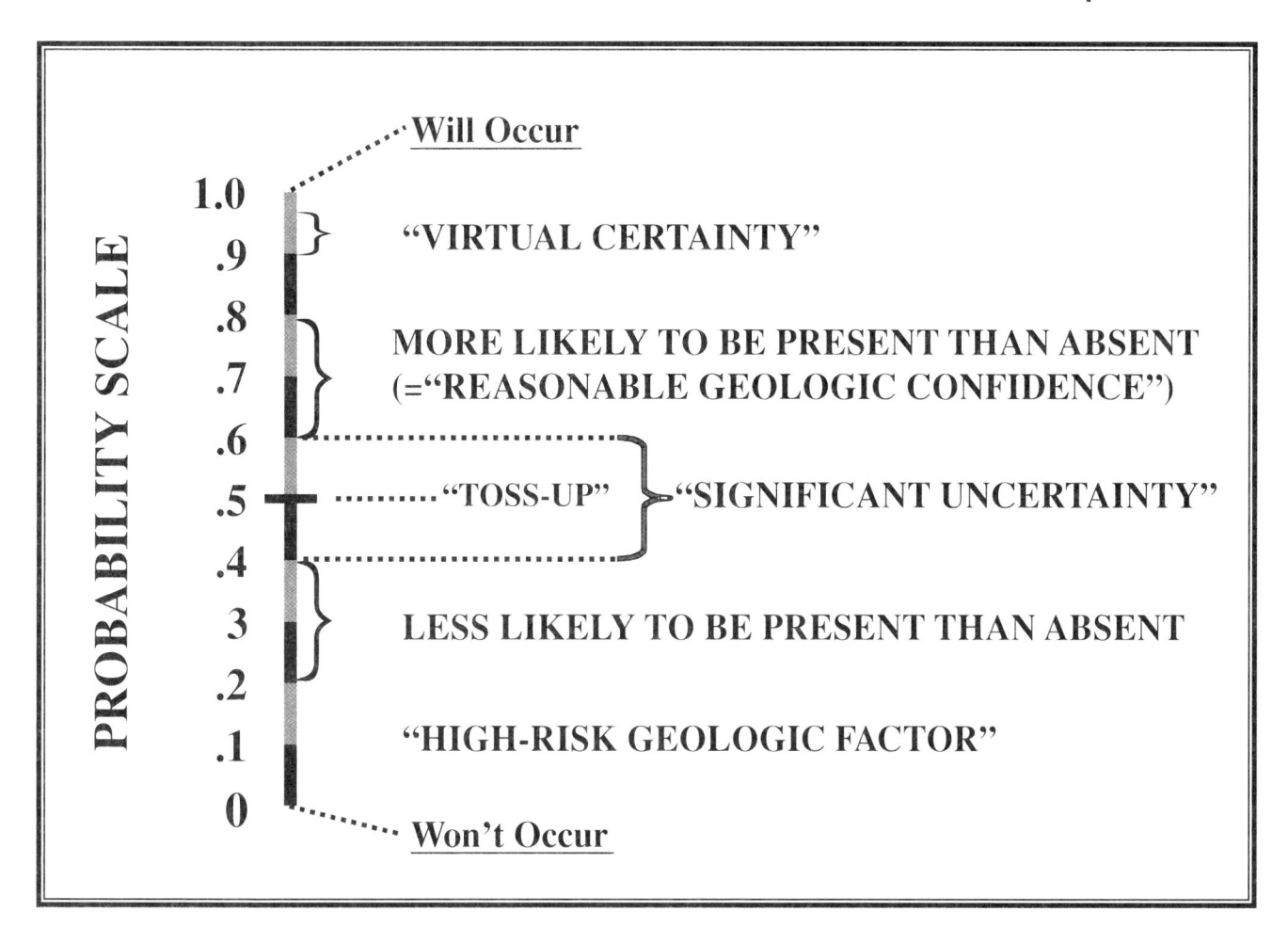

Figure 18 *Subjective expressions of confidence.*

For development wells and most extension and in-field exploratory ventures, the HC source rock, petroleum migration, and trap/seal factors have ordinarily been met. Only reservoir adequacy and the structural aspect remain as serious unknowns.

Rigorous analysis and discussion of real prospects with a peer group are an effective method for acquiring confidence in estimating geologic chance factors and probability of discovery. This also helps explorationists standardize their definitions and procedures.

Naturally, accuracy of predictions on probability of discovery cannot be judged on a single prospect or even on two or three. Only the outcome of a *program* of exploratory ventures can provide a fair indication as to whether the assignment of discovery probability has been optimistic, objective, or pessimistic. Of course, if the program has involved many high-risk wells, a larger sample may be required.

However, results of even a relatively small program can be instructive with regard to correct identification of several geologic chance factors. You should review predrilling projections of dry holes to see whether those geologic chance factors identified as the high-risk factors ("critical risks") did indeed correspond to the geologic reasons why the hole was dry (Rose, 1987). Although dry holes are an inevitable aspect of petroleum exploration, the capable professional will usually—but not always—find that he or she has correctly anticipated the real geologic reasons for failure. If not, this indicates that the geology of prospects is not adequately understood or identified. Again, the writer emphasizes that assessment of geotechnical performance regarding chance requires a completed program of wells, not a single well.

Explorationists can also gain experience by making estimates on wells drilled by competitors operating in the same trend or basin. Commonly, the geoscientist has considerable knowledge about the subsurface conditions attending such wells, which thus provides expanded opportunities for developing a useful experience base for predictive confidence.

Finally, it is difficult to overemphasize the power of independent, multiple judgments in assessing the geologic chance factors and the probability of discovery. Firms are well advised to obtain several different opinions and to combine them into a final estimate of the probability of project success.

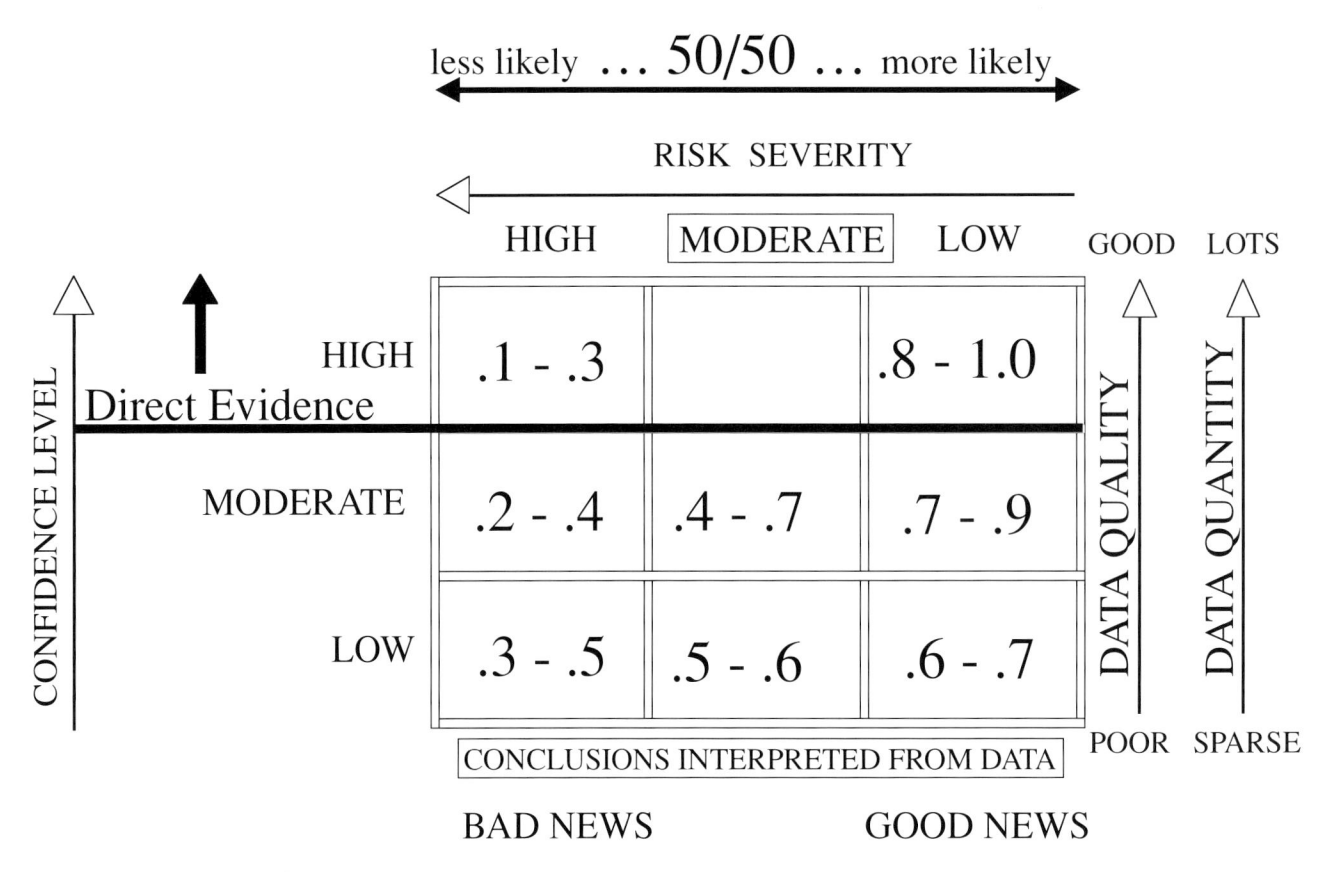

Figure 19 *Chance adequacy matrix.*

Virtues of Geologic Chance Factors

Separation of the various components of geologic chance allows them to be analyzed more thoroughly and objectively, and leads us to better geologic understanding of the prospect. Also, the identification of the geologic chance factor having the lowest probability (= "critical risk") helps exploration management and staff focus on those items of greatest uncertainty. For example, if closure is the critical risk element of a prospect, additional seismic or reprocessing may be warranted. Conversely, when geoscientists see that additional data acquisition can be curtailed because it is not likely to materially increase the chance associated with a given geologic factor, exploration becomes more cost effective and usually more timely. But most important, explorationists cannot really analyze, and thus improve, their performance in predicting the probability of discovery unless they systematically identify, forecast, and inspect the predictive results that attend the several geologic chance factors for a portfolio of exploratory ventures (Rose, 1987).

Geologic, Commercial, and Economic Chances of Success

The relationship between the prospect-reserves distribution, the geologic chance of success, and differing definitions of success was shown on **Figure 17**. Remember that the geologic chance factors (especially reservoir and containment) are purposefully defined to be consistent with the presence of a HC accumulation of at least minimum reserve size (or greater)—"at least enough reservoired mobile oil to sustain flow." Such a definition is equally operative in a mature, inexpensive onshore province such as west Texas, and in an expensive offshore province such as the North Sea.

In a mature, inexpensive onshore province, any exploratory well that flows will probably be completed for production, either as an *economic success*, recovering at least all investments on a full-cycle basis, at interest (or more), or as a *commercial success*, which may only return a profitable investment in tubing, tank battery, and completion. In such theaters, *geologic success (Pg)* and *commercial success (Pc)* may well coincide. But the same onshore commercial subsurface accumulation encountered offshore North Sea would be described only as a show. A very much larger volume of reservoired HCs would be required there to interest the operator in installing an expensive platform and developing the field discovered by the well—enough reservoired, producible oil to cover all exploratory costs, plus platform construction and full development and operation of the new field, as well as a satisfactory return on the total investment. That amount of discovered oil would qualify as an *economic success (Pe)*. If a lesser volume of recoverable oil is discovered, enough to warrant platform installation and development drilling but not enough to recover all exploration costs, then that smaller discovery would qualify as a *commercial success (Pc)*. Any exploratory well that is completed for production therefore qualifies as a commercial success, "commerce" being the production and sale of oil and/or natural gas. Only some of these are economic successes, on a full-scale basis.

Estimating Chance of Commercial and/or Economic Success

Figure 20 represents the concept and process by which geoscientists may progress from chance of geologic success (Pg), to chance of commercial success (Pc), to chance of economic success (Pe).

Let's assume that your geotechnical staff estimate that Prospect Alpha has a 30% chance of geologic success (i.e., that the well will encounter reservoired flowing HCs). The Prospect Alpha cumulative reserve distribution is represented by the solid black sloping line, which has been truncated above P1%. Reserve parameters are:

P99% = 0.05MM bbl
P90% = 0.40MM bbl
P50% = 4.7MM bbl
P10% = 54MM bbl
P1% = 400MM bbl

Mean Reserves* = 20MM bbl
Swanson's Mean = 18MM bbl

*distribution truncated above P1%; refer to **Figure 20** and page 13

As the manager, you have asked the staff to estimate the chance that Prospect Alpha will discover enough oil (or more) to justify completing it for production—the chance of a commercial success.

Your engineering and economic departments estimate that, in this location, at least 0.95 million barrels (MM bbl) must be present to warrant a completion; this is the minimum commercial field size (MCFS). On the reserves distribution, 0.95 MM bbl occurs at P80%, so 20% of the distribution is smaller than the minimum reserves required, and 80% is larger. Therefore the chance of commercial success (Pc) is:
Pc = 0.8 × 0.3 = 0.24.

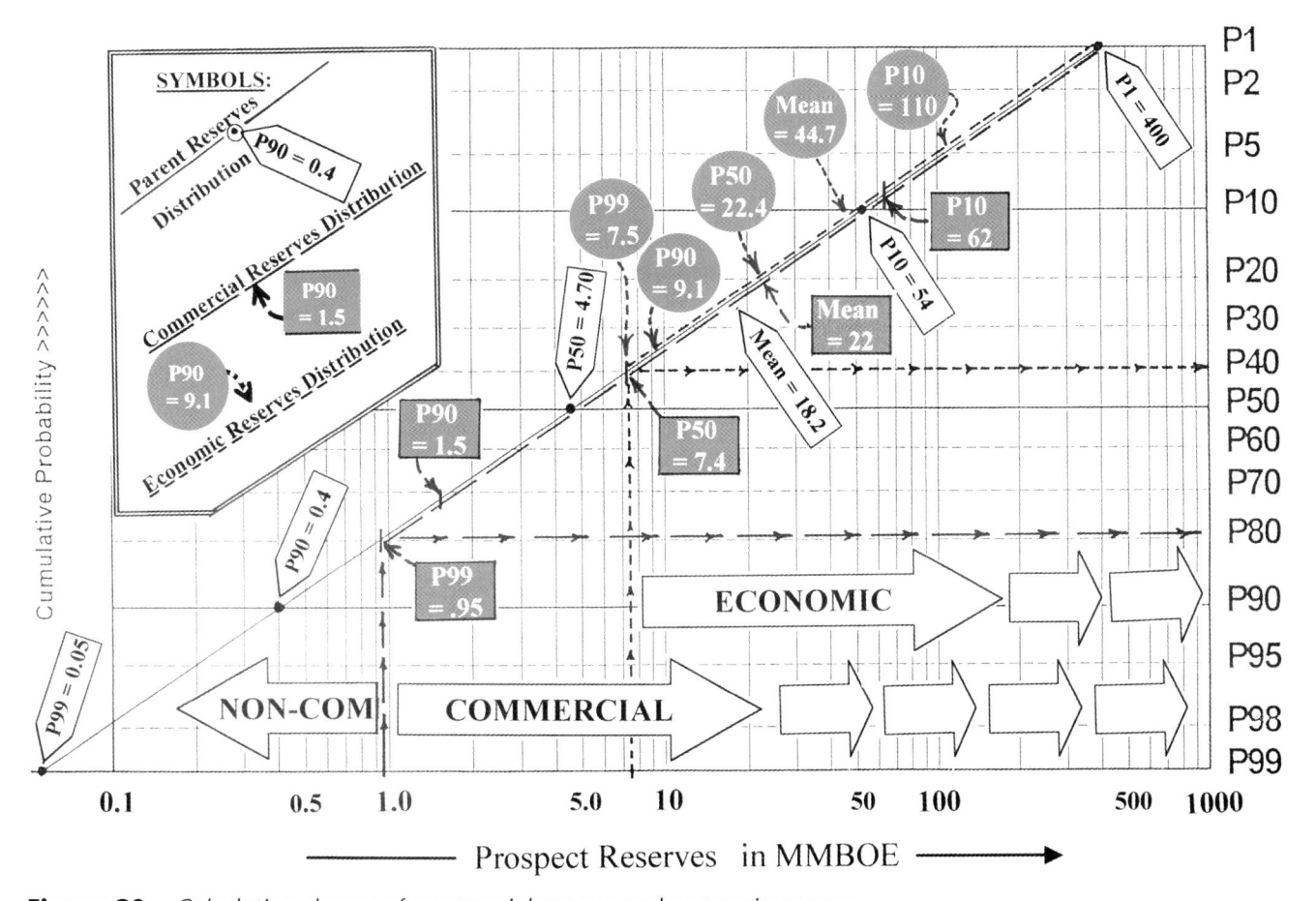

Figure 20 *Calculating chance of commercial success and economic success.*

What is the mean commercial reserve size? Remember that by truncating the original reserves distribution at P80%, your staff deleted the lowest reserves values from the original distribution. That is, a discovered accumulation smaller than 0.95MM bbl will be a dry hole. Furthermore, the surviving distribution is no longer lognormal because the lower part, containing the mode and smaller outcomes, has been removed. What survives has a form that resembles an exponential distribution if plotted in the frequency domain. The mean of the *commercial* reserves distribution must now be recalculated. The new distribution, from P80% to P1%, now has a new set of reserves parameters; note that in moving from geologic chance to commercial chance, chance of success has *decreased* (30% → 24%), whereas the mean of the commercial part of the reserves distribution has *increased* (20MM → 24MM):

Commercial P99% = 0.95MM bbl
Commercial P90% = 1.5MM bbl
Commercial P50% = 7.4MM bbl
Commercial P10% = 62.0MM bbl
Commercial P1% = 400MM bbl

Mean Commercial Reserves* = 24MM bbl
Swanson's Mean = 22MM bbl

*original distribution truncated above P1% and below P80%; refer to **Figure 20**

Next, the Exploration vice president asks you what the chance is that Prospect Alpha will be an *economic* discovery—that is, that the project will find enough oil to earn at least the corporate minimum return on investment on a full-cycle basis and pay for all exploration, development, and operating costs. Again your engineers and economists study the problem and advise that an *economic* discovery will require at least 7.5MM bbl (= MEFS). On the original prospect, reserves distribution, 7.5MM bbl occurs at P40%, so 60% of the distribution is uneconomic, and 40% is economic. Therefore, the chance of an *economic success* is: **Pe = 0.4 × 0.3 = 0.12.**

Again, you must recalculate the mean size of the economic-reserves distribution because you have deleted the smaller, uneconomic accumulations from the parent-reserves distribution. The surviving distribution, from P40% to P1%, now has a new set of reserves parameters:

P99% = 7.5MM bbl
P90% = 9.1MM bbl
P50% = 22.4MM bbl
P10% = 110.0MM bbl
P1% = 400.0MM bbl

Mean Economic Reserves* = 45MM bbl
Swanson's Mean = 45MM bbl

*original distribution truncated above P1% and below P40%; refer to **Figure 20**

So, as the chance of success goes *down* to reflect decreasing chances of finding larger accumulations of a *commercial* or *economic* scale, the commercial and/or economic mean reserves values *increase* because the noncommercial or uneconomic segments have been deleted through truncation.

Understanding Truncation

Geoscientists and engineers seem to struggle with the "Truncation Problem." The procedure described previously is useful because it models the actual decision-behavior involved, after an exploratory well has made a discovery, and management selects the logical next steps.

Implicit in this process is the "sunk-cost" concept—that completion decisions must be made on a "point-forward" basis because funds already invested in seismic, leasing, and exploratory drilling are by then gone—sunk. "Can we make a reasonable profit on our investments in pipe, stimulation, tank-battery, and lateral lines in order to bring the well into production?" For offshore projects, such investments may also include platform cost as well, which is usually so large that the "commercial" threshold may well approach the "economic" threshold. However, in mature producing provinces, like the Permian Basin of west Texas, or the Canadian plains, most wells that flow are likely to be completed, so the "commercial" threshold is likely to be at or just above the "geologic chance of success," and may lie substantially below the "economic" threshold. Obviously no rational investor will continue to drill a series of development wells that are consistently commercial (rather than economic) successes.

Some people are tempted to truncate all projects at the economic threshold, rather than the commercial threshold. This conservative position tends to prevent participation in many projects that could well be profitable. The criterion should be that the *average (= mean)* of the entire reserves distribution above the commercial cutoff is at least economic. For such a prospect, then, we accept that the outcome may turn out to be a small discovery that is commercial but not economic, but the *average* of all outcomes is clearly economic; that is, profitable on a full-cycle economic basis. The project's NPV is greater than 0 at the firm's mandated discount rate.

Each firm should determine its own consistent guidelines to be used in predicting the "commercial" cutoff for an exploratory venture. The "commercial" cutoff is not a precise value, and there is no doubt that producing rate must be considered as well as minimum reserves. Many experienced operators correctly believe that the risk associated with the decision to complete marginal commercial wells is the single most underestimated, potentially dangerous risk involved after exploration has made a discovery. Much care is warranted here.

One-step versus Two-step Method for Estimating a Prospect's Chance of Success

Two methods have commonly been used by modern oil companies to estimate a prospect's chance of success.

The One-step Method is favored by White (1993) and assumes that:

1. Modern explorationists can reliably distinguish large reserves prospects from small reserves prospects, so the geotechnical exploration effort can indeed identify and drill only those prospects capable of containing some designated "significant" reserve size or larger;
2. By setting "significant" limits of closure areas, average net pay, and HC-recovery factor, explorers can screen out unprospective parts of mapped trends; and
3. Prospectors can reliably link "adequacy" of source rocks, migration, closure volumes, and seals to the chance of success. Thus, for chance factors such as source rocks or migration to qualify, the geologist must judge whether they were adequate to provide enough oil to a prospect for it to meet or exceed that reserves quantity deemed to be significant.

Advantages of this method are that explorers don't have to worry about the low-reserves ends of FSDs. Estimating chance of success is a one-step process, keyed to finding at least a field of significant (= economic? commercial?) reserves size or larger.

The Two-step Method is favored by Rose (1995) and is necessitated because all three of White's key assumptions require geologic resolution beyond modern technical capability (i.e., false precision). Instead, in the two-step method Pg is keyed to a very small ("flowable") reserves discovery (= P99%) consistent with documented industry performance. Then, in a second step, the part of the prospect-reserves distribution that is considered to be commercial (the percent of the distribution that is greater than the commercial reserves threshold) is determined and then multiplied by the Pg. As a result, estimation of Pc (or Pe) is a two-step process:

1. Use geologic chance factors to find the chance of a small ("flowable") reservoired accumulation (or larger); then
2. Estimate what percent of the prospect-reserves distribution is of commercial or economic size and multiply the geologic chance by this commercial or economic chance.

Advantages of this method are that the two-step method reflects real industry performance capabilities—there is no false precision. Setting reserves thresholds very low maximizes the likelihood of correctly capturing reality. It allows a company-consistent process to be applied to widely varying economic thresholds in different operating theaters, thus promoting valid ranking and capital allocations. Finally, this method allows reality checks by comparing a consistent geologic chance estimate—usable in all geologic theaters—to a compatible universal public reporting standard. (Most modern companies have now endorsed the two-step method.)

Independent versus Dependent Chance Factors

Many exploratory prospects seek to evaluate a single main reservoir objective on a projected closure. For most such ventures, all the geologic chance factors may be treated as if they are mutually independent. Although there are a few cases where some dependency (either positive or negative) does appear to exist, especially between reservoir presence and structural closure or between seal effectiveness and structural closure, most knowledgeable risk analysts agree that the geologic chance factors, as defined, do not present any serious problems with regard to dependency. However, dependency does become a potential problem in dealing with multiple-objective exploratory prospects or with several prospects contained within one exploration play. Dependency in play analysis is discussed in Chapter 5.

Multiple-objective Prospects

Prospects having multiple objectives tend to be more attractive than one-objective prospects because the combined chance for at least one of the objectives to be productive is higher (see Appendix D). However, a prospect having two objectives will not be *twice* as likely to be successful as a one-objective prospect—nor does its probability of discovery equal the sum of the probabilities of discovery of the two multiple-objective targets. If all the geologic chance factors for the two objectives are independent of one another, then P(discovery) and P(failure) can be derived by binomial expansion as shown in Appendix D.

In most such cases, however, some geologic chance factors are independent and some are dependent (i.e., they are common to both objectives of the prospect). In such cases, Pg and Pf are derived via another two-step process, as shown in Appendix D. Discovery probability (and often EV) for a multiple-objective prospect having independent geologic chance factors is higher than for a multiple-objective prospect having one or more dependent geologic chance factors. Thus, the effect of dependent geologic chance factors is to *reduce prospect discovery probability*. Dependent geologic chance factors (i.e., common to both objectives of the multiple-objective prospect) most often include the structural aspect and the HC-charge and migration aspects. The reservoir and containment aspects tend to be independent. However, exceptions to this pattern are not uncommon.

An additional complication sometimes occurs when a given geologic chance factor contains several subfactors, some independent and others dependent. The task here is to assign relative fractional weights to the subfactors so that their product equals the probability of the parent chance factor. Appendix D shows such a case. In general, dependency among the subfactors is common; that is the primary justification for the "weak-link" approach in establishing confidence levels (see p. 34).

Although having legitimate multiple objectives usually makes a prospect somewhat more attractive economically, aggressive explorationists often are tempted to include secondary objectives that are only of marginal value. The improvement to the prospect's value is illusory, however, for several reasons:

1. For most multiple-objective prospects, several of the geologic chance factors are in fact dependent, thus reducing the apparent chance of success significantly from the independent case.
2. The secondary objective(s) commonly represents only a marginal or incremental completion that may pay for pipe, maintenance, and some part of the drilling cost while not adding substantial new reserves. Such ventures do not add much value and therefore should not be actively sought;
3. Dual-objective discoveries are often completed and produced first in the deeper zone until depletion, then completed in the upper zone. Because of the time value of money, this delayed production often reduces the PV of the upper productive zone significantly; and
4. Dual-objective completions are relatively more expensive and require higher maintenance than conventional completions.

For all of these reasons, a multiple-objective prospect having a high chance of success should be viewed with caution. The most attractive multizone prospects are those in which both or most zones clearly stand alone economically, and production from both zones may be commingled.

Nongeologic Aspects of Success and Failure

Technical and Mechanical Effects

Many variables other than geologic chance factors affect exploration success. For example, firms that use state-of-the-art technology seem to have rates of success much greater than firms that drill without benefit of such advanced geotechnical guidance; this should be taken into account.

Also, mechanical chance factors should be considered, such as the chance of not getting the well down to the objective, the chance of incorrectly locating the well, and the chance of geotechnical errors in mapping, logging, or testing. However, if you anticipate that the well will be redrilled if such difficulties occur, you should make probabilistic provision for such trouble costs in the cash-flow schedule for the project rather than as a chance-of-success factor. Generally, such considerations do not make a substantial difference except in economically marginal prospects.

Some authorities suggest including a chance factor that deals with the probability that the exploratory well has been located and evaluated properly (Baker, 1988). It is certainly true that significant fields are occasionally discovered (or recognized) only after several apparently unsuccessful penetrations. However, the writer's experience is that, for most prospects, this aspect can be covered within the closure or reservoir rock categories; that is, if the well turns out to be improperly located, it is commonly perceived as a failure to adequately assess structural or reservoir risk. However, when dealing with frontier basins and plays, it may be advisable to include a separate chance factor assessing the confidence that the well will be located properly and any productive reservoir zones will be identified and evaluated adequately. Careful review of the stratigraphic column and consideration of active petroleum systems will reduce the chance of overlooking a productive zone while drilling. In other words, "serendipity" may be a euphemism for less-than-thorough consideration of all stratigraphic possibilities and thus for incomplete risk analysis.

Expressing Business and Political Risks

In assessing major projects that require large front-end investments or long elapsed time between expenditure and payout, the firm may wish to appraise the likelihood of a severe and extended drop in wellhead prices (or rise in operating costs or taxes). Basically, the procedure here is to identify what sustained low price levels—or elevated costs—would cause termination of the project, then try to obtain estimates from knowledgeable petroleum economists about the probability and timing of such occurrences. The chance of commercial success (Pc) is then multiplied by (1– the chance of such economic failure). Less severe price and cost fluctuations should simply be considered as variant cases within the project cash-flow model.

Political uncertainty can be expressed similarly. Again, knowledgeable, objective political experts should express their opinions about the likelihood of a change of regulation, law, or regime severe enough to cause a project's termination or change its economic status. Commonly, this probability should be directed to the anticipated time of greatest vulnerability—after large capital investments for development of discovered fields but before recovery of those investments via production revenues—which can then be related to the cash-flow model. The chance of commercial success (Pc) can then be multiplied by (1– the chance of political failure).

Monitoring and Improving Predictive Performance

If the exploration organization is serious about improving staff performance in estimating the chance of success, management themselves must undertake equally serious procedural changes.

Universal Prospect Risking Scheme

Management must insist on adoption and utilization of a consistent geologic risking system that meets the requirements outlined earlier. Geotechnical staff must be trained in its use; periodic management audits and (where necessary) retraining will ensure its consistent, universal application.

Keeping Records

Management should set up procedures whereby forecasts of geologic chance of success (and individual chance factors) are preserved and routinely compared against actual outcomes of exploratory wells. Individual geoscientists should be encouraged to make geologic predictions on competitor wells and to compare them with announced results, as a way to expand the sample size of their predictive experience and reduce the time necessary to begin monitoring, measuring, and improving predictions of chance.

Predicted versus Actual Success Rates

Compare the average *predicted* chance of success for last year's portfolio with the *actual* success rate (Rose, 1987). Is there bias? Are some exploration teams biased more than others? Why? Separate all prospects into three groups—high, medium, and low risk. Then see what the average success rate was of each group—are staff distinguishing high-risk prospects from low-risk ones?

Performance Tracking

The methodology of Clapp and Stibolt (1991) (p. 26 and **Figure 14**) for continuously monitoring reserves additions throughout the annual exploration program may also be applied to chance-of-success forecasts. A P10%–P90% "envelope" of expectations is created, employing Monte Carlo simulation, for the range of numbers of discoveries (**Figure 14c** and **d**). Both the mean and P50% trends may be projected within the P10%–P90% envelope. Then as the exploratory wells of the annual portfolio are drilled, the numbers of actual discoveries are plotted as a line rising from the start of the program toward the completion of the portfolio, and are compared with expectations. Any time the actual performance moves out of the P10%–P90% envelope, management is justified in suspecting professional bias affecting the estimates of chance, and in calling for immediate corrective measures. Although performance tracking is an excellent tool for monitoring geotechnical performance, it does not indicate *why* predictions may be biased. For that, we must turn to dry-hole analysis.

Dry-hole Analysis

Professional staff charged with monitoring and improving geotechnical productive performances should collect and analyze all unsuccessful exploratory efforts. Why were the dry holes dry? Was critical risk (i.e., the geologic chance factor having lowest probability) correctly identified for most dry holes? That is, were most dry holes caused by failure for that chance factor to be satisfied? One U.S. company found that they were correctly identifying reservoir risk but were not recognizing structural risk (Rose, 1987), even though structural errors caused 43% of the company's dry holes—more than any other geologic chance factor **(Figure 21)**. Incorrect predictions of reservoir rock presence were responsible for 40% of the company's exploratory dry holes, but reservoir rock was correctly anticipated as the critical risk in 80% of those dry holes. The same company also found that they were consistently conservative in their chance-of-success estimates (20% predicted vs. 31% actual, over two consecutive years) mostly because their chance estimates of HC-charge were pessimistic (60% predicted vs. 95% actual). In retrospect such conservatism was especially difficult to justify considering that almost all of the company's exploration efforts took place in established petroleum-producing U.S. basins! If this company had properly assessed the chance of HC-charge, its predicted success rates would have matched actual results very closely.

Previously (p. 38) it was emphasized that better estimates of a prospect's chance of success result when the geologic components of chance are analyzed separately. A second advantage of this method is that technology can then be focused on the critical risk—for example, if closure is the greatest risk, additional seismic data may be a cost-effective way to reduce risk. Based on Rose's (1987) experience, a third advantage is apparent: this approach then allows geotechnical staff to improve their predictive performance by identifying and correcting prevalent patterns of error. Amoco (McMaster, 1998), Santos (Johns et al., 1998), and Unocal (Alexander and Lohr, 1998) report analogous learning from their results.

Industry Experience in Estimating Prospect Chance of Success

Actual Industry Performance

In international theaters, NFW success rates since about 1960 have been remarkably consistent at about

STRUCTURE
- INCORRECT STRUCTURAL INTERPRETATIONS WERE CHIEF CAUSE OF 43% OF DRY HOLES
- RISK CORRECTLY ANTICIPATED IN 23% OF CASES

RESERVOIR ROCK
- INCORRECT PREDICTIONS OF RESERVOIR ROCK WERE CHIEF CAUSE OF 40% OF DRY HOLES
- RISK CORRECTLY ANTICIPATED IN 79% OF CASES

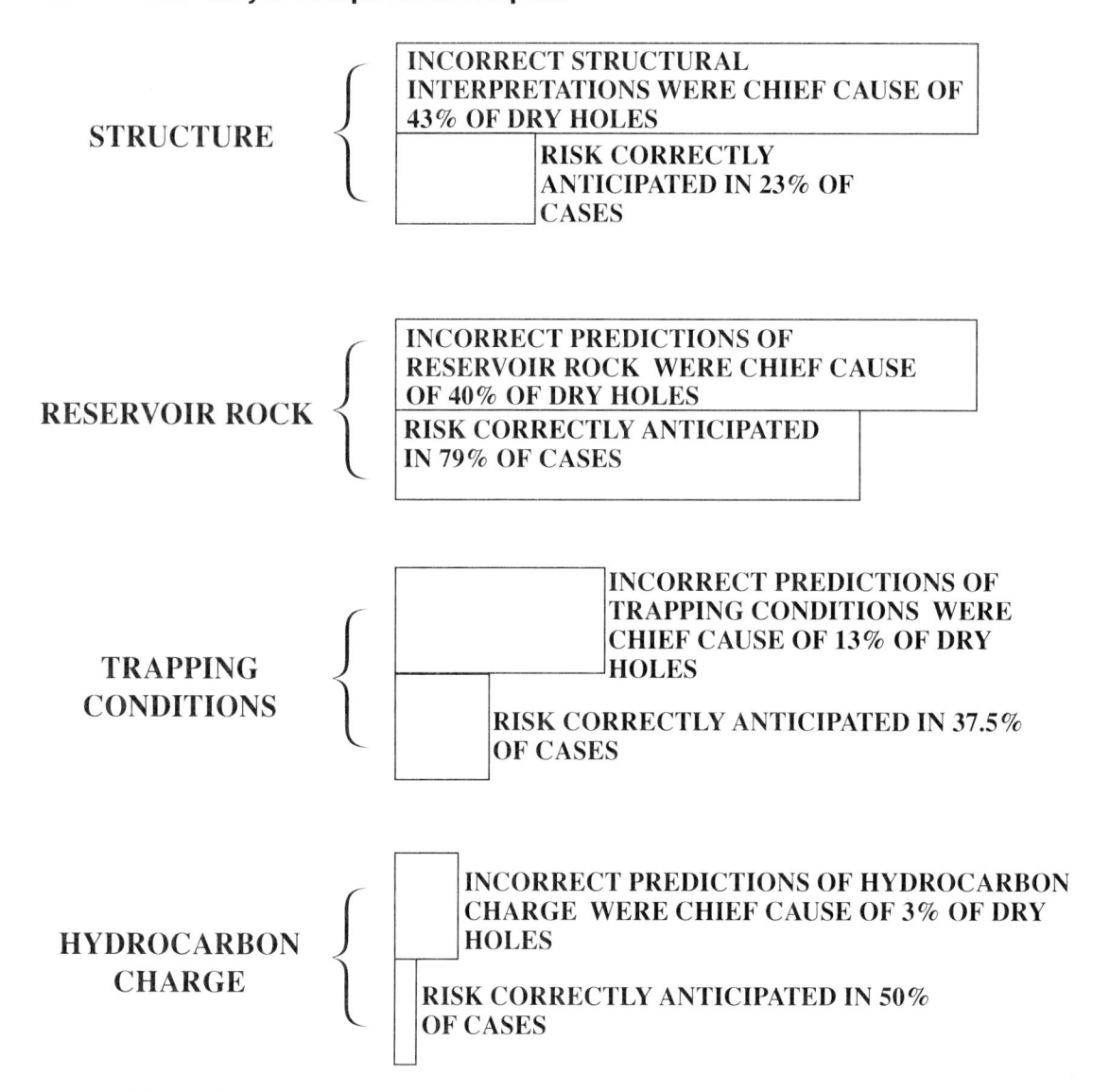

TRAPPING CONDITIONS
- INCORRECT PREDICTIONS OF TRAPPING CONDITIONS WERE CHIEF CAUSE OF 13% OF DRY HOLES
- RISK CORRECTLY ANTICIPATED IN 37.5% OF CASES

HYDROCARBON CHARGE
- INCORRECT PREDICTIONS OF HYDROCARBON CHARGE WERE CHIEF CAUSE OF 3% OF DRY HOLES
- RISK CORRECTLY ANTICIPATED IN 50% OF CASES

Figure 21 *Relative frequency of four geologic chance factors causing dry holes during a company's 1977–1978 exploration programs, plus performance by company geologists in correctly anticipating which geologic chance factor indeed represented greatest technical risk (from Rose, 1987).*

25% overall **(Figure 22)**. U.S. exploration success rates during the 1980s (before 3-D seismic) for all exploratory wells were commensurate (20–30%), but showed considerable variation among different classes **(Table 9)**. In particular, annual success rates for U.S. NFWs (onshore and offshore) ranged from 13% to 18% during the 1980s.

Impact of 3-D Seismic Data

In those geologic provinces in which 3-D seismic data collection is feasible, discriminating, and cost-effective, it improves exploration performance in three different ways, especially where DHI technology is also incorporated.

1. First, by improving their prospect chance-of-success estimates, explorers can be more selective and thus improve their exploration success rates. This is accomplished through clearer resolution of geologic structure (which leads to improved location of exploratory test wells) and better discrimination of reservoir rock and sealing rock distributions. Also, positive DHI indicators allow enhanced confidence regarding the presence of reservoired HCs in the traps. During the 1990s, provinces such as the North Sea and deep-water Gulf of Mexico report prevailing NFW exploration success rates of 30% or more.

2. Second, estimates of prospect reserves can be improved through improved resolution of geologic structure and reservoir thickness and extent. Also, DHI signals can reduce uncertainty (variance) on trap volume by indicating approximate position of oil/water or gas/water contacts.

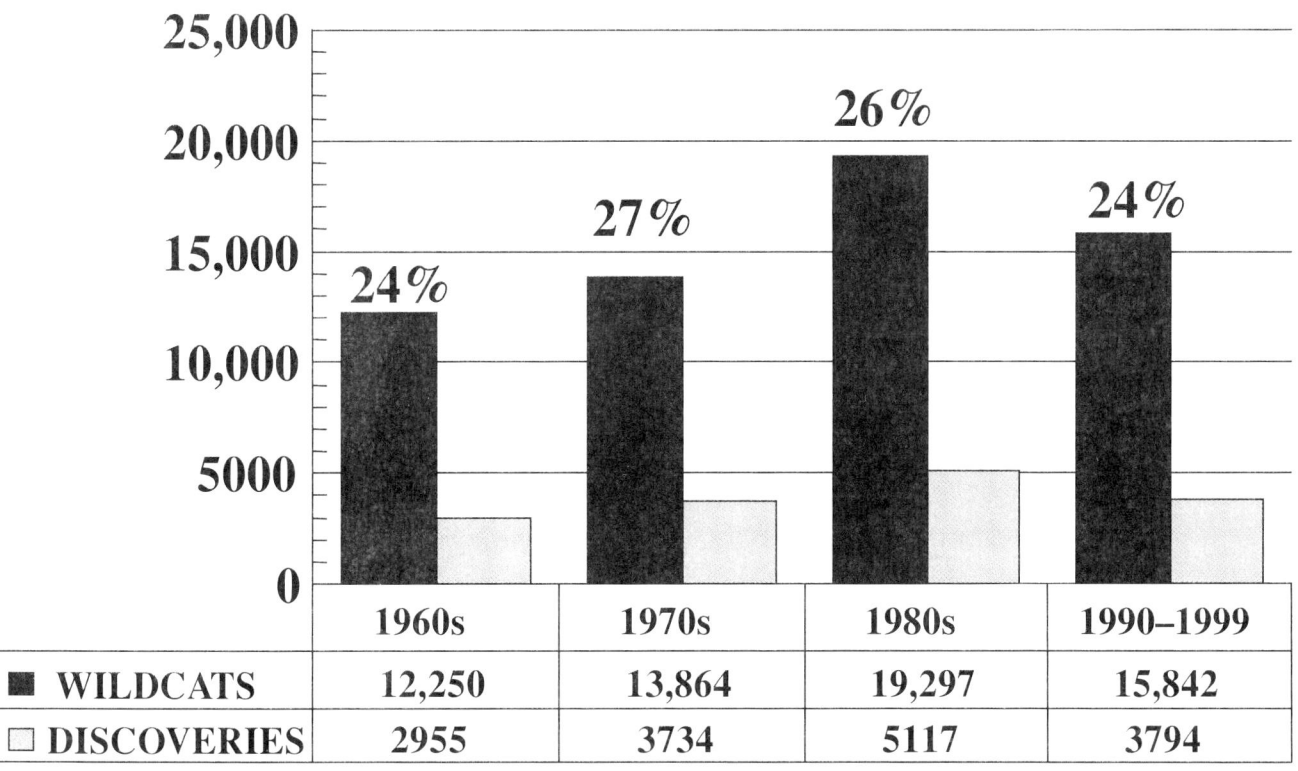

	1960s	1970s	1980s	1990–1999
■ WILDCATS	12,250	13,864	19,297	15,842
□ DISCOVERIES	2955	3734	5117	3794

Bar chart percentages: 1960s 24%, 1970s 27%, 1980s 26%, 1990–1999 24%.

Source: Petroconsultants

"WILDCAT CHANCE" (RATIO OF DISCOVERIES TO WILDCATS) HAS REMAINED REMARKABLY CONSTANT THROUGH TIME.

Figure 22 *Global discovery percentages through time (excludes the U.S. and Canada).*

3. Third, prospect profitability may be improved through optimum location of exploration and development wells, which results in higher initial production rates, larger individual well ultimate recoveries, and fewer required development wells. Nevertheless, 3-D seismic may not be feasible or cost-effective in many onshore provinces, *especially in the early stages of exploration.*

However, characterizing seismic anomalies as "DHIs" should be rigorous and calibrated against actual experience and should call for the presence of multiple attributes if they are to represent a discriminating basis for elevated Pg estimates, rather than just routine amplitude anomalies.

Characteristic Patterns of Predictive Bias in Estimating Chance of Success

Several international exploration organizations that have adopted companywide geotechnical risk analysis of all prospects report that, during the first year or two, a prevalent performance pattern emerged: for high-risk NFW prospects, geotechnical staff were overly optimistic and overestimated true chances of success (Otis and Schneidermann, 1997; Alexander and Lohr, 1998). This will be addressed further on page 47. For intermediate-risk NFWs, those in the 20–35% range, actual success rates were generally about right and matched predicted success rates fairly closely. For low-risk exploratory ventures, those in the 35–60% range, actual success rates were conservative—more of these ventures were successful than predicted. But for high-confidence ventures—those in the 60–90% range—actual results were notably lower. Apparently, prospectors tend to be overoptimistic when identifying an exploration venture as a sure thing!

Table 9 *Generalized success rates of various well classes drilled in the U.S. onshore and offshore during the 1980s as reported by the CSD (Rose, 1992a).*

Well Class	Percentage Successful
Development wells	75–80
All exploratory wells	20–30
Extensions (outposts)	40–45
In-field wildcats	25–35
New-field wildcats	13–18

46   Risk Analysis of Exploration Prospects

However, by maintaining (and circulating) records of predictions vs. outcomes, by making geotechnical professionals aware of the causes and consequences of predictive bias, and by constructively addressing the reasons for error and bias in specific prospects, we can improve forecasts of a prospect's chance of success, and reduce predictive bias if not eliminate it.

Using Trend or Basin Success Rates

In some cases, where geotechnical staff or management mistrust geologically derived prospect success estimates (or lack the geologic skill to reliably derive them), observed success rates (number of discoveries ÷ total number of exploratory wells) have been used as a proxy. In some geologic settings, this procedure is acceptable, especially in "statistical plays" where reservoirs are lenticular and beyond predictive geotechnical resolution. But in most trends, such observed success rates are a poor substitute for prospect-specific chance-of-success determination and tend to give misleading results that are either overly pessimistic or optimistic.

There are at least five important unknown aspects of dry-hole ratio trends:

1. Were the concepts and geotechnical skills of those prior operators commensurate with yours?
2. Was the quality of their data commensurate with yours? (This particularly applies to vintage and acquisition parameters of seismic data.)
3. Remember that all wells drilled through the subject zone are counted as valid exploration tests of that horizon, even if they simply passed through the subject zone on the way down to a deeper exploration objective. Therefore, such wells may not have been legitimate exploratory tests of the subject zone.
4. Why were the completed wells completed? Were the economic parameters of those operators similar to yours? Remember that not all completions are legitimate economic attempts, and a small company may complete a well that a large operator would abandon.
5. Trend success rates tend to decrease with time **(Figure 23)**; ignoring this pattern may lead to overly optimistic expectations from trend success rates, especially if your venture is in a fairly mature exploration theater.

Accordingly, caution is recommended in substituting observed trend success rates for geologically derived prospect estimates of the chance of success. Certainly they should not be ignored, but their best use is as a reality check after the responsible geoscientist

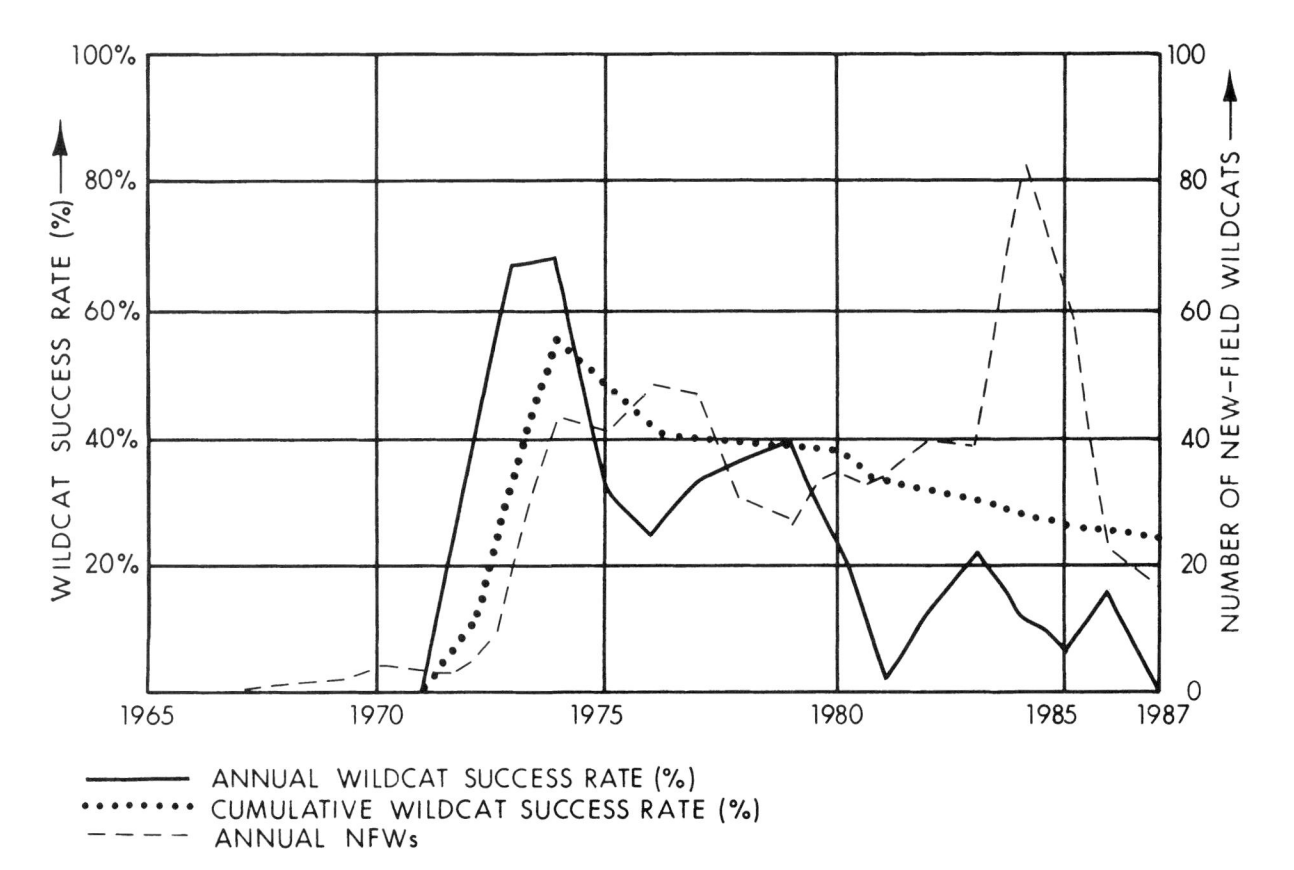

Figure 23   *Success rates change with maturity—annual and cumulative success rates compared with annual drilling, Niagaran Reef Trend, Benzie and Manistee Counties, Northern Michigan (Rose, 1992a).*

has carefully reviewed and edited such data so that those ventures from which the edited trend success rate was calculated are truly comparable to the prospects in the trend you are exploring.

Historical Changes in Trend Success Rates

In most exploration theaters (basins, trends, and plays), wildcat success rates change through time. Success rates are characteristically high during the early phases of exploration while larger and more evident fields are being found, then decline as the industry searches for fields that are smaller and/or harder to find. **Figure 23** shows actual data from a segment of the Niagaran (Silurian) Pinnacle Reef Trend of northern Michigan. Although the discovery probability should certainly be estimated based on the geotechnical characteristics of the prospect itself, the prudent explorationist will also consider the trend's state of exploration maturity in arriving at a final estimate of Pg, Pc, and Pe.

The Trouble with High-risk Exploration

During the 1980s, large, international corporate explorers, such as Shell, Amoco, and Mobil, experienced a disturbing result from their high-risk exploration ventures: *within the category of all NFWs having a predicted chance of success of 10% or less, less than 1% of those ventures resulted in discoveries.* Amoco (McMaster and Carragher, 1996) indicates that, since 1982, such high-risk exploration ventures have *destroyed* corporate value, not created it.

The same pattern was reported by all three companies independently, and the total number of wells in each company's sample was more than 200. These results cannot be ascribed to vagaries of random sampling—Amoco reports that the probability of such a result occurring by chance alone is only about 1%. Clearly, major company geoscientists and managers dealing with high-risk exploration ventures tend to be seriously overoptimistic in predicting chance of success, so such ventures are often overvalued as investment ventures to the detriment of corporate economic performance and the stockholder.

Causes

Some probable reasons for these difficulties have been summarized by Boccia (1996):

1. Most large companies (the kind that carry out most high-risk, high-potential exploratory ventures) systematically favor such projects because they offer the potential for large, new reserve additions—big new fields that represent opportunities for long-lived, large-profit projects because of applications of advanced technology and efficiencies of scale. Such big companies, having large reserves bases and corresponding cash flows, are—without realizing it—actually exhibiting risk-prone behavior with respect to such exploration ventures. Their managers desperately want to find such large, new fields, so they are prone to approve such ventures whenever they appear. Ambitious geotechnical staff are therefore prone to overestimate the value of such ventures in their efforts to respond to perceived management needs. This is especially true when exploration organizations have the wrong priorities—when they confuse the need to *drill wells* with the need to *add value.*

2. Risk-analysis tools and methods for evaluating such high-risk, high-potential ventures are operating at the extremes of the risk spectrum—reserves anticipated are very large, whereas chances of success are very small. Both theory and experience suggest that our ability to responsibly assess uncertain events begins to deteriorate at the extremes of either *chance* or *magnitude.* For example, most geotechnical professionals are better able to judge whether the chance of occurrence is 50% or 25% than they are at distinguishing between a 5% chance and a 10% chance. Because people are conservative processors of fallible information (Edwards, 1982), we tend to set the ranges of our predictive limits too narrow (Capen, 1976). Also, technologic risk-reduction in certain areas may actually encourage managers to take still higher risks elsewhere. Finally, Boccia suggests that the economics of higher-risk ventures are more sensitive to underrisking than are lower-risk projects. The *relative* negative impact of overoptimism becomes progressively more severe as the probability of success decreases—"It hurts more, on a per-dollar investment basis, to be wrong by the same degree when the risks are high. Our ability to clearly discern risk is the weakest for exactly those kinds of prospects where it needs to be sharpest."

3. In order to have an acceptable chance of making such large discoveries, many trials must be undertaken. Such high-risk, high-potential ventures are not easy to identify and are expensive to carry out. "In effect, high-risk exploration may be failing because companies are underestimating the time and money they need to commit to the high-risk game" (Boccia, 1996). Accordingly, such companies may have difficulty adequately diversifying high-risk ventures within their overall exploration portfolios.

4. A fourth possible cause, not identified by Boccia, is more fundamental—explorationists and their managers have not come to grips with the reality that the remaining world endowment of undiscovered fields is getting smaller, simply because petroleum exploration has tended to find the

giant fields preferentially (see **Figure 1**). Accordingly, exploration costs must be constrained, consistent with the potential profits of smaller fields. It is not that exploration for large fields must cease—rather, it cannot proceed in the same ways it did in the 1950s through the early 1980s. We must figure out how to be profitable while exploring for (and finding) smaller fields.

5. Yet another probable cause has to do with inadequate geotechnical verification of *coincidence* (p. 34). All geologic chance elements must coincide in time and space if reservoired petroleum accumulations are to occur in a basin or trend. Especially in frontier areas, it is essential to map the areas where the various geologic chance elements are present (or probably present) and to restrict exploration to those areas of probable coincidence.

Remedies

What are some remedies to counter these problems?

1. Geotechnical staff must be vigilant with respect to *coincidence*—all geologic chance factors must *coincide* in time and space in the area of the prospect (p. 81). In the case of petroleum generation and migration, their *effects* must coincide with the presence of reservoirs, closures, and seals in the prospect area.
2. Actively employ *reality checks*—analogous experience from other basins, FSDs, and credibility of high-side projections (P1%–P10% range of values). Also, actively consider that all prospects may (unfortunately) result in only a small subeconomic field, and the prospect P99% and P90% forecasts should reflect this!
3. Solicit independent, multiple estimates, by peer and expert review and/or exploration committee review. Look at such high-risk prospects very carefully, employing Petroleum System Analysis.
4. Take on geotechnically proficient partners both as a risk-spreading measure and as a way to get independent confirmation of geotechnical and economic merit.
5. Verify positive expected value and economic feasibility of such projects, assuming a lower chance of success and significantly lower prospect reserves—i.e., what is the economic sensitivity relative to reduced chance and reserves values?

Are some remedies to be avoided? Although geotechnical staff should be admonished to give special technical scrutiny to high-risk prospects, it is probably a mistake for management to select a "chance hurdle"—an arbitrary lower limit for a prospect's chance of success. For example, if a company announced that henceforth, no exploration venture with a chance of success less than 20% would be undertaken, it might only encourage geotechnical staff to find creative ways to elevate what might legitimately be a 15% prospect to one rated 20% or 25%. Also, geotechnical staff must be accountable, and any official prospect review committee should not have power to approve or condemn prospects presented to them. Otherwise, no one is accountable! The expected value concept is a useful screen here. If the prospect-reserves distribution and geologic-chance estimates are well documented and venture EV is strongly positive (even though a scrutinized credible chance of success is only 10%), then the prospect should probably be drilled.

Chapter 4

Economic Analysis of Exploration Ventures

Introduction

It is essential for geoscientists to understand how the results of their technical work are used in estimating the economic value of the ventures in which they have been involved. Otherwise, they may invite incorrect use or manipulation of their professional geotechnical product. This understanding requires that they have a good working knowledge of economics and finance integrated into their geotechnical expertise.

Time Value of Money and Discount Rates

Corporations invest in petroleum exploration ventures, anticipating receipt of a series of future annual cash flows from production revenues (Megill, 1988). To assess the value of such future cash flows requires understanding of the time value of money, especially the concepts of future value, compounding, present value, and discounting.

Discounting is "compounding in reverse." The discount rate has one use and one use only: *to express the time value of money.* Arbitrarily elevated discount rates are not useful screening measures nor are they a proxy for risk.

The discount rate selected by the firm should be consistent among all classes of ventures ("it's all the same money"), and it should reflect the firm's average weighted cost of capital. Part of that cost of capital consists of interest on bank loans, part is the return realized by corporate investors as dividends and stock appreciation. As an alternative to the cost-of-capital approach, some authorities believe that the chosen discount rate should approximate the firm's actual long-term average annual rate of return—the "corporate reinvestment rate" (Capen, 1995).

When companies deliberately choose a high discount rate—one substantially higher than their cost of capital (or average reinvestment rate), they in effect select against long-term projects (which are typically associated with large-reserve opportunities) by assigning little or no value to cash flows beyond about 15 years. Instead, short-term projects are preferentially introduced into the portfolio, projects with high earning rates, but short lives, which are difficult to replace. On the other hand, choosing a low discount rate results in portfolios containing long-term, large-reserve projects. Even though they may create large values, such projects may depress the overall present value of the portfolio somewhat, although not as much as the short-term projects will (Capen, 1984). The selection of a discount rate that is too low is not as detrimental to portfolio value as the selection of a discount rate that is too high.

Exploration Cash-flow Models and Discounted Cash-flow Analysis

The cash-flow model of a proposed exploration venture is a quantified scenario for the exploration, discovery, development, and producing life of an oil or natural gas field.[5] It models the complex cash flows involved in a successful venture. *The cash-flow model assumes success.* This scenario must be geologically reasonable using the mean-reserves case and compatible values for per-well ultimate production: initial production rates; percentage decline rates; numbers of wells; costs for exploration, development, and well operations; taxes and tax provisions; wellhead prices; field life; salvage costs; and expected contract terms. To have meaning, the cash-flow model must be based on actual geotechnical estimates of ultimately recoverable reserves, field area, numbers and depths of wells,

---
[5]The reader is referred to books by Megill (1988), Stermole and Stermole (1990), and Wright and Thompson (1985) for detailed discussions about cash-flow models and economic analysis of projects.

and existing surface conditions. This model should not be unduly optimistic (in order to sell it to management) or unduly pessimistic (in order not to be wrong). The responsible geoscientist/prospector should strive for objective realism, recognizing that unbiased geotechnical predictions are a professional goal.

As previously stated (p. 24), discounted cash-flow (DCF) models for most prospects should also be run on the P10%, P50%, and P90% reserves cases, with the goal of generating a probabilistic distribution of net present values (NPV) for the venture. In other words (because NPV/BOE may vary with reserve sizes), we want to determine the mean of all NPV outcomes rather than the NPV of only the mean-reserves outcome. Naturally, geologic and engineering parameters such as area, well numbers, net pay thickness, HC-recovery, reserves, well initial production (IPs), and field life must be compatible with the corresponding P10%, P50%, and P90% reserves cases.[6] The key result from the cash-flow model is the discounted cumulative net cash flow (= "present value" or "present worth") over the projected life of the field.

Exploration costs and development costs constitute the *net investment cash-flow stream* (Megill, 1988); analysts are encouraged to calculate these costs on an after-tax basis, taking depreciation and investment tax credits into account. The *net income cash-flow stream* (also on an after-tax basis) is influenced by production revenues (declining), net revenue interest, wellhead taxes, operating costs, and income tax provisions. For production-sharing contracts, further modification may be required to correctly provide for the state's share of production revenues, cost recovery, and special tax provisions. For each year, the difference between *after-tax investment cash flow* and *after-tax income cash flow* is *annual after-tax net cash flow*. Ordinarily, annual net cash flows are negative in the first years of a project and positive in middle and later years when the field is fully developed and wells are in their producing (but declining) lives. Sometimes a project may anticipate a second stage of investment in a field's midlife to install an enhanced oil recovery (EOR) program or additional infill drilling. By adding all the annual after-tax net cash flows for the life of the field, we derive the field's cumulative after-tax net cash flow (CNCF).

Annual net cash flows are discounted using the appropriate annual present-value factor for the selected discount rate **(Table 10)**. By adding them for the period of the cash-flow model, we derive the key value of the cash-flow analysis: the cumulative net present value (= NPV), which is the sum of the discounted annual net cash flows for the project, using the appropriate annual present-value factor for years hence and the selected discount rate. This is, in essence, an after-tax profit number, incorporating investments, costs, taxes, wellhead revenues, production decline rates, operating costs, and the time value of money.

The cumulative NPV for any proposed prospect thus represents the venture compared against the perspective of the firm's present performance, i.e., How much better is this project than our present performance (or average weighted cost of capital)?

Problems with DCF Valuation of Exploratory Ventures

For more than 50 years, the petroleum industry has routinely used DCF analysis to value producing properties and exploratory ventures. One difficulty with the procedure has been that deterministic values were used, even for parameters that were known to be highly uncertain. Multiple runs using different values for some parameters gave a spread or range of possible outcomes; this process has been called "sensitivity analysis." But no probabilistic values could be assigned to the ranges. Software add-ins, especially Lotus® with @Risk®, or Excel® with Crystal Ball®, utilizing Monte Carlo or Latin Hypercube simulation, now allow probabilistic expression of such parameters so that the cumulative NPV can be expressed as a probability distribution. Even so, most firms at year-end 1999 still utilized multiple runs of deterministic cash-flow models.

Another problem is that each cash-flow model represents only one sequence of events from project inception to abandonment, often spanning 30 years or more. It is not possible to build into one cash-flow model the possibility of several alternative scenarios that might develop during the life of the field. This difficulty can now be partially addressed through a combination of "segmented" cash-flow models and decision-tree analysis.

But the most fundamental difficulty with DCF analysis of exploration ventures is that the observed business behavior of most major companies indicates that they place much more intrinsic value on large-reserve, long-term prospects than is consistent with their DCF valuation of such projects (Boccia, 1996). The reason, of course, has to do mostly with discounting: using prevalent discount rates of 10% to 12%, PVs of annual production cash flows beyond the first 15 or 20 years of a project's life are reduced to practically zero. But most companies specifically seek large new fields having long-term, stable production potential—just the

---

[6]To match the appropriate area, average net pay, and HC-recovery factor to the P90%, P50%, and P10% reserves cases, remember that multiplication of the product of the three P23% cases for area, pay, and HC-recovery results in the P10% reserves case, just as the product of the three P77% cases for area, pay, and HC-recovery yields the P90% reserves case. The product of the three P50% values yields the P50% reserves (Appendix B).

Table 10 *Present value factors.*

$$\text{Present Value of 1} = \frac{1}{(1+i)^n}$$

Discount Rate

Years Hence	1%	3%	4%	5%	6%	8%	10%	12%	15%	20%	30%	40%	50%
1	0.990	0.971	0.962	0.952	0.943	0.926	0.909	0.893	0.870	0.833	0.769	0.714	0.667
2	0.980	0.943	0.925	0.907	0.890	0.857	0.826	0.797	0.756	0.694	0.592	0.510	0.444
3	0.971	0.915	0.889	0.864	0.840	0.794	0.751	0.712	0.658	0.579	0.455	0.364	0.296
4	0.961	0.888	0.855	0.823	0.792	0.735	0.683	0.636	0.572	0.482	0.350	0.260	0.198
5	0.951	0.863	0.822	0.784	0.747	0.681	0.621	0.567	0.497	0.402	0.269	0.186	0.132
6	0.942	0.837	0.790	0.746	0.705	0.630	0.564	0.507	0.432	0.335	0.207	0.133	0.088
7	0.933	0.813	0.760	0.711	0.665	0.583	0.513	0.452	0.376	0.279	0.159	0.095	0.059
8	0.923	0.789	0.731	0.677	0.627	0.540	0.467	0.404	0.327	0.233	0.123	0.068	0.039
9	0.914	0.766	0.703	0.645	0.592	0.500	0.424	0.361	0.284	0.194	0.094	0.048	0.026
10	0.905	0.744	0.676	0.614	0.558	0.463	0.386	0.322	0.247	0.162	0.073	0.035	0.017
11	0.896	0.722	0.650	0.585	0.527	0.429	0.350	0.287	0.215	0.135	0.056	0.025	0.012
12	0.887	0.701	0.625	0.557	0.497	0.397	0.319	0.257	0.187	0.112	0.043	0.018	0.008
13	0.879	0.681	0.601	0.530	0.469	0.368	0.290	0.229	0.163	0.093	0.033	0.013	0.005
14	0.870	0.661	0.577	0.505	0.442	0.340	0.263	0.205	0.141	0.078	0.025	0.009	0.003
15	0.861	0.642	0.555	0.481	0.417	0.315	0.239	0.183	0.123	0.065	0.020	0.006	0.002
16	0.853	0.623	0.534	0.458	0.394	0.292	0.218	0.163	0.107	0.054	0.015	0.005	0.002
17	0.844	0.605	0.513	0.436	0.371	0.270	0.198	0.146	0.093	0.045	0.012	0.003	0.001
18	0.836	0.587	0.494	0.416	0.350	0.250	0.180	0.130	0.081	0.038	0.009	0.002	0.001
19	0.828	0.570	0.475	0.396	0.331	0.232	0.164	0.116	0.070	0.031	0.007	0.002	
20	0.820	0.554	0.456	0.377	0.312	0.215	0.149	0.104	0.061	0.026	0.005	0.001	
21	0.811	0.538	0.439	0.359	0.294	0.199	0.135	0.093	0.053	0.022	0.004	0.001	
22	0.803	0.522	0.422	0.342	0.278	0.184	0.123	0.083	0.046	0.018	0.003	0.001	
23	0.795	0.507	0.406	0.326	0.262	0.170	0.112	0.074	0.040	0.015	0.002		
24	0.788	0.492	0.390	0.310	0.247	0.158	0.102	0.066	0.035	0.013	0.002		
25	0.780	0.478	0.375	0.295	0.233	0.146	0.092	0.059	0.030	0.010	0.001		
26	0.772	0.464	0.361	0.281	0.220	0.135	0.084	0.053	0.026	0.009	0.001		
27	0.764	0.450	0.347	0.268	0.207	0.125	0.076	0.047	0.023	0.007	0.001		
28	0.757	0.437	0.333	0.255	0.196	0.116	0.069	0.042	0.020	0.006	0.001		
29	0.749	0.424	0.321	0.243	0.185	0.107	0.063	0.037	0.017	0.005			
30	0.742	0.412	0.308	0.231	0.174	0.099	0.057	0.033	0.015	0.004			
31	0.735	0.400	0.296	0.220	0.164	0.092	0.052	0.030	0.013	0.004			
32	0.727	0.388	0.285	0.210	0.155	0.085	0.047	0.027	0.011	0.003			
33	0.720	0.377	0.274	0.200	0.146	0.079	0.043	0.024	0.010	0.002			
34	0.713	0.366	0.264	0.190	0.138	0.073	0.039	0.021	0.009	0.002			
35	0.706	0.355	0.253	0.181	0.130	0.068	0.036	0.019	0.008	0.002			
36	0.699	0.345	0.244	0.173	0.123	0.063	0.032	0.017	0.007	0.001			
37	0.692	0.335	0.234	0.164	0.116	0.058	0.029	0.015	0.006	0.001			
38	0.685	0.325	0.225	0.157	0.109	0.054	0.027	0.013	0.005	0.001			
39	0.678	0.316	0.217	0.149	0.103	0.050	0.024	0.012	0.004	0.001			
40	0.672	0.307	0.208	0.142	0.097	0.046	0.022	0.011	0.004	0.001			
41	0.665	0.298	0.200	0.135	0.092	0.043	0.020	0.010	0.003	0.001			
42	0.658	0.289	0.193	0.129	0.087	0.039	0.018	0.009	0.003				
43	0.652	0.281	0.185	0.123	0.082	0.037	0.017	0.008	0.002				
44	0.645	0.272	0.178	0.117	0.077	0.034	0.015	0.007	0.002				
45	0.639	0.264	0.171	0.111	0.073	0.031	0.014	0.006	0.002				
46	0.633	0.257	0.165	0.106	0.069	0.029	0.012	0.005	0.002				
47	0.626	0.249	0.158	0.101	0.065	0.027	0.011	0.005	0.001				
48	0.620	0.242	0.152	0.096	0.061	0.025	0.010	0.004	0.001				
49	0.614	0.235	0.146	0.092	0.058	0.023	0.009	0.004	0.001				
50	0.608	0.228	0.141	0.087	0.054	0.021	0.009	0.003	0.001				

kinds of fields that build companies and provide steady, reliable, low-cost production revenue streams for many years. Yet these are the kinds of long-term, steady cash flows whose value beyond about 20 years is shown to be nearly zero by conventional DCF analysis!

One solution to this difficulty has been to employ artificially reduced discount rates when evaluating such opportunities. Of course, the choice of the proper low discount rate is arbitrary. A better approach would be to run all DCF analyses for all candidate projects in the inventory at a low discount rate that represents the fundamental interest for the "hire of the money"—perhaps 4% to 5%—one that does not include any provision for inflation of costs or prices. By using the current mean of "real" historical oil prices, the company could compare all projects for its portfolio and rank them on that basis. This would be internally consistent, reducing the negative effect that discounting has on long-term cash flows and eliminating the possibility that some projects could be made to appear more attractive through biased selection of elevated price-escalation schedules. Use of the historical mean of real oil prices (corrected to present day for inflation) recognizes the long life of most large oil and gas fields and tends to correct for short-term price influences. Such a simplified procedure would likely optimize the ranking of projects and would select for growth.

But the most promising solution to "the DCF problem" lies in adoption of an alternate method of valuing exploration ventures: Option-pricing Theory.

Option-pricing Theory and Valuation of Exploration Ventures

The sequence of characteristic business decisions that attend discovery, development, and operation of large oil and gas fields represents classic option behavior **(Figure 24)**. Companies acquire leases or contract areas, then invest in additional geotechnical data to refine their risk/reward perception—which, if encouraging, leads them to exploratory drilling. If drilling is successful, the company confirms and delineates the discovered field, which, if it is judged to be economic, the company then develops and produces. Enhanced recovery projects may be added during the field's producing life, followed by abandonment when production revenues decline below operating costs. Depending on the prevailing economics, technologic developments, political trends, and contract terms, the company may choose at various decision points to invest further, to defer action, to sell part or all of their interest, or to abandon the venture. Each stage in the venture thus represents an option.

The Black-Scholes model (Brealey and Myers, 1988; Bernstein, 1996) for valuing a stock option depends on four parameters: time, price differential between current price and strike price, interest rates, and variance of price. But there are four important differences between options in the stock market or commodities market and options in the oil business.

1. When a stock option is exercised the benefit is realized immediately, but when an oil company exercises its option by developing a property or installing new EOR procedures in an existing field, additional revenues may not be realized for one to four years. This can be handled by discounting those future cash flows back to the time of the decision, but price fluctuations may introduce substantial uncertainty.
2. In the case of stock options, economic benefits are realized because the current price exceeds the strike price. However, most large oil fields have lives of 20 to 100 years, and the price of oil or gas behaves as a typical fluctuating commodity, oscillating widely through a max-min price envelope. Therefore, any price differential at the time of option-exercise will change many times, positively and negatively, during the field's life. Thus the benefit in oil and gas field options usually relates not to elevated oil *prices* but to improved *operating profits*, which result from reduced costs to find, develop, and/or operate fields. In general then, oil exploration option behavior depends on waiting for new data or technology that may lower costs and/or reduce risk, not on sustained higher oil or natural gas prices.
3. Calculating the variance (or standard deviation) in price of a given stock is easy. Moreover, it would be easy to calculate the historical standard deviation in the real price of crude oil (approximate 2000 estimate = ±$7.00 bbl). What is not known is the variance in prices of oil *properties*, such as exploration prospects or discoveries that have not yet been developed.
4. There is a large and continuous market for trading common stocks—any time an owner wishes to sell his or her common stock, a trade may be effected almost instantly. But sales of oil properties commonly require months of preparation, analysis, and negotiation, during which ongoing developments may cause major changes in the perceived value of the property (Lohrenz, 1988).

Most major international oil companies are now developing some form of option-pricing procedure to replace conventional DCF analysis for establishing the monetary value of oil and gas ventures, especially long-term, large-reserve projects (Chorn, 1999; Dixit and Pindyck, 1994; Lehman, 1989; Mann et al., 1992; Paddock et al., 1983; Pickles and Smith, 1993).

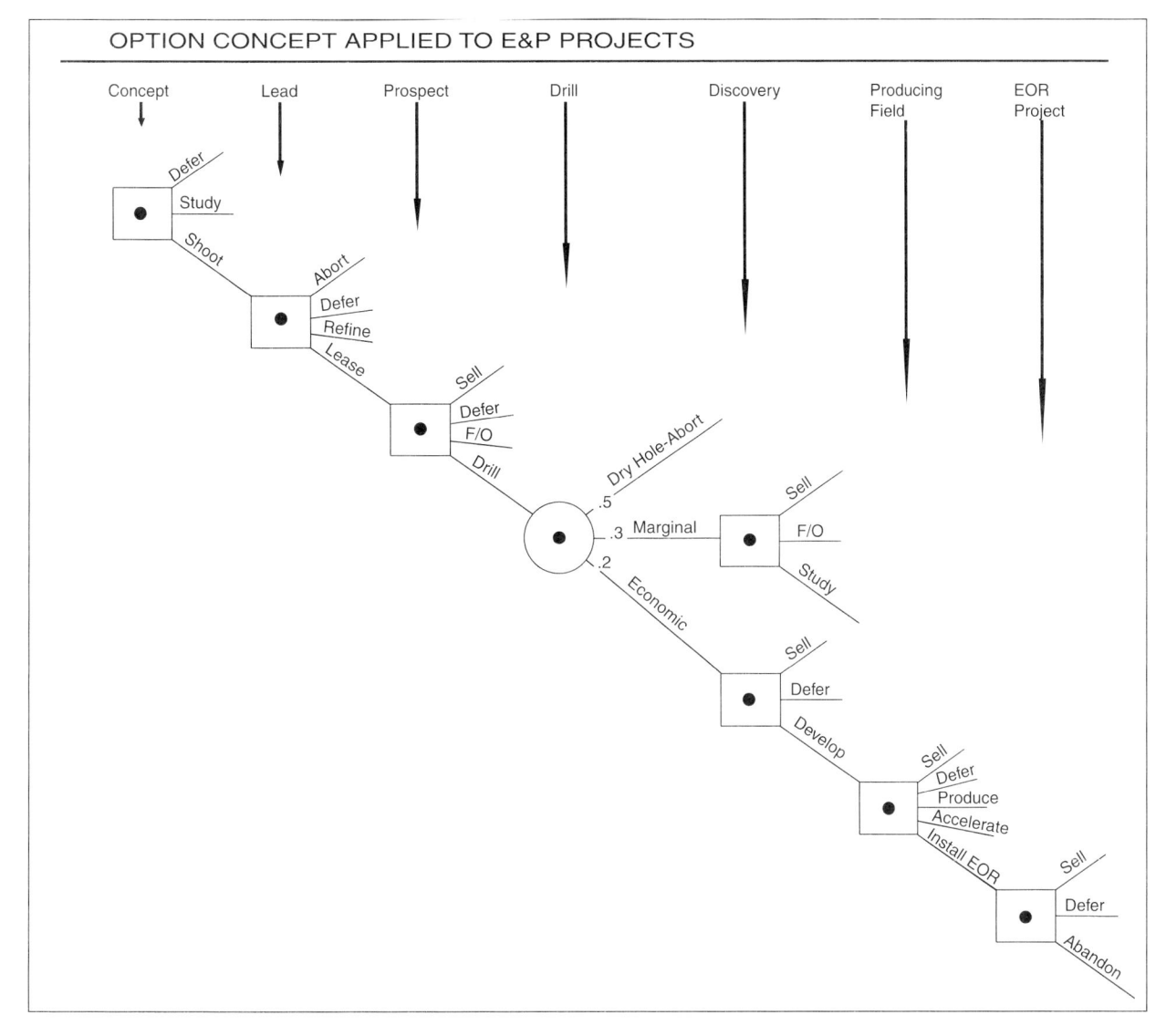

Figure 24 *Option concept applied to E&P projects. F/O = farm-out; EOR = enhanced oil recovery.*

Recommended Economic Measures

Once the cash-flow model or models of the proposed venture have been run, there are many different ways to measure the venture's attractiveness (Megill, 1988, 1992). Use and diversity of these measures have evolved as companies and analysts have become increasingly sophisticated about oil and gas investments. Different companies have developed minor variations on the main measures to suit their individual needs.

However, all current and widely used industry measures depend on the fundamental expression of project value—cumulative NPV (see p. 50)—which of course assumes project success.

Discounted Cash-flow Rate of Return

Discounted cash-flow rate of return (DCFROR) may be expressed in two different ways: (1) the exact earning rate of the project during its full life, expressed as an annual average rate of return; or (2) that discount rate that sets the value of the cumulative net cash flow stream to be discounted, over the life of the project, at zero. DCFROR is not useful for comparing different projects. It has only one legitimate use: to serve as a minimum qualifying standard, or "hurdle rate," which any project must clear if it is to be considered further for corporate funding. Once DCFROR has been used in this way, other economic measures should be employed to compare and rank exploratory ventures. Employment of arbitrarily elevated DCF hurdle rates does not compensate for risk;

moreover, it selects *against* long-term, large-reserve ventures.

Maximum Negative Cash Flow

Maximum negative cash flow (MNCF) is the "turnaround" point on the project's cumulative discounted net cash flow profile—that point at which the cumulative net cash flows have reached their maximum negative level and will turn back upward toward the break-even line and increasing profitability **(Figure 25)**. MNCF is a discounted value, and for exploratory ventures, where a new field may be developed if there is a discovery, MNCF represents the net of investments and partially offsetting production revenues. It is useful in capital budgeting and planning because it represents the amount of money that actually will be needed from the corporate treasury. In firms that have short-term capital constraints, it may be useful for comparing and choosing projects. It also serves as a "time focus" for concerns about political risk because it represents the time of greatest economic vulnerability for project life. But the most significant use of this parameter is as a proxy for investment in investment efficiency, one of the most useful common economic measures (see this page).

Expected Net Present Value

As introduced in **Equations 1** and **2**, ENPV is the chance-weighted NPV of a venture, in which the product of the chance of failure and the cost of exploratory failure is subtracted from the product of the chance of success and the NPV of the mean-reserves case **(Equation 3)**. For prospects (rather than plays), it integrates prospect reserves, DCF values, and commercial chance of success, thus allowing comparison of high-risk, high-potential prospects with low-risk prospects having only a moderate reserves potential. It is useful in portfolio analysis primarily because the sum of all project expected values is the expected value of the entire portfolio. The drawback of expected value is that it implies that the firm is risk-neutral: two projects might have identical ENPVs even though one project requires a much larger initial capital investment (= dry-hole cost) than the other (see p. 92). In fact, however, most firms recognize that exploration decisions commonly involve provisions against loss (= risk) as well as ENPV **(Equations 6** and **7)**.

(3)
$$ENPV = \begin{cases} \text{Chance of Commercial Success} \\ \text{(NPV of Mean Commercial} \\ \text{Reserves Distribution) minus} \\ \text{Chance of Commercial Failure} \\ \text{(Net Cost of Exploratory Failure)} \end{cases}$$

In its simple form, ENPV makes no provision for *risk* (as distinguished from *chance*). However, ENPV does form the basis of an expanded economic measure that considers project utility and corporate loss-aversion, called risk-adjusted value (RAV) (Cozzolino, 1977, 1978), which is discussed further below and on page 92.

Investment Efficiency

Investment efficiency (IE) is the most discriminating form of profit/investment ratio, in which profit is the project's NPV and the investment is maximum negative net cash flow (MCNF) **(Equation 4)**.

$$IE = \frac{\text{PRESENT VALUE}}{\text{INVESTMENT (MNCF)}} \quad (4)$$

Figure 25 shows the relationship of the key terms involved in investment efficiency. Investment efficiency produces the same project ranking as does another preferred measure: growth rate of return (GRR) (Capen et al., 1976), in which net cash flows are considered to be reinvested as received, at the company's real rate of return, and projected out to some preselected target year (often 10 or 12 years). For longer-term projects, annual net cash flows extending beyond the target year are discounted back and then combined with accumulated earnings. Even though generally acknowledged to be a superior economic measure, GRR has not received the wide usage of its derivative, investment efficiency (Clapp, 1995).

Another advantage of investment efficiency is that it can easily be risked—that is, it can be modified to chance-weight all outcomes **(Equation 5)**:

$$IE_{RISKED} = \frac{Pc\,(NPV) - Pf\,(DHC)}{Pc\,(I) + Pf\,(DHC)} \quad (5)$$

where

I = maximum negative cumulative discounted net cash flow, and
DHC = net cost of exploratory failure (literally, dry-hole cost).

Exploration portfolios ranked using risked investment efficiency are optimized for the creation of value. Unfortunately, such portfolios sometimes present unacceptable degrees of risk, and this may require the company to surrender some attractive high-risk prospects in exchange for some less risky but smaller ventures.

Risk-adjusted Value

Cozzolino's (1977, 1978) equation for RAV combines the expected value concept with principles of utility theory, which is generally acknowledged to follow an exponential form **(Equation 6)**.

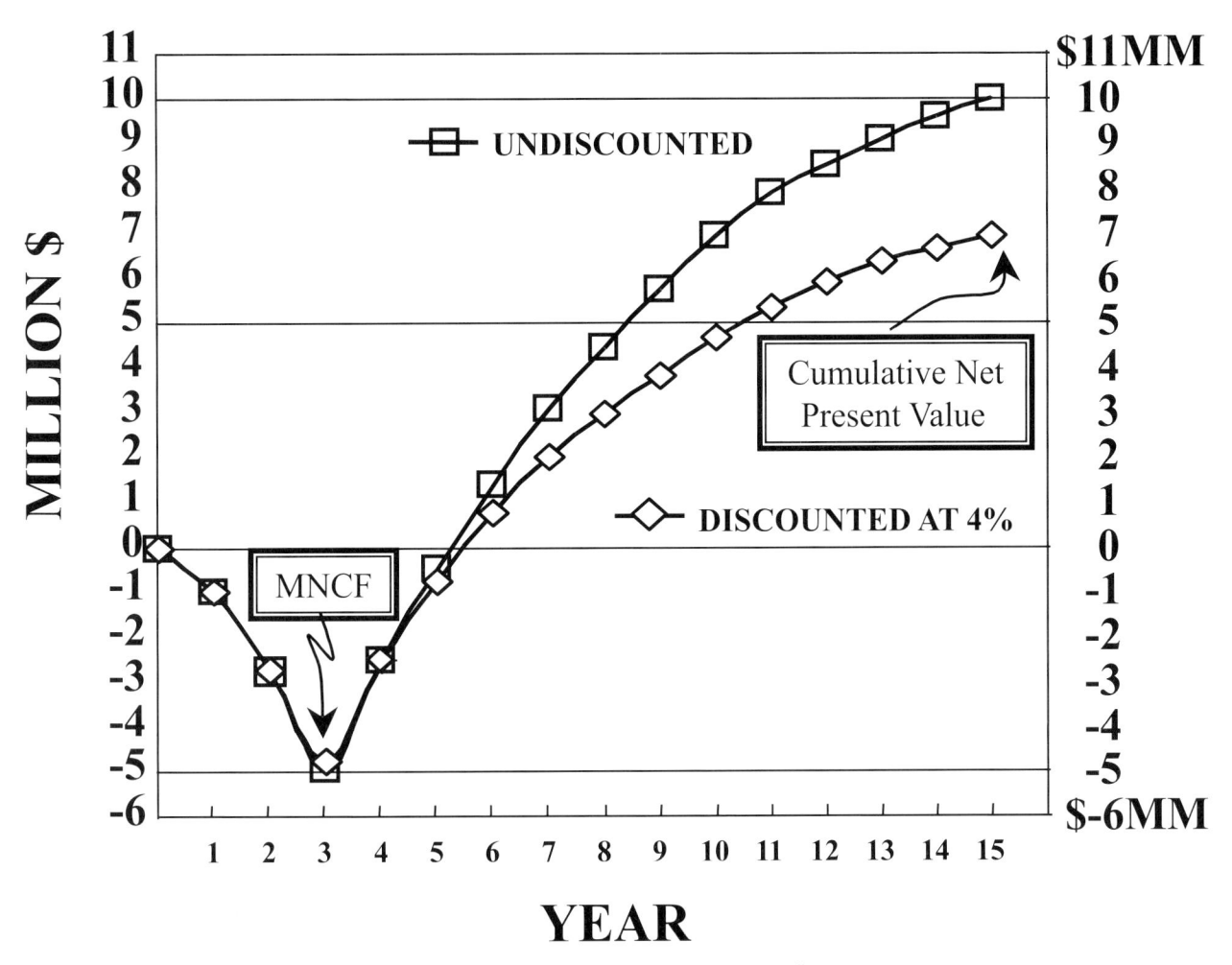

Figure 25 *Cumulative net present value and maximum negative net cash flow.*

$$\text{RAV} = \frac{-1}{r} ln\left[\text{Pc} \times e^{-r(\text{PV})} + (\text{Pf}) \times e^{r(\text{DHC})}\right] \quad (6)$$

Where

Pc = chance of commercial success
Pf = chance of commercial failure
PV = prospect present value
DHC = dry-hole cost
r = company risk quotient

Optimum Working Interest

If the company's risk-quotient (r) is known,[7] every venture can be shown to have an optimum working interest (OWI)—i.e., that proportional share at which the RAV is greatest (MacKay, 1995). However, further work by MacKay and his colleague Ian Lerche has generated a direct method for determining OWI **(Equation 7)** using the concept of risk tolerance, generally represented as $1/r$.

$$\text{OWI} = \frac{\text{RT}}{\text{Cost} + \text{PV}} \times ln \frac{\text{Pc} \times \text{PV}}{\text{Pf} \times \text{Cost}} \quad (7)$$

where

RT = risk tolerance
PV = prospect present value
Cost = cost of failure
Pc = chance of commercial success
Pf = chance of failure

If a company wishes to include considerations of utility theory or risk aversion in ranking its various projects for inclusion in the annual portfolio, it can calculate OWI for each venture, then calculate ENPV and risked IE (see this page) at the predetermined share (or actual share, where the exact OWI is not available).

---

[7]Cozzolino suggested that a rough approximation of (r) was 1/annual exploration budget ($MM); thus (r) for a firm with a $50MM annual budget would be 1/50 or 0.02. Later observations and calculations by Walls (1993, personal communication) suggested that 5/annual budget was a more representative value for average oil companies, so Walls's (r) for a $50MM firm would be 0.10. Each company should be able to determine approximately what its (r) value really is, based on recent previous joint ventures and expressed share preferences for its current joint ventures.

Considerations of OWI have two main applications in exploration. Small firms are often quite sensitive to risk because of their limited capital and the correspondingly small number of drilling ventures that are possible for them. Such firms may employ OWI calculations to ensure that participation levels in the several ventures comprising their annual portfolios are consistent and appropriate to their modest financial resources.

The second OWI application arises from the nature of annual drilling portfolios. Ideally a company would assemble an inventory of candidate prospects for ranking and selection to make up the next year's drilling portfolio, and appropriate shares of joint ventures would be determined as part of the calculations that lead to portfolio optimization. But many companies do not have the luxury of assembling a full year's supply of prospects 12 months in advance. Instead they make decisions serially on prospects that appear throughout the program year, hence they cannot predetermine the appropriate share based on portfolio considerations. Here OWI offers an alternative approach that, however, may actually function in a somewhat more risk-averse way and thus reduce portfolio value more than necessary. This topic will be revisited in Chapter 6, in the section on prospect and play portfolios.

Chapter 5

Exploration Plays—Risk Analysis and Economic Assessment

Introduction

The Problem with Most Exploration Contracts

No rational investor wants to make a large payment for a purchase whose quantity, quality, and longevity are largely unknown. However, that is essentially what is required of most modern petroleum firms that seek to explore and develop new prospective areas.

To obtain contractual rights to explore for and develop petroleum resources in most countries, a corporation usually must commit to spending millions of dollars, either through work commitments (line-miles of seismic surveys, number of drilled wells, and the like) or front-end payments (bonus bids, fees, and the like), or both. Frequently, such financial commitments are undertaken with only minimal knowledge about the prospectivity of the contract area—how many new fields may be discovered; how much oil and/or gas they may contain; how much it may cost to find, develop, and produce them; how profitable they may be; how long it may take to establish production; and how long the productive life of the fields may be.

Ideally, such exploration would be *staged*: progressive investments would be closely related to the ongoing acquisition of geotechnical, economic, and political information bearing on evolving perceptions of risk versus reward, thus minimizing unnecessary expenditures. However, the form of most existing international contracts prevents such prudent investing.

Thus the most critical decision in modern petroleum exploration is not which *prospect* to drill. Rather, it is which new *trend* or *area* to go into, because that decision commits the organization to millions of invested dollars, years of involvement, and hundreds of man-years of professional and technical effort. If the selected new area proves to contain economic petroleum reserves, then substantial value has been acquired by the firm. Yet such commitments commonly have been made without disciplined, integrated geotechnical and economic evaluation. Almost every large oil company can relate disastrous experiences with international contract areas, in which dramatic economic losses were experienced over multiyear contract periods, commonly stemming from undisciplined, even haphazard entry decisions into new trends or basins.

Fortunately, the problem is tractable. Explorationists recognize that oil and gas fields occur in "families"—groups of fields of common geologic origin, usually in geologically definable areas or trends. These groups of fields have similar producing attributes and similar economic patterns. We call such related groups of fields and prospects "plays" (p. 3). And plays can be evaluated as full-cycle economic ventures.

History and Development of the Play Concept

The era of modern petroleum exploration began in 1859 in Pennsylvania (Owen, 1975; Pees, 1989; Yergin, 1991). As drilling for oil spread in the United States and in eastern Europe during the late 19th century, and then more widely around the world during the first half of the 20th century, petroleum exploration focused on the prospect: *"A documented set of anomalous geological criteria that, in combination with related economic circumstances, justifies the capital investment of drilling an exploratory well to discover a hypothecated commercial accumulation of oil and/or natural gas"* (modified after Levorson, 1967).

By 1935 geologists recognized several different types of petroleum accumulations—anticlinal traps, fault traps, stratigraphic traps, combination traps, hydrodynamic traps, and so on. Moreover, experienced geologists knew that certain types of petroleum accumulations were characteristic in some basins or trends but rare or even unknown in others.

Beginning in the 1950s, petroleum exploration researchers began to focus on stratigraphy and depositional systems, trying to understand and predict the origin and distribution of sedimentary facies as they relate to the occurrence of reservoirs, seals, and hydrocarbon source beds. That research campaign, directed in substantial part at modern depositional processes, constituted a revolution in sedimentary geology, especially with regard to industry knowledge about different types of reservoir bodies.

In the late 1960s another new subdiscipline—sedimentary basin analysis (Miall, 1984)—arose in petroleum exploration, abetted in part by the emerging revelations of plate tectonics (Dickinson, 1974; Klemme, 1975, 1980; Bally and Snelson, 1980) and in part by computer-processed CDP seismic data, which could now sense and depict the subsurface configuration and internal geometry of specific sedimentary sequences (Vail et al., 1977a, 1977b). Now geologists could relate the distribution of reservoir and sealing rock bodies to geologic structure, in terms of (1) origin, provenance, and regional setting, as well as (2) subsequent structural evolution and present configuration.

These geotechnical concepts and tools all contributed to the development of the *exploration play concept*, first used by the Geological Survey of Canada in 1972 (McCrossan, 1973; Roy, 1975; Miller, 1986) and later well described by Baker et al. (1986): *a group of prospects as well as oil and/or gas fields, all having similar geologic origins—a family of geologically similar traps*. Fields comprising a play contain similar reservoir rocks that arose from similar depositional processes, and the constituent field reservoirs exhibit similar production patterns. Prospects and fields in a play have similar structural configurations and structural histories. They have similar top seals and seat seals. Also, fields in a play form a coherent lognormal distribution of ultimately recoverable reserves. Other names for the same thing include genetic trend, geologic fairway, petroleum zone, complex of fields, and producing trend.

Exxon geologists published important papers on various aspects of play analysis during the 1975–1995 period, especially David White (1980, 1988, 1992, 1993) and R.A. Baker (1986, 1988). Sluijk and Nederlof (1984) described Shell's complex system for prospect and play analysis. Serial publications by the Texas Bureau of Economic Geology staff during 1985–1995 described and summarized many plays in Texas. Otis and Schneidermann (1997) published an excellent and detailed summary of Chevron's exploration risking procedure.

Perceptive prospectors recognized that when companies carried out exploration campaigns along structural or stratigraphic fairways, they were usually engaged in play exploration. Geophysicists could lay out regional seismic grids and stratigraphers could deal with depositional trends. This was a much more efficient way to conduct exploration. Once the key geologic and geotechnical patterns and relationships became understood—once a company had "cracked the exploration code" and discovered the first field—discovery of other fields in the play was greatly facilitated. Thus, play exploration was a form of geotechnical leveraging, and it often led to multiple discoveries and highly profitable "core areas." Moreover, field development became more efficient because the fields in a play usually had similar reservoir conditions, thus similar development and production techniques could be applied to the related fields in the play. Learning facilitated profitability.

But exploration economics tended to focus on the single prospect as the *economic unit of exploration*, even though companies didn't ordinarily explore on the basis of isolated, unrelated prospects. Instead they directed their attention to the play as the *operational unit of exploration*. And the unifying attribute of the play was the overall similarity of traps—reservoir rocks, structural and stratigraphic configurations, and sealing facies. The U.S. Geological Survey and U.S. Minerals Management Services employed the play concept in carrying out several assessments of remaining onshore and offshore U.S. oil and gas resources during the 1990s. Their databases are now available to the public, at no charge, on CD-ROM (1995, 1997, 2000).

Plays and Petroleum Systems

In the early 1970s ongoing research in petroleum geochemistry began to bear fruit, leading to the widespread recognition that oil and natural gas could be classified into distinct geochemical types, and that they were generated from kerogen-rich, generally fine-grained sediments in petroleum-generative depressions (Demaison, 1984) through processes that were time- and temperature-dependent (Waples, 1980). Later geochemical work recognized that kinetics played a dominant role in the generation process (Hunt et al., 1991; Waples, 1994). Nevertheless, integrated geologic methods of analysis and mapping could identify such thermally mature basins, or "kitchens," as well as the probable timing and directions of subsequent migration of generated petroleum.

With these geochemical capabilities, explorationists could now demonstrate what had long been suspected—that fields in a play also had similar histories of hydrocarbon type, origin, emplacement, and preservation. Armed with these powerful geochemical concepts and analytic tools, explorationists began to exploit the play concept worldwide.

By about 1975, regional explorationists began to develop yet another unifying concept, employing the concepts and techniques described previously: the concept of the petroleum system (Magoon and Dow, 1994). Here the focus was on the entire petroleum-generative basin complex of petroleum source rocks, carrier beds and conduits for migrating petroleum, and traps containing the reservoired hydrocarbons. A petroleum system often contains multiple plays with several different types of traps, all charged from a common petroleum source rock in a petroleum-generative depression, or kitchen **(Figures 26** and **27)** (Demaison, 1984). Magoon's emphasis on the "critical

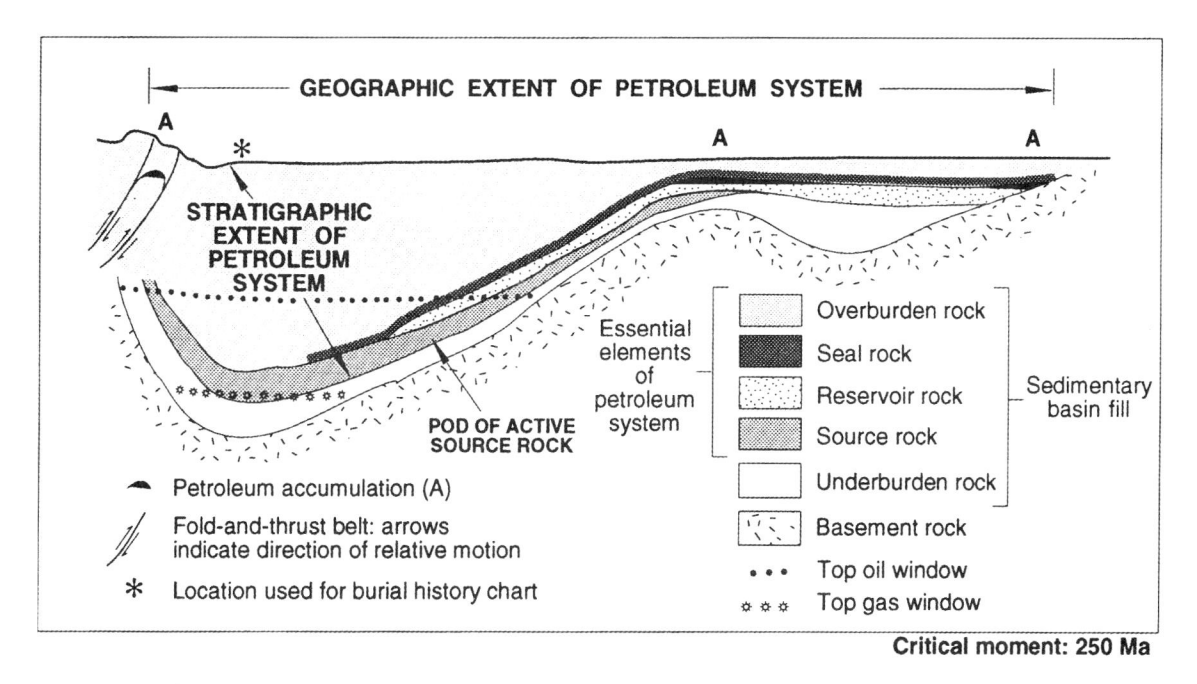

Figure 26 *Hypothetical geologic cross section of a basin showing the essential elements of a petroleum system. From Magoon and Dow (1994).*

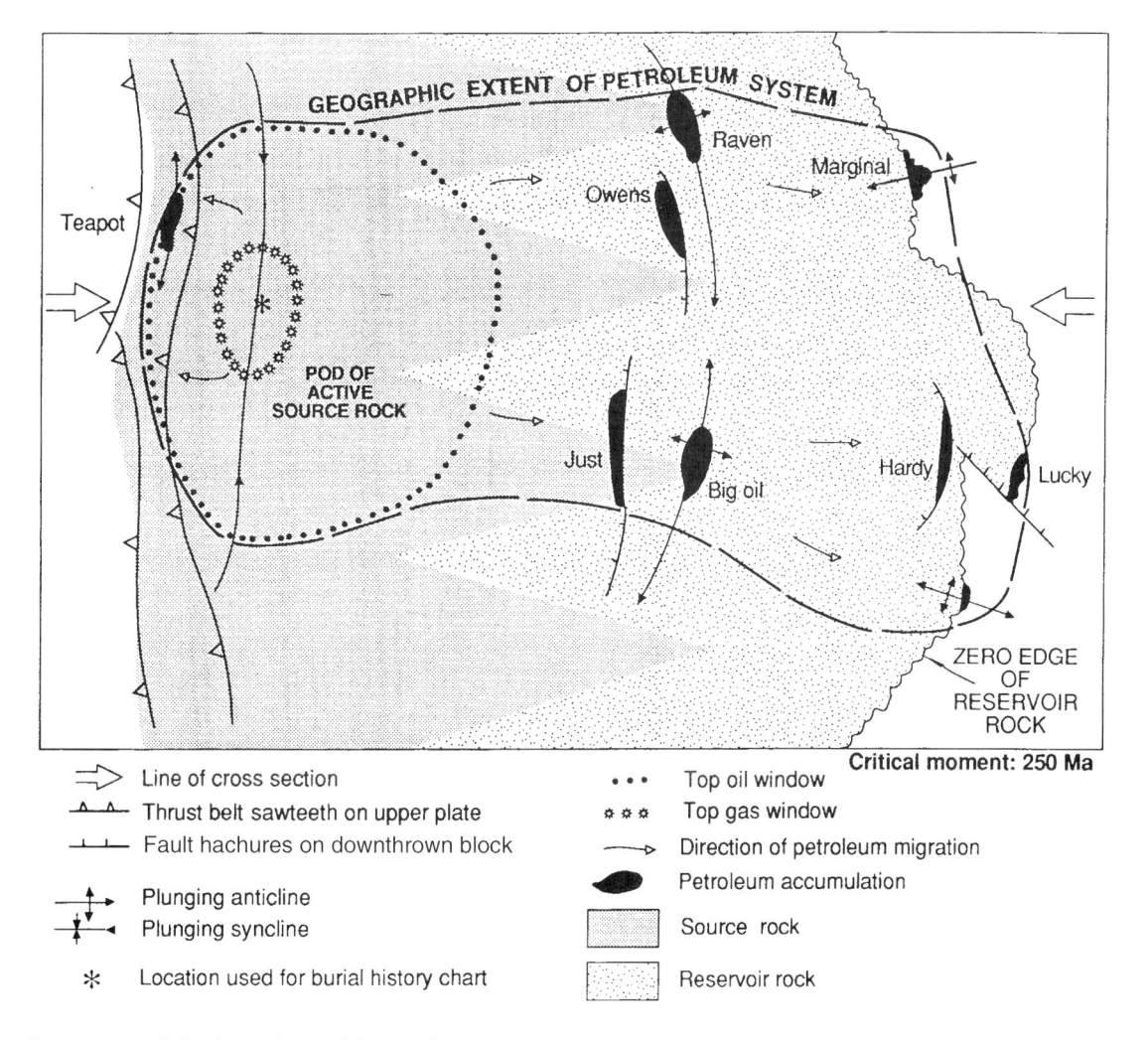

Figure 27 *Map of the hypothetical basin showing areal extent of the petroleum system. From Magoon and Dow (1994).*

moment" **(Figure 28)** facilitates critical thinking and investigations bearing on time of peak hydrocarbon generation and probable migration routes to traps available at that time. Accordingly, the petroleum system approach provides a very powerful framework for understanding the basin's "plumbing system," and it stimulates and encourages the development of new exploration ideas and targets **(Table 11)**. However, it does not lend itself to economic analysis because of the complexities attendant upon the multiple and dissimilar constituent plays **(Figure 29)**.

Possibly because of their geoscience research focus, leading petroleum system authorities define the geologic play differently than do most practical petroleum explorationists. Magoon and Dow (1994), for example, conceive of the petroleum system as including only those elements that are known—proven source rocks, identified carrier beds and conduits, and discovered fields whose analyzed oils and natural gases are clearly related to the source rocks. Following that definition, a play is only that part of the petroleum system that is undiscovered (Magoon, personal communication, 1997).

To the practical explorationist, such a definition causes substantial problems: First, it allows several different families of traps, if charged from a common mature source rock, to be included within a single play. This presents extremely complex consequences for companies that wish to analyze an entire play as a full-cycle business venture because of very wide variances caused by the diversity of trap types, geologic dependencies, and profitabilities. Second, it makes use of field-size distributions (FSDs)—a very powerful predictive tool in economic play analysis—much less discriminating because different genetic trap types must be included in the same distribution. This is a serious statistical drawback. Third, it artificially separates prospects and leads from discovered producing fields in the play and thus hinders our use of field analogs and models in exploration. Finally, the preferred definition of the play, *a family of geologically related fields, prospects and leads, all of similar geological origin and charged from common petroleum source beds*, does not in

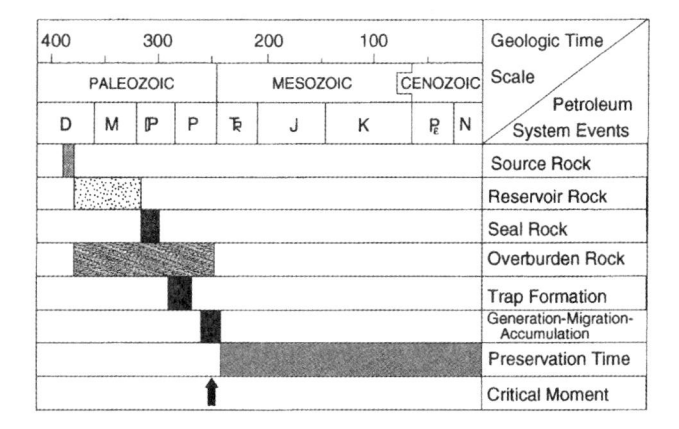

Figure 28 *Events chart showing relationship between essential elements and processes as well as preservation time and critical moment. From Magoon and Dow (1994).*

any way hinder the employment of the petroleum system as an extremely useful exploration concept. The writer strongly urges active explorers to follow the above-recommended definition of the exploration play.

Play Selection as the Critical Exploration Decision

With the previous considerations in mind, and recognizing the prevalence in international exploration of large contract areas obtained through various combinations of costly work commitments and/or front-end bonuses, it is clear that the most important decision in international exploration is not which prospect to drill. Instead, the key decision concerns which new play to enter because it involves much larger commitments of money, time, and personnel. The economic consequences of choosing a bad play can be serious to a medium-sized international explorer; to a smaller firm such an outcome can be financially disastrous.

Table 11 *Factor comparison in the four levels of petroleum investigation (Magoon and Dow, 1994).*

Factor	Sedimentary Basin	Petroleum System	Play	Prospect
Investigation	Sedimentary rocks	Petroleum	Traps	Trap
Economics	None	None	Essential	Essential
Geologic time	Time of deposition	Critical moment	Present-day	Present-day
Existence	Absolute	Absolute	Conditional	Conditional
Cost	Very low	Low	High	Very high
Analysis & modeling	Basin	System	Play	Prospect

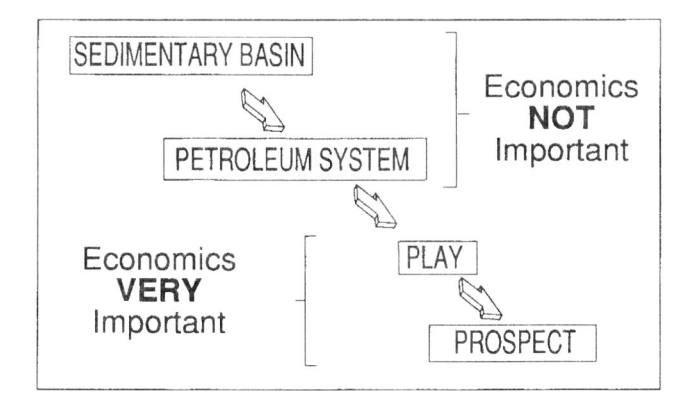

Figure 29 *Four levels of petroleum investigation. From Magoon and Dow (1994).*

an exploration play are identical to, derived from, or analogous with those employed in prospect risk analysis **(Table 12)**.

For example, just as a series of successful development wells prove up the discovered field, so do successive discoveries prove up the successful play (Baker et al., 1986). The prospect-reserves distribution allows probabilistic prediction of reserves expected, given that the *prospect* proves to be a discovery; similarly, the FSD allows probabilistic reserves prediction for the new *play*, given at least one discovery. Either distribution can be used to help estimate the chance of commercial success (see p. 39) and/or the chance of economic success, given the presence of flowable hydrocarbons. For distributions of both prospect reserves and field sizes, it is important to determine minimum commercial field size (MCFS) or minimum economic field size (MEFS) and the probabilities associated with them (Pmcfs and Pmefs). No prospect should be drilled unless the operator has a legitimate reason to expect the venture to be profitable on a full-cycle economic basis (i.e., the mean-reserves case is at least minimally economic). However, the operative decision to complete the discovery well, made after the well has been drilled, is based on the MCFS simply because the decision to complete the discovery well considers all prior costs as "sunk" and thus depends only on whether costs of completion and operation allow an acceptable profit-making investment on a point-forward basis. For plays, however, MEFS is preferred because no rational company is purposefully going to *continue* to explore for and develop new fields in a play where the discovered fields are not economic on a full-cycle basis. For both prospects and plays, we

The good news is that, because of (1) similar reservoir types and trap geometries, (2) commonality of hydrocarbon charge, (3) consistent exploration and development methods, and (4) uniform contract terms, it is possible to carry out economic evaluations of exploration plays as full-cycle economic ventures. Such evaluations utilize regional geologic, geochemical, and geophysical studies (see Appendix E), and they are carried out using basic principles of prospect risk analysis, as described in Chapter 3.

Risk Analysis of Prospects and Plays Compared

For the most part, the logic and procedures used in conducting risk analysis and economic assessment of

Table 12 *Exploration risk analysis—prospects versus plays.*

PROSPECTS	vs.	**PLAYS**
• Development wells prove up the discovered *field*		• Successive discoveries prove up the successful *play*
• Prospect-reserves distribution		• Field-size distribution
• Pmcfs → Pcommercial and Pmefs → Peconomic		• Pmefs → Peconomic
• Cash-flow model for full-cycle economics of field life		• Cash-flow model for full-cycle economics of "core producing area"
• Geologic chance factors: —Independent for 1-objective wells —Shared + Indep. for 2-objective wells		• Geologic chance factors: —Shared (= "Play Chance") —Indep. (= "Local Chance")
• "Staged" development potential is *limited*		• "Staged" development potential is *substantial*
• HC generation & migration usually more assured		• HC generation & migration highest priority to satisfy

HC = hydrocarbon

must construct detailed cash-flow models based on parameters estimated through objective and reliable geotechnology and contract analysis to assess project profitability on a full-cycle economic basis, first for the anticipated new fields (prospects) and then for the anticipated new core producing area (the play).

However, there are also some important differences between prospect and play risk analysis. For single-objective wildcats, the geologic chance factors used to estimate the chance of encountering flowable hydrocarbons (= geologic success, Pg) are treated as if they were independent of each other. This assumption allows serial multiplication of the individual components of geologic chance to yield Pg. However, for exploratory wells having multiple objectives, risk analysis recognizes that some chance factors are *common* to all the objective zones, whereas other chance elements *vary* among the different objective zones (p. 41 and Appendix D). The chance factors that are *shared* (that is, common to all the objective zones) frequently include petroleum generation and migration, including the elements of timing and preservation. The *independent* chance factors typically include reservoir, closure, and containment. To correctly estimate the chance of various combinations of discoveries for such multiple-objective prospects, it is necessary to calculate the chance of success of the *shared* factors separately from the *independent* chance factors.

This same principle is also consistently employed in risk analysis of plays, simply because there are, characteristically, elements of geologic chance that apply equally to every prospect in the play (= "shared chance"); similarly there are also elements of geologic chance that vary among the different prospects (= "average prospect chance" or "local chance"). To make things even more complicated, we may also deal with partial dependencies, where a given geologic chance factor is partly shared and partly independent.

In carrying out risk analysis of plays, especially new plays, the elements of geologic chance associated with hydrocarbon generation, migration, and timing are usually of paramount importance to address and satisfy. However, for plays having greater exploration maturity or plays in known petroliferous basins, concerns about hydrocarbon charge commonly are diminished, whereas concerns about reservoir, closure, and containment are greater. Nevertheless, all chance factors are theoretically of equal importance in the sense that all must have been satisfied in order for a reservoired accumulation to exist. As pointed out previously (p. 34), the chance factors should be thought of as if they were equal links in a circular chain: if one link is broken, the chain is broken.

Another significant difference between plays and prospects concerns the strategies involved *after* discovery: generally, it is important to develop the newly successful prospect promptly and begin generating production revenues as soon as possible because of the time value of money. But most successful plays involve several sequentially discovered and developed fields. Moreover, early production revenues may themselves generate funds required for subsequent development of fields within the play or core area. Construction of pipelines and/or development of markets for production may take several years. Accordingly, in some plays there may be legitimate reasons for staging the exploration and development, consistent with maximum long-term profitability. Often such delays may constitute pragmatic, nonquantitative applications of option-pricing theory (see p. 52).

Integration of Geotechnology, Economics, and Management in Play Analysis

There are many ways to convert a viable play into either an economic loss or an unappreciated, rejected investment opportunity. Whether the error has to do with bad geotechnology, bad engineering, bad economic evaluation, or bad acquisition strategies, the consequences are the same. That's why successful risk analysis of exploration plays requires thorough synthesis of multidisciplinary topics: geostatistics, geology, geophysics, reservoir engineering, drilling and completion technology, economics, decision analysis, contract analysis, political analysis, industrial operations, and business strategies. These specialties take on greater or lesser importance at different stages in the life of the successful play, but their successful integration is required if the play is to succeed as a full-cycle economic risk venture.

Accordingly, the most common organizational pattern adopted by the modern petroleum industry for analyzing and exploring new plays is the multidisciplinary exploration team. The composition of such teams may change in both numbers and specialties as the play evolves.

Important Geologic Concepts for Play Analysis

Appendix E outlines topics, procedures, and key steps in carrying out a geologic synthesis of an exploration play. Such a synthesis—"total geology"—integrates all geologic elements bearing on the likelihood of petroleum accumulations, their possible volumes, spatial distribution, and geologic character. Such integrated studies form the basis for any subsequent legitimate attempt at risk analysis and economic assessment of a new exploration play, or entry into an ongoing one.

It is far beyond the scope of this book to delve deeply into the subject of geologic basin analysis or even to summarize such a complex topic. Appendix E is, however, a useful flow sheet to guide explorationists

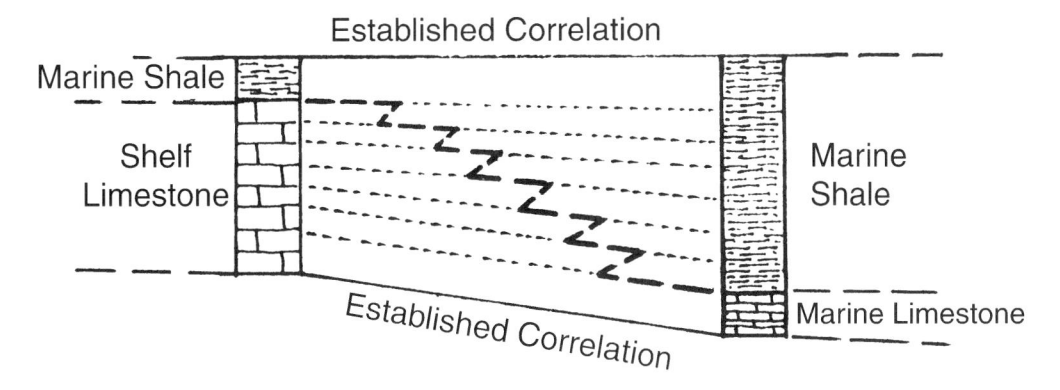

Figure 30a *Traditional facies interpretation indicates that the shelf limestone and marine shale are coeval.*

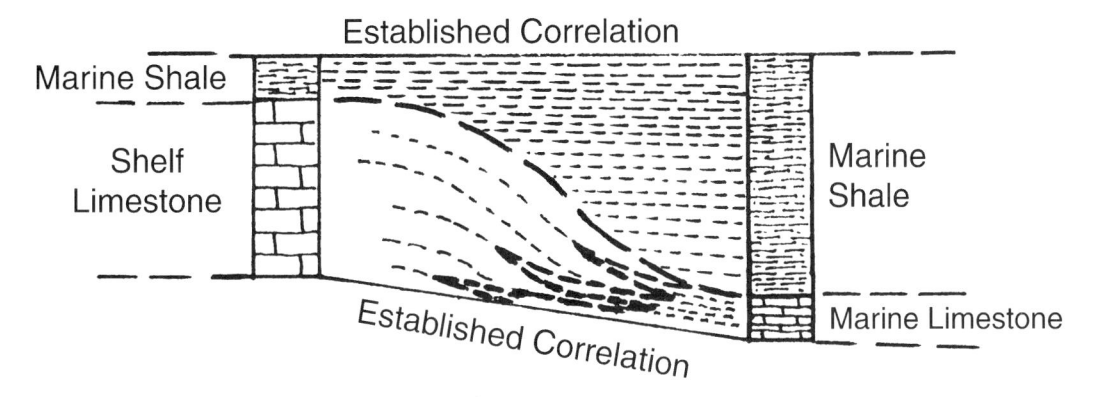

Figure 30b *Depositional topography interpretation indicates that all of the shelf limestone is older than any of the marine shale. The only facies relationship is between the shelf limestone and marine limestone, with basin starvation inferred.*

through the process, so that they will end up with the key maps, cross sections, and data necessary for the estimates and calculations required in the sequential steps of formal play analysis. In addition, several geologic concepts are especially important to consider in conducting a sound play analysis.

Stratigraphic Sequences in Play Analysis

The topic of sequence stratigraphy has been a rapidly expanding field of geologic study since the mid-1970s. Utilizing the principles of sequence stratigraphy is extremely important in carrying out geotechnical reviews and syntheses of new basins and plays.

L.L. Sloss (1963) published the first comprehensive treatment of continental-scale stratigraphic sequences, identifying six unconformity-bounded "packages" of sedimentary rocks on the North American continent. Sloss's original sequences each represented about 50 to 120 million years of geologic history. Later work by Sloss's student, Peter Vail, and his Exxon associates led to the recognition of a hierarchy of ordered sequences—cycles spanning diminishing intervals of geologic time (Vail et al., 1977a, 1977b). For petroleum geoscientists concerned with efficient evaluation of basins and plays, sequence stratigraphy is important for three reasons.

Regional Mapping

One of the first tasks facing the geoscientist who is entering a new basin or play is to identify natural cycles—unconformity-bounded stratigraphic units—and to make maps and cross sections using such natural sedimentary packages and especially the unconformable surfaces bounding them. The true spatial and geologic relationships between source rocks, reservoir rocks, and sealing rocks are best understood in context with these natural chapters of earth history. In particular, sedimentation related to contemporaneous structural events and sedimentary provenance is most readily deciphered at a regional scale when geoscientists think in terms of stratigraphic sequences and subsequences.

Depositional Topography

Traditional stratigraphy has not dealt comfortably with depositional topography in sedimentary sequences. **Figure 30a** shows how the characteristic changes in rock type and thickness are conventionally interpreted as facies changes of coeval sedimentary deposits, whereas **Figure 30b** deals more realistically with the same rock patterns, as a combination of different facies and depositional topography. Depositional topography is significant and important to recognize in play scale geologic analysis because it allows the geoscientist to understand the true spatial relationships of various constituents of the petroleum system—source rocks, carrier beds, reservoir rock, and seals. These are most readily detected where the cross section or mapping datum is a regional unconformity, either at the base or the top of the subject sequence or subsequence.

Predictions Based on Sea-level Stands

Modern sequence stratigraphers understand that sea level has risen and fallen, often dramatically, in the geologic past, and—in context with depositional topography—has produced characteristic depositional models and lithologic patterns. Stratigraphers may look for and predict certain combinations of petroleum facies associated with highstand, transgressive, and lowstand deposits. In particular, just the awareness of the possibility of lowstand events can be an insightful guide in the search for new plays, and modern seismic surveys are a powerful tool for detecting and delineating key reservoir and sealing units.

Worldwide versus Provincial Petroleum Source Rocks

Arthur and Schlanger (1979) recognized the existence of "global anoxic events," of Cretaceous age (Albian and Turonian), and speculated that they represented widespread organic-rich marine deposition. Klemme and Ulmishek (1991) identified six such events (which occurred in the middle Silurian, Late Devonian, Late Pennsylvanian–Early Permian, Late Jurassic, middle Cretaceous, and the Oligocene-Miocene), and showed that more than 90% of the world's oil and gas production and reserves originate from these six preferred stratigraphic intervals. The implications for exploration strategy are obvious—high priority should be given to those basins and plays containing marine sedimentary rocks of any of those six ages.

At the same time, the geoscientist must not ignore petroliferous source-facies that are more provincial or even local in origin and extent, such as foundered structural basins, euxinic back-reef depressions, and lacustrine deposits. However, such secondary source-rock units may often be understood only in context with sequence stratigraphy, basin tectonics, and geologic history.

The Kitchen—Geochemical Modeling

Demaison (1984) demonstrated that most of the world's petroleum occurs in "petroleum-generative depressions" and recorded four important characteristics of such generative basins:

1. Such trends and areas typically have high exploratory success ratios;
2. They are mappable by integrated geologic/geophysical/geochemical methods;
3. Large petroleum accumulations tend to occur near the center of such petroleum-generative basins, or on adjacent structural high trends; and
4. Migration distances commonly range in tens rather than hundreds of miles and are limited by the drainage areas of individual structures.

Sluijk and Nederlof (1984) provide an excellent illustration of these basic ideas **(Figure 31)**. Murris (1984) and Sluijk and Parker (1986) demonstrated that synthesis of these integrated geochemical/geologic methods (in combination with trap-size considerations) results in greatly improved exploration results **(Figure 32)**. Later refinements of Lopatin's and Waples's ideas on time-temperature index as an indicator of petroleum generation, through realization of the strong kinetic influence on the process (Hunt et al., 1991; Waples, 1994) and sophisticated probabilistic computer modeling of the oil-generative process (example: "Basin-Mod" software and others), have now enabled geoscientists to make more reliable predictions about the time and relative quantity of petroleum generation, as well as the probable direction of migration out of the kitchen toward the basin margins.

Explorationists engaged in play analysis must understand thoroughly the genetic relationships between the family of related traps we call a play and the kitchen from which the traps were charged with oil and gas. Fortunately, the petroleum system concept facilitates that analysis and understanding.

Total Geology and Geologic Play Maps

In order to understand, analyze, and make geotechnical predictions for purposes of exploration in oil and gas plays, geoscientists must integrate all aspects of *stratigraphy* (reservoir rocks, source rocks, sealing rocks), *structural geology* (burial history, tectonic events, structural styles), *geochemistry* (source rock richness and volume, generation amount and time [the "critical moment"], migration routes and impedance), *geophysics* (trap detection and measurement), and *petroleum occurrence* (fields, production data, shows). We call such synthesis "total geology." The petroleum system concept encourages such integration.

Many diverse tasks are involved in conducting thorough, integrated risk analyses of exploration plays. Many geologic, geophysical, and geochemical facts must be gathered, interpreted, assimilated, and displayed, to be evaluated along with geostatistical,

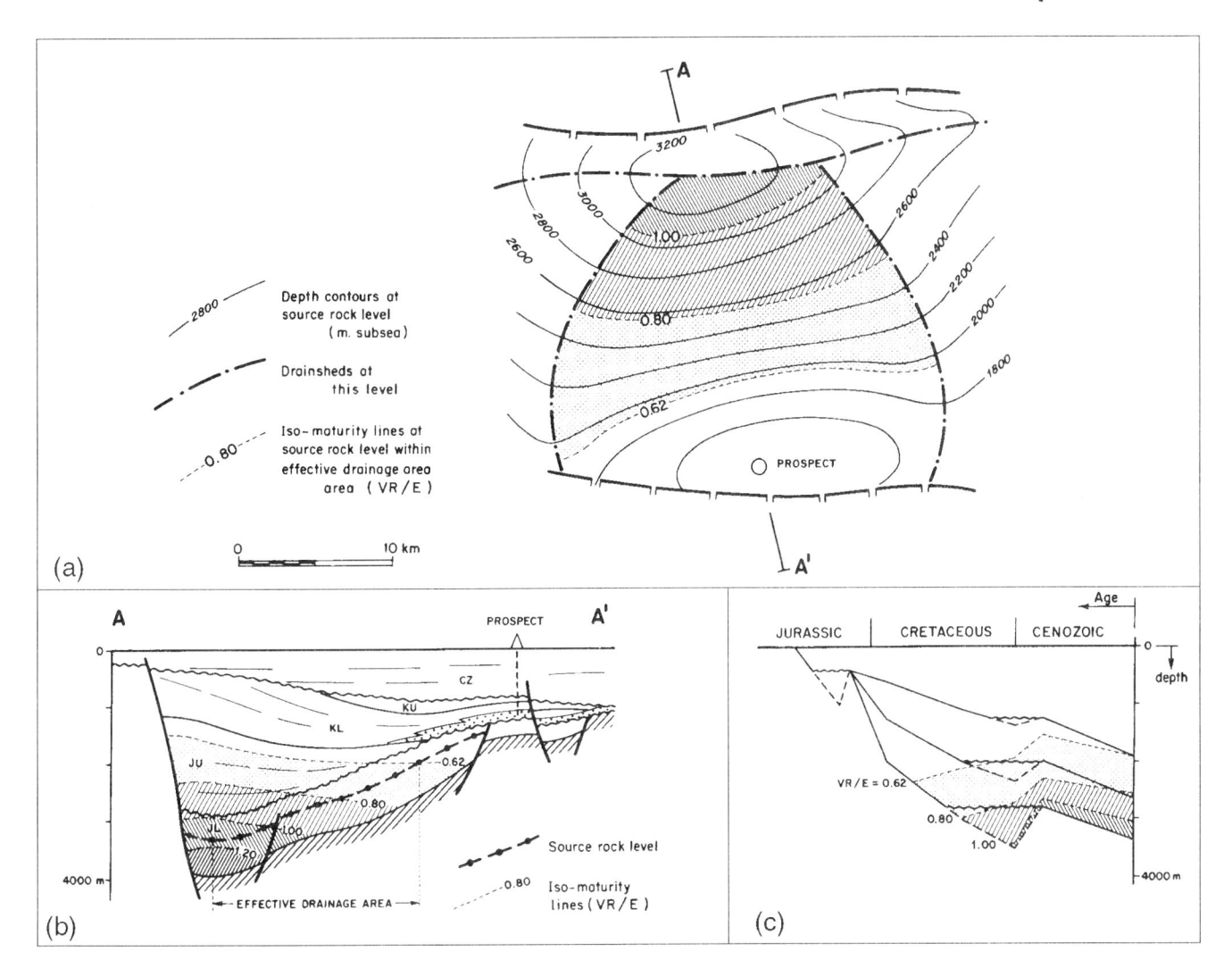

Figure 31 *Hydrocarbon charge model. From Sluijk and Nederlof (1984).*

financial, and operational considerations. Moreover, the procedure should be carried out in consistent ways throughout the organization, for purposes of completeness and comparison with other plays being considered. Accordingly, many firms have developed play-analysis checklists to guide geoscientists in the investigation, analysis, and representation of such plays and trends. Appendix E is an example of such a checklist. When such a checklist is properly used, the result is that all available significant geotechnical information has been gathered for use in the risk analysis of the play as a full-cycle business venture. Such a play risk analysis, however, usually is carried out as a separate flow sheet or software program.

It is also desirable for geoscientists to develop consistent, expressive symbologies and mapping techniques that contribute to such synthesis, represented as play maps (White, 1988), which convey to exploration decisionmakers the key geologic relationships and uncertainties that bear on a play's definition, prospectivity, uncertainties, and risks. Each company should adopt a consistent geologic style by which essential information may be synthesized objectively for management's consideration.

Use of Analogs in Play Analysis

Exploration play analysis requires geoscientists to make informed geologic and geostatistical predictions under conditions of great uncertainty. Frequently, *direct* evidence bearing on key geologic criteria is simply not available. However, knowledgeable geoscientists may make surprisingly accurate *indirect* forecasts by using appropriate analogs.

An example of the effective use of analog FSDs, adjusted appropriately for geologic differences and exploratory maturity, is presented later in a west Texas case where the two subject areas were indeed geologically analogous.

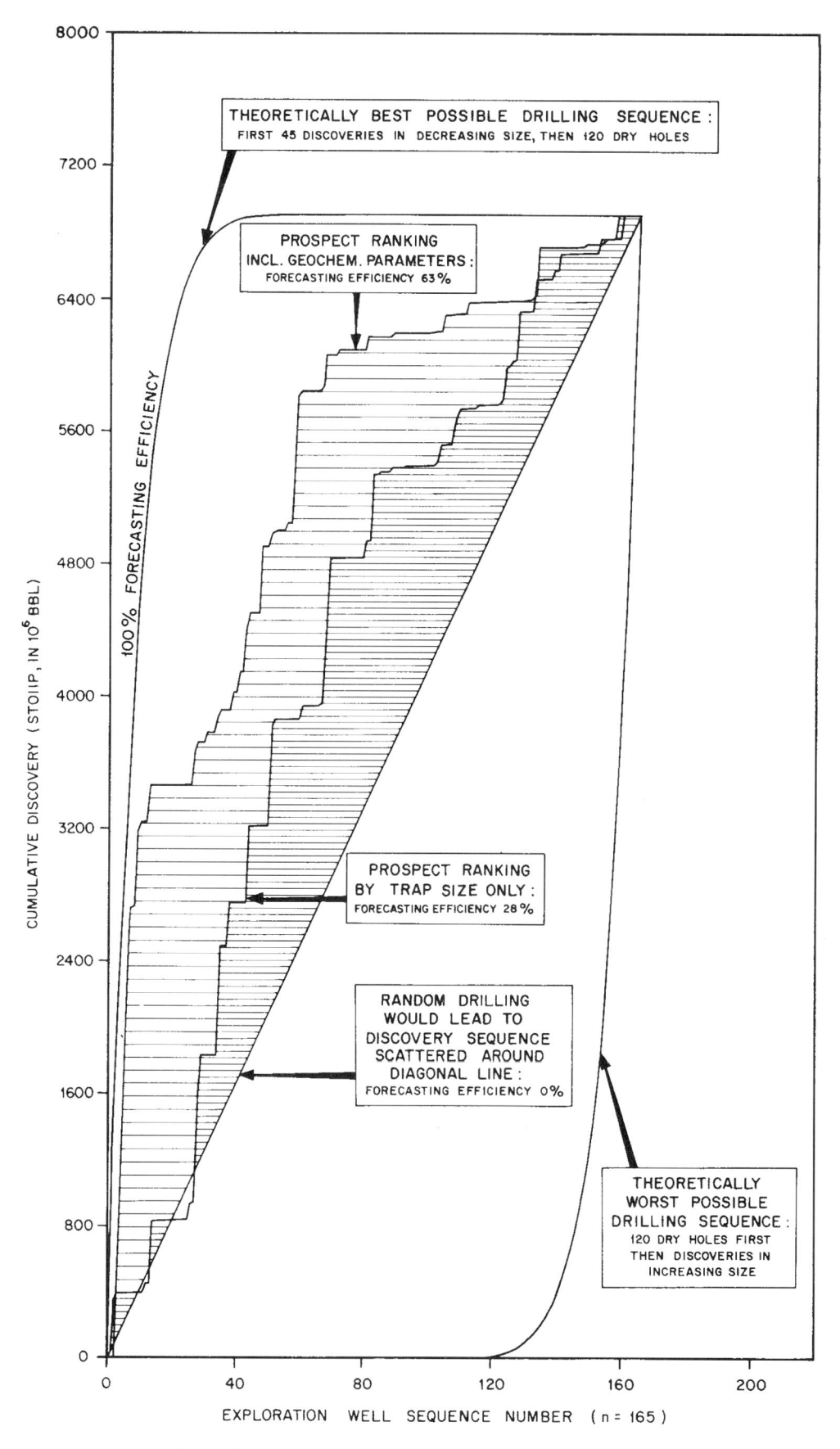

Figure 32 *Integrated methods produce more efficient exploration results. From Sluijk and Parker (1986).*

In a broader context, explorationists should always be alert for documented analog examples of the basins, plays, and fields they are studying in the course of evaluating new plays. The international geologic literature is rich in classifications and documented studies of basin types, classes of plays and trends, types of different fields, FSDs, and other geostatistical data.

To maximize the effective use of analogs, three conditions must be met:

1. Geoscientists must have ready access to the international geologic literature. A qualified geotechnical librarian, with keen organizational and computer-search skills, greatly facilitates such capabilities;
2. Statistical databases, organized to be geologically discriminating, allow geologic class and type to be related to pertinent geostatistics; and
3. Geoscientists must adopt a working philosophy that recognizes the likelihood of substantial uncertainty and embraces the use of analogs to help make estimates where direct evidence is absent.

Key Concepts and Techniques for Risk Analysis of Exploration Plays

Field-size Distributions

The topic of FSDs was introduced in Chapter 2, relative to prospect risk analysis, where the FSD was used as a reality check (p. 12). In play analysis, knowledgeable manipulation and utilization of FSDs, in combination with estimates of total fields to be found in the play, is an extremely powerful technique that allows surprisingly accurate forecasts of total play reserves, and prediction of approximate field sizes present in new plays.

Concepts and Principles

The FSD is the statistical expression of all fields found within a basin or play *to date*. It represents the effective natural synthesis of three factors:

1. The natural petroleum endowment of a play, including
   - the abundance and efficiency of hydrocarbon generation and migration, and
   - the number and capacity of traps
2. The relative maturity of exploration in the trend, including
   - numbers of exploratory wells and discoveries, and
   - optimization of current geotechnology in exploration, drilling, and development.
3. The relative efficiency with which industry can sense and discover larger, richer fields early and leave smaller, less profitable fields to be found in the later stages of the exploration cycle.

Discovery Process Modeling

Item 3 above touches directly on the concept of discovery process modeling, first expressed in 1958 by Arps and Roberts: *the likelihood of discovering a field of a given size class is proportional to the geometric probability of its discovery and to the efficiency of exploration* (**Equation 8**).

$$F_A(w) = F_A(\infty)(1 - e^{-CAw/B}) \qquad (8)$$

where

$F_A(w)$ = cumulative number of discoveries estimated to be made in size class A by the drilling of w wells
$F_A(\infty)$ = ultimate number of fields in size class A that occur in the basin
B = area of basin
A = average areal extent of the fields in the given size class
w = cumulative number of wildcat wells, and
C = efficiency of exploration

It is important to understand that *C* is a dimensionless number estimated for each size class, and that *C* may vary, being higher for the larger size classes and declining gradually as size class diminishes unless new concepts or technology cause temporary increases in exploration efficiency.

When $C = 1$, discovery is random. For 1.5 to 3.0 MMBOE fields in the Denver Basin and Texas Gulf coast, $C \approx 2.0$ (Drew, 1990). The commonly observed pattern is for C to increase (as size class of fields increases) ultimately to values approaching 6 or even greater for very large fields. Four very important conditions must be emphasized:

1. Sampling without replacement is assumed;
2. The area of the play remains constant;
3. Exploration technology is either constant or its improvement is regular; and
4. There is a consistent proportion between field ultimate recovery and field productive area—that is, fields with large reserves have large surface areas. Generally this is a valid assumption.

A good way to estimate Cs for each of the significant field-size classes of a *future* play would be to calculate C for analog field-size classes for several well-explored analogous plays or basins, and to apply it to the anticipated exploration campaign. Obviously, you must have some idea of the natural endowment of oil and gas accumulations that are undiscovered in the play (FSDs and estimated field numbers provide that) and apply analog C values to that data set. For perspective, here are some documented values for C:

- $C = 1$ where discovery is random;
- In mature petroleum plays such as Miocene-Pliocene of the onshore U.S. Gulf Coast, typical C values range from less than 2 for small fields (0.1 MMBOE → 10 MMBOE) to as much as 5 for very large fields (≈ 300 MMBOE).
- For west Texas fields of 1.5 → 3.0 MMBOE, C was 2.0; similar values for C were calculated for Denver Basin fields.
- If there have already been some discoveries in the play, you can usually use those data to project roughly what future discoveries will be, for field number and size—that is the basic premise of discovery process modeling. Keep the basic assumptions and conditions in mind, however!

Discovery process modeling can be useful in play risk analysis because it provides a method by which estimates of numbers of future discoveries can be independently confirmed or supported. In a partially explored play, $F_A(w)$ is the total number of fields discovered of size class A, and that value is easily derived just by counting the number of such field discoveries to date. $F_A(\infty)$ is the projected ultimate number of fields of size class A that exist in the play—this value is the "unknown" in the equation. The difference between $F_A(w)$ and $F_A(\infty)$ is the number of fields of size class A remaining to be found, theoretically. The critical parameter, C, cannot be determined—only estimated—which may constitute a serious drawback to the method. Moreover, results are extremely sensitive to the estimated area of the play.

Further discussion of discovery process modeling is beyond the scope of this book. Readers interested in more detail are referred to papers by Kaufman (1980, 1983), Andreatta and Kaufman (1986), and Drew (1990).

Creaming Curves

During the course of exploration in a play, there is a clear tendency for the larger fields to be found in the earlier stages, whereas during subsequent stages steadily smaller fields are discovered. Geotechnically guided exploration is more efficient than random drilling, especially during the early stages of play exploration. Exploration inefficiencies result mostly from the fact that, while geoscientists generally can identify prospects too small to contain a *large* petroleum accumulation, they cannot reliably predict whether a prospect of large area or volume actually contains *small* reserves (because of leaky traps, poor reservoir quality, or falsely optimistic seismic data or interpretations).

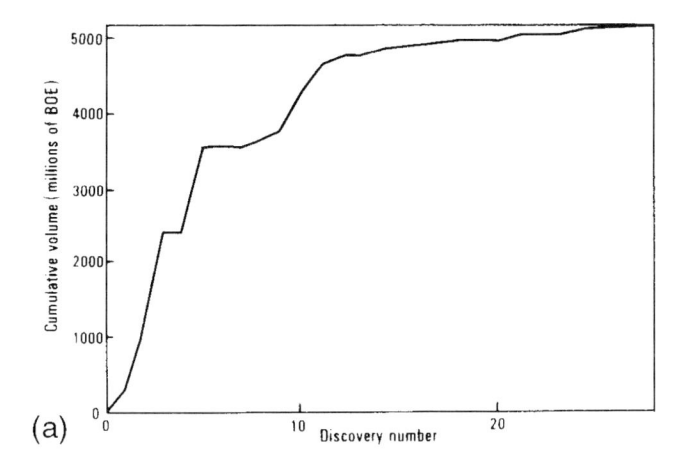

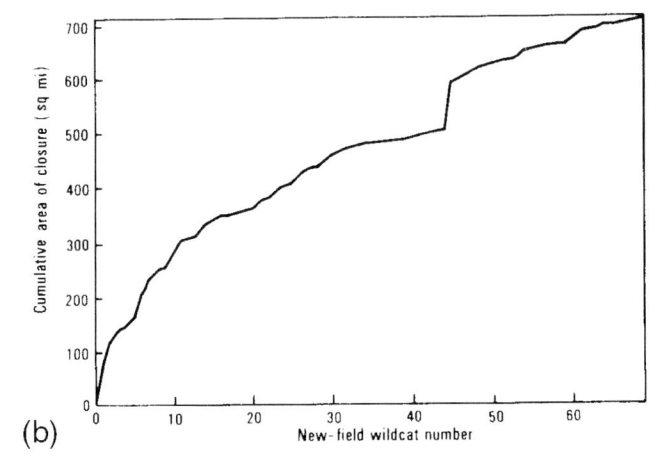

Figure 33 *Creaming curves. From Forman and Hinde (1986).*

This pattern has been recognized by authorities who present and analyze "creaming curves" (Forman and Hinde, 1986). By plotting cumulative reserves discovered by successive discoveries (or successive exploratory wells), relative exploration maturity of a play is indicated. When the discovery curve is rising steeply, exploration is efficient and profitable because large reserves are being found by relatively few wells. However, when the discovery curve flattens out, relatively small reserve additions are being added during later-stage drilling **(Figure 33)**.

Creaming curves express the relationship between average exploration efficiency among all size classes and the natural endowment of oil and gas accumulations in the play or basin. The flattening slope of the creaming curve through time reflects decreasing average exploration efficiency among all size classes, acting on the natural endowment of oil accumulations of differing sizes, which as we know takes a natural log-normal form. Because more small accumulations are developed onshore than offshore, we expect creaming curves to be more pronounced in onshore trends.

An interesting example of efficiency variations in international exploration was presented by Shell (Murris, 1984) and previously introduced as **Figure 32**. Here, random exploration (C = 1) is represented by the straight, sloping line from lower left to upper right. Use of only the selective factor of estimated trap size generated forecasting efficiency that was 28% better than random. However, use of geochemical parameters plus trap size produced forecasting efficiency that was 63% better than random. Note that this expression of efficiency can be calculated at any stage of maturity, and it applies to discovery of all size classes, not individual size classes. Efficiency is expressed graphically as the percentage of all space between the diagonal random line and the optimum efficient case on the left. By analogy, exploration efficiency in the Gippsland Basin was clearly greater relative to trap volumes than to trap areas **(Figure 33)**.

Shift of Field-size Distributions

As previously pointed out (p. 11 and **Figure 5**), when we separate a given play into earlier and later groups of field discoveries and plot them on a single log-probability graph, we can see the "daughter" FSDs shift steadily toward smaller field sizes during the life of the "parent" play. **Figures 5a and 5b** illustrate this tendency, where more than 100 fields in the Minnelusa Trend (northeastern Wyoming, U.S.A.) were separated into (1) the earliest one-third of all discovered fields; (2) the middle one-third; and (3) the latest one-third of all fields found.

Although there is considerable overlap in field sizes among the three daughter distributions, the overall reduction in field size is significant: mean field sizes drop from 4.58 MM (first third) to 2.17 MM (second third), to 0.76 (last third), for complete, untruncated distributions. For distributions truncated at the commercial limit (0.1 MMBOE), the respective differences in mean reserves are larger: 5.51 MM, 2.98 MM, and 1.06 MM.

Estimating Field Numbers

One of the essential geotechnical tasks required to carry out meaningful play analysis is to estimate how many petroleum accumulations remain to be found in the play area. Although the development of such estimates may be reviewed with skepticism by novice explorationists or non-geoscientists, useful projections can indeed be generated using several tested approaches outlined as follows.

Counting Visible Anomalies

If a seismic grid is available over part or all of the play area, estimates of the number of fields can be derived simply by counting all anomalies and reducing their number via estimates of the chance of geologic success (Pg) and of economic success (Pmefs). Where surface geology relates to numbers of prospects, landsat images may indicate the density of anomalies.

Probabilistic Range of Field Number Estimates

Of course, we cannot know just how many petroleum accumulations are present, awaiting discovery, in a play fairway. But we can develop plausible predictions by using analog basins and trends, employing different independent reality checks, and expressing our estimates as probabilistic ranges. For example, we might be quite confident (P90%) that at least one field is present (given that an active petroleum system exists in the play area), with a best guess (P50%) of four fields, and be 10% confident in as many as 16 fields. Note that this distribution is probably lognormal.

Such a probabilistic expression can be combined with the projected FSD for the play to give a probabilistic distribution of play reserves, a key goal for play analysis.

Field Density in Analog Plays

Careful counts of the numbers of fields in one or more analog plays usually yields characteristic ranges of field numbers per unit area (i.e., 1.5 to 5.0 fields per 100 square miles [260 km^2] or the reciprocal expression, 1 field per 20 to 67 square miles [52–174 km^2]). Obviously, the desired value represents the ultimate number of fields, so the stage of exploration of the analog play must be taken into account. Note that such ranges lend themselves to probabilistic expression.

Field Area versus Field Reserves in Discovery Process Model

For analog plays and trends, graphs can be made showing the relationship between documented field areas and the associated projections of ultimate recoveries from those fields. Use those graphs to assign appropriate areas to the different field-size classes **(Table 13)**. For different field-size classes, use the possible exploration efficiencies as outlined on page 68. The final step is to utilize the appropriate area for each field-size class in the discovery process model **(Equation 8)**, which will yield the expected number of remaining fields in each size class. The resulting value should be viewed as an independent reality check of your other probabilistic estimates of field number that you derived by analog experience.

Pragmatic Approach for Field Number Estimates

A useful rule-of-thumb approach to estimating field numbers has been suggested by Dr. Jeff Brown (personal communication) based on the observation that in thoroughly explored play fairways, approximately 10% of the trend/area will be under closure. Given that the average wildcat success rate is approximately 25%, we can thus expect about 2.5% of the

Table 13 *System of graduated size classes used currently by the U.S. Geological Survey (after Drew, 1990).*

Size Class	Size Range (Million BOE* recoverable oil and gas)		
1	0.0	to	0.006
2	0.006	to	0.012
3	0.012	to	0.024
4	0.024	to	0.047
5	0.047	to	0.095
6	0.095	to	0.19
7	0.19	to	0.38
8	0.38	to	0.76
9	0.76	to	1.52
10	1.52	to	3.04
11	3.04	to	6.07
12	6.07	to	12.14
13	12.14	to	24.3
14	24.3	to	48.6
15	48.6	to	97.2
16	97.2	to	194.3
17	194.3	to	388.6
18	388.6	to	777.2
19	777.2	to	1554.5
20	1554.5	to	3109.0

*BOE = barrels of oil equivalent

trend/area to consist of productive closures. Given common incomplete trap fill-up, averaging perhaps 40% of the closure areas, this suggests that about 1% of any productive play should be occupied within productive field outlines. Utilizing the graphs showing the relationship between field reserves and field area (p. 68), and the expectation of lognormality for the FSD, we can "back out" reasonable estimates for the field numbers and their associated sizes. This can often be done by trial-and-error methods as well.

Observed Estimating Patterns

As pointed out previously, most geoscientists tend to underestimate the numbers of fields that will ultimately be found in a prospective play (given success) and overestimate the sizes of the those fields.

Use of Field-size Distributions in Play Analysis

It is not possible to carry out a geologic and economic play analysis without generating a projected FSD for the subject play, whether it represents an undrilled play in a frontier area or a later-stage entry into a proven play that is thought to still have economic potential.

The basic principles outlined earlier provide the basis by which explorationists can analyze and shift projected FSDs for those plays that are being considered for possible entry and participation by their companies. Manipulation of FSDs can be classified and discussed usefully in relation to play maturity.

Where Production Is Well Established

Companies may consider entering an existing play where they identify remaining profitable exploration potential, often anticipating changes in

- regulation, taxation, or oil prices;
- new technology enabling higher success rates, or increased discrimination regarding field reserve sizes;
- increased profitability via reduced drilling costs, more effective stimulation/completion techniques, or more efficient production operations; or
- new geologic concepts or perspectives about the trend.

In such areas, the *existing* play FSD should form the basis for the *projected* FSD for purposes of play analysis. Where new areas of the play appear prospective, the parent FSD itself can be employed. But where anticipated additional exploration will take place in the *existing* play area, the projected FSD should be compatible with the most recent 10 to 20 discoveries, depending on the timeframe involved. It is important that analog FSDs reflect the use of similar geotechnical techniques and concepts. That is, if new technologies demonstrate or promise a clear improvement in average discovery size, it is permissible for explorationists to shift the FSD toward slightly larger average field sizes. However, in most cases, projected FSDs in established basins should reflect recent discoveries, or shift toward slightly smaller average fields. In such cases, a reliable and complete catalog of producing fields provides the basis for constructing the projected FSD.

Where Limited Production Exists

In petroliferous trends where previous production consists of small fields because of poor reservoir performance, new tools (that allow areas of higher porosity and permeability to be detected) may generate discovery of larger fields for a limited time. Similarly, improved stimulation techniques and/or more optimal well locations may allow greater per-well recoveries, resulting in larger fields. Such expectations, if prudent and documented, should be reflected through manually shifted FSDs. New tools such as 3-D seismic and/or direct hydrocarbon indicators (DHIs) may allow explorers to sense traps that were previously invisible. Although the population of the remaining trend FSD will not change, it is likely that, for a limited period, discoveries will preferentially include the larger remaining fields, rather than the smaller ones, as previously discussed under Creaming Curves.

Another common class in this category applies to those trends in which only a few fields have been discovered but have not been developed to the point that reasonable predictions can be made for their approximate reserves sizes, or the key data bearing on reserves sizes are proprietary and not available. In such cases, geoscientists must use whatever data can be obtained to make range-type estimates of key parameters such as *areas of closures* (land-sat images, air photos, geologic maps, seismic data, etc.); *average net pay thickness* (outcrop studies, stratigraphic projections, well logs, reported perforation intervals, seismic data); and *HC recoveries* (sources reported above, plus analog fields, test reports, and extrapolations made therefrom). It may be possible to estimate a range of possible field numbers based on anomalies present on air photos, geologic maps, or subsurface seismic maps. It is often helpful to identify other producing areas that appear to be geologically analogous, utilizing FSDs, field numbers, and field densities from such counterpart areas, as well as more specific analogs bearing on prospect areas, reservoir thickness and character, and producing characteristics. The final product of such studies should be a catalog of projected field sizes that follow a lognormal distribution and a probabilistic distribution of possible field numbers.

Where Production Has Not Been Established

Three approaches can provide guidance here. The first uses ranges of geologic parameters from available outcrop or well data, air photos, seismic lines, and the like, as discussed previously. The second method relies on analog trends and plays in adjacent basins or geologically similar basins elsewhere, even on different continents. The key requirement here is that the subject basin and the analog basin must be geologically similar with respect to traps (structural style, reservoir lithology, and origin), sealing rocks, and petroleum endowment. The third approach may be applied in desperation—only when time or data limitations prevent the construction of a projected FSD for an unexplored, nonproductive new trend as described earlier. In this approach, the geoscientist constructs a generic FSD, represented at the low end (P99%) as a small, noneconomic or noncommercial field. Conceptually, this value might represent a small trap that was not correctly sensed by explorationists or a large trap containing only a thin attic-type oil accumulation resulting from a deficient HC-charge, absence of effective seal, fracture leakage, or extremely thin or poor-quality reservoir rock. Recommended values for such situations must be credible; they should generally lie in the range of 0.01 MMBOE to perhaps 2 MMBOE, depending on geometry and structural/stratigraphic style. At the upper end, the projected P1% value should represent the largest field that could credibly be expected in the trend, based on existing geologic knowledge. Generally this value will range from about 100 MMBOE to perhaps as much as 1 to 4 BBOE, if such a large discovery is indeed remotely possible. Both the P1% and P99% values must be credible. A straight line drawn on a cumulative log-probability graph then represents the projected FSD for the subject trend. This method should be used *only* for new, non-productive frontier trends where there is very limited information, and the projected values must be compatible with available geologic knowledge. Again, this method represents a last resort.

As a broad reality check the reader is referred to **Figure 34**, which shows the FSD of all oil and equivalent gas fields in the world. It is instructive to note the probabilistic distribution of world field sizes: P99% = 0.018 MMBOE, P90% = 0.25 MM, P50% = 5.4 MM, P10% = 143 MM, P1% = 1,917 MM, with the mean = ~ 100 MM. The writer is indebted to Richard Nehring and Petro-Consultants, Inc. for these data.

Manipulation of an analog FSD—by shifting it to reflect the expert's opinion that the subject play will be either more or less petroliferous—may reflect the following expectations:

1. *More and larger fields*, because traps are thought to be larger, reservoirs thicker and/or more permeable, and top-seals more numerous and effective; or *fewer and smaller fields*, for the opposite reasons;
2. *More and larger fields*, because petroleum source rocks are thought to be thicker, richer, or more favorably situated with respect to migration pathways and/or timing, or *fewer and smaller fields* for the opposite reasons;
3. *More and larger fields*, because the subject play is thought to be at an immature stage of exploration compared with the analog play; or *fewer and smaller fields*, because the subject play is thought to be more mature than the analog play.

Prediction Using Analog Trends and Interpretive Shifts—An Example FSD

The Permian Basin of west Texas and eastern New Mexico is a world-class oil-producing province. In 1945, its northern extent (Area X) was poorly known, very lightly drilled, and essentially unproductive. Adjoining Area X on the south, however, was an area of similar stratigraphy and structural history and comparable size,

GLOBAL FIELD FAMILY

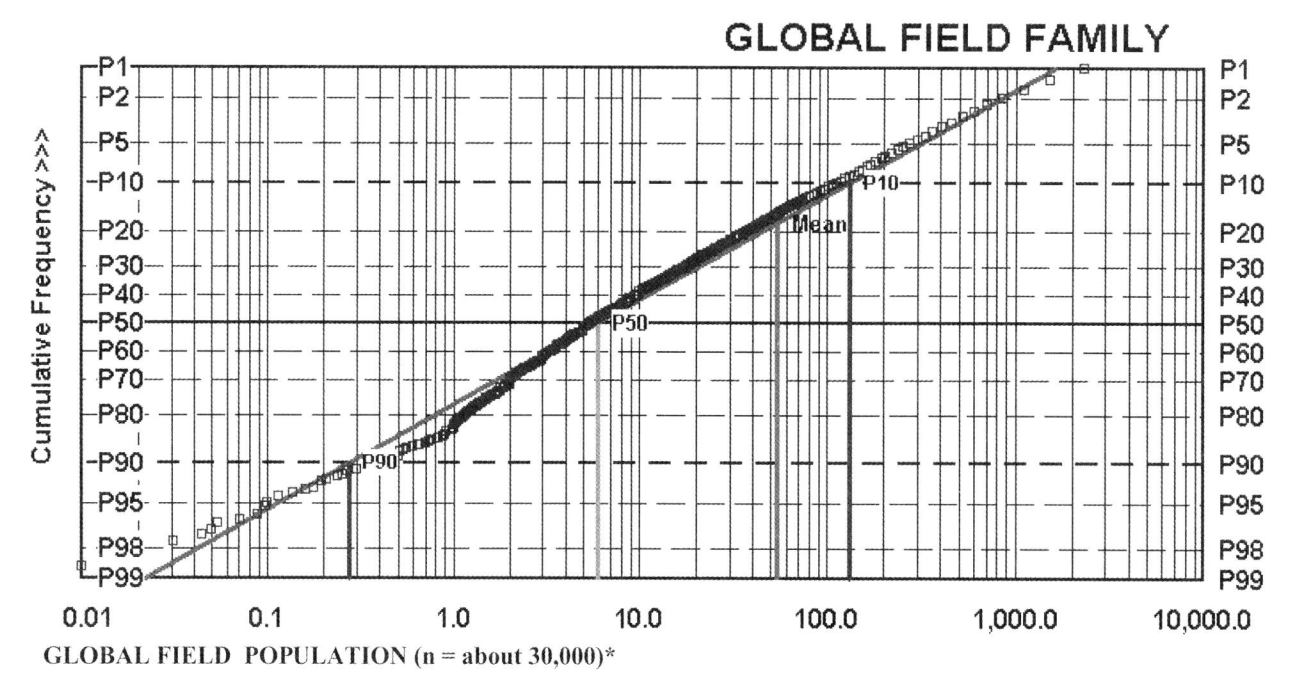

FIELD SIZES IN THE WORLD ARE LOGNORMALLY DISTRIBUTED

*Every 100th field plotted

Source: Nehring, Petroconsultants

P99 =	0.018	MMBOE
P90 =	0.250	MMBOE
P50 =	5.40	MMBOE
P10 =	143	MMBOE
P1 =	1917	MMBOE

Figure 34 *Global field-size distribution.*

Area Y, which contained 32 producing fields, nearly all with structural-stratigraphic traps in Permian-Pennsylvanian shelf-sandstone and carbonate reservoir rocks.

In order to construct a predicted FSD for Area X, the FSD for analog Area Y was first adopted as a proxy **(Figure 35a)**. Then the proxy was assessed for plausibility. In this case the geoscientists concluded that Area X was probably not as petroliferous as Area Y because (1) one of two regional source-rock horizons was absent; (2) Area X was less deeply buried and cooler, and therefore less petroleum might have been generated, and then migrated and emplaced; (3) many of the Middle Permian porous carbonate formations of Area Y seemed to have been replaced in Area X by evaporites and tight dolomites through facies change; and (4) finally, the geoscientists did not believe Area X would prove to contain a field as large as the largest field in Area Y (Slaughter, 1,000 MMBOE).

Based on these geologic considerations, and working from the Area Y FSD, the geoscientists chose a projected P1% field size of 400 MMBOE as plausibly the largest field that Area X was likely to contain. Recognizing that the low-side field size observed for the Area Y FSD (P99% = 1,500 BOE) probably would be similar for the Area X FSD, the geotechnical team then constructed a predicted FSD for Area X, using P99% = 1,500 BOE and P1% = 400 MMBOE **(Figure 35b)**.

In 1945 the original Area Y FSD had an arithmetic mean field size of 45 MMBOE, with a median of about 1.5 MMBOE (see **Table 14**, column 1). Swanson's mean field size was 22 MMBOE. After downward adjustment for the aforementioned geologic reasons, the predicted FSD for Area X had a median field size of 0.8 MMBOE and Swanson's mean field size of 8.0 MMBOE (**Table 14**, column 2).

Compared with those 1945 predictions, what was the actual outcome in Area X (**Table 14**, column 3)? Fifteen fields were actually discovered in Area X during the next 12 years (1945–1957). The largest field was Anton-Irish (212 MMBOE); the smallest was West Petersburg (30,000 BOE). The actual FSD for these 15 fields is shown on **Figure 35c**, for comparison with the original Area Y proxy as well as the Area X prediction. All 15 fields are formed by structural and structural-stratigraphic traps in Permian-Pennsylvanian shelf sands and carbonates located along an irregular east-west regional transcurrent fault trend, the Matador Arch.

Figure 35a

Figure 35b

Figure 35c

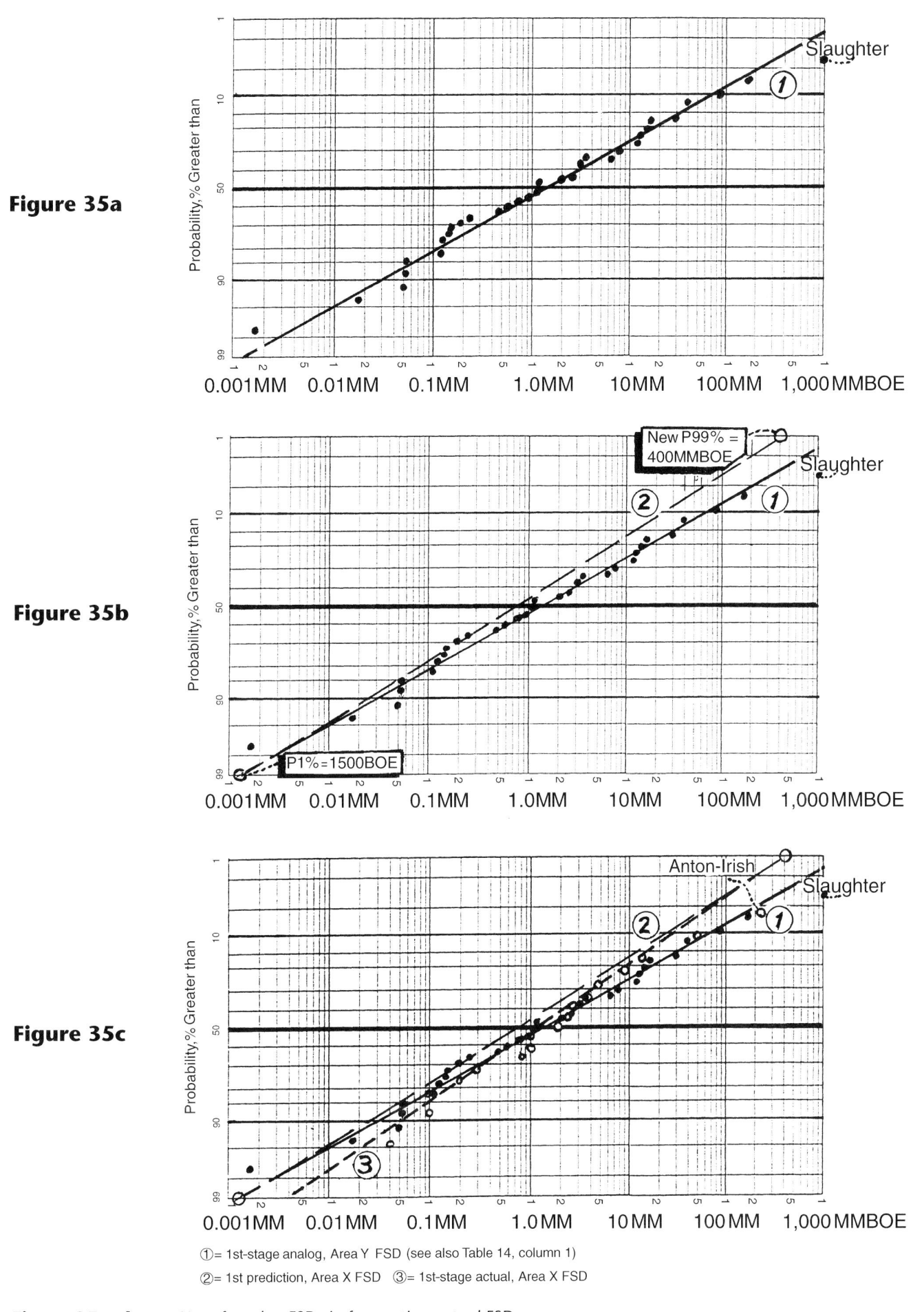

① = 1st-stage analog, Area Y FSD (see also Table 14, column 1)
② = 1st prediction, Area X FSD   ③ = 1st-stage actual, Area X FSD

Figure 35 a, b, c *Use of analog FSDs in forecasting actual FSDs.*

Table 14 *Comparison of analog (area Y), predicted (area X), and actual (area X) FSDs.*

Reserves Parameters (BOE)	① 1945 Area Y FSD (1st Analog)	② 1945 Area X FSD (1st Prediction)	③ 1945–57 Area X FSD (1st Actual)	④ 1945–57 Area Y FSD (2nd Analog)	⑤ 1957–95 Area X FSD (2nd Actual)
P99%	1,500 BOE	1,500 BOE	4,000 BOE	650 BOE	800 BOE
P90%	30,000 BOE	25,000 BOE	50,000 BOE	8,900 BOE	10,000 BOE
P50%	1.5MMBOE	0.8MMBOE	1.3MMBOE	0.34MMBOE	0.24MMBOE
Swanson's Mean	22MM	8MM	9.5MM	2.4MM	1.58MM
Arithmetic Mean	45MM	N/A	15.4MM	6.76MM	0.76MM
P10%	72MM	23MM	30MM	7.1MM	2MM
P1%	1,100MM	400MM	400MM	225MM	55MM
Largest field	Slaughter 1,000MM	N/A	Anton-Irish 212MM	Levelland 485MM	4.7MM
Pmefs	64%	56%	33%	43%	37%
Smallest field	1,641BOE @P97%	N/A	5,000BOE @P93%	179BOE @P99.7%	30,000BOE @P98%

How well did this described predictive method actually perform? How do the predictions compare with the actual outcomes? **Table 14** facilitates comparison by showing statistical parameters of the Area Y analog FSD (Column 1), the Area X Predicted FSD (Column 2), and the Actual Area X FSD (Column 3), as recorded 14 years later. In fact, the median field size was actually 1.3 MMBOE (vs. 0.8 MMBOE predicted), and Swanson's mean field size for Area X was actually 9.5 MMBOE (vs. 8.0 MMBOE predicted). The arithmetic mean field size for Area X proved to be 15.4 MMBOE. So the method generated reasonably accurate predictions, as documented by **Table 14** and illustrated by **Figure 35c**.

Second-stage Example

Additional confirmation of the validity of this method for predicting FSDs in new areas is provided by the next stage of exploration in the region. In analog Area Y, 292 additional fields were discovered during 1945–1957. Arithmetic mean field size was 6.76 MMBOE, and the median field size was 0.34 MMBOE. Swanson's mean field size was 2.4 MMBOE (**Table 14**, Column 4). So, as **Figure 36a** demonstrates, fields discovered in Area Y (FSD 4 vs. FSD 1) were notably smaller in the 12 years after 1945 than previously. Comparison of **Figure 36a** with columns 1 and 4 of **Table 14** quantifies this substantial reduction in field sizes: the Area Y FSD shifts to the left, toward smaller field sizes, by roughly one order of magnitude, in the second stage of exploration.

With such supportive data, the geotechnical professional staff of the exploration team began to have confidence that Area Y could indeed be used as an analog for Area X, given the appropriate adjustments for the geologic differences. To provide an independent test of this approach, we might reasonably expect that the shift in Area X FSDs from the 1945–1957 discoveries to the next cycle (1957–1995) would be comparable to the observed shift in analog Area Y FSDs between 1945 and 1957. In fact, **Figure 36b** confirms this expectation: the correlation is striking—the downward shift is of very similar magnitude, and slope changes are also quite comparable, providing compelling evidence for the applicability of this method.

During the period 1957–1995, 52 new fields were discovered in Area X. The arithmetic mean field size was 0.76 MMBOE and the median was 0.24 MMBOE. Swanson's mean field size was 1.58 MMBOE, based on the projected trend line of the FSD data points; based on actual field sizes, Swanson's mean field size was 0.82 MMBOE (**Table 14**, Column 5).

Four Additional Examples

Further evidence of the overall validity of such FSD manipulation is provided by the consistently downward

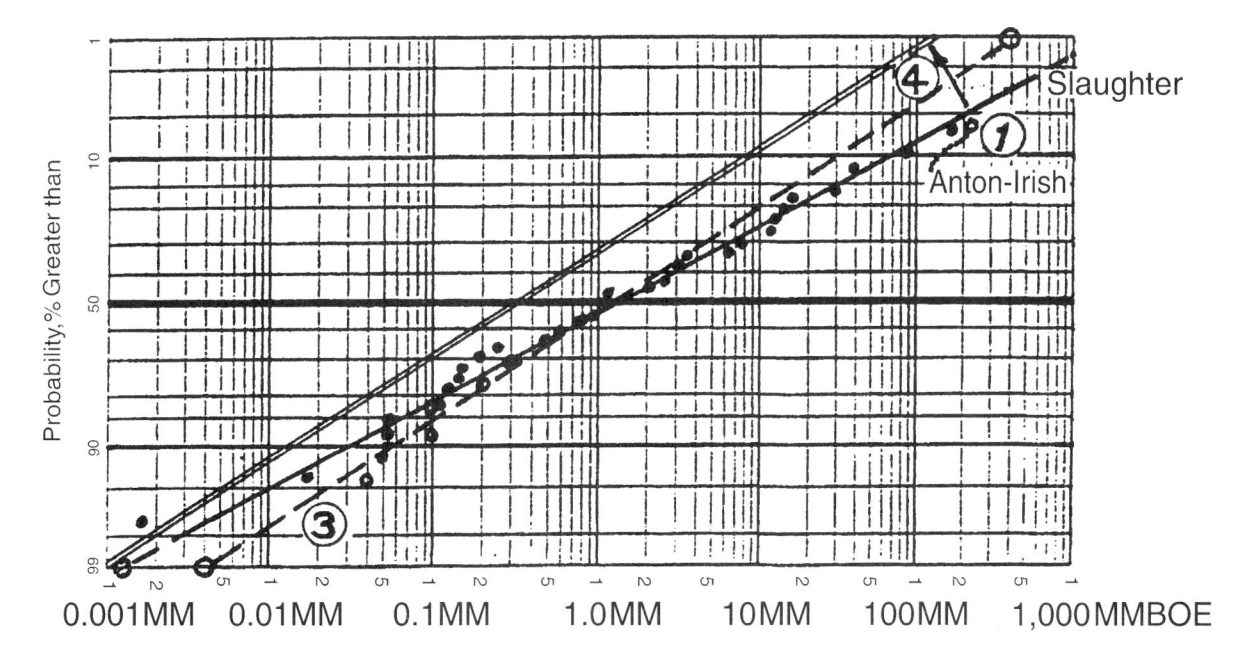

Figure 36a

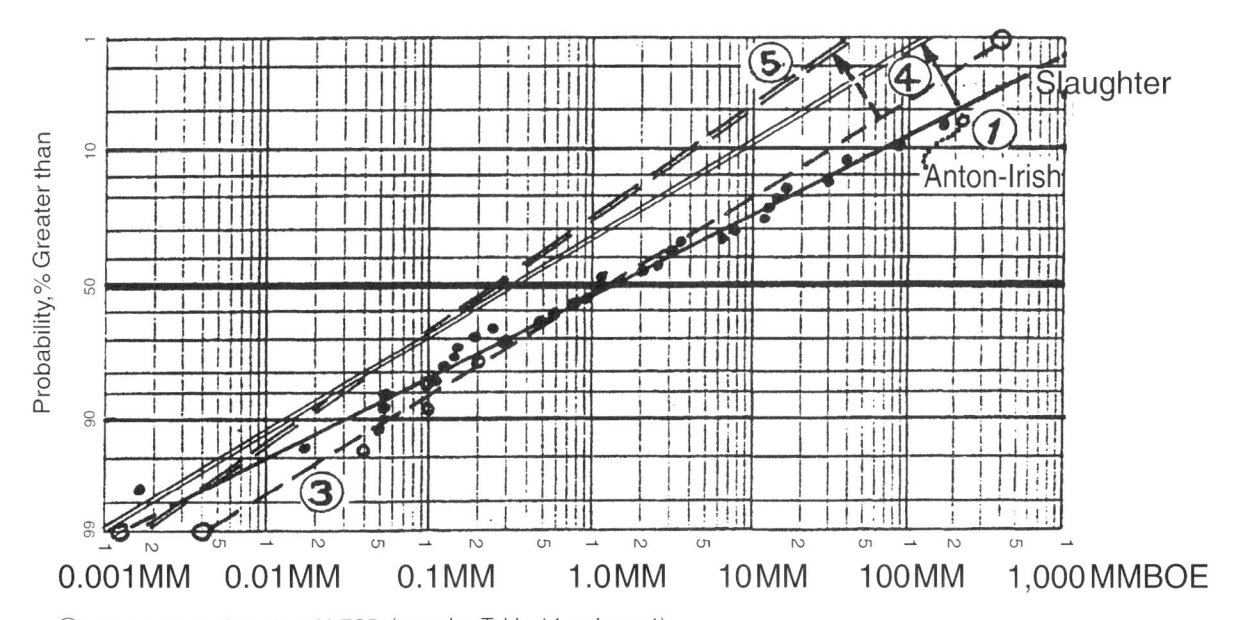

Figure 36b

①= 1st-stage analog, Area Y FSD (see also Table 14, column 1)
③= 1st-stage actual, Area X FSD
④= 2nd-stage analog, Area Y FSD
⑤= 2nd-stage actual, Area X FSD

Figure 36 a, b *Use of analog FSDs in forecasting actual FSDs: second stage.*

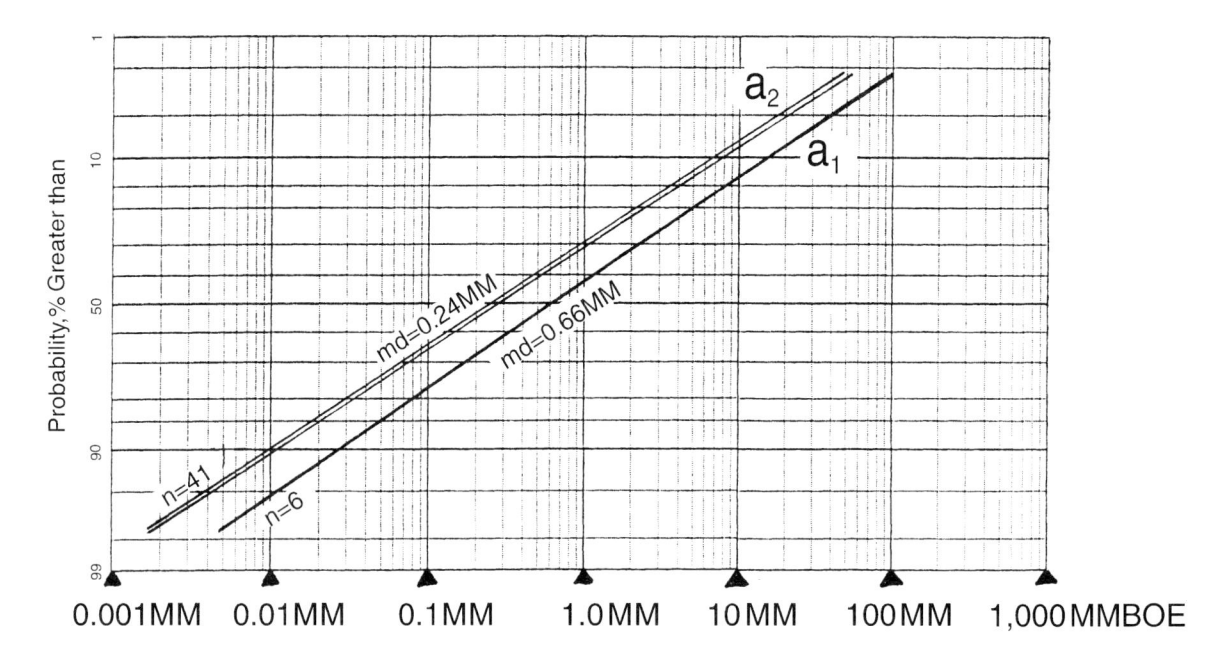

76 Exploration Plays—Risk Analysis and Economic Assessment

Figure 37a

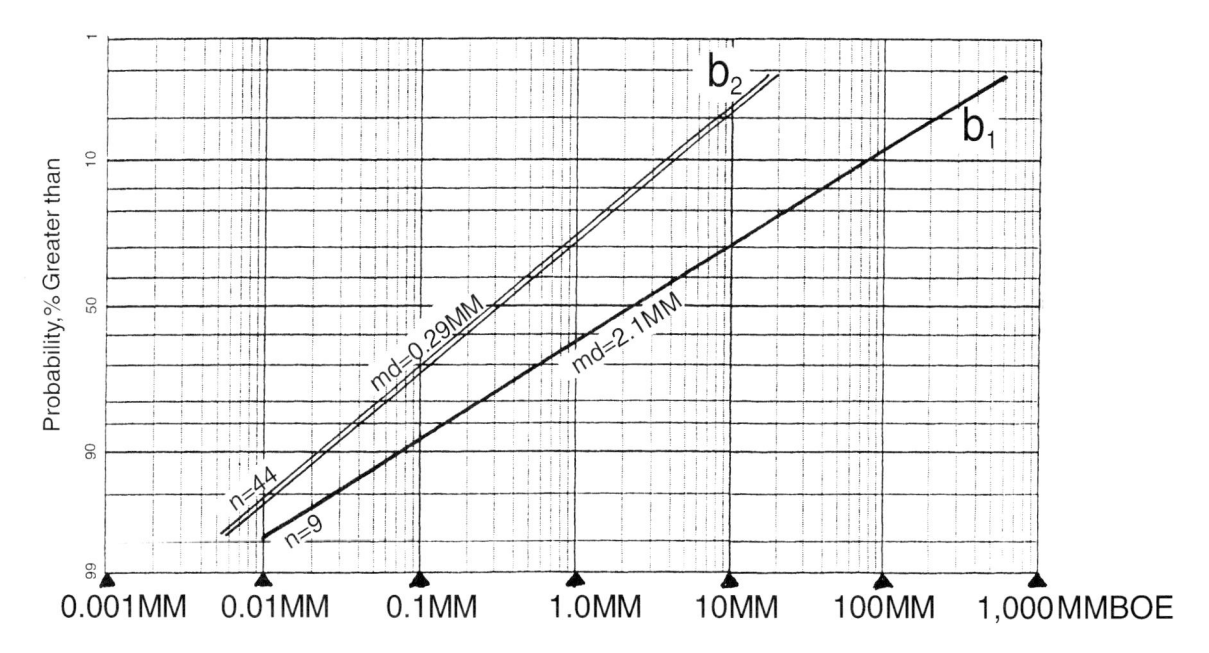

Figure 37b

Figure 37 a, b, c, d *Downward shifts in FSDs in area Y between first cycle of exploration (pre-1945: a_1, b_1, c_1, and d_1) and second cycle (1945–1957: a_2, b_2, c_2, and d_2), for four plays.*

shifts in FSDs of four plays in Area Y between 1945 and 1957 **(Figure 37a, b, c,** and **d)**. Changes in the median values are substantial, averaging about 85% reduction between the two exploration stages. One partial departure should be noted: Leonard Dolomite FSDs show a marked steepening from the first to the second cycle, as expected. However, although there was a sharp *decrease* in the size of *large* fields found of this type, there was also an unexpected sharp *increase* in the size of *small* fields in this play. The result is that the mean field size actually *increased* slightly (0.18 MMBOE → 0.35 MMBOE) in the second exploratory cycle. This anomaly may be caused by the small sample size (n = 5) of the first cycle FSD; in any case, the *economic* significance was borne out that fewer large fields were found, *as predicted.*

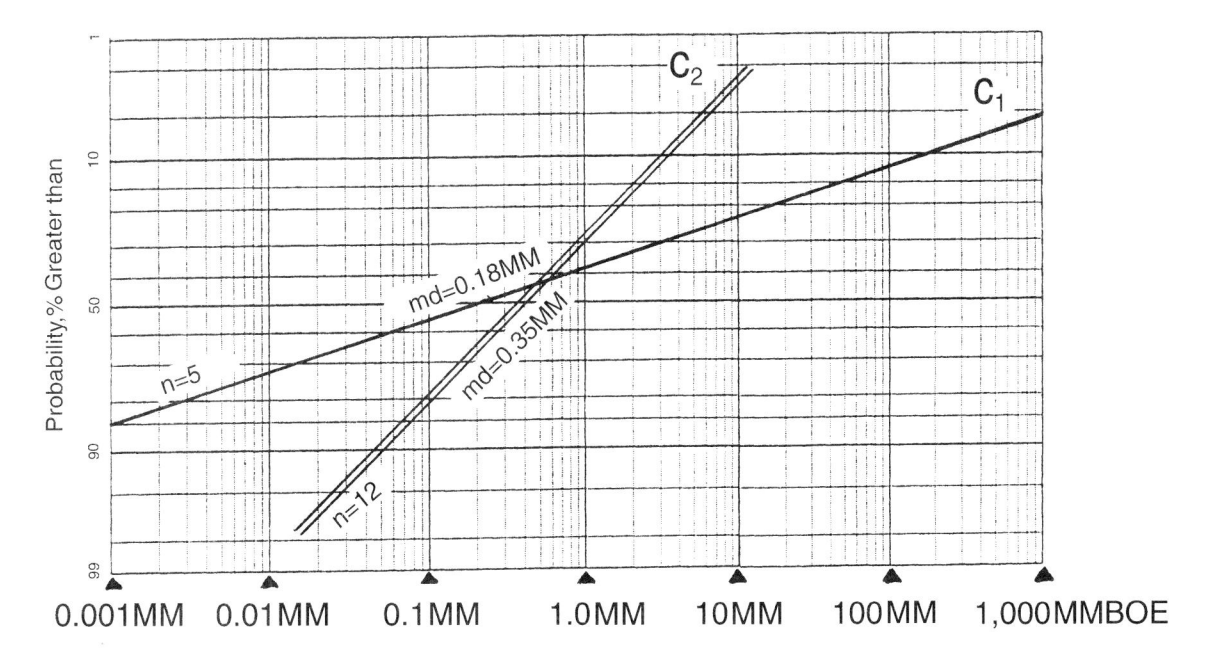

Figure 37c

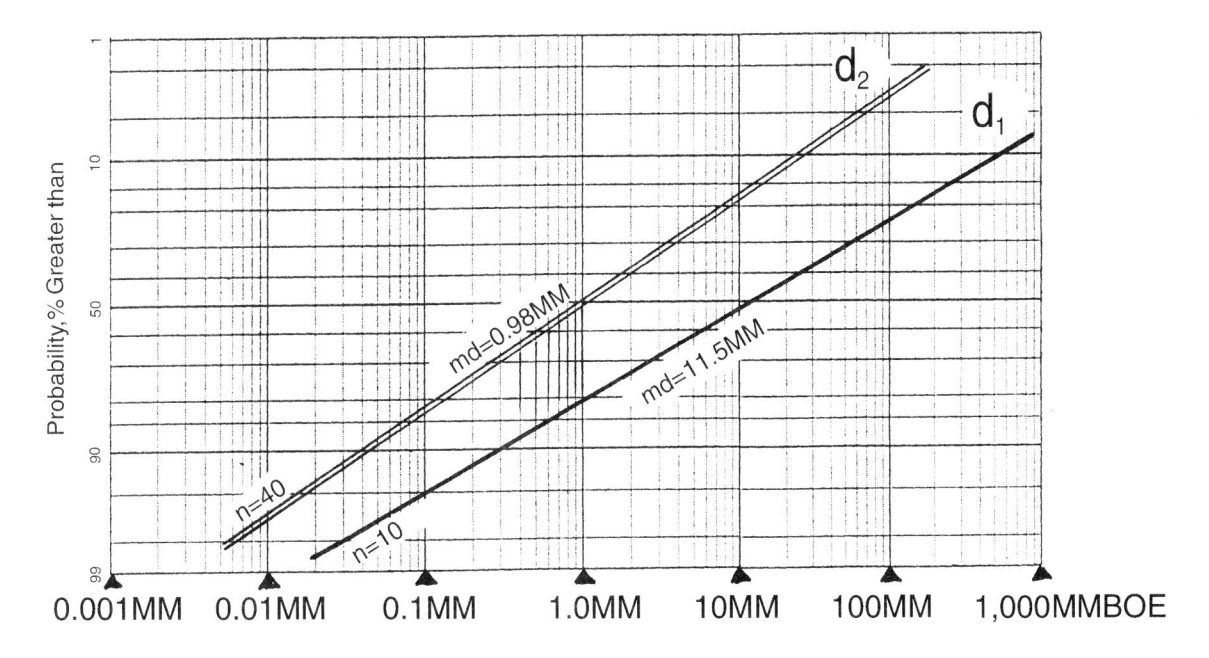

Figure 37d

Figure 37 a, b, c, d (continued)

Minimum Economic Field Size

The reader was introduced to the concept of minimum economic field size (MEFS) earlier, and its importance in play analysis has been discussed briefly. Early in the process of conducting a modern risk analysis of a proposed new play, it is necessary to estimate MEFS, which is defined as the threshold amount of producible oil and gas sufficient to recover—with interest—all exploratory capital investments required to establish the play as a profitable venture—or an economic failure. Ordinarily, the investments recovered include geologic and geophysical project costs (including seismic), lease or contract-area acquisition costs (such as bonuses, fees, etc.), costs of exploratory drilling and completion, and overhead, plus required interest. If one or more delineation or confirmation wells are

> **Equation 9** *Calculating minimum economic field size.*
>
> *Concept:* How large a field (or fields) must we find to recover all exploration investments, including interest?
> *Considerations:*
>
> 1. Money has a time value.
> 2. Some discovered small, noneconomic fields may be developed as commercial discoveries.
> 3. Several small but economic fields are a more likely outcome than one large field.
> 4. $4.50 PV/BOE determined from P10%, P50%, and P90% cash-flow models, considers contract terms, includes development costs.
>
> **
>
> $$\text{MEFS} = \frac{\text{After-tax Costs (G\&G, Exploratory Drilling + Land + Transportation + Overhead)}}{\text{Minimum Number of Discoveries (P90\%)} \times \$\text{PV/BOE (After-tax)}}$$
>
> *Example:*
>
> $$\text{MEFS} = \frac{\$2\text{MM Seis} + \$1.8\text{MM Expl.Drlg.} + \$.7\text{MM Lease Bonus} + \$1.5\text{MM PL} + \$1.2\text{MM OH}}{2 \text{ discoveries} \times \$4.50 \text{ PV10\%/BOE}}$$
>
> $\text{MEFS} = 0.8\text{MMBOE}$

required to warrant field development, those costs must also be included along with the anticipated costs to develop the discovered field. In other words, the discovered new field(s) must be at least large enough to generate, through production revenues, an after-tax NPV sufficient to pay for all investments required to establish the fact that profitable production does exist (PV > $0).

The use of $PV/BOE is a practical convention that includes development costs of successful discoveries because it is directly derived from DCF analysis of the discovered and developed field. Accordingly, where $PV/BOE is being used to establish MEFS, no *additional* provision should be made for development costs unless they are required to prove that an economic discovery has been made. In some cases, necessary pipeline costs may be included for product transportation. Reasonable and expectable initial production rates and percentage decline should be employed in the cash-flow analysis, which should also utilize the legal provisions, terms, and price structures of the anticipated contract. It is important for all estimates used in the cash-flow analysis to be rigorously and objectively evaluated, thereby eliminating bias of any kind—whether optimistic or conservative. Estimating ranges may be used where there is uncertainty about certain parameters, and probabilistic project NPVs may be calculated through Monte Carlo or Latin Hypercube simulation. **Equation 9** provides an example calculation of MEFS for an onshore play in a mature trend, assuming two fields.

One of the most harmful conservative biases concerns the practice of requiring a single discovery to cover all exploration investments—that is, for MEFS to apply only to a single field. This usually results in the requirement that one large field be discovered. In fact, however, if a company is successful at all in a new play or large contract area, the usual outcome is the discovery of several new fields. Accordingly, it may be a more likely scenario to require three 10-million-barrel discoveries or two 15-million-barrel discoveries rather than one 30-million-barrel new field. This leads to the concept of minimum economic reserves required (MERR), to provide minimum profits sufficient to cover exploration investments. The practical result of such an enlightened criterion is to prevent more large-area projects from being rejected because of unrealistic, conservative biases.

Economic Truncation of Field-size Distributions

In mature onshore U.S. petroleum provinces, FSDs of plays or basins contain constituent "fields" ranging down to as small as a thousand barrels each, or even less. In fact, such fields really represent shows of oil or gas that were completed only for business reasons, or from geotechnical or financial imprudence, but nevertheless must be included among all production, which is regulated by the state.

The useful terms commercial and economic were defined and discussed on page 38, as they applied to prospect-reserves distributions. Procedures for truncating such distributions were also reviewed. The same procedures apply to FSDs. Appendix F provides additional detail.

Pmcfs and Pmefs

By estimating MCFS and/or MEFS and finding the location of those reserves values on the FSD, we can

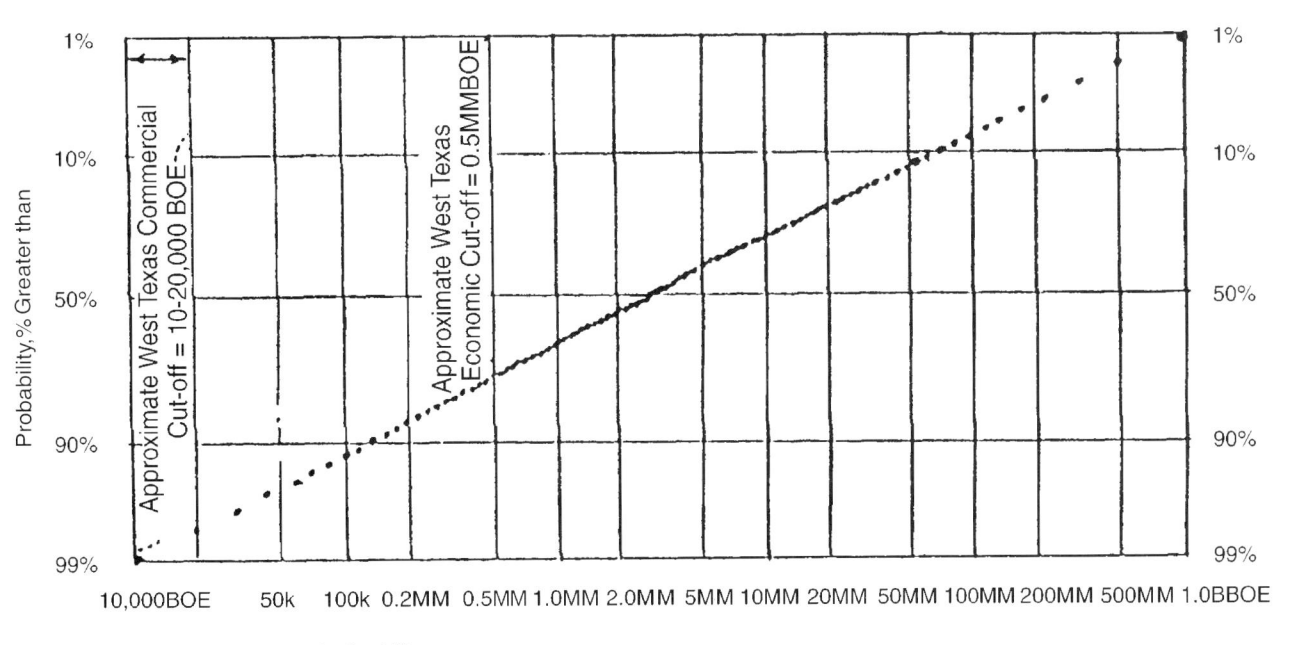

Figure 38a

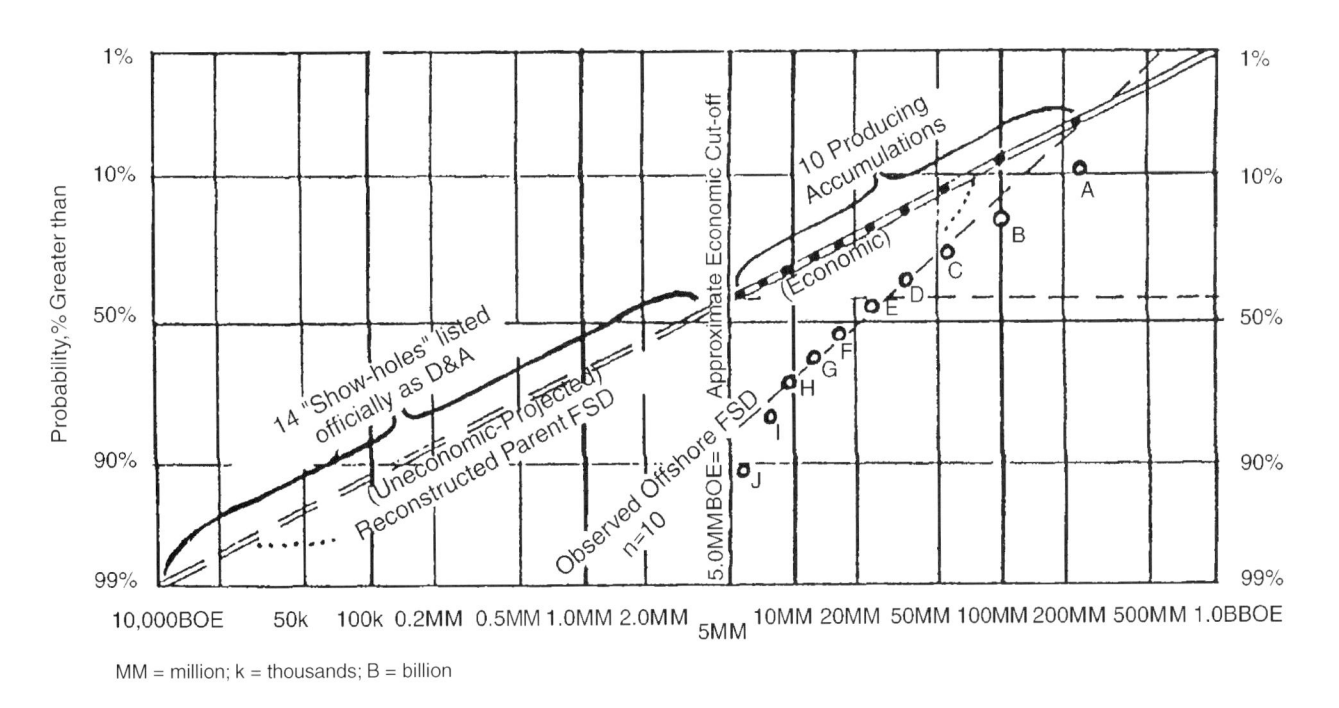

Figure 38b

Figure 38 a, b *Offshore FSDs are truncated by platform cost.*

estimate the probability of a commercial field (or larger) or an economic field (or larger) in the play, given at least one discovery of sufficient reservoired hydrocarbons to at least sustain flow. Those probabilities are Pmcf and Pmef, respectively.

Figure 38a shows an FSD of all fields in part of the prolific northern Midland Basin, west Texas: fields in the distribution range from 10,000 BOE (P99%) to 1,000 MMBOE (P1%). Generally, a well that encounters an accumulation of at least 10,000 to 20,000 BOE will flow.

In that area, any well that flows will probably be completed for production, if a reasonable profit can be expected on the investment in stimulation, tubing, and production equipment. Of course, such a commercial well would not recover the investments in seismic, leasing, or drilling—they would be classed as sunk costs. Accordingly, the commercial threshold in such a province might be approximately 10,000–20,000 BOE; naturally, that threshold might vary depending on the details attending any particular well, especially flow rate. So, for the Northern Midland Basin, Pmcfs equals about 99% to about 96% **(Figure 38a)**.

However, for an exploration venture to be *economic* it must recover all investments involved to bring it into production, plus a reasonable profit, taking into account also the time value of money. To estimate the proportion of fields in the northern Midland Basin that are economic, we must first estimate the approximate reserve size required to generate such a profit (about 500,000 BOE),[8] and then determine the proportion of the FSD having that reserves value, or larger (Pmefs = 75%). By excluding the noneconomic segment of the parent FSD, the remaining segment has been truncated economically, just as previously described for prospect-reserves distributions (pp. 39–41). The smaller, noneconomic fields have been excluded, therefore the mean of the remaining distribution of economic fields will be larger than the mean of the parent FSD, just as previously described.

Offshore FSDs Are Already Truncated

Now, suppose the Midland Basin actually was located offshore, in waters up to 600 ft (~200 m) deep. The parent endowment of accumulations would be no different, but the actual FSD would be greatly attenuated. Because of the expense of offshore production facilities, FSDs of offshore plays reflect *de facto* truncation **(Figure 38b)**. Ordinarily such truncation is *commercial* rather than *economic*. However, because the cost of offshore production facilities is generally very large in relation to exploration costs, the commercial threshold usually approaches the economic threshold for offshore plays. The same principle holds true for all plays in which very substantial financial commitments are required to bring a new field into effective production—for example, remote, ultra-deep, hazardous, or hostile provinces. It is important to emphasize this point because many explorationists seem to overlook it. Reconstruction of the parent FSD is possible, however, by reviewing all pertinent well data and logs in the play area, and by distinguishing dry holes that were uncompleted show holes from dry holes that did not encounter flowing hydrocarbons in the reservoir objective. Appendix F provides more detail on the particular procedures involved in such reconstructions.

Chance of Play Success

Geologic Chance Factors

A system of five discrete geologic chance factors was presented in Chapter 3, pertaining to prospect chance of geologic success (Pg), including definitions and descriptions of subcomponents involved in each of the five main categories (p. 34–36). The importance of the chance factors applying to plays as well as prospects was emphasized. **Table 15** summarizes this recommended system.

Coincidence of Geologic Chance Factors

In order for the geologic chance factors to work, their influence must be operative in a common area—that is, their effects must coincide in time and space (pp. 34 and 48). **Figure 39** depicts a hypothetical basin to illustrate the problem. Petroleum source rocks are present only in the eastern end of the basin bottom. Because buoyant migrating hydrocarbons move updip, at right angles to structural contours, it would be difficult (even impossible) to charge the faulted closures on the southwestern flank of the basin. Moreover, primary reservoir sands do not extend far enough southwest (updip) to be present in the area of the faulted closures. Also, the regional evaporate seal is not present in the western half of the basin. The result is a greatly reduced chance of success because the key geologic elements controlling the occurrence of reservoired petroleum accumulations do not coincide anywhere in this hypothetical basin.

Coincidence is one of the most significant elements that explorationists must assess, especially for new plays in frontier basins. It is probably one of the most commonly overlooked problems, which leads to very low industry success rates for high-risk new plays. Play maps, as described previously, provide an excellent way to address the coincidence problem.

Shared versus Independent Chance Factors

Earlier work by Baker et al. (1986), Baker (1988), and White (1993) discussed independent and shared chance factors, and the concept was reviewed on pages 41 and 62.

Consider the five elements of geologic chance—some will apply to all prospects in the play area, whereas others will *vary* among all prospects in the

---

[8]Naturally, we must recognize that 500,000 BOE should not be considered as a precise value. The economic threshold will vary according to the influence of depth, completion costs, flow rates, transportation, wellhead price, and operating costs, including taxes. Nevertheless, it is possible to generate an approximate minimum economic field size for fields in a play because plays are generally constrained by similarities in the above factors.

Table 15 *Geologic chance factors required for play and prospect success.*

Confidence (%) that thermally mature **HC-source rocks are present** in adequate volume, richness, and type to provide an HC-charge to the play area. Components:
- quantity [thickness, extent, richness]
- HC-type [oil, mixed, gas]
- thermal maturity

Confidence (%) that **hydrocarbons have migrated**, utilizing conduits and carrier beds, along migration pathways into the location of existing closures in volumes adequate to charge them. Components:
- conduits [carrier beds or zones]
- migration routes
- efficiency [concentration and transmission versus dispersion]
- timing

Confidence (%) that **reservoir rock is present** in adequate volume, porosity, and deliverability to support one or more flowing wells in the play area. Components:
- storage capacity [thickness, extent]
- porosity
- reservoir performance [permeability, drive mechanism]

Confidence (%) that structural and/or stratigraphic **closures of adequate area and vertical relief are present** in the play area and can be detected. Components:
- adequate closures exist
- confidence in mapping

Confidence (%) that **effective sealing rocks are present** and that **emplaced hydrocarbons have been preserved (= containment)**. Components:
- effectiveness [thickness, differential permeability, absence of open fractures]
- preservation from subsequent spillage [fault leakage, fracturing, breaching, tilt-and-spill]
- preservation from degradation [biologic, oxidation, thermal]

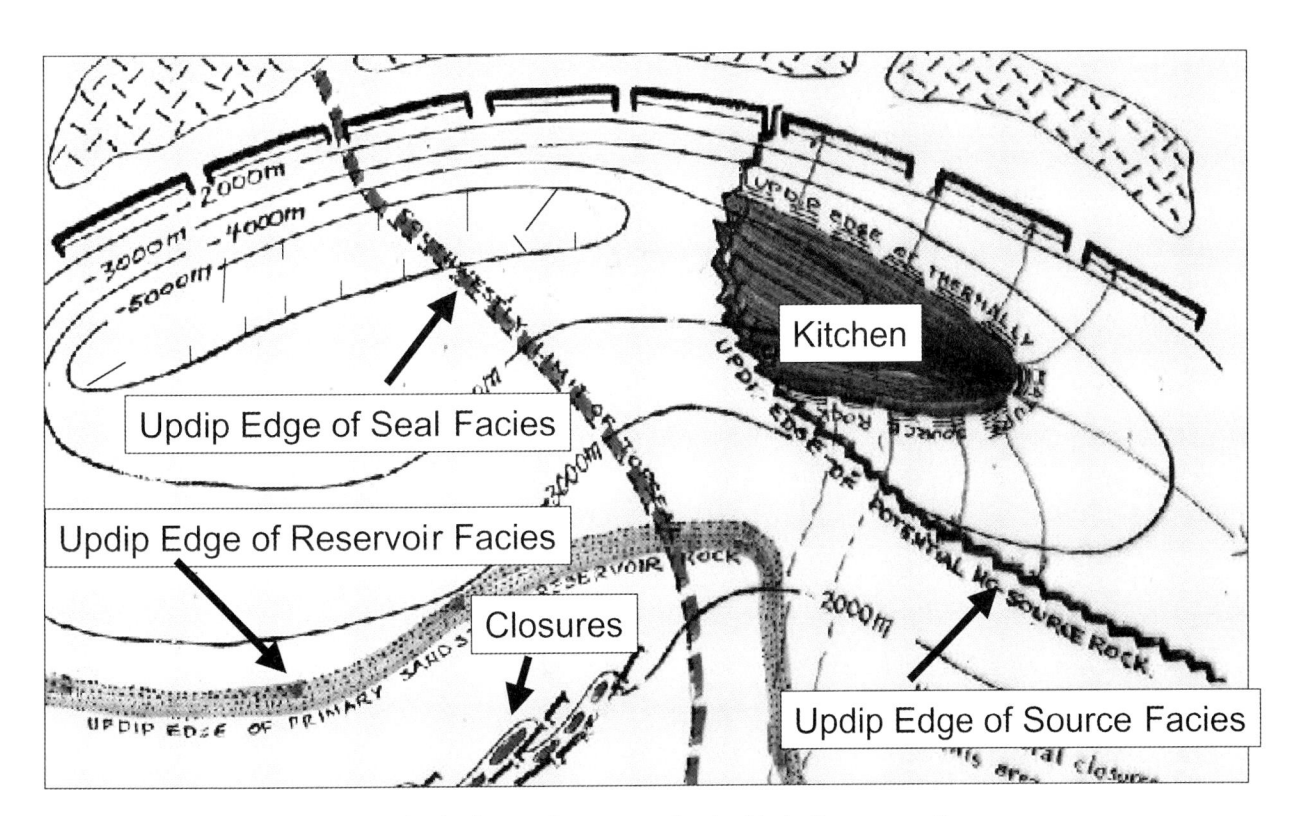

Figure 39 *Effects of operative geologic chance factors must coincide in the prospective area.*

play area. Examples of frequently shared chance factors include the presence of mature hydrocarbon source rocks, hydrocarbon migration into the play area, and timing. Independent chance factors commonly include reservoir rock, closure, and containment. In some cases, subsidiary elements of each main chance factor may vary—for example, seal effectiveness (such as fault leakage) may be independent, causing some prospects in the play to be dry, but not all, whereas the regional preservation history (absence of biologic or thermal degradation) may be common among all prospects and therefore shared.

This leads, then, to the separation of geologic chance factors for purposes of play analysis. Those elements are *shared* that affect all prospects in the play area. If a valid test establishes clearly that a shared chance factor does not exist in the play area, it condemns all prospects in the play area—or it forces significant revision of the play area outline (area of possible coincidence).

Finally, it is common to recognize partial dependencies—elements of geologic chance that are partially shared (= dependent) and partially local (independent).

Chance of Play Success Is Economic, Not Commercial

As previously discussed, the criterion for success of the exploration play is that the play must be economic, rather than commercial. The reason, of course, is that no responsible organization is going to continue to drill for fields that are merely commercial—after several such marginal discoveries in a play, management will perceive the folly of continuing to explore in a play that cannot be economic on a full-cycle basis. That is, they will not continue to drill for fields that do not generate production revenues sufficient to exceed the invested capital plus interest. Accordingly, such a play will be abandoned even though some marginal fields have been found.

A further complication is presented by the play which contains at least one economic field, but additional dry holes or seismic costs incurred in subsequent exploration for other counterpart fields add sufficient expense to transform the play from economic to commercial on a full-cycle basis. The solution to this problem is to identify, for various reserves cases, the maximum costs for additional drilling and seismic that can be incurred before the entire project, on a full-cycle basis, deteriorates from economic to commercial. After discovery of the first economic field, each subsequent discovery should bear the costs of the number of dry holes that would be consistent with the independent chance of economic success; i.e., if Pe (independent) is .25, each anticipated discovery should carry the cost of three dry holes, in addition to the cost of the discovery well.

Integration: Calculating the Chance of Economic Play Success

The purpose of this section is to explain and illustrate one of the mathematical procedures involved—utilizing various geologic and economic estimates—to calculate the estimated chance of economic play success **(Equation 10)**.

Part 1 of **Equation 10** shows the basic form of the equation, with the shared chance factors separated from the independent chance factors. Given that the play exists (shared chance = 1.0), the steps shown for the independent chance factors allow successive determination of:

1. average local chance of a prospect's geologic success (one test),
2. average local chance of a prospect's economic success (one test),
3. average local chance of a prospect's economic failure (one test),
4. chance of all economic failures in n local trials, and
5. chance of at least one economic discovery in n local trials.

This equation expresses the generally recognized truth that, if the *play* really does exist (i.e., the product of the shared factors = 1.0), then the chance of at least one discovery increases as the number of wells testing the independent chance factors also increases.

Part 2 of **Equation 10** lists the estimates and assumptions required to carry out the calculation. For most established plays—even "undercharged" trends—there is usually more than enough hydrocarbon source rock and generated/migrated oil to supply the traps in the play, i.e., the adequacy of source rock and generated/migrated oil is usually not a critical problem. *However, in frontier basins and plays, especially those requiring very large discoveries in order to be economic, the play analyst may be justified in assigning a probability to the likelihood that source rock and migration processes have been adequate to supply at least one economic field.*

Part 3 of **Equation 10** tracks the actual calculation using the equation from Part 1 and the values provided in Part 2. Play (= shared) chance is estimated to be 0.54: the analyst is quite confident of source rock presence (0.9), and moderately confident about generation/migration adequacy (0.6). Given that the play does exist, the average chance of prospect success (flowing hydrocarbons) is 0.28, and the average chance of *economic* prospect success is 0.112. Therefore the average chance of economic prospect failure is the complement, 0.888. The chance of drilling four consecutive economic failures from such prospects is 0.622. Therefore the chance of making at least one economic discovery among four such prospects is again the

Equation 10 *Calculating estimated chance of economic play success.*

1. BASIC EQUATION:

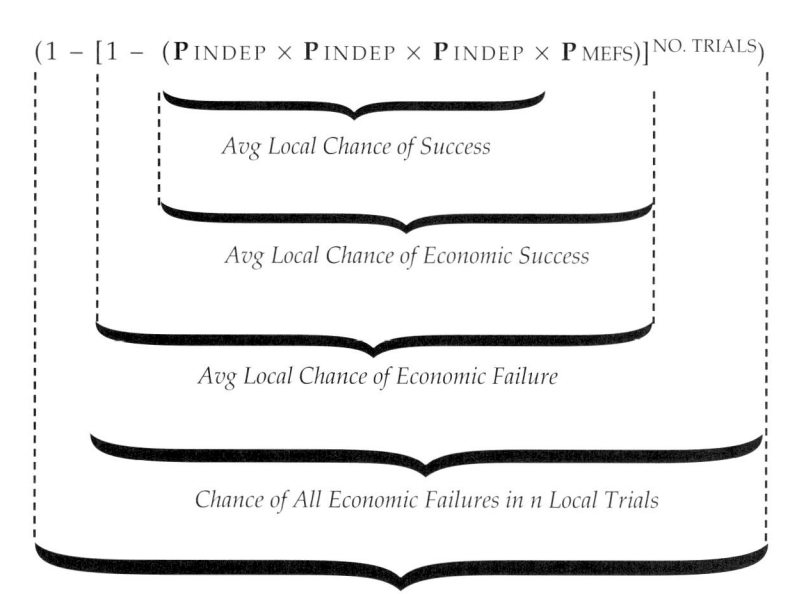

$$\underbrace{P_{SHARED} \times P_{SHARED}}_{\substack{\text{PLAY CHANCE} \\ (= \text{shared chances})}} \; \left(1 - [1 - \underbrace{\overbrace{\underbrace{(P_{INDEP} \times P_{INDEP} \times P_{INDEP}}_{\textit{Avg Local Chance of Success}} \times P_{MEFS})}^{\textit{Avg Local Chance of Economic Success}}}_{\textit{Avg Local Chance of Economic Failure}}]^{\text{NO. TRIALS}}\right)$$

$\underbrace{}_{\textit{Chance of All Economic Failures in n Local Trials}}$

$\underbrace{}_{\textit{Chance of at least 1 Economic Discovery in n Local Trials}}$

2. REQUIRED ESTIMATES AND ASSUMPTIONS FOR SUBJECT PLAY
   a. MEFS = 3 MMBOE, Pmefs = 40%
   b. SHARED GEOLOGIC CHANCE FACTORS = 54%
      1) HC source rocks = 90%
      2) HC generation/migration = 60%
   c. INDEPENDENT GEOLOGIC CHANCE FACTORS = 28%
      1) Reservoir = 70%
      2) Closures = 80%
      3) Containment = 50%
   d. NUMBER OF SUCCESSIVE DRY HOLES BEFORE PLAY IS ABORTED = 4
      (Assumes shared chance factors are verified by tests 1 or 2)
   e. HC SOURCE ROCKS AND HC GENERATION/MIGRATION ARE JUDGED TO BE ADEQUATE TO CHARGE AT LEAST ONE 3-MMBOE FIELD

3. EXAMPLE CALCULATION

   $$\begin{aligned}
   Pe(play) &= [Phc \times Pgen] \times [1 - (1 - [Pres \times Pclos \times Pcont \times Pmefs])^{WELL\ NO.}] \\
   &= [.9 \times .6] \times [1 - (1 - [.7 \times .8 \times .5 \times .4])^4] \\
   &= [.54] \times [1 - (1 - [.112])^4] \\
   &= [.54] \times [1 - (.888)^4] \\
   &= [.54] \times [1 - .622] \\
   &= [.54] \times [.378] \\
   Pe(play) &= .204 = \text{Chance of Play Economic Success}
   \end{aligned}$$

complement, 0.378. Finally, the product of the shared and independent economic chance factors is 0.204, which represents the chance of making at least one economic discovery before quitting the play.

Note that these estimates of geologic and economic chance should be expected to change with successive wells, depending on what is learned from each test, as Baker (1988) explains. This is a very important point.

84 Exploration Plays—Risk Analysis and Economic Assessment

Table 16 *Geotechnical parameters required for play analysis.*

Primary Parameters

1. Shared Chance (= Play Chance)
2. Independent Chance (= Average Prospect Pg)
3. Cost of Exploration (= "Failure Costs")
4. Projected Field-size Distribution (= Play FSD)
5. Projected Numbers of Fields (= Distribution of Field Number)
6. Number of Exploratory Tests (= How Many Successive Dry Holes before Quitting?)
7. $PV per BOE of Discovered Reserves (May Vary with Field Sizes)
8. Minimum Economic Field Size (= MEFS)

Secondary Parameters (Derived from Primary Parameters)

1. Pmefs (= % of FSD > MEFS)
2. Projected Numbers of Economic Fields (= Field Numbers × Pmefs)
3. Chance of Economic Play Success:

    (Pshared × (1 − [1 − Pindependent × Pmefs]$^{\text{No. Tests}}$)

4. Projected Economic Field-size Distribution (= Truncated FSD)
5. Projected Distribution of Economic Play Reserves

    (= Truncated FSD × Economic Field Numbers)

6. Distribution of $PV OF Economic Play Reserves
7. Play Expected $Present Value:

    ([Pplay success × $PVmean reserves] − Pplay failure × Play Failure Cost])

Summary of Geotechnical Data Required for Play Risk Analysis

After completing the studies required to carry out the geotechnical assessment of the new play (see Appendix E) and the resulting assimilated maps and compilations of pertinent data, our next step is to conduct the actual play analysis, the principal product of which is the evaluation of the play as a full-cycle economic venture. As previously described (p. 62), such analyses are usually carried out in a systematic way, using either a flow sheet or interactive computer software that is based on such a flow sheet.

In any case, 15 key geotechnical values are required to carry out the analysis **(Table 16)**. Eight of these parameters are *primary* estimates made on the basis of geotechnical studies, or analog data. The seven remaining parameters are *secondary* values derived from arithmetic manipulation of the primary estimates. Risk analysis of the exploration play cannot proceed without these parameters, which in all cases should be compared with various reality checks for credibility.

Primary Parameters

Play (= Shared) Chance

Play chance is a confidence statement—the probability that in the area of the play, those geologic chance factors that apply to all prospects in the play are actually satisfied. *Play chance is the product of the probabilities of the shared geologic chance factors that must be satisfied if there is to be at least one field large enough to sustain flow.* It is not tied to economics or commerciality. A useful alternative definition might be the explorationist's confidence that an active petroleum system exists somewhere in the area and within the stratigraphic interval of the play. Theoretically, if a valid test establishes that one of the shared chance factors is not operative, it kills the entire play—or it requires significant revision of the prospective play area (p. 82). Characteristic elements of play chance often include (but are not limited to) generation, migration, timing, and preservation **(Table 17)**.

Average Prospect (= Local) Chance

Another confidence statement, prospect chance is the likelihood (expressed as a probability) that those

Table 17 *Form: flow sheet for play risk analysis (modified from Baker et al., 1986; White, 1992, 1993).*

FLOW SHEET FOR PLAY RISK ANALYSIS

Play Name: _____ Play Location: _____.

1. GEOLOGICAL CHANCE FACTORS REQUIRED FOR PLAY AND PROSPECT SUCCESS

   Shared Chance   Average Independent Chance
   (= Confidence - %)   (= Confidence - %)

   _____ .... (A) HYDROCARBON SOURCE ROCKS   (J)_____
           _____ 1. Quantity (Thickness, Extent, Richness)
           _____ 2. HC-Type (Oil, Mixed, Gas)
           _____ 3. Thermal Maturity
   _____ .... (B) HYDROCARBON MIGRATION   (K)_____
           _____ 1. Conduits Exist
           _____ 2. Routes Toward Closures
           _____ 3. Efficiency
           _____ 4. Timing Correct
   _____ .... (C) RESERVOIR ROCKS   (L)_____
           _____ 1. Volume (Thickness, Extent)
           _____ 2. Porosity
           _____ 3. Deliverability (Permeability, Drive-type)
   _____ .... (D) CLOSURES (Structural, Stratigraphic, Etc.) (M)_____
           _____ 1. Adequate Area and Vertical Relief
           _____ 2. Confidence in Mapping
   _____ .... (E) CONTAINMENT and PRESERVATION   (N)_____
           _____ 1. Seals Effective (Thickness, Differential Perm.)
           _____ 2. Subsequent Spillage Insignificant
                      (Fault leakage, Fracturing, Breaching, Tilting)
           _____ 3. Degradation (Biologic, Oxidation, Thermal)

2. ESTIMATED PLAY CHANCE (A x B x C x D x E)
   (Note: This value is 1.0 if Play is proved, ongoing, *and* existence of at least   _____
   one more field is assured.)   PLAY CHANCE (= SHARED)

3. ESTIMATED PLAY SUCCESS RATIO OR AVERAGE PROSPECT P_S (J x K x L x M x N)
   (Compare with analogs, from history, geologic "look-alikes" or "prospect-grading."   _____
   Note: This assumes Play chance = 1.0).   AVERAGE PROSPECT CHANCE = (LOCAL)

---

geologic chance factors that are *independent* (that is, that may vary locally, among all the prospects in the play) are, *on average*, satisfied in the area of the play. *If the play really does exist (play chance = 1), then prospect chance is the average geologic success ratio of all prospects in the play area.* It is the average product of the independent geologic chance factors. Common independent chance factors include reservoir, closure, and some elements of containment **(Table 17)**. Remember that prospect chance equates only with discovery of a reservoired accumulation capable of sustained flow. It has no economic or even commercial implications—those constraints are derived values, considered later in the analysis.

Cost of Exploration

The cost of exploration is the sum of estimated prudent expenditures for seismic surveys (including processing), other geophysical data, other necessary maps, surface data acquisition, geologic and geochemical analyses, leasing costs (including bonuses and fees), exploratory drilling and testing, and overhead. It is the total amount that must be recovered (at interest) from future production revenues if the venture is to be at least minimally profitable (= PV > $0). This is the amount of money you are going to have to spend to know whether the project is a success or failure. In some conservative project evaluations, this amount is projected to be recovered through production revenues from only one discovery; in more reasonable evaluations, it may be recovered from several discovered fields (see p. 78). Conceptually, it also can be considered as the cost of a failed exploration play—and as such it should be tied to your minimum exploration program.

Projected Field-size Distribution

The construction of an estimated FSD for the subject play has already been described at length, whereby informed manipulations (= shifts) consider geologic attributes and exploratory maturity and efficiency. Regardless of the methods employed, the projected FSD represents a responsible estimate of the fields that will be found, *given the discovery of one or more fields*, and it is a key parameter for risk analysis of any exploration play. It is expressed as a lognormal cumulative probability distribution.

Projected Numbers of Fields

Another required primary estimate is the number of fields that will ultimately be discovered in the play area (p. 69). Note that such fields need not be economic. Ordinarily this is expressed as a lognormal cumulative probability distribution. The projected field number is usually determined by comparison with analogous areas, taking into account relative maturity of exploration, but it may also be estimated using the principles of discovery process modeling or other methods. Obviously this estimate assumes at least some future success in the play.

Number of Exploratory Tests

Given that the shared chance factors turn out to be satisfied in the play area (play chance = 1), then the probability of success is a function of the independent or local chance and the number of consecutive unsuccessful trials (dry holes) the firm is willing to drill before giving up. Usually, this number is partly political, based on management's preferences, but it is also a function of what specifically is learned from each trial. This involves considerations of Bayesian mathematics[9] (see Baker, 1988). In general, companies experiencing two consecutive tests that indicate deficiency in the shared chance factors are probably justified in abandoning the play. Consecutive dry holes that confirm the play chance factors, but appear deficient regarding the independent chance factors, might be allowed to number two to four or five, depending on what is learned from each dry hole and the anticipated capacity for geotechnical learning, adjustment, and improvement.

$PV per BOE of Discovered Reserves

The play analyst needs to be able to translate projected prospect reserves into present value in order to be able to estimate the present value of the entire play as a full-cycle economic venture. In some plays, a useful approximation of this parameter can be made from the median or mean field-reserves case and applied to fields of all sizes in the play. In most plays, however, the analyst is advised to prepare economic analyses (cash-flow models) of key field sizes (P10%, P50%, P90%, Pmean), using the contract terms and tax schemes expected in the area. This is because in most plays, especially those with production-sharing contracts or offshore areas requiring expensive production platforms, $PV (in dollars) per BOE is not a constant. Variables such as initial production, decline rate, and wellhead price can be considered via such reserves cases. The ultimate product required is a simple graph showing field $PV as a function of field reserves and/or $PV per BOE for different field sizes.

Minimum Economic Field Size (MEFS)

MEFS has already been discussed in detail, and **Equation 9** shows the method of calculation, which utilizes (1) cost of exploration; (2) $PV per BOE; and (3) minimum number of required discoveries.

Secondary (Derived) Parameters

Probability of Minimum Economic Field Size (Pmefs)

Pmefs refers to the probability, *given a discovery in the play*, that the discovered field will be equal to or larger than the MEFS. If several equal-size fields are anticipated to reach break-even economics, Pmefs is the probability of either of them (but not both). This parameter is derived using MEFS in conjunction with the projected FSD for the play, as described on page 79.

Projected Numbers of Economic Fields

This parameter is expressed as a cumulative probability distribution, ordinarily lognormal, derived from the projected number of fields distribution (p. 69), reduced by multiplying by Pmefs.

Chance of Economic Play Success

This parameter has already been discussed in detail (p. 82 and **Equation 10**). It is derived using (1) play chance; (2) average prospect chance of success; (3) Pmefs; and (4) number of exploratory tests. Note that this requires Pmefs to be combined with the other independent geologic chance factors.

---

[9]Following the concepts and formulae of Thomas Bayes, an 18th-century English mathematician, "the primary application of [Bayesian mathematics] is to use new information—'learning'—to revise probabilities based on old information, that is, to compare posterior probability with the priors" (after Bernstein, 1996). In other words, we revise inferences about old information as new information arrives. Dealing with conditional probabilities requires employment of Bayesian principles.

Projected Economic Field-size Distribution

This FSD is derived from the original projected FSD for the play, economically truncated at Pmefs and redistributed through 98%. It is necessary to determine the new P10%, P50%, P90%, and Pmean of the truncated distribution as described previously and in Appendix F.

Projected Distribution of Economic Play Reserves

This distribution is the product of two distributions: (1) projected numbers of economic fields, and (2) projected economic field sizes. These two distributions are combined by Monte Carlo or Latin Hypercube simulation or by employing the analytical/graphical method described in Appendix B. The result is a cumulative probability distribution of economic play reserves. The mean of that distribution (mean economic play reserves) is statistically the best representation of economic play reserves.

Present Value of Economic Play Reserves

This distribution is the product of two distributions: (1) $PV/BOE, and (2) distribution of economic play reserves. The mean of the distribution is statistically the best expression of economic play present value.

Play Expected Present Value

The expected value concept was discussed previously. It is the chance-weighted present value of a project—it represents the play as an entire, full-cycle economic venture. It is one of the important economic measures by which competing plays can be usefully compared. It may be derived using (1) chance of economic success; (2) mean $PV of economic play reserves; and (3) cost of exploration (= cost of a failed play). As explained earlier, its weakness is that it assumes the firm is risk-neutral.

Process for Systematic Risk Analysis of Exploration Plays

Now we will set out the various steps and calculations required to carry out a geologically responsible, statistically sound assessment of the economic value of a given play, as previously discussed (p. 84). Note again that the values used in the flow sheet must be based on a sound and thorough geotechnical review of the subject plays, as outlined in Appendix E.

Many exploration firms utilize comprehensive computer software, or a standardized flow sheet, to carry out systematic play risk analysis. Either approach can bring companywide consistency to the process, which then leads to play inventories that, in turn, yield legitimate optimized values to those plays selected for execution—the play portfolio. However, geotechnical staff must be trained to understand the principles of play analysis if they are to use software (or flow sheets) responsibly.

Recommended Procedure

The following discussion, which also draws on prior work by Baker et al. (1986) and White (1992, 1993), is intended to guide the explorationist/analyst through the proper steps of economic play analysis.

Model and Map the Play as if It Already Exists

Depict all the requisite geologic elements in the contemplated area, *as if they already exist*—the following analysis is then designed to estimate the likelihood that your picture is essentially correct. In particular, you must show the areal and spatial distribution of geologic features, on maps and sections, in relation to the play fairway and to locations of specific prospects—if you have that much data. Remember what you are risking geographically: the chance that at least one flowable petroleum accumulation (having the geologic attributes described) really does exist in the play area, in the stratigraphic succession identified.

Estimate the Play (= Shared) Chance

Based on **Table 17**, circle those geologic chance factors that are *shared*, i.e., common to all prospects in the play, and enter your confidence (probability = decimal fraction) that each factor will indeed prove to operate or exist in the play area. If you are essentially certain that a shared factor exists throughout the trend area, assign it a probability of 1.0. Then multiply the circled chance factors—the product is *play chance* or *shared chance*. NOTE: Individual chance factors may be partly shared, and partly independent, indicating partial geologic dependency.

Estimate the Average Prospect Chance

Under Item 1 of the flow sheet **(Table 17)**, circle those geologic chance factors that are *independent*, that is, that vary among the prospects in the play area. Assign to each your confidence (= probability) that the chance factors will be satisfied for *average prospects*, and multiply them. Some chance factors may be partially dependent, so you may enter decimal fractions in both the shared and the local columns. If you have sufficient data, determine from several prospects in the play area your average confidence (= probability) in the existence of each of the independent chance factors and multiply them.[10] Their product is *average prospect chance (prospect Pg)*. If the play proves to exist (i.e., play chance is 1.0), then the average prospect chance will be the overall

---

[10]However, see page 46 for additional perspective on this scenario.

> **Equation 11** *Prospect grading procedure (White, 1993).*
>
> (a) *Step 1* = Grading Prospects
>
> A = grade for highest-chance prospects
> C = grade for intermediate-chance prospects   } Consider all Geologic Controls
> F = grade for lowest-chance prospects
>
> ---
>
> (b) *Step 2:*
>
> $$\text{Approximate Future Success Ratio} = \frac{1 + (\text{No. of A Prospects}) + (\text{No. of A + C Prospects})}{\text{Total no. of A + C + F Prospects}}$$

success rate of prospects in the play. Some reality checks are:

- If the play is a future projection of an ongoing play, is the historical exploration success ratio compatible with your estimate?
- If the play is undrilled but you have a comparable productive analog, what is the average prospect success rate of the analog play? Be sure you take modern technological capabilities into account.
- Use White's "prospect grading scheme" if you have enough data to identify the location of many of the prospects in the play, as shown in **Equation 11**. The problem with this approach is that commonly, if you have sufficient data to be able to identify and grade so many prospects, *you're already in the play!* That is, you have already invested capital for geotechnical information—the decision to enter the play has already been made!
- If you have absolutely no idea about the average prospect success rate, remember that the world average for the petroleum exploration industry has been consistently about 25% for the past 40 years (Pcommercial, not Pgeologic!).
- *Reality check*: If you have an inventory of prospects in the play, be sure the average Pg of such identified prospects is consistent with average Pg for the play.

How Many Consecutive Exploratory Dry Holes before your Firm Quits?

Based on your firm's risk propensity and past history and assuming your wells establish that the play chance factors appear to be satisfied (play chance = 1.0), estimate the number of consecutive dry holes your management would be likely to drill before abandoning the project. *Reality check:* Following Baker (1988), this number ordinarily should be more than one and usually no more than four or five. *Key question*: What do you expect to learn from each dry hole? *Important note:* This assumes only one play concept to test.

Estimate the Cost of Geotechnical Exploration

What is the area of the play? How much will regional gravity and magnetics cost? Interpreted landsat imagery or air photos? Surface geologic mapping and/or sampling? How much seismic data (regional 2-D, local 2-D, and 3-D data) will be required? At what cost? How many successive exploratory dry holes would your company drill in the play before declaring the venture a failure? What will they cost? Remember to include nonrecoverable bonus and lease costs here, as well as overhead, and make all estimates on an after-tax basis. *Reality check:* Another term for this value is *the cost of exploration failure.*

Estimate the Number of Fields in the Play

Based on the size of the play area, structural and stratigraphic grain or complexity, and field density in analog trends, forecast the total number of fields that will be discovered in the play area, *given that there is at least one discovery*. This forecast should take the form of a probabilistic range with a lognormal distribution (see p. 69). An alternative method is to employ discovery process modeling principles to derive these estimates (see p. 69). Remember the common biases: Most explorationists *underestimate* the *number* of future fields in plays and *overestimate* the *reserves size*s of those fields, especially in onshore areas.

Analyze the Terms of the E&P Contract

Be sure to incorporate all relevant terms, including taxes, into cash-flow models that you develop for possible project scenarios. Identify particularly critical, sensitive, and useful provisions that should influence your negotiations and/or business decisions.

Construct a Field-size Distribution for the Play

Details have been discussed (pp. 67–76 and Appendix F). Subject the projected FSD to reality checks.

Find Net Present Value for Different Field Sizes

Run cash-flow models on P10%, P50%, P90%, and Pmean reserves cases under the operative contract terms and using the current company discount rate. Construct a graph showing the relationship of NPV to recoverable reserves (p. 86). Also run cash-flow models for the total failure case and at least one partial failure case to determine the negative NPV for those outcomes. All values should be estimated on an after-tax basis.

Estimate Minimum Economic Field Size (MEFS)

Use the graphs and data from the previous item to estimate the minimum economic reserves required (MERR) to recover the cost of exploration *at interest*. Then, given at least one economic discovery, what is a reasonable low-side outcome—one field discovery? Two? Three? Whichever is the most reasonable outcome will determine MEFS. *Reality check:* Large play areas and geologic complexity both encourage field numbers larger than one, but prudence suggests that this field number should not exceed three. Short exploration time periods (contractual), limited exploration budgets, and risk-averse management all drive the estimated field number downward toward one.

Find the Probability of a Field of Minimum Economic Size (Pmefs)

On the FSD, find the probability associated with a field of minimum economic size. Pmefs is the proportion (%) of the FSD that is of MEFS *or larger* (see pp. 79 and 86).

Find NPV/BOE for Different Field Sizes

Using the data and graphs from net present value, construct a graph and/or table that shows the NPV per oil-equivalent barrel to your firm, as operator (p. 86). This will allow your prospectors to readily assign an approximate value to every prospect, based on mean reserves, *given discovery* (and also to calculate expected value, by incorporating average prospect chance and assuming play chance = 1.0). All values reflect an after-tax basis.

Estimate the Number of Economic Fields in the Play

This estimate is derived from the distribution of number of fields in the play by multiplying each of the P10%, P50%, P90%, and Pmean field numbers by Pmefs to generate a new probability distribution for numbers of economic fields, *given at least one discovery*. Since these estimates represent statistical values, it is permissible for these values to be decimal fractions.

Find the Chance of Economic Play Success

This calculation has already been discussed and illustrated (p. 82 and **Equation 10**). It is derived using the following:

- play chance = product of shared factors
- average prospect chance = product of local or independent factors
- number of consecutive dry holes before failure
- probability of MEFS (Pmefs)

Construct the Economic Field-size Distribution

This distribution of economic field sizes is derived by truncating the original FSD constructed for the play (p. 87). It is essential to determine the new P10%, P50%, P90%, and the Pmean reserves values for the *economic* part of the FSD, as described on page 79, and in Appendix F.

Find the Mean Economic Play Reserves

The next step is to construct a cumulative probability distribution of economic play reserves. This is accomplished by combining the distribution of economic field sizes and the estimate of the number of economic fields in the play, ordinarily through conventional Monte Carlo simulation or the Latin Hypercube method (p. 94). An analytical method to combine either two or three such distributions, using graphical procedures, has been developed and described by Capen (1992), Megill (1992), and Rose and Thompson (1991), as discussed in Appendix B. The mean of the economic play reserves distribution is the best statistical expression of play reserves potential, but the whole range of possible outcomes can be calculated.

Find the Mean NPV of Play

This range of values, which assumes economic play success, is derived on the basis of the following:

- mean play economic reserves
- NPV/BOE for different field sizes

This may be generated as a probability distribution, with P90%, P50%, and P10% values determined. However, the mean value is the best statistical expression of play NPV and should be calculated on an after-tax basis.[11]

---

[11]For the anticipated P50 or P10 numbers of fields, we must also account for the costs of exploratory drilling (especially the unavoidable dry holes) and additional leasing costs associated with such a successful play. Therefore, the mean play NPV must include such costs to be correctly represented.

Calculate the Play Expected Value (ENPV)

This value is the chance-weighted statistical value of the play. Play ENPV utilizes the following parameters:

- chance of economic play success and chance of failure
- the mean NPV of the play (including additional exploration costs associated with P50 and P10 field numbers)
- play cost of failure

It should be calculated on an after-tax basis.

Determine the Lease/Acquisition Price

This determination will vary widely, depending on the method by which contract rights are to be acquired—sealed bid, oral auction, performance bid (= work commitment), serial negotiations, or private treaty. This topic is discussed in more detail in Chapter 6, in the section on Acquisition Strategies (pp. 93–99). There are several cautionary notes:

- If there is a reasonable likelihood that the host government or landowner will allow subsequent renegotiations of contract terms, the fundamental strategy of competitive sealed bidding, based on bidding a fraction of project expected value, is negated (see p. 99). In such situations, a winning strategy may very well involve tactics of deliberate overbidding to obtain the license, followed by later negotiations. This is a dangerous game, however, and disavows the sanctity of contracts.
- The widely described (Capen, Clapp, and Campbell, 1971; Thaler, 1992) systematic reduction of ENPV (.35 × ENPV) utilized by ARCO and others in the Gulf of Mexico (to guard against the Winner's Curse) is compatible with chances, reserves variances, and values of that petroleum region. But in many new play areas, chances are lower, and reserves variances even higher, justifying a more severe reduction, even lower than 35%, to perhaps 25% or even 20% of ENPV. On the other hand, in acquisitions having higher anticipated chances of success and smaller reserves variance, the 35% reduction should be relaxed to 50% or perhaps even 60% or 70% for producing properties.
- It is also extremely important to consider the overall distribution of bid amounts by competitor companies in previous offerings and sales, in the area of interest, in analog areas, and in other recent sales. Often, especially in marginal or high-risk plays, the actual prevailing bid levels expressed as dollars per acre (or any other area measure) may be much less than your 35% or 25% reduced bid determination!
- In estimating cost of geotechnical exploration (= cost of geotechnical failure), it may be necessary to perform several iterations to develop an appropriate value representing the land portion of costs (= winning bid). Such iterations may impact values of MEFS, Pmefs, etc.

Calculate the Key Economic Measures for the Play

To provide a basis for evaluating the play as a business venture, or to compare it with other opportunities, it is useful to calculate the anticipated values for key economic measures, such as:

- discounted cash flow rate of return (DCFROR) (calculate at P10%, P50%, P90%, and Pmean economic reserves level). DCFROR is only useful as a minimum qualifier, or hurdle—it is not useful to compare projects;
- investment efficiency (calculate on a risk-adjusted basis; see p. 54);
- cost of finding (calculate on a risk-adjusted basis, i.e., include the costs of dry holes).

Allocate Play Reserves, ENPV, Exploration Costs, and Bids among Prospective Blocks

By subjectively ranking the various acreage blocks within the play area, it is then possible to allocate play reserves, ENPV, exploration costs, and bids among the prospective blocks. This will be useful in carrying out various negotiations and business operations as the play is carried out.

Chapter 6

Management of Exploration Projects as Business Ventures

Introduction

We have now reviewed all the necessary considerations by which exploration prospects and plays may be objectively measured with respect to potential reserves, chance of commercial or economic success, and range of profitability given success. The remaining tasks concern how the inventories and portfolios of such opportunities may be managed as business ventures, taking into account the financial and human resources of the firm.

Dealing with Risk and Risk Aversion

Practical Expressions and Applications

The term "risk" implies the threat of loss. A proposed project becomes a risk venture only when we assign economic consequences—gains and losses—to the various possible outcomes. The fundamental attribute of all risk ventures is that the threat of loss outweighs the prospect of gain—people will take a greater chance to avoid a loss than to make a gain of the same size. This is the essence of utility theory. Except for compulsive gamblers and those who purposefully remain ignorant, the normal human condition is to be risk-averse whenever a proposition involves things that are precious—life, health, money, reputation, human relationships, social status, and so on.

Accordingly, we try to "hedge" our position in such ventures by finding ways to increase our safety, either by giving up some interest in the deal or by delaying our commitment until the probable outcome of the venture is more apparent.

Biases Affecting Risk Decisions

Pioneering work by Tversky and Kahnemann (1974) provided good examples of common biases affecting our everyday judgments about risk ventures. **Table 18** outlines seven such biases, all of which tend to cause our evaluations of such ventures to be inconsistent. One of these biases is especially important to understand: the fear of anticipated criticism that may impede individual-enterprise decisiveness. This is just an organizational expression of risk aversion, in which the perceived threat jeopardizes status, position, even one's continued employment. In especially authoritarian companies, such bias may effectively paralyze the organization, thus shifting even the most trivial decisions upward to upper management.

It is important for geotechnical staff, as well as exploration management, to be aware of such biases and to know how to detect and correct for them, as shown in the following section.

Risk-adjusted Value, Risk Tolerance, and Optimum Working Interest

The economic parameter risk-adjusted value (RAV) was defined in Chapter 4 (p. 55) and shown to be a modification of the expected value (EV) equation, in which the function that expresses the risk preferences of the decisionmaker is exponential. The relative degree of risk aversion expresses itself as variations in "r"—larger r's indicate an increasing degree of risk aversion.

Calculated values for RAV have been intuitively hard for planners and decisionmakers to deal with because they combine objective economic values with subjective behavioral responses. Subsequent developments made applied utility theory more useful to exploration management:

1. Walls (1993, personal communication) found that characteristic r's of oil and gas firms approximated 5/(annual exploration budget), rather than 1/(annual exploration budget). In other words, exploration firms actually behaved in a more risk-aversive way than Cozzolino had anticipated (p. 55).
2. Following Cozzolino (1977 and 1978), Lerche and MacKay (1999) showed a more comprehensible and useful form of r, called risk tolerance (RT) (**Equation 7**, p. 55).

Table 18 *Biases affecting risk decisions (modified after Tversky and Kahnemann, 1974).*

Type of Bias	Common Example
Framing effects	Decision makers will take a greater gamble to avoid a loss than to make an equal gain.
Existence of a prior account	Decision makers are more inclined to take a risk at the beginning of a project than later in the project's life.
Maintaining a consistent reference frame	Decision makers are most likely to invest during a "run" of good fortune, and less likely to invest during a "run" of bad fortune.
Probability of success	A venture having a perceived high chance of success is preferred over a second venture having a low chance of success, even though the expected value of the second venture is clearly superior.
Wrong action versus inaction	Managers prefer to take a risk by not making a decision, rather than taking action that could result in the same loss.
Number of people making decision	Groups are more prone to take risks than individuals.
Workload and venture size	Large-volume ventures are preferred over smaller ones, especially when decision makers are busy.
Personal familiarity	The "comfort bias"—decision makers are more risk-prone in deals or environments with which they have good experience.

Table 19 *EV implies "risk-neutral."*

PROJECT A

P_c = 20%;
Mean reserves = 50MM bbl
DHC = $30MM; PV/BOE = $3.00
EV = .2(50MM × $3/BOE) − .8($30MM)
 = .2($150MM) − .8($30MM)
 = $30MM − $24MM
EV = +$6MM

PROJECT B

P_c = 50%;
Mean reserves = 5MM bbl
DHC = $3MM; PV/BOE = $3.00
EV = .5(5MM × $3/BOE) − .5($3MM)
 = .5($15MM) − .5($3MM)
 = $7.5MM − $1.5MM
EV = +$6MM

Pc = commercial chance of success
DHC = dry-hole cost
EV = expected value

Risk tolerance was intuitively easy to grasp as that threshold value whose anticipated loss is unacceptable to the corporation. Pragmatically, RT could be thought of as the investor's choke-point—the value that motivated the investor to find a co-investor with whom to share the risk of loss—even at the prospect of giving up some of the gain.

The EV concept (p. 54) ignores the pervasive, powerful force we call risk aversion. **Table 19** compares two dissimilar projects that happen to have the same EV ($6.0 million) but vastly different front-end costs ($30 million vs. $3 million).

3. Again, following Cozzolino (1977), Lerche and MacKay (1999) showed that, for every venture, RAV would be maximized at some specific working interest, through a trial-and-error process. They then transformed the RAV equation to allow direct calculation of the optimum working interest (OWI) for any venture, given that the firm's RT is known.

$$OWI = \frac{RT}{Cost + PV} \times ln\left(\frac{P_c \times PV}{P_f \times Cost}\right) \quad (12)$$

Example:

1) Firm's RT = $10MM
2) PV of mean-reserves case = $42MM
3) PV of cost = $6MM
4) P_c = 0.3; P_f = 0.7

$$OWI = \frac{\$10}{\$42 + \$6} \times ln\left(\frac{0.3 \times \$42}{0.7 \times \$6}\right)$$

OWI = 0.2287 = 23% = Company should take about one-quarter of this venture.

The power of the OWI calculation is that it allows the most common response to unacceptable risk—reduction of one's share—to be optimized for each venture, consistently throughout the company. That is, the firm can behave consistently in its response to risk propositions, by taking appropriate shares of the diverse ventures in its portfolio. This is particularly important where companies seek to spread risk by participating widely in many joint ventures and thereby broaden their exposure, but they do not have the luxury of assembling a full inventory of opportunities, more than a year in advance, from which to select the optimum combination and share of ventures for the upcoming year's drilling program. Using OWI offers a legitimate alternative for converting the common process that many companies use to determine their share—management's intuition—to a valid and consistent procedure that optimizes value to the firm.

Common Business Conventions for Mitigating Risk

The petroleum exploration business has developed many different procedures and devices for alleviating excessively risky ventures. Basically, all such conventions, as they apply to individual ventures, involve one of three key elements influencing risk ventures:

1. improve the odds;
2. reduce the capital at risk; or
3. alleviate risk through diversification.

Improving the Odds

The most common method of improving the odds is to acquire additional geotechnical information such as seismic or geochemical data, either by purchasing or trading data. But other more imaginative methods also are used, such as bottom-hole or dry-hole contributions, which involve the acquisition of additional geotechnical information illuminating your own prospect, by encouraging another operator to drill a well near your leasehold and then share key well data (logs, cores, tests, etc.) that bear on your own prospect, in exchange for some agreed-upon monetary benefit. This benefit is ordinarily paid on reaching the necessary depth and/or if the well proves to be a dry hole. Another way to improve the odds is to contract for terms that allow you to enlarge your interest in the venture in the event it appears to be successful. Receiving a larger share after the venture pays out, or purchasing additional interest at preestablished favorable terms after additional information is available, are common examples.

Reducing the Capital at Risk

There are two main approaches to reducing the front-end costs of any venture. The first method is to obtain especially beneficial terms through effective negotiations, or by leverage, because of an inherent advantage stemming from (1) available funding, (2) favorable leasehold relative to the prospect, or (3) proprietary knowledge, tools, or skills without which the prospect is unattractive.

The second method by which cost can be reduced involves the voluntary surrender of some share of the venture in exchange for a proportional reduction in front-end exposure. Common examples of the second method are provided by conventions such as farm-outs, where the leaseholder exchanges a substantial share of the interest in the leasehold for the commitment of another company to test the acreage by drilling an exploratory well. Companies also carry out joint ventures with other firms, often cross-assigning interests in several deals.

All such conventions are perfectly legitimate methods of mitigating risk, with one important *caveat:* it is essential that dealmakers understand clearly just how much value they are giving up in exchange for the desired financial safety. Many times the tradeoff is, in fact, inappropriate, and the value surrendered is much greater than the incremental safety warrants. This is especially true where a diversified portfolio provides additional risk protection.

Alleviating Risk through Diversification

Diversification is a well-known concept in the securities investment business, leading to the wide employment of portfolios of common stocks, bonds, precious metals, and other securities. The same principle applies to portfolios of exploration ventures, which are covered later in this chapter.

Common Methods for Acquiring Petroleum Rights

Staged Exploration

Theoretically, the most efficient economic process for petroleum exploration and development is staged, where capital is invested over time in a series of systematic risk decisions, each decision weighing investment level against the risk and reward that are perceived to attend the project at that stage of its evolution **(Figure 40)**.

But pure, staged exploration is rare. In trends where many companies are competing simultaneously for acreage, high front-end payments—caused by competitive leasing or sealed bonus bidding—force firms to make early investments that are commonly larger than pure, staged exploration could justify. Also, companies properly use geotechnology, such as seismic, reservoir studies, and geochemistry, to acquire knowledge bearing directly on the risk-reward question. For reasons of competitive advantage, such geotechnical knowledge is held confidential. Unfortunately, such

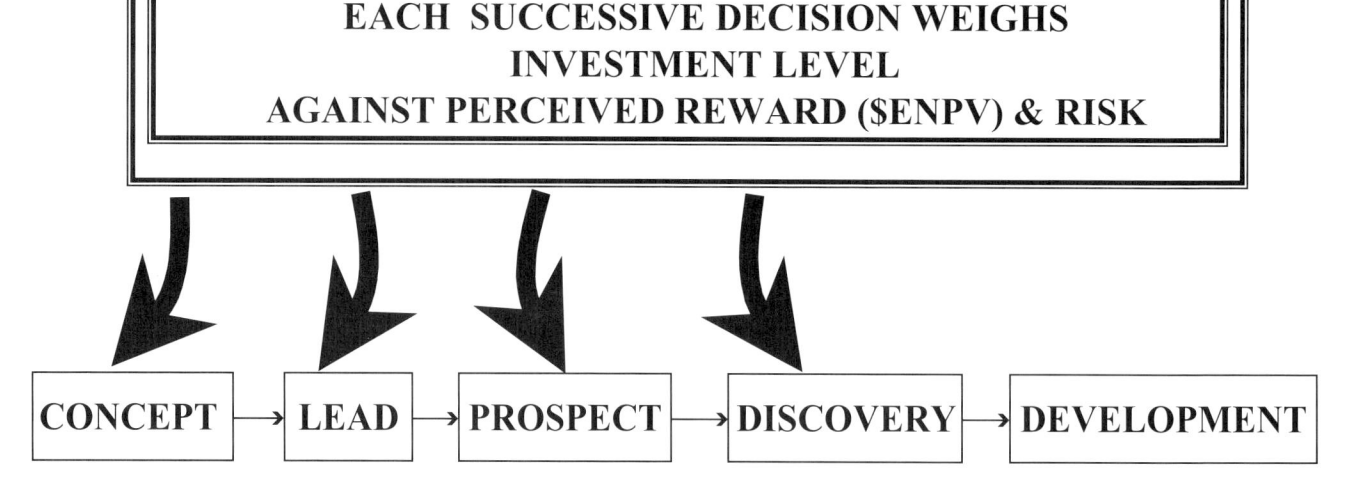

Figure 40 *Staged exploration.*

competitive advantage is fleeting, so companies have learned to act quickly on their confidential findings of geotechnical information. "The secret is, there are almost no secrets—and they don't stay secret very long."

In large international contract areas within which the operating company has no competitors, staged exploration is compromised because large signature bonuses and/or work commitments are ordinarily required before the operator can even begin to acquire critical geotechnical data that address the risk-reward questions. Once a large block is acquired, the freedom from competition within the acreage block may induce a certain amount of complacency, thus encouraging delays that reduce exploration efficiency from the optimum. In some cases, however, there may be real benefits in such delays, as suggested by option pricing theory (p. 52). Finally, unique contract terms may distort and impede efficient decision making.

Conditions of Acquisition

Except for most of the U.S. and parts of Canada, minerals are ordinarily owned by the state rather than by private individuals or companies. Rights to explore for and produce such minerals are acquired in at least six different ways, as discussed previously. However, except for some uncommon situations where mineral prospectivity is seen to be quite unpromising or state representatives are in collusion with favored firms, private companies usually compete for mineral rights. Such competition takes many forms, but it ordinarily involves proprietary data and/or interpretations as to (1) resource size, chance of project success, and profitability; (2) terms designed to appeal to the grantor of the license; and (3) some specified timeframe for offers and decisions. *In one form or another, companies bid for mineral rights, but the particular method of acquisition itself has substantial impact on the overall profitability of the venture.*

Sealed Bonus Bidding

Sealed bonus bidding is common in the U.S. and Canada, as well as in some international theaters such as Venezuela. It is the method that is most detrimental to operators and most advantageous to mineral owners. Sealed bonus bidding has two main drawbacks—the "Winner's Curse," and the "Ubiquitous Overbid."

The Winner's Curse

The phenomenon of the Winner's Curse, first recognized and discussed by Capen, Clapp, and Campbell in 1971, has been incorrectly characterized as, "If you won the bid, you paid too much." A more accurate articulation is, "If you won the bid and the tract turns out to be productive, you probably overestimated the value, expressed as net present value (NPV), and therefore you probably won't make your anticipated return. If the tract turns out to be dry, you probably overestimated expected value and paid too much for it on a risk-reward basis."

The uncertainty surrounding prospect reserves is the primary cause of the Winner's Curse: given the high variance of the lognormal reserves distribution, and the likelihood of several unintentional overestimates among any group of competitive bidders, it follows that the firm that overestimates by the most is likely to be the highest bidder **(Figure 41)**. Because of the award procedure and competitive secrecy, group wisdom about the tract value doesn't prevail. In fact, the bidder who most exceeds group wisdom usually wins the bid. Moreover, firms can't average-out their estimates with overestimates and underestimates on other tracts because underestimates usually generate bids too low to win tracts!

What are the effective remedies to counteract the Winner's Curse? Most important is to revise the criterion

Reserves are lognormal, so bids are lognormal

It's easy to overestimate

"Group wisdom" doesn't prevail

Bidder who most exceeds group wisdom wins bid

Sealed-bid method prevents "averaging out"

(M = million in this figure)

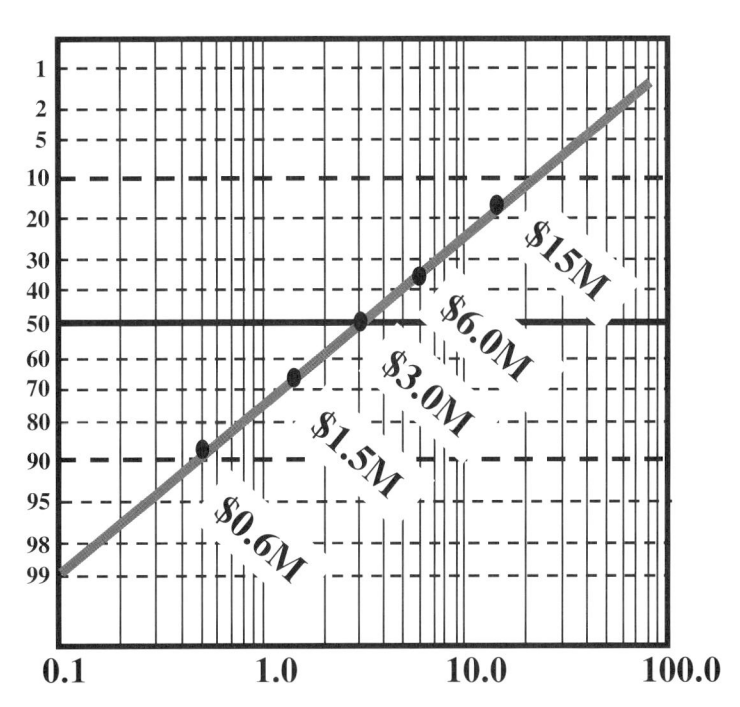

Figure 41 *Sealed bidding for uncertain reserves leads to the Winner's Curse.*

for success: *The goal is not to win the tract; the goal is to add value—to make money.* Secondly, limit the bid to some deep discount of the tract expected net present value (ENPV): the more uncertainty, the deeper the discount. Naturally, this presupposes that anticipated competitive bid levels for the particular sale are expected to rise above threshold trend per-acre prices of, say 5–10% of ENPV or anticipated minimum bid levels, as they did in the 1996–98 Gulf of Mexico sales. Third, bid widely: recognizing the large uncertainties inherent in exploration, firms should bid on all blocks perceived to have positive expected value. Fourth, encourage a detached, disciplined bidding attitude, to wit, *"If we can't get this tract for our price, we don't want it."* Fifth, as our industry was able to do in 1983, encourage the state to reduce the intensity of competition by offering very many tracts, as the U.S. Minerals Management Service (U.S.M.M.S.) does through area-wide sales. Finally, seek other ways to acquire mineral rights, such as with private treaties and through farm-ins, trades, or acquisitions.

Adoption of the area-wide leasing procedure by the U.S.M.M.S. in 1983 reduced the intensity of competition for Gulf of Mexico leases. Before 1983, competing companies like Shell, Arco, and Chevron were using deep bid discounts and bidding widely **(Figure 42)**. They were bidding efficiently—acquiring their acreage for fewer dollars than others like Exxon, Mobil, Gulf, Tenneco, and Texaco, who were concentrating their bids and paying top dollar.

After area-wide sales began, overall bid prices dropped to 12.5% of their former level.[12] Some companies, such as Shell, Chevron, and Amoco, continued to bid efficiently and kept acquiring offshore acreage for proportionately fewer dollars **(Figure 43)**. Others, such as Exxon, Texaco, and Mobil, had apparently learned from their prior bidding experience and switched to efficient bidding. On the other hand, a few firms, notably Arco/Vastar and Unocal, apparently lost their corporate memories and now became inefficient bidders. Some latecomers, such as Kerr-McGee and Amerada, bid very aggressively but inefficiently.

The Ubiquitous Overbid

The second operative drawback of sealed bonus bidding is the Ubiquitous Overbid of Megill and Wightman (1984), defined simply as "the money left on the table"—the difference between the winning bids and the second bids, as a percentage of the winning bids. From the company's point of view, the overbid represents a totally wasted investment. Although counterintuitive, the fact is that with less competition the average percentage overbid tended to *increase*, from about 50% pre-1983 **(Figure 44)** to about 75% post-1983 **(Figure 45)**. When we deal only with

---

[12]This compares average bid prices on a nominal dollar basis; on a "real" basis, i.e., taking inflation into account, the average per-acre reduction of bids is much greater, probably to about 4% to 5% pre-area-wide sales average.

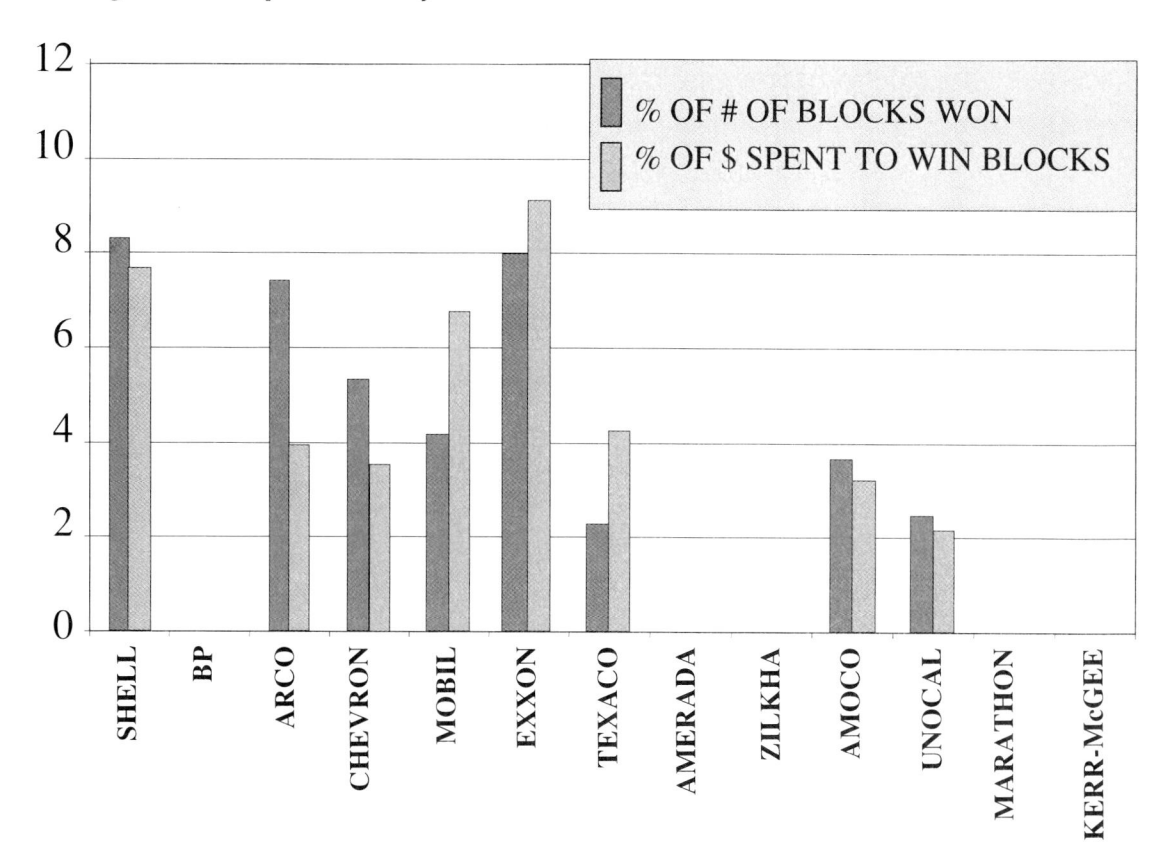

96 Management of Exploration Projects as Business Ventures

Figure 42 *Net purchases by company: Gulf of Mexico sales, 1972–82 (figure courtesy of Robert Clapp). Compare with **Figure 43**.*

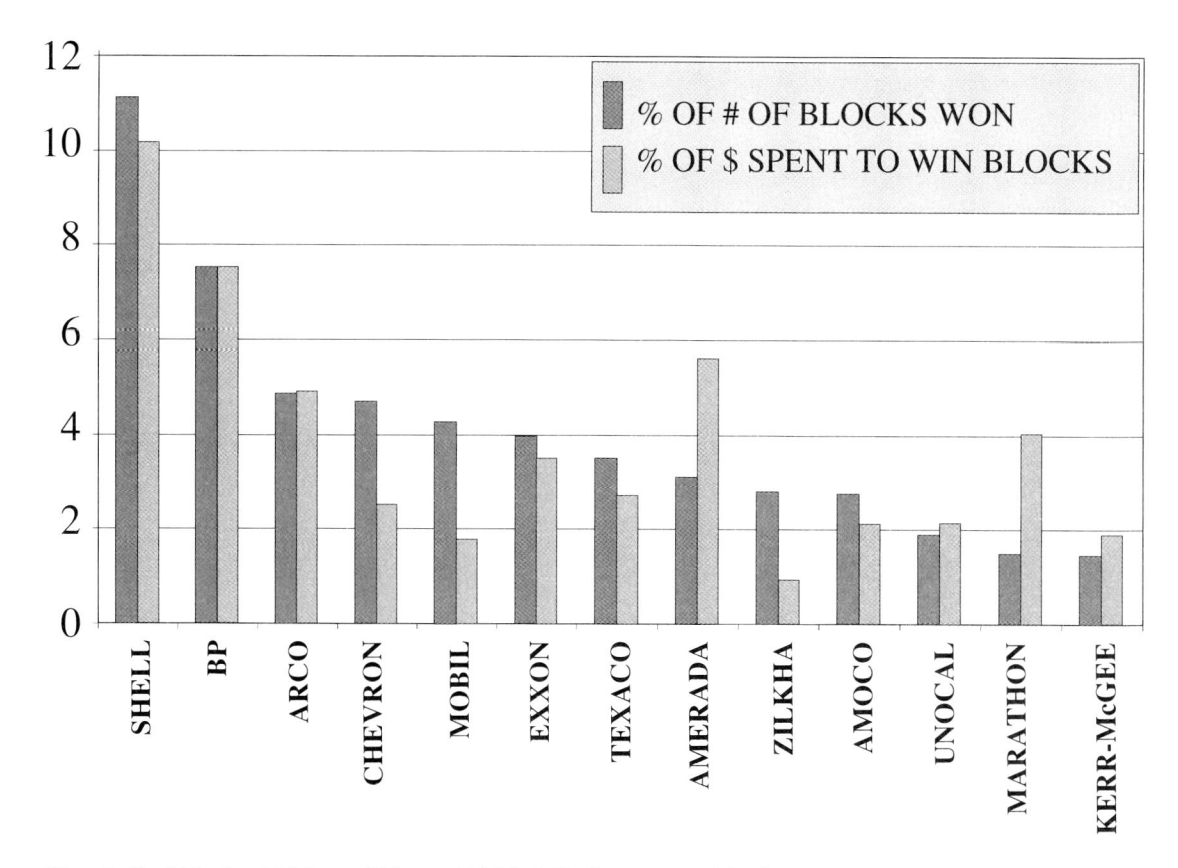

Figure 43 *Gulf of Mexico bidding efficiency (1988–95). Compare with **Figure 42**.*

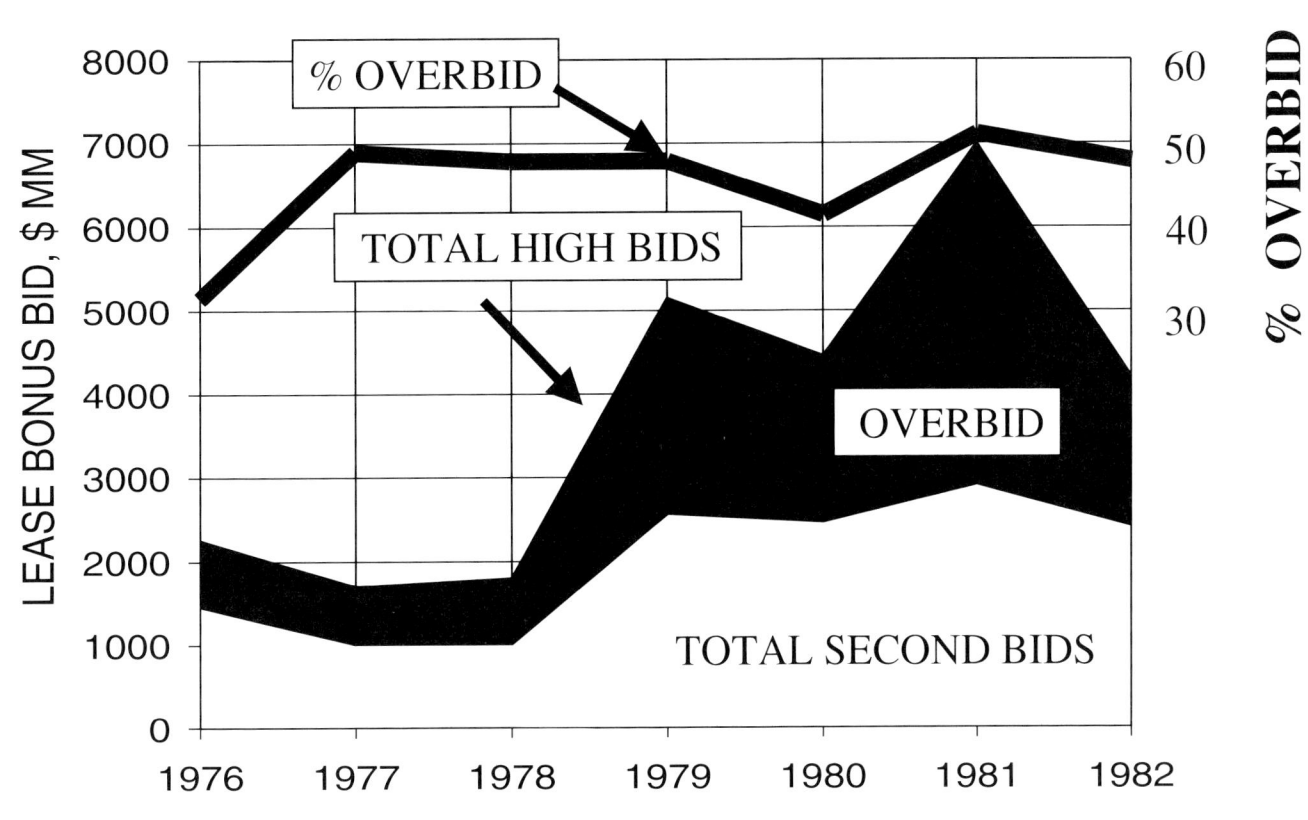

Figure 44 *High bids and second bids; GOM lease overbids averaged about 50% pre-1983 (from Megill, 1984).*

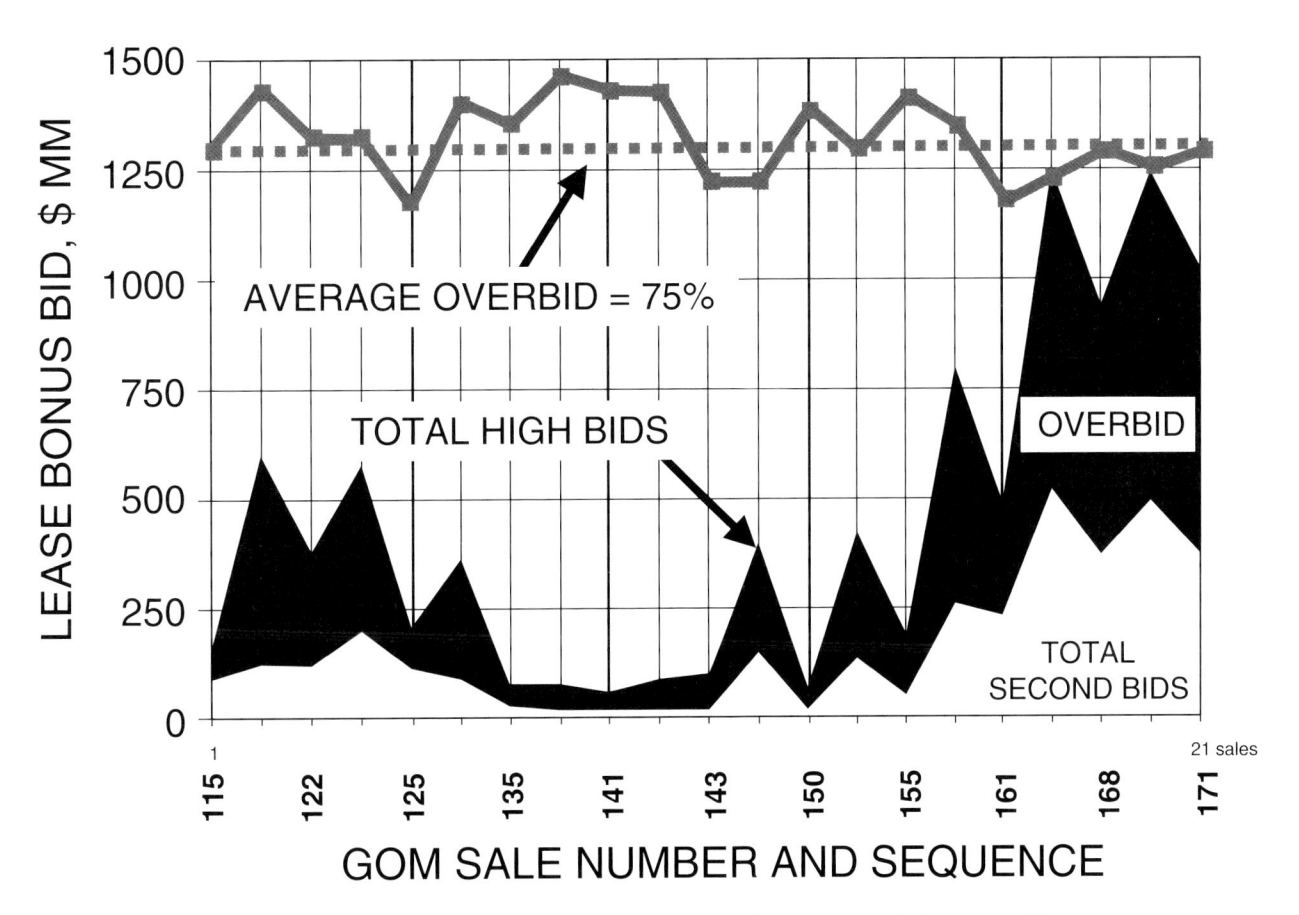

Figure 45 *High bids and second bids; area-wide GOM lease overbids averaged 75% post-1983.*

multiple-bid tracts, the percentage overbid becomes smaller—45% pre-1983 and 57% post-1983. Now, overbids are characteristically large, simply because bids—based mostly on reserves potential—are log-normally distributed, hence the difference between the first and second bid is generally large, compared with, say, the fifth and sixth bids, because of the log scale. As Megill and Wightman pointed out, prospectors and their managers must understand that the overbid is intrinsic to the sealed bid process. Overbidding is part of the mathematics and can't be eliminated.

It is instructive to compare levels of overbidding before and after the adoption of area-wide sales: **Figure 44** was made by Bob Megill in 1983 and shows that the average overbid before area-wide sales was about 50%, whereas **Figure 45** (Rose, 1999) shows that the average overbid rose afterward to around 75%. However, since the entire bidding level had been so greatly reduced, as it was starting in 1983, the pain of the increased overbid could be accommodated more easily.

Summary

Thus sealed bonus bidding has these two main drawbacks: the Winner's Curse and the Ubiquitous Overbid. However, their negative effects can be ameliorated by substantially discounting the tract's expected value to determine appropriate bid levels, and by reducing the intensity of competition on individual tracts so the net impact is economically tolerable. Nevertheless, even after area-wide sales began, the key to success in bonus bidding remains to persuade executives that their intuition cannot beat the effects of the Winner's Curse and the Ubiquitous Overbid.

The actual effect of the Winner's Curse and overbidding on the overall profitability of U.S. oil companies operating in the Gulf of Mexico is chilling—Lohrenz (1988) reported that the total industry investment in the Gulf had not yet paid out and likely would not ever achieve actual profitability. Furthermore, if area-wide bidding had not been adopted, it is quite possible that the economic development of deep-water discoveries in the Gulf of Mexico during the late 1980s and 1990s would never have been possible.

Serial, Time-constrained Auctions

The second common method for acquiring petroleum rights is the serial, time-constrained confidential auction, in which a deal is shown individually and privately to several potential buyers over a short period, with an announced deadline in the near future. Such deals function like sealed-bid sales, with the same drawbacks to purchasers and advantages to the deal seller. Whichever potential buyer values the deal the most is likely to submit the best offer, and confidentiality discourages the outside input that might indicate overestimation. Near-term deadlines promote similarity to sealed bonus bidding. However, if the deal seller sells a fractional share, a limit is thus set on the upside potential, and the inherent advantages of competitive confidential bidding have been eliminated.

Oral Auctions

The third common method is the oral auction, which is still used by some U.S. states and onshore federal lease sales, and in privately managed sales of producing properties. Theoretically this method should be more attractive to deal buyers because there is no need for more than a fractional difference between the high bid and the second bid, thus eliminating the overbid and the inherent waste associated with it. However, competitive egos often seem to produce the same effect as the Winner's Curse, generating bids that indicate greatly over-valued tracts. So success in oral auctions requires disciplined bidding, as well as the recognition that the behavior of other bidders may provide useful on-site information about your own valuation of the tract—whether it may be too high or too low.

Performance Contracts

Performance bidding (or so-called work-contracts) should eliminate both the Winner's Curse and the Ubiquitous Overbid because, theoretically, operators should limit their bids to whatever a prudent explorer would spend to explore any given block, based on tract size, geology, and geophysics, not on perceived reserves potential. This sounds good in principle; in practice, however, the competitive desire to obtain the block often translates into extra wells or better terms. Such measures are not necessarily bad, as long as decisionmakers recognize that the Winner's Curse is operating on all such overages and extras. Obviously, the worst of both worlds is represented by acquisition procedures combining performance bidding as well as competitive sealed bonus bidding.

Private Treaties

The best method for the deal buyer to acquire petroleum rights is through private treaties or simple bilateral negotiations, where a given deal is shown to only one buyer at a time and multiple buyers are never looking at the same deal simultaneously. This is the method traditionally employed in conventional onshore U.S. exploration. It is best for the deal buyer because it avoids the Winner's Curse as well as the Ubiquitous Overbid, and it's worst for the seller for the same reasons. Such deals may approach staged exploration if the deal involves a new concept or tool and competition is as yet minimal. Such situations, however, don't last long.

Corporate Acquisitions

Our final method for acquiring petroleum rights is through corporate acquisitions—buying another company's reserves by buying the company. Friendly takeovers function like private treaties, generally being most favorable to the buyers. Unfriendly takeovers that lead to bidding wars function more like sealed-bid sales—the more bidders, the more favorable to the company being bought. However, the impact of the Winner's Curse may be relatively less because there is generally less variance surrounding a company's true worth than there is around an offshore exploration block.

Sanctity of Contracts versus Subsequent Renegotiations

All of the observations and comments have assumed the sanctity of contracts—"a deal's a deal." If it's possible to renegotiate a deal later, after disappointing results have been confirmed, then all bets are off and advantages and disadvantages of the previous six methods are obviated. This by itself may suggest a seventh method of acquiring rights through subsequent renegotiations. Such methods are anathema to most Western corporations, perhaps because when such subsequent renegotiations took place in the past they represented violations of existing contracts. However, perhaps this is a limiting Western cultural value—suppose we approach international exploration, from the start, as an uncertain business that should logically be carried out through agreements that expressly allow for changes in terms, depending on what the results of exploration turn out to be?

This may represent the last, best way to improve exploration profitability—to develop new, flexible types of contracts that allow us to approach the efficiency of staged exploration. Of course, such contracts presuppose that an informed landowner or state must be able to verify the legitimacy of the critical geotechnical expenditures and findings that impact the changing risk-versus-reward picture, and thus, the changing terms. Some aspects of production-sharing contracts contain such flexibilities.

Conclusion

Small companies or independent operators especially should realize that the method of sale itself plays a big part in the profitability of the purchase or sale. Stated simply, when you're selling, try to utilize the sealed bid or auction model. When you're buying, buy through private treaty or performance bidding.

Prospect and Play Portfolios

Requirements

A prospect portfolio (Rose, 1992a) is selected from an inventory of exploratory prospects. The portfolio listing displays their respective costs, chances of commercial success, estimated mean reserves and mean NPVs, risked mean reserves and risked NPVs (the latter are derived by multiplying estimated mean reserves and NPVs each by chance of commercial success), and preferred economic ranking measures such as ENPV and risked investment efficiency.

Each of the prospects in the inventory may be effectively compared and ranked with the other prospects because the same processes for estimating reserves, chance of success, and profitability have been used for all. Consistent corporate hurdles and discount rates have been applied to each prospect, and meaningful economic measures have been consistently used to rank the various ventures in the inventory. So the inventory represents those prospects that the firm is *considering*; the portfolio represents the exploratory wells that will actually be *drilled*.

Inventories become another selective screen in choosing prospects for the company's annual or semi-annual exploration portfolio, but only if the various candidate ventures considered for entry can be evaluated quickly and efficiently, both geotechnically as well as economically.

Similarly, a portfolio of exploration plays may be selected from an inventory of candidate exploration plays. Ordinarily, however, play inventories and portfolios are considerably smaller than prospect inventories and portfolios; moreover, prospects and plays are segregated into separate inventories and portfolios. Because of their inherent differences in scope and timeframe, plays and prospects should not be included and compared in the same inventory. It is far better to maintain two separate inventories, one for plays and another for prospects.

Benefits

If these conditions are met, the assembly of a prospect or play portfolio from an inventory of qualifying prospects or plays can significantly improve corporate exploration performance, for at least six reasons:

Optimizing Capital Allocation

If the selected portfolio contains those projects that rank highest, using risked investment efficiency (see p. 54), it will produce the highest possible capacity to create value for the firm. A ranking based on ENPV will produce a portfolio having the highest ENPV, but because investment costs may vary among ventures, that ranking may ignore venture risk; at the same time it may not maximize value. Any economic measure that includes a provision for risk aversion, such as calculation of OWI, will necessarily reflect value reduced from optimum, in consideration of the reduced vulnerability to loss.

Forecasting Performance

Prospect portfolios **(Table 20)** are one of the most effective tools to improve exploration performance. Objective professional estimates of an individual prospect's chance of commercial success, in combination with reliable forecasts of mean reserves (and thus prospect mean ENPV), provide the basis for predicting the following:

1. approximate number of discoveries from a given multi-well program;
2. approximate total new commercial reserves added (p. 33) and their present value; and
3. approximate program cost-of-finding, using project cost forecasts.

Naturally, the accuracy of such program forecasts is keenly sensitive to (1) average prospect discovery probability; (2) variance in individual prospect-reserves distributions; (3) the predictive skill and lack of bias of the geoscientists; and (4) the number of prospects in the inventory. Accordingly, the predictive ability of the play portfolio is much inferior to prospect portfolios. However, play inventories are quite useful because they facilitate the comparison of different exploration plays.

Guiding Geotechnology

Provisional risk analysis may be carried out on emerging prospects and plays before they are ready for drilling to identify those ventures that seem to have the greatest economic promise. To maximize cost-effective use of geoscientists and their tools, specific exploration technologies should then be focused on the highest-ranked anomalies, leads, and trends, and especially on the critical geologic chance factors (see p. 38).

Assessing Predictive Performance

In order to construct an inventory (from which are selected the best ventures for the company's drilling portfolio), estimates of reserves, chance of success, critical risk, initial production rates, percentage declines, and drilling and completion costs must already have been estimated for each venture. Thus half the task of geotechnical performance evaluation has already been carried out—and preserved! After the results of each venture are known—successful or unsuccessful—the actual results can be assembled by the exploration team from drilling and completion reports and postdrill reviews and compared with the predictions. So the inventory/portfolio process helps promote systematic performance review. This approach is not as readily applied to play analysis, however, simply because of the long time elapsed between forecasts and discernible results common to play development.

Eliminating Predictive Bias

Motivational bias expressing overly optimistic or overly conservative estimates of reserves, chance, and profitability, can, with a reasonable number of trials (wells), be detected, analyzed, and corrected through feedback and subsequently modified procedures by geotechnical staff. By reducing such bias we can improve portfolio performance and create added value for the company.

Scheduling Future Work

The selected portfolio forms the basis for planning and scheduling the work necessary to carry out the constituent ventures over the period of the portfolio.

Lognormality and Performance of Prospect Portfolios

Most knowledgeable explorationists and many of their managers now accept the principle that prospect-reserves distributions are lognormal, reflecting natural processes of multiplication [area (acres) × average net pay (feet) × HC-recovery (bbl/acre-foot)]. Accordingly the distribution of most corporate balanced portfolios is also approximately lognormal.

What is remarkable is that many corporate officers and high-level exploration managers have not grasped the implications of this principle as it impacts the magnitudes and timeframes of corporate exploration results. In particular they do not seem to understand the expected natural pattern of annual portfolio outcomes: predominantly mediocre annual results punctuated occasionally by exceptionally good years and bad years. It can be demonstrated that such fluctuations may have nothing whatsoever to do with geotechnical or managerial skill; rather, they may be the natural consequence of repeated sampling from natural lognormal prospect-reserves distributions.

A common manifestation of management's misunderstanding of the lognormal principle is their continual and excessive reorganization of ongoing exploration programs, in the well-intentioned but mistaken belief that such adjustment and interference (= "tweaking") will improve year-to-year exploration results. But exploration is inherently a sustained, long-term process plagued in most corporations by short-term interferences. There are indeed effective criteria by which exploration performance can be judged, to distinguish luck from skill; however, prediction of annual discovery volumes is not an effective criterion unless the exploration portfolio contains 60 to 100 or more trials.

Table 20 *A model prospect portfolio (prospects are ranked in this list by ENPV).*

Prospect	Dry-hole Costs ($MM)	Chance of Success	Reserves (MMBOE) if Successful P10%/P90%	P10%/P90% Mean	Mean NPV ($MM)	Risked Mean Reserves (MMBOE)	Expected Investment ($MM)	OWI	ENPV ($MM)	Investment Efficiency	RAV
A	6.2	0.05	5.0	50.0	112.5	275.0	2.5	15.0	0.03	7.86	7.86 / 15.0 = 0.52	0.103
B	5.4	0.10	2.4	24.0	54.0	120.0	2.4	8.8	0.07	7.14	7.14 / 8.8 = 0.81	0.224
C	3.2	0.20	2.2	8.0	16.0	32.0	1.6	6.0	0.26	3.84	3.84 / 6.0 = 0.64	0.445
D	4.0	0.15	1.0	10.0	22.5	45.0	1.5	7.2	0.14	3.35	3.35 / 7.2 = 0.47	0.214
E	1.8	0.15	0.6	6.0	13.5	24.0	0.9	3.3	0.33	2.07	2.07 / 3.3 = 0.63	0.305
F	2.0	0.20	1.1	4.0	9.0	14.0	0.8	2.0	0.35	1.20	1.20 / 2.0 = 0.60	0.197
G	0.8	0.25	0.3	2.0	4.4	6.0	0.5	1.8	1.00	0.90	0.90 / 1.8 = 0.50	0.516
H	1.5	0.20	0.5	3.0	6.6	9.0	0.6	6.1	0.39	0.60	0.60 / 6.1 = 0.10	0.111
I	0.5	0.30	0.2	1.0	2.2	2.5	0.3	0.8	1.00	0.40	0.40 / 0.8 = 0.50	0.309
J	0.4	0.40	0.1	0.5	1.0	1.0	0.2	1.0	1.00	0.16	0.16 / 1.0 = 0.16	0.137
N = 10	25.80	2.00		108.5		528.5	11.3	52.0	4.57	27.52	IE program = 0.53	2.56
		Avg = .2							Avg = .46			

NOTES: 1) Dry-hole cost includes exploratory drilling and completion, land, G&G, and overhead.
2) Firm's r=5/50MM=.1.
3) Firm's RT=1/r=1/.1=10.
4) Order of prospects changes if ranked on investment efficiency (IE) or RAV.

ANTICIPATED RESULTS: This portfolio of 10 exploratory wells is a balanced program including three lower-risk extension wells (G, I, & J), five medium-risk trend wildcats (C, D, E, F, & H), and two high-risk new-field wildcats (A & B). The most probable outcome of this program is: two discoveries, totaling 11.3 MMBOE reserves, having a total mean program expected value of $27.52MM. Cost of finding should be about 25.8/11.3 = $2.30/BOE. Program EPV/Investment = 27.52/52 = 0.53.

Chapter 6   101

Table 21 *Simulation of results for a prospect portfolio.*

We have an inventory of 20 exploratory prospects. The prospects have varying chances of success, and each has a lognormal distribution of reserves (if successful) with P10% divided by P90% = 13. In this exercise, we will use the given probabilities and simulate the results of drilling the inventory. To sample randomly from the lognormal reserves distribution of each successful prospect, multiply (Mean Reserves if Successful) by (Multiplier).

Prospect	Chance of Success	Mean Reserves if Successful (MMBOE)	Expected Reserves (MMBOE)	Actual Outcome Multiplier	Reserves (MMBOE)
A	0.5	0.87	0.44		
B	0.1	4.96	0.50		
C	0.3	2.17	0.65		
D	0.5	0.56	0.28		
E	0.1	7.61	0.76		
F	0.3	2.44	0.73		
G	0.2	3.64	0.73		
H	0.4	1.18	0.47		
I	0.1	10.82	1.08		
J	0.3	1.74	0.52		
K	0.4	1.37	0.55		
L	0.2	3.16	0.63		
M	0.5	0.72	0.36		
N	0.2	2.81	0.56		
O	0.2	4.24	0.85		
P	0.5	0.39	0.20		
Q	0.1	5.96	0.60		
R	0.4	1.01	0.40		
S	0.4	1.53	0.61		
T	0.3	1.94	0.58		
n = 20	6 Discoveries Expected		11.50 MMBOE		

Accordingly, assessing exploration performance based on annual portfolios may require 1–5+ years, depending on the size and aggressiveness of the firm and the number and character of ventures in the annual portfolio.

Predictability versus Portfolio Size

Assuming that the staff's estimates of prospect reserves and chance of success are geotechnically responsible and unbiased (utilizing the estimating concepts and procedures described previously), the number of prospects in the portfolio influences the precision and reliability of forecasts about portfolio results. The average chance of prospect success and the prospect-reserves variance also influence portfolio predictability.

But understandably, management commonly wants to know how many wells are required to make useful forecasts of portfolio outcomes. However, in providing a proper answer, management must be asked, *What level of confidence do you require?—50%? 68%? 80%? 90%? 95%? or 99%?*

A useful answer can be provided in at least two different forms:

1. A range of new reserves or NPV added, such as "80% confidence in new reserves of 3.5 to 18.5 million BOE (barrels oil equivalent)"; or
2. 50% confidence (or some other probabilistic confidence level) that "*at least* 8 million BOE or $25MM NPV will result."

Table 21 represents a model 20-well exploratory portfolio for a domestic U.S. firm. Prospect discovery probabilities are 10%, 20%, 30%, 40%, and 50% (four

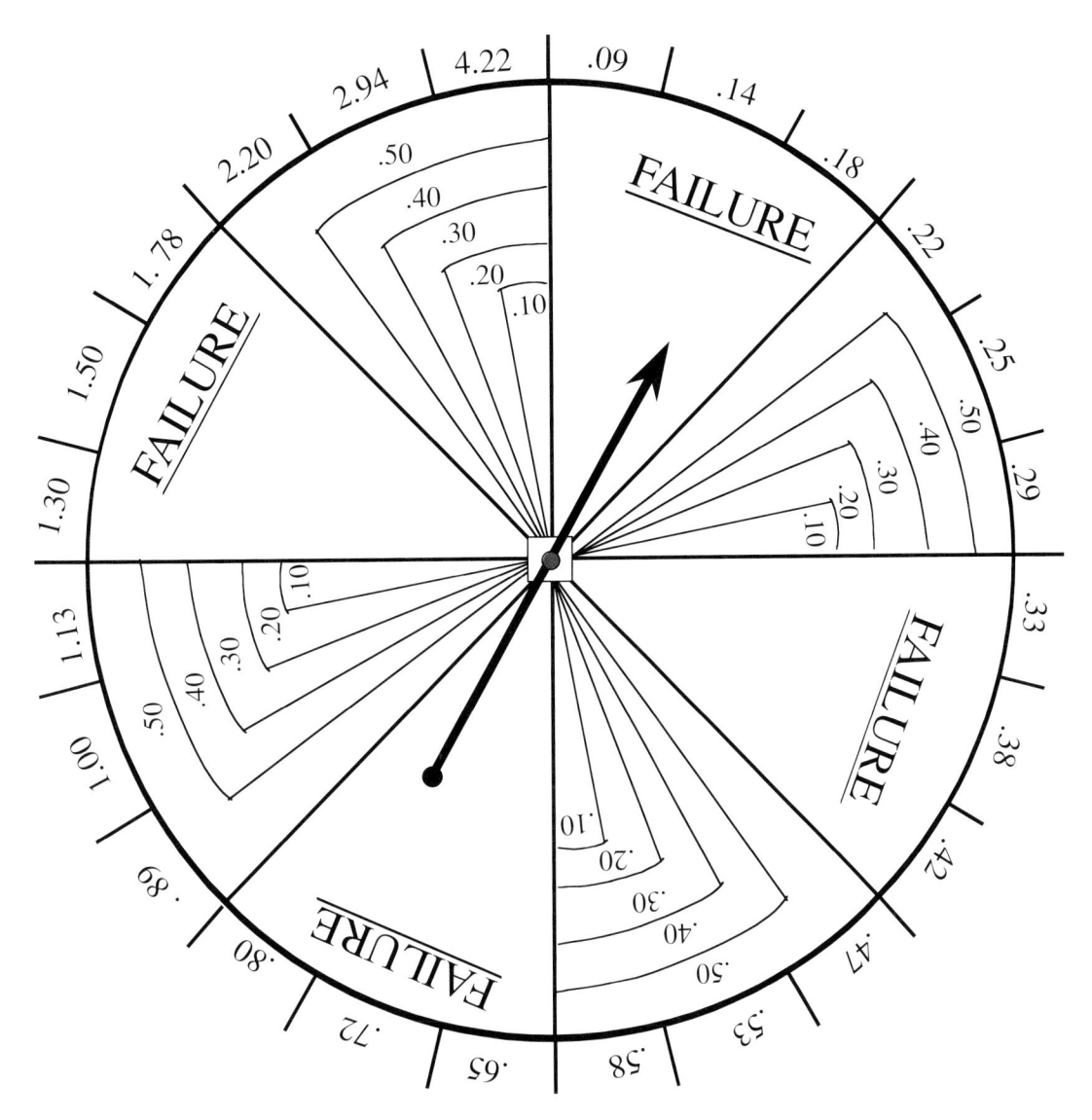

Figure 46 *Spinner for simulating chance of success and reserves discovered.*

prospects in each chance class), with a portfolio average chance of success of 30%; all chance categories are represented by a mechanical spinner **(Figure 46)**. All prospect-reserves distributions are lognormal, with estimated prospect mean reserves of 11.5 MM bbl and an 80% range (P90%–P10% estimates) of 3.0 MM bbl to 22.6 MM bbl. Median (P50%) is 8.8 MMBOE.

All prospects have P10%/P90% ratios of 13, as established by the outer multiplier ring on the spinner **(Figure 46)**. This represents a minor inconsistency because variance typically increases among high-risk, large-potential prospects. To operate this simulation, each prospect is first tried for success or failure, using the graduated inner ring. If a prospect is a discovery, the next spin determines the amount of new reserves found (outer ring). If the prospect is a dry hole, the next spin determines success or failure on the next well. Obviously, employing a spinner is a visually satisfying alternative to a computer-driven Monte Carlo simulation, which may not be understood.

Figure 47 shows that as such a portfolio increases from 20 wells to 100 wells, the confidence in forecast results improves, the P10%–P90% range becoming relatively narrower with respect to the mean.

Practically speaking, as many as 80 trials (four successive **Table 21** portfolios) may be required to provide 80% predictive confidence in new discovered reserves volumes equal to ±50% of the predicted mean of 4 × 11.5 = 46 MMBOE, if that is the level of confidence management desires. If a more conservative portfolio were selected, one in which the wells had lower-variance reserves and higher chances of success, perhaps as few as 40 wells would be enough to deliver an equivalent level of predictive confidence. At the other end of the scale, for a company involved in high-risk (Pc = 10%), large-reserve (100 to 500 MMBOE), high-variance

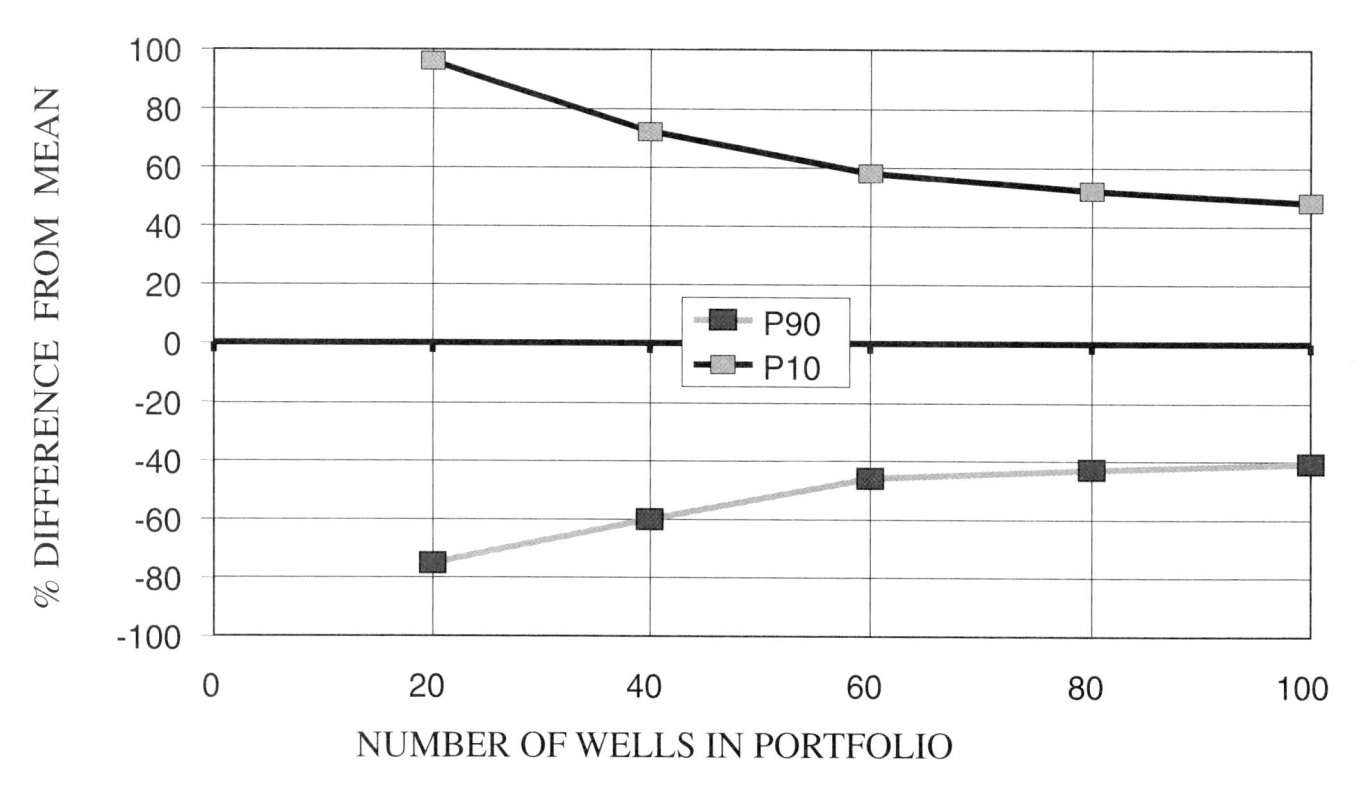

Figure 47 *Predictive accuracy of portfolio performance improves with the number of wells in the portfolio.*

prospects, an inventory of 250 wells or more might be required to provide adequate confidence in the forecast outcomes (Schuyler, 1989).

If the portfolio's size is inadequate to deliver the confidence in forecast outcomes that management expects, at least six possible solutions exist:

1. Add more wells to the portfolio (which of course will increase exploration expenditures proportionately);
2. Expand the portfolio by drilling more joint-venture wells (this increases sample size without significant increase in total exploration expenditures);
3. Consider the portfolio over a multi-year period, i.e., the forecast might cover a 3-year or 5-year prediction with running averages;
4. Modify the character of the portfolio by including more low-risk wells at the expense of some high-risk wells (of course this usually also entails substantial reductions in reserves potential);
5. Focus geotechnical exploration tools on high-risk prospects, to either:
   - improve confidence in critical risk geologic factors and raise Pc; or
   - condemn such prospects in favor of other, more attractive ventures; or
6. Management may revise its expectations for the level of confidence required in portfolio forecasts, i.e., they may accept a more realistic, increased level of risk consistent with real exploration variance.

The key point for management to realize is that any portfolio can be routinely analyzed by Monte Carlo simulation to provide various confidence levels associated with corresponding reserves outcomes. Then management can decide how the portfolio should be adjusted to provide the predictive confidence they require. Obviously, if prospect parameters are biased, the portfolio will lose much of its effectiveness.

For companies operating in a variety of exploration theaters, especially those desiring a diversified, balanced portfolio, it is important to recognize that divisions operating in mature provinces may be expected to provide prospects for the smaller-reserve, low-risk end of the overall portfolio, whereas divisions exploring in frontier basins may provide ventures for the high-potential, higher-risk part.

Principles of Exploration Portfolio Management

It is far beyond the scope of this book to review the principles of modern portfolio management (Bernstein, 1996; Markowitz, 1952). The key point here for both explorationists and their managers to realize, however, is that the same principles of risk-reward optimization apply to an exploration portfolio that apply to portfolios of various common stocks and to other financial ventures.

Exploration management can be provided with a risk-reward diagram showing many possible portfolios

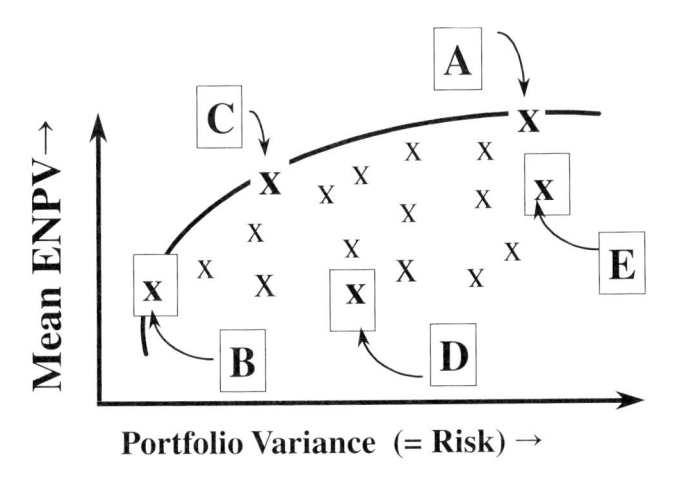

Figure 48 *The efficient frontier.*

in which the mix of constituent prospects is varied (Figure 48). The horizontal axis expresses *risk*, usually as the variance or standard deviation of each possible portfolio combination, or more pragmatically, as the chance of some unacceptably low program outcome. The vertical axis expresses *reward*, usually as the expected mean reserves added (or equivalent NPV). Management can then select the portfolio that best balances their need for value addition with their need to minimize risk.

For example, combination A would represent a portfolio that maximizes ENPV but also represents an unacceptably high level of risk. Combination B would minimize risk but would also reduce ENPV to only about one-third the ENPV of combination A, which also might be unacceptable. Combination C might be a choice that maximizes value consistent with acceptable risk. However, portfolio combinations such as D or E should never be chosen; instead, selected portfolios should always lie along the "efficient frontier" whose value is maximized consistently with acceptable risk.

However, it is essential for both exploration management as well as the professional geotechnical staff to realize that a portfolio selected exclusively to *maximize value added* (one using prospect risked investment efficiency) may be associated with risks unacceptable to management. Such a portfolio may need to be modified in favor of another mix of prospects that provides the desired safety and accepts the accompanying reduced value.

Problems with Exploration Portfolios

Most modern oil companies try to construct and maintain prospect portfolios. Nevertheless, characteristic difficulties must be addressed.

Obligatory Wells

Prospect selection for portfolio optimization is the guiding principle in inventory and portfolio management, and this requires ranking, selecting, and rejecting individual ventures. However, many exploration contracts require that certain wells be drilled regardless of how those wells compare with other prospects in the portfolio.

Most firms include such wells in the portfolio for purposes of forecasting portfolio performance and for assessing staff performance in making geotechnical predictions. If they include such obligatory wells in the ranking process, it is only for purposes of general comparison and to allow them to drill the better obligatory wells earlier rather than later. Skillful employment of play-analysis principles and proper sequencing of exploration tasks will greatly reduce the number of obligatory wells that rank low in the inventory rank order.

Maintaining Geotechnical Consistency

In order for the portfolio to function properly, the geotechnical staff must be confident that the ranking of prospects from all divisions and theaters is equitable and consistent, because they correctly recognize that such a portfolio system causes competition for corporate capital. Such equity can be ensured by various means:

1. use of a consistent, geotechnically valid evaluation process and software, by all groups in the firm;
2. annual comparison of predictions versus results, to reveal any groups that consistently demonstrate bias in their prospect forecasts, and whose geotechnical performance therefore needs improvement;
3. deployment of a risk-normalization team of respected senior professionals (geologist, geophysicist, engineer, economist) that reviews all new major prospects and randomly reviews smaller ones;
4. annual exploration conference where each group presents one or two prospects to peer groups from all other units, thus demonstrating a broad application of consistent standards and procedures; and
5. management that demonstrates its commitment to the process by rewarding professional accuracy and integrity of predictions.

Static versus Dynamic Portfolios

All companies would like to have the luxury of selecting their annual exploration portfolio from an inventory of identified, drillable prospects. Such a portfolio would allow them to maximize risk, in part through the discriminating determination of venture shares. As previously discussed, however, portfolios tend to be *dynamic* rather than *static*, and prospects are commonly drilled as they are identified. In order to achieve the benefits of portfolio management, companies may identify several classes of exploratory

Table 22 *Uncertainty leads to common underperformance of exploration portfolios (after Horner, 1990).*

	Estimated Rate of Return (% p.a.)												
Actual Rate of Return	70	60	50	40	30	20	15% cutoff	10	0	–10	–20	–30	
10 ventures at 50%	1	2	4	2	1			Excluded, but really turn out to be attractive					Attractive
20 ventures at 40%		2	4	8	4	2							
50 ventures at 30%			5	10	20	10		**5**					
100 ventures at 20%				10	20	40		**20**	**10**				15% cutoff
200 ventures at 10%	Included, but really turn out to be unattractive				**20**	**40**		80	40	20			Unattractive
500 ventures at 0%						**50**		100	200	100	50		
1000 ventures at –10%								100	200	400	200	100	
	These prospects included							**These prospects excluded**					

prospects they wish to include, and then try to secure such a model portfolio as the year unfolds. The result is to diminish some of the theoretical advantage of portfolio selection. Another aspect of dynamic portfolios is to preselect preferred participation levels in certain classes of prospects, or to employ OWI to indicate the appropriate share for the company (pp. 55 and 92).

Timing Considerations

A second possible goal of portfolio management has to do with optimizing *timing of cash flows.* Ideally, projects should be timed so that excess cash from production revenues will be available when large development projects are expected to begin, and large-scale exploration projects are available when the company has cash flows to use in increasing asset value. Such timing may require precision beyond our present levels of geotechnical and predictive skill, however, and some companies endorse a simpler procedure: rank the portfolio to maximize value, then if money is needed for development, it can be borrowed or derived by selling existing, less profitable properties.

An alternative approach to the dual corporate needs of (1) cash flow and (2) growth could be to set up two noncompeting portfolios, one composed of low-risk ventures that could generate needed cash flows near-term; and the second, composed of higher-risk, large-potential projects that could provide growth. Then the question is, What is the appropriate relative level of funding for the two portfolios?

"Theory of Inevitable Disappointment"

Identification of this fascinating phenomenon is ascribed to Dr. Dennis Horner of Royal Dutch Shell. He recognized that companies assemble portfolios of drilling prospects on the basis of some form of predicted economic ranking, such as investment efficiency (IE), ENPV, or even discounted cash-flow rate of return (DCFROR), and he realized that *actual* performances of the individual constituent ventures would vary, both up and down, from *predicted* mean performance because of the substantial uncertainty that attends exploration ventures (Horner, 1990). That is, some estimates would turn out to be too high and some would be too low. To model what may actually happen in nature if estimators are unbiased, he constructed a table comparing estimated rates-of-return (ROR) with actual rates-of-return for a portfolio in which the economic cutoff was 15% ROR **(Table 22)**.

As Horner pointed out, the portfolio cutoff (vertical line) must be made under conditions of uncertainty, where prospects estimated as less than 15% ROR are excluded. Because predictions vary from actual results, however, some *included* ventures will inevitably underperform expectations, and some *excluded* ventures would have outperformed expectations. Thus the vertical cutoff is wrong, but inevitable, whereas the horizontal cutoff is correct but unattainable. So those ventures shown in bold type in the northeast and southwest quadrants of the diagram will be incorrectly dealt with. The consequence is that the actual performance of the original portfolio will inevitably be lower than the estimated performance— *even if estimates are unbiased.* The prevalent tendency of explorationists to overestimate prospect reserves (optimistic bias) has the effect of aggravating this problem.

Although Horner indicated this to be a problem without a practical solution, there may be at least a partial solution that can be described as the "pilot-fish" concept (pilot-fish are small fish that accompany sharks, deriving their living off the crumbs and morsels not swallowed by the shark during feeding). If large companies can identify small exploitation firms that may be willing to develop small or marginal fields, and can prenegotiate basic deal structures with them, then a discovery that is recognized to be below standard may be promptly conveyed to the smaller, more efficient firm. Such business practices allow the large company to avoid the development cost of a marginally profitable field, and may allow it to recover some incremental cost as a transfer payment from the small firm.

Managing Exploration Plays

Matching Play Attributes to Business Strategies

Successful exploration is the lifeblood of the international oil and gas business. New fields must be found on a regular basis in order to replace the firm's steadily depleting producing fields. But petroleum accumulations usually occur in geologically related families, which we call *plays,* and modern petroleum exploration is characteristically carried out at play scale rather than prospect-scale. Accordingly, the critical exploration business decision concerns which new play to enter, not which prospect to drill. It follows, therefore, that any dedicated modern oil and gas company should have a strategy and process under which it systematically and continuously identifies and evaluates candidate new plays.

Business Consequences of Play Choices

Competent exploration play analysis and play selection involve not only the synthesis of petroleum geoscience, statistics, and economics but also require consideration of (1) present and future business conditions (local and international), and (2) business patterns and requirements that are unique to the firm.

It is clear that successful development of new exploration plays generates a steady supply of new and attractive prospects, which in turn lead to the successive discoveries of profitable oil and gas fields to sustain and even increase the company's reserve base. But there are consequences of participating in a bad play:

1. poor return on invested time, staff, and capital (often an actual loss of capital);
2. the company may miss out on good profits from an alternative play in which it did *not* participate; and
3. competitors benefit from a successful play in your company's absence.

For unsuccessful plays, there are two polar end-members: every company should fervently wish that play failure will occur quickly and unambiguously, leaving geoscientists and management content that a promising idea has been evaluated and disproved efficiently and relatively cheaply. The alternative negative outcome is correctly dreaded—the play that was poorly chosen and improperly negotiated, requiring unnecessarily long and expensive efforts and with tantalizing but ultimately fruitless results.

Negative Impact Is Inversely Proportional to Firm Size

Generally, the negative impacts of a bad play choice are inversely proportional to company size. To very large firms like Exxon-Mobil, Shell, or BP/Amoco, which evaluate dozens of new plays each year and enter perhaps five or ten, a bad play can be shrugged off and balanced against other successful plays, which are expected to carry the cost of unsuccessful ventures so that the overall annual new-play portfolio creates substantial new value.

To intermediate-sized firms, which may evaluate five to ten new plays each year and enter perhaps one or two, a bad play choice usually causes a long-lasting reduction in the company's annual production stream and puts more pressure on the organization to find and enter successful plays or even to purchase existing producing properties. Thus the consequences are inconvenient or even serious, but ordinarily can be tolerated.

For small firms, which may evaluate only a few new plays each year and actually enter a new play every two to five years, the consequences of a bad play choice can be disastrous. As a result, smaller companies tend to choose new plays in more established petroleum-producing areas, participating as minority partners, or choose simply to drill a series of independently submitted individual prospects in areas where they already have expertise, thus foregoing the efficiencies of regional exploration, as well as the likelihood of making large new discoveries (see the discussion on creaming curves, p. 68).

Of course, the consequence of a successful new play is to add a new core producing area, which can then be expected to provide a significant and long-lasting incremental increase to the company's production revenues. Because large new fields are typically found early in the exploration cycle, large firms have usually placed a high premium on exploration in new trends and basins. Unfortunately, during the 1980s overall industry participation in such high-risk, high-potential new plays did not add to corporate net worth—it actually destroyed value.

Learning to Make Money Finding Smaller Fields

Incorporation of exploration statistics and the principles of exploration risk analysis into decision making has had a substantial, positive impact on the selection of new plays by modern petroleum companies. Especially compelling are data indicating that, despite continuing development of superb new geotechnical tools and concepts that have kept average exploration success ratios constant at about 25% **(Figure 22)**, annual volumes discovered worldwide have been decreasing since about 1965 **(Figure 49a)**. Moreover, the new fields being found by the international industry are

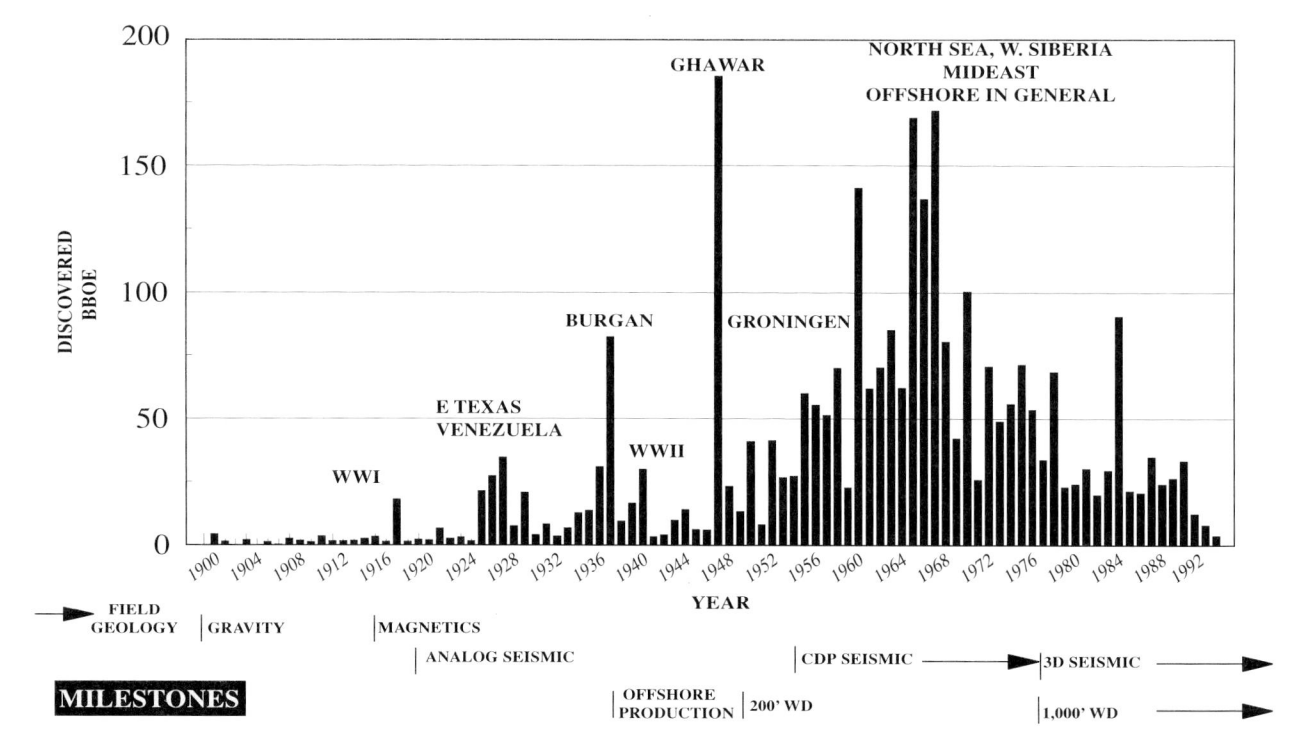

Figure 49a *Post-1900 BBOE discovered by year.* Source: Petroconsultants

Figure 49b *Discovery data, 1990–1999 (excluding U.S. and Canada).*

steadily decreasing in size **(Figure 1)**, so that the chances of making a very large discovery are getting very small indeed **(Figure 49b)**. The message is clear: Given that (1) most of the world's possible petroleum basins are increasingly well-known, and (2) the rate of discovery of super-giant fields ("elephants") has been decreasing since the 1960s, successful oil companies must organize themselves and conduct their E&P business to make money by discovering and developing oil and gas fields in the 10–100 MMBOE categories. *They must become more efficient in order to find and produce smaller fields profitably.*

Fortunately, the new principles of exploration risk analysis (and especially play analysis) provide methods by which a firm's entire exploration effort can be made more efficient, greatly reducing the likelihood of selecting a bad play and providing a greatly improved basis for predicting reserves, chance, costs, and profitabilities of new ventures being considered for entry.

Special Business Requirements May Dictate New Play Attributes

Different companies have differing financial circumstances and business constraints. These special conditions may place special limitations on their requirements of play choices. However, it is important to distinguish between short-term (one to three years) and long-term (four to eight years) constraints, remembering that the time required to identify, evaluate, secure, prove, execute, and develop a new play is usually not less than three years and often as much as six to eight years. Obviously, the astute exploration firm will not allow short-term constraints to prevent it from taking part in a play that is likely to be entirely compatible with the business circumstances expected to exist when the play actually comes to fruition.

Nevertheless, here are some special business conditions that may influence new play choices:

1. A company with legal contracts that require it to deliver specified volumes of natural gas to customers may attach higher priorities to gas plays capable of increasing deliverable gas in the short-term, especially if the company fears a possible shortfall.
2. A company with a limited exploration budget may give preference to plays located near producing infrastructure, or to those whose primary objectives are relatively shallow. Alternatively, such a company may choose to invest in specialized professional staff and state-of-the-art geotechnical tools and methodologies, which can be expected to develop new play concepts that can then be leveraged into substantial shares of multiple new-play ventures. The problem with the latter approach, however, is the substantial time required to build such staff and generate the necessary new concepts.
3. Some companies may be constrained from operating in certain countries or geographies, either by internal organizational restrictions or limitations or by external circumstances. Similarly, any limited geotechnical skills of the professional staff may prevent consideration of some plays. Sometimes a previous negative experience by senior management in a given location or in a play of a certain type may prejudice them against objectively considering an otherwise valid play venture.
4. For smaller companies that typically generate new plays, promote them, and thereafter operate as minority partners, certain types of plays may be currently in or out of favor in the marketplace. For example, it is currently very difficult to sell a play or prospect in the U.S. Gulf Coast unless it involves wide 3-D seismic coverage.
5. Given that taxation of oil and gas production has substantial impact on project profitability, and that tax ramifications may apply to a firm's other ventures, certain plays that offer special tax circumstances may be preferable to other equally valid plays that do not. In the U.S., there has been an unfortunate tendency for firms to pay more attention to such "if-success" tax benefits than to the geotechnical and economic merit of the play itself. *Working rule: First priority should go to geotechnically sound, economically superior plays; then consider ancillary tax benefits.*

Concurrent Geotechnical, Economic, and Business Evaluations of New Plays

In order to achieve efficient, thorough, and objective assessments of new exploration plays, many geoscientists have recognized the need to adopt a consistent procedure that uses either a manual flow-sheet or computer software to perform all the geotechnical tasks and attendant calculations needed to carry out a risk analysis of a new exploration play.

However, a common and unfortunate industry pattern has been to conduct the geotechnical evaluation first, and perform an economic assessment only at the end of the investigation. This often leads to poor and/or delayed business decisions. A much better approach is for the geotechnical, economic, and business assessment to proceed simultaneously, with frequent and detailed integration of such information among team members. This approach results in more reliable estimates and more innovative business plans. It is also more efficient because proposed plays that have severe economic or business limitations may be detected early, and expensive but unpromising geotechnical work may be curtailed, allowing scarce manpower and a limited budget to be used in more promising projects elsewhere. An excellent general summary of long-range exploration planning is provided by Megill (1985).

Specific business circumstances that should be explored and assessed include:

Product Transportation

Are there pipelines in the areas? Do they have available capacity? Will their owners allow your product to be shipped in the areas? Are there transportation tariffs? Are there calendar restrictions? If a pipeline must be constructed, what is the lead time? cost of construction? minimum new reserves to justify pipeline construction? Can you make additional profits by shipping gas for other producers as well as your own? What is the cost and capacity for temporary transportation (truck or ship)? hazards?

Markets

Especially for natural gas, you must consider market volumes, lead times, stability, and growth potential. Always explore the possibilities of ancillary profitable businesses connected with other aspects of oil and gas production.

Contract Terms

Understand in detail the terms of the typical E&P contract in the area and their ramifications regarding different types and patterns of production. Look for negotiating topics that offer positive tradeoffs acceptable to the host government and favorable to the geotechnical character of the play and the specific economic and business attributes of your company. Consider when unleased prospective areas may become available for acquisition of E&P rights. Moran (1992) and Johnston (1997a, 1997b) offer excellent treatments of this topic.

Government Tax Law, Legislation, Regulations, and Incentives

You should have extensive knowledge of the existing and impending tax laws, legislation, regulations, and government incentives, all of which may exert substantial influence on the value as well as conduct of a proposed new play. Such knowledge should be available before making final play valuations or entering into contract negotiations. Johnston (1997b) provides guidance on this topic.

Personnel Needs and Availability

What professional expertise will be needed (and when) to carry out the play? Where should they be located? What about support staff? lead times? What about geotechnical services, such as seismic crews, logging and completion capabilities, and production services? costs? lead times? government permits?

Political and Economic Stability

The traditional approach to political and economic stability addresses the likelihood of a political or economic crisis in the host country sufficient to result in substantial loss of monetary value or property during the life of the project. However, a more realistic approach focuses the question of political/economic risk on the two- to four-year period when substantial capital investments have already been made, but before project pay-out, i.e., recovery of invested capital. Marlan Downey (1993, personal communication) has outlined another approach to assessing political risk: Using experienced international petroleum experts, assess the degree to which the *real* infrastructure of the host country (not just politicians) really wants the firm to participate in the long-term economic development of their country, as opposed to just wanting the firm's money.

Expected Terms and Reputations of Potential Partners

For later-stage entry into existing contract areas, the firm should consider carefully any previous experiences with the company holding the license, and discreetly explore its reputation as a competent operator and reliable business partner. Terms of any participation agreement should be evaluated as outlined earlier under Contract Terms.

Likelihood for Renegotiated Contract Terms

One of the most significant potential impacts on play profitability concerns the likelihood that the original contract terms agreed upon with the host government may be renegotiated, either because the play has proved to be much less profitable than first thought or because the host government wishes to modify the contract terms because of changed circumstances.

Let us first consider such contract changes initiated by the company. These arise most commonly from new geotechnical information indicating that the area has a smaller petroleum resource endowment than originally thought—fields are smaller, fewer, or less profitable than expected. Sometimes the host country is willing to renegotiate terms to encourage the company to develop and produce these smaller, less profitable fields and to continue exploration. Sometimes, such changes may be mandated because of new regulations, economic conditions, or political situations. In all cases the tradeoff for the host country involves its genuine desire for the operating company to remain and continue to produce (under the changed terms), versus the consequences to the country's international business reputation if the operating company decides to exit.

In some cases, the proposed contract changes may be initiated by the host country. Common motivations for such renegotiations include:

- *a change of governments,* where the incoming government has different priorities for petroleum development. This can include different tax structure, different regulation schemes, different ownership proportions, and the like. Confiscatory government actions risk rejection by the world petroleum community and deterioration of international relations;
- *substantive changes in the world price of oil,* either through external market forces, political developments, or new technologies;

- *a perception of excessive profits by the company,* in which production potential of the contract area turned out to be much greater than originally anticipated; and
- *a desire by government to keep the company in the host country,* in hopes of developing more extensive petroleum resources.

Comparing Plays and Planning Exploration Campaigns

Assumptions

Most substantial, long-lived international oil companies recognize that they must add new core producing areas as their existing large-producing properties deplete. Regardless of whether such new core areas are generated internally through original prospecting skills or by joining into a partnership venture generated by another company, all firms should have a systematic basis by which they can identify, analyze, select, and execute profitable new exploration plays on a continuing basis. This book has previously enumerated five principles of modern exploration play analysis:

1. The most critical decision in petroleum exploration is the choice of which new play to enter (pp. 3, 57, and 60);
2. Exploration plays may be analyzed systematically with respect to geotechnical risk and economic profitability, as full-cycle business ventures (pp. 3, 57, and 61);
3. Successful play analysis requires thorough integration and iteration of diverse geotechnical, economic, and business skills, through multi-disciplinary professional teams (pp. 62, 113, and 114);
4. Play recognition, analysis, and ranking should be an ongoing, centrally coordinated corporate activity that generates an evolving, dynamic play inventory, from which desirable plays should be selected to form an annual play portfolio (pp. 99 and 113); and
5. Economic evaluations and business considerations should be linked with geotechnical play analysis from its inception, with special emphasis on contractual negotiation strategies, whether such negotiations are with host governments or companies offering partnership participations (pp. 109 and 111).

The following discussion assumes that all of these five principles are being utilized by the firm.

Constructing a Framework for Comparing Prospective New Plays

The problem in choosing new plays is that many significant criteria must be assigned in order to optimize the selection process. The most important criterion, however, is to estimate the likely profitability of the play venture, given discovery. Other criteria then should be considered:

Ranking by Risked Investment Efficiency

Ideally, new exploration plays should be ranked on one criterion only—risked investment efficiency (RIE) (p. 54)—if the firm is constrained by available capital for investments and the only criterion is to maximize economic value (Capen et al., 1976; Clapp, 1995). In practice, however, many other factors commonly turn out to be great influences in play selection. Often it pays to conduct a quick review of all attributes of the candidate play just to ensure that some requisite attribute is not absent, thus making even a profitable play unwise to pursue further. Such secondary factors may include:

1. expected net present value;
2. front-end costs and/or development costs;
3. chance of economic success;
4. corporate risk aversion and optimum working interest;
5. finding cost;
6. political risks;
7. critical geotechnical risks;
8. special business needs;
9. present value and actual value of net cash-flow stream (the mean-reserves case);
10. preferred partners; and
11. portfolio requirements unique to the company.

Play-ranking Matrix

Accordingly, most firms employ a matrix for comparing and ranking plays, in which plays are listed in horizontal order and the various selective criteria are arrayed vertically. Appendix G is an example of such a matrix, which in effect serves as an efficient and practical inventory. All candidate plays in the inventory can be ranked by different criteria, as selected by management; however, companies are well advised to rank candidate plays first on the basis of value as indicated by risked IE.

Optimum Working Interest

For companies whose standard mode of operation is to participate in many international ventures as minority working-interest partners, it is desirable to rank projects based on their actual working interest in the various plays under consideration. Unfortunately, because the choice of the working-interest share is usually made subjectively, this constitutes one of the largest sources of inconsistent corporate decision making (pp. 55 and 93).

Designing Exploration Campaigns

The most practical publications dealing with the design of exploration campaigns—how to plan and carry out successful play exploration—have been written by Megill (1985), Downey (1992), and St. John (1992).

Well-planned plays save money by identifying unsuccessful ventures quickly and efficiently. They make money by identifying potentially successful plays with high probability, optimum participation, and minimal investments, before success can be claimed with certainty. *Successful play exploration represents the ultimate geotechnical leverage.* But good play-planning starts with:

1. discriminating, reliable geotechnical work, investigating petroleum systems;
2. sound play risk analysis; and
3. integrated concurrent business assessments.

The writer has already pointed out the common, counterproductive industry pattern of waiting until the end of the geotechnical play evaluation before carrying out the economic assessment of the venture. Alternatively, the most efficient way to generate a properly evaluated exploration venture is to periodically perform provisional risk analysis, economic evaluation, and business planning as the new play evolves from concept to provisional play to committed venture. In this way, large geotechnical uncertainties can be related to economic and business circumstances, to highlight critical business issues and negotiating strategies. For any new play that is finally selected by the firm for participation, a series of provisional economic and business assessments should have been carried out, which attached values to the new play during its emergence as a valid business venture.

This calls for close, ongoing, and effective liaison and integration among geoscientists, engineers, planners, economists, negotiators, and decisionmakers, considering especially the topics raised in the previous sections of this chapter.

The planning process is graphically represented by **Figure 50**, originally developed by Megill (1985). It begins with sound geotechnical work and objective risk analysis of the prospective play as a full-cycle economic venture. A provisional economic evaluation of the emerging play is carried out, often using rough estimates and based on the play's projected means-reserves case. Simultaneously, the availability of contractual rights to the play area is assessed and integrated with:

1. the play risk analysis;
2. play economics for different reserves outcomes; and
3. probable methods and tactics for lease acquisitions.

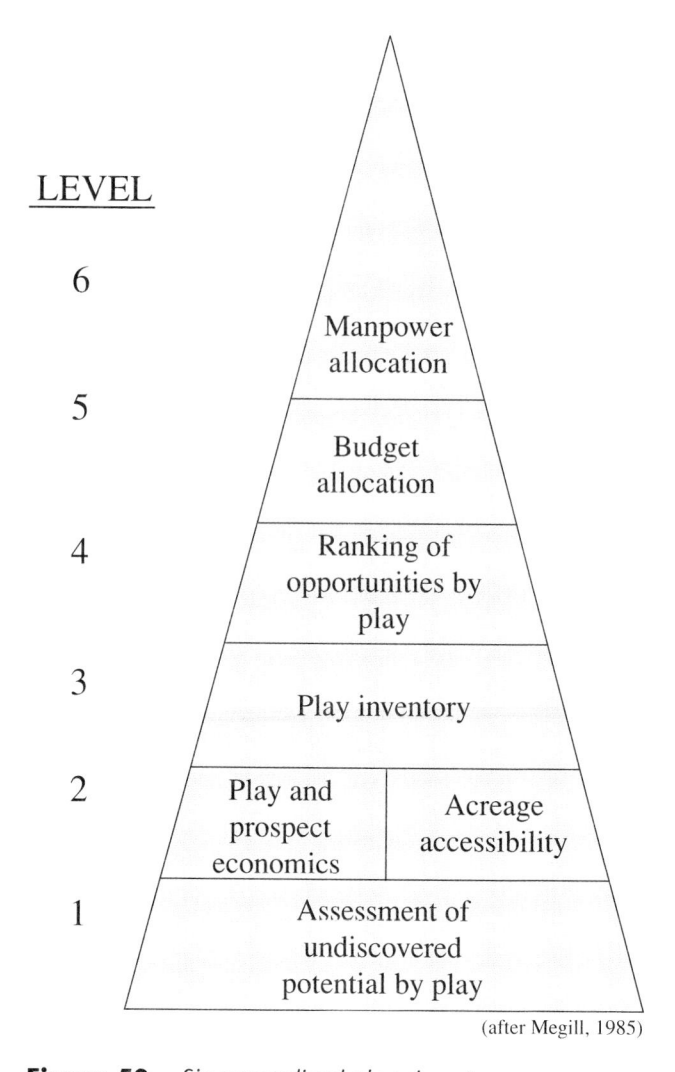

Figure 50 *Six generalized planning steps.*

Concurrently, the integrated exploration team should identify critical or sensitive factors that may affect play profitability (or demonstrate the need for early exit), for early use by negotiators and business agents, and for additional geotechnical studies that provide cost-effective ways to clarify the risk-reward ratio of the project.

Using reasonable assumptions, the emerging play then takes its place in the existing play inventory. If it appears to compare favorably with the firm's other contemplated or actual plays, the next stage of geotechnical, economic, and business studies should be initiated following the most cost-effective paths for project improvement by reducing geotechnical risk, reserves uncertainty, and project costs, or by improving profitability through more efficient development, streamlined business arrangements, and favorable contract terms. Economic evaluations should be carried out periodically as critical new geotechnical and business information is acquired.

If the play appears clearly to be inferior to other ventures being considered, it should be filed for later review (one to two years). If the play appears to be marginal, a brief analysis should be carried out to indicate those factors that could be improved and the likely degree of improvement.

Superior plays should be selected from the play inventory to form the annual play portfolio. This selection should give strong weight to the risked investment efficiency of the constituent projects, but it is also appropriate to consider other criteria as well. Required investments will be apparent at this stage.

Once the play portfolio is selected, budget allocations must be made. These allocations should be planned provisionally over at least a five-year period, covering several possible outcomes. Decision points should be clearly denoted in the five-year budget plan, following contingent developments.

The final step in the planning process involves manpower planning, which has three essential aspects:

1. What skills are likely to be needed, for what time periods, and where?
2. Who are the existing staff members who represent the required expertise? What vacancies must be filled by recruitment, and when?
3. Construct a provisional plan for staff succession and promotion.

The final step involves management's decision to carry out the new play, with early priority given to both advantageous negotiating tactics and the formation of a play team based on the previous manpower considerations.

Overview of Successful Play Management

Successful, cost-effective play development is a continuously evolving, multidisciplinary staff effort that requires dedicated professional skill, unselfish cooperation, thorough communication, objective evaluations, and courageous execution. Properly organized and managed profitability, play selection, and development provide—on a regular basis—new prospects to populate the firm's annual drilling portfolio, and therefore new discoveries of economic reserves to replace produced reserves. Orderly new play development is impeded by frequent reorganizations or personnel instability. Properly executed, the exploration play is the ultimate form of leveraged geotechnical risk venture. But an essential aspect of successful play generation and analysis is another ongoing process—the rigorous assessment of geotechnical as well as economic performance. That is the subject of the final section of this chapter.

Assessment of Exploration Performance

Most of the critical parameters that influence valuation and ranking of exploration plays and prospects are, in fact, estimates made under varying degrees of uncertainty. This places a heavy professional burden on the corporate technical staff to consistently generate responsible, unbiased estimates, and on exploration decisionmakers to utilize such estimates wisely and consistently. When technical estimates are overly optimistic, the firm is encouraged to invest in inferior projects. Overly conservative estimates discourage the firm from realizing the full profit potential of underestimated projects. Thus either error has the potential to cause loss; either error reduces staff credibility. When company decisionmakers do not know the relative reliability of technical estimates, they are encouraged to rely on their intuition (which usually causes great inconsistency) and to improperly use expensive geotechnical data bearing directly on project risk versus reward.

The only way for corporate decisionmakers to improve the overall exploration performance of the firm is to monitor and preserve, on a systematic and routine basis, the technical and economic predictions made by their professional staff, and to compare them against actual outcomes. Without such ongoing calibrations, technical and economic forecasts are analogous to one-way rockets launched into outer space—there is no feedback! Without comparisons, exploration companies continue to make the same mistakes year after year, and performance of neither staff nor decisionmakers can be measured properly; accountability is thus greatly diminished. *What gets measured, gets done.*

Technical Performance versus Economic Performance

It is important to recognize that positive results from excellent technical predictions can be nullified by inept economic forecasting, and vice versa. Technical staff should not be penalized for the poor performance of the economic staff and managers. Accordingly, for both plays and prospects, two different aspects of performance should be monitored. Technical performance compares all geotechnical, engineering, and cost/price forecasts with actual outcomes. Some examples are reserves; chance of completion; initial production rate; decline percentage; drilling, completion, and operation costs; and wellhead prices. Economic performance measures forecasts of project profitability in relation to actual profitability; both forecasts and actuals must be related to preselected corporate standards. Some useful economic measures adaptable as success criteria include predicted project ROR in relation to actual ROR and to corporate hurdle rates; projected venture NPV and IE compared with actual NPV and IE; actual early-term investment costs compared with predicted investment costs; projected exploration cost of finding (COF, expressed in $/BOE) compared with actual COF and established corporate

COF goals. Making economic comparisons on the basis of actual monetary value (rather than present monetary value) may facilitate the process. Also, cost-of-finding results should be normalized by distinguishing between increased drilling efficiencies, stimulation and completion efficiencies, and exploration skills. Finally, try to separate economic influences that lie within the purview of professional staff and managers from external influences over which technical and management staff had no control.

For all prospects, scenarios outlining various technical and economic outcomes *and their consequences* should accompany any project recommendations. For possible economic events *external* to the project (world price fluctuations, international political developments, new technologies, etc.), project planners should also outline scenarios, impacts, and possible responses.

Measuring Performance: Plays versus Prospects

Papers by Rose (1987), Clapp and Stibolt (1991), Capen (1992), Otis and Schneidermann (1997), Alexander and Lohr (1998), Johns et al. (1998), McMaster and Carragher (1998), and McMaster (1998) presented different but complementary methods for evaluating and expressing staff performance in geotechnical predictions related primarily to prospects rather than plays. For many corporations that participate in 20 to 100 exploratory prospects each year, such methods provide an acceptable basis for assessing and improving geotechnical predictive performance, either on an annual or multi-year, moving-average basis.

Assessing predictive performance for plays is much more difficult than for prospects. Variance (uncertainty) within plays is generally much greater, and the number of predictions at play scale are far fewer than predictions at prospect-scale. For plays, elapsed time between technical predictions and measurable results is commonly four to eight years; economic forecasts commonly require six to 12 years before useful comparisons can be made. Normal personnel changes over such timeframes reduce staff continuity and preserved histories of projects. Fear of criticism (on the parts of both technical staff and managers) leads to incomplete preservation of key records and reports. Changes in technical and economic definitions produce inconsistent data sets.

Moreover, there is great organizational pressure for early and correct assessments—for example, that an emerging play is mediocre, or that it has great potential. Understandably, companies do not want to wait four to eight years to decide that a given play is not worthwhile. Opposed to this pressure is another truth: *Beware the premature exit, the abandonment of a promising play after only one dry hole!* Naturally, the key issue here is to focus on what was learned from that dry hole—does it apply throughout the play area (as a shared attribute) or does it apply only to the specific prospect (as an independent factor)?

Criteria Indicating Competence in Play Analysis

Because indirect and subjective criteria must be used to assess the technical performance of play teams, the writer has developed 10 criteria that help to indicate the relative skill level with which such teams are functioning in the critically important activity of generating and evaluating new exploration plays. He has used these criteria for more than eight years in reviewing play development teams for many different international exploration companies.

1. *Some team members have previously been closely associated with discoveries.* Successful past experience brings an essential sense of scale and scope to the geotechnical process, especially to keep the effort focused on practical (rather than scientific) problems. Play analysis is best carried out by seasoned, capable professional geoscientists and engineers.
2. *Routine use is made of the petroleum system approach.* All geotechnical aspects of hydrocarbon occurrences are routinely integrated, with special emphasis given to understanding the HC kitchen (see Appendix E). Integration of petroleum system thinking with regional tectonic expertise and broad knowledge of basin classification provides additional creative insight and power.
3. *Routine use is made of geostatistics and databases.* Thoughtful, thorough acquisition, organization, and regular analysis of critical and current statistical data is necessary, such as:
   - field production catalogs;
   - routine construction of FSDs, including FSD shift studies (see pp. 71–75);
   - success-rate studies in analog trends, including show-holes, economic discoveries, and dry-hole causes; and
   - field number and density studies (including creaming curve data) for analog trends.
4. *Staff has easy access to comprehensive petroleum references.* Staff must have ready access to the international literature on petroleum exploration, production engineering, economics, finance, and law. Many data are free, in the public domain. Proprietary reports and databases provide additional information. Successful play analysis requires efficient sifting through of copious quantities of data. A competent technical librarian is a valuable member of any play-generating group.
5. *A consistent process is routinely used for formal play analysis.* Routine use is made of a simple, consistent flow sheet or of software to estimate chance of economic play success and reserves potential.
6. *There is demonstrated continuous integration of provisional economic criteria and business considerations with the emerging geotechnical picture.* It is important that each play group have a modicum

of economic and business expertise, or have routine access to (and interactions with) such expertise.

7. *An open, dynamic play inventory is maintained.* A continuously changing inventory of new and existing plays should be ranked consistently by investment efficiency and show status of the projects. Appendix G is an example. The constituents of the inventory should include plays having reserves potential that is appropriate to the company's needs, in diverse geologic settings, and of an adequate number to ensure a satisfactory annual flow of new trends into the firm's exploratory effort.
8. *Technical work is organized and orderly.* There are visible planning calendars and evidence of:
   - efficient and timely work performance;
   - accurate forecasts of costs;
   - geotechnical costs that are competitive with industry standards; and
   - systematic preservation of regional geologic compilations, in a usable format.
9. *Systematic criteria are used for measuring the accuracy of technical forecasts.* There is an ongoing, open process for recording forecasts of emerging data focus in the areas and comparing them with actual results, as well as periodic review of predictive performance and sharing of lessons learned.
10. *Routine group procedures are used for peer reviews and the generation of new ideas.* There is an open, interactive working atmosphere where professionals informally review each other's emerging work and stimulate new ideas through routine group interactions.

Attributes of Good Play Managers

Good managers of the process of exploration play generation and analysis are by nature generalists and integrators. They must be able to motivate individuals of diverse technical expertise and personality types, to listen and communicate effectively, and to keep projects on schedule and within budget. They must strike a working balance between accepting large, irreducible uncertainties and using expensive state-of-the-art technologies to reduce risk where they are cost-effective. Good play managers must be willing to make decisions on imperfect information, being cognizant that some of their decisions may turn out to be wrong. They must understand clearly that early rejection of a considered play for technical and/or economic reasons does not constitute failure. Such managers know that money can be made in two ways: by finding profitable new plays and by staying out of unprofitable ones. Such managers must have an inherent sense of:

1. the known facts that are critical;
2. the unknown facts that need to be determined; and
3. the acceptable level of irreducible uncertainty and risk, given project costs and potential rewards.

Play Analysis: Organizational Patterns and Principles

Common Patterns and Procedures

The writer has observed and noted several common biases, patterns, and useful procedures of corporate risk analysis that are practiced by capable explorationists around the world:

1. Most geoscientists with medium to large companies tend to overestimate the reserves sizes of future discoveries, especially in onshore plays.
2. Conversely, they tend to underestimate the number of future fields, especially in onshore plays.
3. Pmefs for new plays commonly lies between P30% and P70%. As Pmefs rises above 50–60%, the chance of economic play failure increases rapidly.
4. If the required geotechnical data are available and organized (see pp. 65 and 84 and Appendix E), a discriminating play analysis can be carried out in one or two work days.
5. Many of the critical supporting data on exploration plays are in the public domain and therefore are quite inexpensive—use them!
6. Reasonable estimates of future field numbers can be derived from analog producing areas and verified using discovery process modeling or other pragmatic methods (pp. 69–70).
7. Intelligent manipulation and utilization of FSDs (combined with estimates of field numbers) allow useful forecasting of play reserves.
8. Items 4 through 7 demonstrate the importance of having, in every play-analysis organization, qualified technical staff—especially a librarian and statistical technician—to assist in data acquisition, organization, and analysis.
9. Full-cycle economic analysis of exploration plays allows discriminating business decisions to be made early in the exploration cycle.
10. Play analysis does not provide perfect answers, but it will prevent serious mistakes at either extreme, both the positive and the negative, and that level of precision is usually sufficient.
11. The play only works where all the geologic chance factors coincide. Your job as play analyst is to delineate the area of coincidence (and possibly the more apparent prospects in it). Make overlay maps showing degrees of confidence in the various elements of geologic chance.
12. Pay very close attention to the kitchen—and recognize that "shows are the footprints of migrating oil."

13. Using the petroleum system concept, think critically and imaginatively about potential reservoir/seal couplets to help recognize potential new plays.
14. Identify and focus on the critical data that will prove or disprove the play.
15. "The early bird gets the worm"—usually, the larger fields in a new play are found early in the exploration cycle.
16. Play exploration requires routine application of geotechnical analogs, *but be sure your analog is valid!*
17. Try to nurture creative and/or unconventional ideas in the face of contrary opinions, especially in older trends.

Tips on Basic Working Principles for Exploration Play Analysis

Following are some pragmatic and even philosophic tips for explorationists involved in play generation and analysis.

1. Don't be afraid of "quick and dirty" methods (pragmatic rules of thumb)—sometimes such approximations are all you can do anyway, and they are often reasonably accurate and cost-effective.
2. Accept the necessity of making subjective decisions, using uneven and qualitative data.
3. Honor nature's envelopes—lognormality, known limits of parameters, and reality checks.
4. Remember the power of independent multiple estimates.
5. Hydrocarbon generation/migration is important—pay attention to the kitchen and what's in it when.
6. The Earth is trying to speak to us, and geology and geostatistics are her language—listen for the message (see item 7).
7. Don't get lost in the technical forest; the details may be complex, but the basic message is usually simple.
8. Geoscientists behave as if they know more than they really do, usually stating uncertainty substantially—widen your ranges!
9. There are two kinds of unknowns—the good unknown and the bad unknown. Allow for both.
10. Control front-end costs vigorously—don't overpay for opportunities, and evaluate proposed data acquisitions for cost-effectiveness (see item 11).
11. Remember that the objective is to make a reasonable profit. Accomplish this by limiting your losses on failures and making large profits on your successes.
12. The expected value concept is always a useful yardstick for consistency. When EV is positive, you're investing—when it's negative, you're gambling. Invest!
13. There are two simultaneous and interactive evaluations: geotechnical and economic—don't ignore either one.
14. In competition, the Winner's Curse always looms. Know how to avoid it—above all, avoid blind competitiveness.
15. It is not as if you know nothing—you usually know more than you think you do!

Chapter 7

Petroleum Industry Practices of Exploration Risk Analysis

The "Prospector Myth" versus Systematic Exploration: Dealing with the Dilemma

Introduction

The Prospector Myth is the petroleum explorationist's version of the Hero Journey. We are informed and inspired by the image of the courageous lone prospector who struggles against Mother Nature, financial hardships, skeptical associates, and repeated rejection by investors, before finally succeeding through persistence, faith, and luck, to achieve vindication, wealth, and fame. Most of us know personally—or know of—one or more such individuals. We call them "wildcatters," "oil finders," "visionaries," and other dramatic names reflecting the respect they are accorded in our industry.

Uncertainty, Intuition, and Overoptimism

Geoscientists select (or are assigned) basins or trends in which to explore for petroleum. Such endeavors are characterized by daunting uncertainty, which can be reduced (but not eliminated) through costly geotechnology and seasoned judgment. Explorationists must peer through Nature's fuzzy lenses, searching for cryptic clues. They must invest intense physical and intellectual energy, over extended periods, patching together possible portraits of the subsurface, then selling and defending the proposed risk ventures that arise from their imagination and labor. Because exploration is dominated by subjectivity and uncertainty, it invites the exercise of intuition. And, of course, when geotechnical intuition is rewarded by exploration success, the prospector's ego is affirmed and even extolled. But most exploration projects fail, so most seasoned prospectors have learned to live with repeated failure. It is no wonder that petroleum exploration cherishes the Prospector Myth.

It is also not surprising that most explorationists are overly optimistic about their basins, trends, and prospects. After all, such dedicated prospectors could hardly be expected to be rigorously objective about their prospects! The Prospector Myth is the primary reason why explorationists persistently overestimate the reserves potential of their prospects.

But the process by which oil and gas prospects are translated into economic ventures also contributes to overoptimism. In the early days of petroleum exploration—the glory days—many prospectors were indeed individuals or small firms, and their investors were private third-party investors and corporations, more or less knowledgeable about petroleum exploration. *Caveat emptor* was the prevailing ethic because the subscribing sponsors were expected to be able to judge the true merit of each deal. So the operative criterion for success was to sell the deal, to get the well drilled. And that pattern still today characterizes many smaller firms that generate prospects and turn them over to larger companies to be drilled. *"Have faith—success will eventuate, given persistence and sufficient trials: one real success will carry a dozen failures."* Unfortunately, the same value system still operates in some offices—even throughout entire companies—even though the professional employees of these publicly owned corporations are selling their deals to their own managements (and thus their own stockholders). Because of our sympathy for the Prospector Myth, we tend to dismiss more benign examples of this as motivational bias. More flagrant examples, however, we are bound to label as conflicts of interest.

Times Change

The increasing employment of geoscientists and the rise of large, publicly held corporations after World War II gradually began putting a crimp in the freewheeling presentation of oil and gas prospects. Scientific objectivity, professional ethics, the declining petroleum resource base, and the need to deliver

- **FREQUENCY**

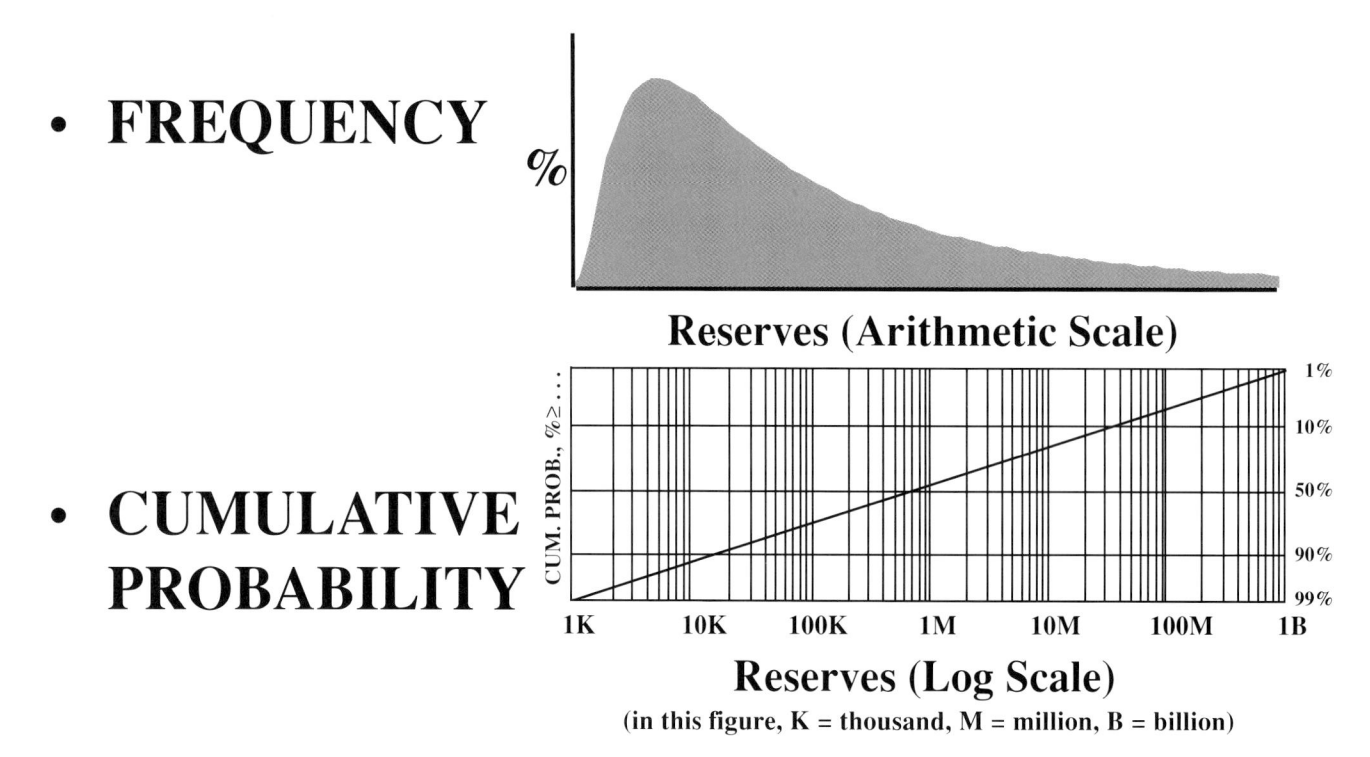

Reserves (Arithmetic Scale)

- **CUMULATIVE PROBABILITY**

Reserves (Log Scale)
(in this figure, K = thousand, M = million, B = billion)

Figure 51 *Lognormality—two modes of portrayal.*

promised exploration performance together collided with the Prospector Myth and salesmanship. Even so, influenced by the Prospector Myth, the world petroleum industry wasted a lot of money on exploration in the late 1970s to early 1990s. Shell, Mobil, and Amoco independently reported that exploration for high-risk, high-reserves targets in this period destroyed value, rather than creating it. While we kept looking for elephants, sizes of discoveries were steadily diminishing **(Figure 1)**. We lost credibility with directors; we lost money for stockholders. By the 1990s the industry was becoming global in scope and needed to become much more efficient. To be sure, improvements in seismic technology and drilling and completion methods improved our success ratios substantially. But consistent, objective, technically sound procedures for assessing prospects also led to the adoption of systematic prospect risk analysis procedures. The recognition of the lognormal distribution as the prevailing natural pattern of oil and gas field-reserves distribution **(Figure 51)**, together with the development of refined methods of estimating geotechnical uncertainties, began to constrain the optimistic exuberances that had been indulged by intuition and the Prospector Myth.

Today, most modern petroleum exploration is carried out by multidisciplinary geotechnical teams, not individual prospectors. Most substantial companies consider an inventory of many candidate prospects, from which they select their annual drilling portfolio, which comprises only those prospects that together maximize economic value consistent with company goals and risk tolerance. We try to manage exploration by managing the exploration portfolio. With this concept comes the realization that, if portfolio management is to succeed, each prospect must be assessed consistently and objectively. The inherent uncertainties can be dealt with via improved geotechnology and with geostatistics. What kills the portfolio is bias, which overvalues some prospects so that the value of the portfolio is not optimized **(Figures 15 and 16)**. The stockholder is shortchanged by the Prospector Myth. Systematic portfolio management is more effective than intuitive prospect selection—or "cherry-picking." This is a blow to the egos of most prospectors, as well as many managers.

Imperfect Remedies

Since the 1950s, our industry has tried to reconcile the dilemma in various ways. A common approach—thankfully now diminishing—pitted geoscientists against engineers, tacitly accepting and reinforcing the proposition that geologists were expected to be overly optimistic, which required engineers to be correspondingly overly conservative. Another remedy was to artificially inflate economic criteria—notably the discount rate—under the mistaken notion that "those

MOST PROBABLE OUTCOME = SMALL FIELD

BUT:

THERE'S A SMALL CHANCE OF A VERY LARGE FIELD

Frequency - %

Arithmetic Scale
PROSPECT RESERVES →

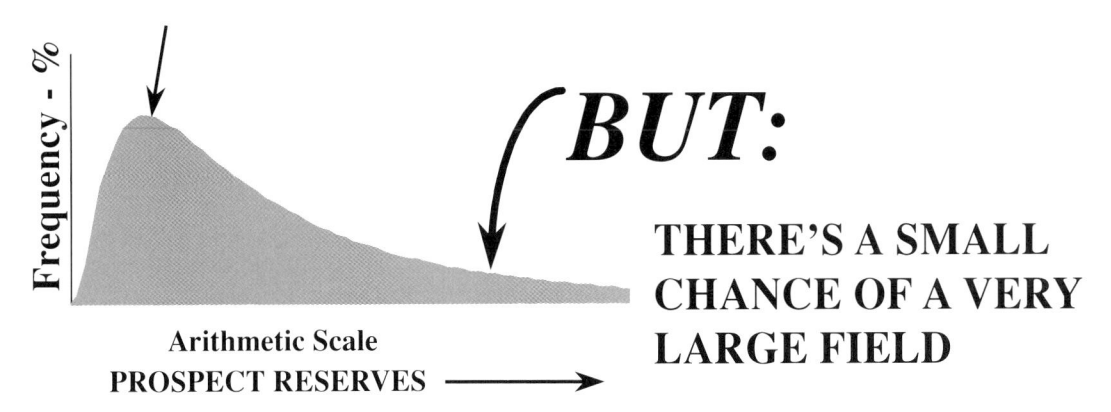

Figure 52 *Exploration reality.*

prospects that still have positive expected monetary values (EMVs) under inflated discount rates must be better prospects than those that don't." A third technique was to employ hidden hurdles (p. 123) in the higher levels of the decision chain: managers at headquarters routinely cut prospect values by half (or more), based on their observations of past exploration overoptimism. In response, explorationists became adept at sniffing out such arbitrary screening measures and devising ingenious ways to generate geotechnical numbers that were adequate to get their prospects drilled. In particular, many explorationists in top management exercised their own version of the Prospector Myth by applying their privileged intuition—and egos—to the prospect selection process. Understandably, such managers found it difficult to surrender the intuitive style that had advanced their successful exploration careers to date, in favor of probabilistic expressions and reliance on systematic prospect selection.

Since almost no one kept systematic records documenting actual prospect results (compared against geotechnical predictions), everyone in the chain—prospectors, engineers, local managers, and senior executives—usually did not have to confront the consequences of systematic bias. The urgency of drilling the next well far outweighed the value of objectively and purposefully assessing our mistakes from the last well. *We were too busy drowning to take time to improve our swimming ability.* Instead we put our greater reliance on geotechnology (especially seismic surveys), which often did reduce the impact of large uncertainties regarding prospect reserves and present value and the discouragingly low chances of prospect economic success. But most of us steadfastly refused to address the glaring problem of bias **(Figures 15** and **16)**.

Response of Systematic Exploration

Companies eventually began to employ institutionalized systematic procedures for continuous improvement, which required objective comparison of geotechnical predictions versus actual outcomes. Geoscientists began to learn from their mistakes and to calibrate their predictions. Corporate explorers began to employ a different criterion for success: *adding value* versus *getting the prospect drilled.* The need for objectivity generated a long-overdue appeal for geotechnical professionalism as a requisite to objectively identifying and selecting those projects that together maximize the value of the portfolio, consistent with the organization's strategies and risk tolerance. Geoscientists could take pride in being professional.

Today, some prospectors mourn the diminished influence of the Prospector Myth, even though the lognormal distribution still allows them to dream **(Figure 52)**. But increasingly, astute explorationists are recognizing the necessity for heightened exploration efficiency as the global resource base continues to shrink. Systematic risk analysis, professional objectivity, and performance tracking must go hand-in-hand with sophisticated geotechnical methods.

But the Prospector Myth still lingers, and properly so if it can inspire our courage, persistence, and imagination in petroleum exploration, *without biasing portfolio selection.* All too often, however, the entrenched intuitive preferences of management as well as some geoscientists—and inappropriate concern about preserving budget share—warp exploration performance through bias or double-risking. The ongoing challenge for geotechnical professionals is to harness the energy of the Prospector Myth without compromising the scientific integrity and business objectivity now required for successful management of the exploration portfolio.

Characteristic Corporate Process for Exploration Risk Analysis

Most organizations have settled on using a consistent process to assess all exploration prospects and plays for management evaluation and decision. Procedures, underlying concepts and principles, and helpful suggestions are carefully organized into handbooks or manuals, which in turn relate to and explain computer programs or flow sheets by which geotechnical staff in all office locations can readily, systematically, and consistently carry out risk analysis of all exploration ventures. Some companies have developed their own risk analysis software, using various forms of Lotus® or Excel® spreadsheets and risking software such as "@Risk"® or "Crystal Ball."® Other companies have licensed customized software from several different vendors or consulting groups. A useful byproduct of such standardized approaches is that all geotechnical predictions and forecasts are preserved, thus facilitating subsequent project review for purposes of performance analysis. Such data are rolled up and compiled by central staff to facilitate portfolio selection and analysis and to analyze overall company performance.

Prospects are identified by name, location, trend, reservoir, objectives, originator, and the like. Then interactive risk analysis software guides the explorationist(s) through the process of developing the prospect-reserves distribution, honoring the lognormal distribution and expressing projected prospect ultimate recovery probabilistically, as P10%, P50%, P90%, and mean reserves. Many firms have incorporated interactive graphics capabilities that allow the reserves distributions to be depicted in either frequency and/or cumulative probability format and to be shifted at will. Reality checks help common errors to be identified throughout the estimating process. Many programs contain analog field data, providing a perspective against which the prospect can be viewed. The software promotes trial fitting and testing of data and early estimates, resulting in repeated iterations and reiterations of data until best-fit distributions emerge and are finalized.

In a detached procedure, cash-flow models utilizing the differing probabilistic reserves level (and ancillary well numbers, initial production rates and percentage decline curves, costs, and contract terms), are used to calculate the present value of different reserves outcomes. Uncertainties such as initial production rates, percentage decline rates, and wellhead prices are variables within the cash-flow models. Based on these several reserves cases, (P10%, P50%, P90%, and the mean), minimum *commercial* and *economic* field sizes are derived. These figures are used in connection with the prospect-reserves distribution to estimate the chances of minimum commercial and minimum economic field sizes (given a discovery).

Accepted economic measures, such as net present value (calculated at the corporate discount rate), discounted cash-flow rate of return, investment efficiency, and growth rate of return, are calculated for each reserves case.

The next step is to estimate the chances of success, utilizing a consistent set of well-defined geologic chance factors. Again, flow sheets or software takes the explorationist(s) through the estimation of geologic chance in a step-by-step manner, with useful questions, reality checks, and questioned errors appearing throughout the process, thus encouraging iteration and reiteration of estimated values before settling on final forecasts.

Once sound estimates of prospect reserves and chance have been made, the next step is the generation of risked prospect parameters, such as expected net present value, risked investment efficiency, and prospect optimum working interest, by which prospects under consideration may be ranked for possible inclusion in the company's current prospect portfolio. These values are used to help determine appropriate bid levels for acquisition, keyed to the anticipated methods for offering and sale.

Ordinarily, portfolio selection is carried out as a separate computerized procedure that may employ the efficient frontier concept, using preselected corporate values for acceptable portfolio risk (variance of economic results) versus portfolio rate of return. Some portfolio management systems consider and balance growth with timing of cash flows. Probabilistic expression of portfolio results allows senior management to assess and evaluate various portfolio tradeoffs before settling on a final selection of prospects to constitute the final portfolio. *However, it cannot be overemphasized that meaningful portfolio analysis absolutely depends on responsible and unbiased estimates of prospect reserves and the chance of success.*

Another distinct computer module or standardized activity is ordinarily devoted to performance analysis. Predictions of prospect parameters are routinely entered and preserved, keyed to the parent play, location, objective formation, and prospect name. Results of exploratory drilling are then entered into the inventory to be used in compiling and analyzing the predictive capabilities of the geotechnical staff and the overall exploration performance. Frequent feedback and discussion of specific learnings and remedies between portfolio management and exploration teams allows steady improvement of professional geotechnical performance.

Play Analysis

Some exploration companies have also formalized procedures for conducting risk analysis and economic evaluations of new exploration plays, along comparable lines to the procedures outlined in Chapter 6's section on Play Analysis. Many firms have software or flow sheets that systematize and standardize the process of exploration play analysis. A limited but useful literature outlines many of the common concepts, procedures, and pitfalls in risk analysis of exploration plays: Baker (1988); Baker, Gehman, James, and White (1986); Brown and Rose (2000); Jones and Smith (1983); Rose (1995, 1996a, and 1996b); and White (1988, 1992, and 1993).

Implementation of Risk Analysis in Exploration Organizations

Introduction

Exploration firms that have been utilizing a consistent system for risk analysis of all ventures in their exploration program already know that it improves economic performance by:

1. identifying and deleting prospects unlikely to be profitable;
2. promoting consistency in allocation of capital among competing ventures, according to merit;
3. improving cost effectiveness and manpower utilization by highlighting those emerging exploration leads having the greatest profit potential;
4. forecasting future results of current prospect inventories and delivering on those forecasts; and
5. encouraging systematic improvement of exploration predictive performance.

Over the past 10 years, many domestic and international companies have made the purposeful decision to set up consistent, companywide exploration risk analysis procedures. When they take this step, it inevitably changes the corporate culture, operating values and tactics, and reward system. Adoption of exploration risk analysis goes hand-in-hand with reorganization (Rose, 1994).

Each company that undertakes this move usually encounters about 9 to 18 months of turmoil, during which time it believes itself to be plowing new ground. In fact, however, there are characteristic—almost expectable—organizational behaviors and responses that tend to recur among all firms. Prior awareness of such patterns can help make the transition much smoother and more efficient.

Fundamental Requirements for Implementation Success

In the end, five fundamental requirements must be met for successful adoption of an organizational risk analysis system:

1. Top management must understand the basis of risk analysis, commit to its consistent application in decision making, and support implementation of the risk analysis system by inspection, follow-through, and enforcement;
2. Exploration staff must thoroughly understand risk analysis concepts and their proper geologic/economic applications, and accept responsibility for unbiased predictive performance;
3. There must be a consistent system by which risk analysis is carried out on all prospects and plays considered by the company;
4. There must be a centrally coordinated prospect inventory leading to objective selection of the annual drilling portfolio, which is keyed to meet corporate goals; and
5. An effective process must be operating that measures predictive performance, learns lessons from experience, and passes them on to exploration staff efficiently.

Effective Techniques for Implementation

Several techniques for implementing exploration risk analysis have proved to be effective in many different organizations.

Champions

In every exploration location, it is important to have at least one knowledgeable geoscientist who is available to all prospectors and engineers, and who can help them understand the principles of risk analysis, apply them correctly, and execute risk analysis software programs properly. Such champions also serve as facilitators for project reviews by exploration teams and peer groups, and assist in postdrilling project reviews. They often function as bridges, communicating results and their implications between the geotechnical staff and exploration management.

Most firms do not appoint champions. Instead they wait until a geotechnical professional exhibits the voluntary interest and skill and manifests inherent interest in compiling and analyzing data that express the company's true exploration performance. As such professionals emerge and are recognized, they are appointed to act as champions. Ordinarily such assignments are of two to three years' duration and are seen as a natural stepping-stone toward exploration management status.

Company-consistent Play and Prospect Portfolios

Companies assemble annual, semi-annual, or biannual inventories containing plays or prospects from various exploration divisions. All ventures have been assessed using consistent techniques of risk analysis and ranked using the same economic measure. These inventories are then ranked and cut, and surviving projects are combined to form a portfolio that can be optimized for added value (risked investment efficiency) or portfolio risk-weighted value (expected net present value). If the firm has concerns about risk aversion, these measures can be calculated at optimum working interest for each included venture. Alternatively, the ventures can be chosen to optimize management's declared preference regarding risk versus reward, following the efficient frontier concept. In this approach, risk aversion considerations apply not to each project but to the overall portfolio. In either method the process generally results in capital allocation based on merit, consistent with the firm's risk preferences.

Depending on the number of ventures in the portfolio, their reserves variance, and the average chance of success, it is possible to predict the probabilistic results of drilling the portfolio. Naturally, the more wells in the portfolio, the more accurate will be its predictive power.

Most companies do not include plays and prospects in the same portfolio.

Portfolio Scrutiny by Educated Management

The key to success in corporate risk analysis lies in support and utilization by knowledgeable managers, often supported by high-level staff. To be effective, management must understand the basis for risk analysis, accept its indications of appropriate constraints, and use appropriate economic measures consistently to assign values to the constituent ventures. By reviewing portfolio results frequently, managers can reward geotechnical staff whose predictions are unbiased and objective, as well as correct those explorationists whose forecasts are overly optimistic or overly conservative.

Honoring Nature's Envelopes

Geotechnical predictions are made by professional geoscientists and engineers who have learned how to improve their estimating techniques. They employ the expectation of lognormality, known ranges of geologic parameters, and reality checks such as field-size distributions, edited success ratios, and credible upper and lower values.

Independent Multiple Estimates

Companies employ multidisciplinary exploration teams, thus promoting consideration of independent multiple estimates and multiple working hypotheses. The teams generate several versions of many geotechnical maps. They invite peer reviews of emerging projects and utilize exploration committees that provide experienced counsel and mentoring, but not at the expense of project accountability by the originating staff.

Positive Postdrill Reviews

We learn best by constructive examination of our own errors. The learning process is optimized by a spirit of open, objective inquiry, which may be difficult to sustain because dedicated professionals often find their mistakes painful and may fear criticism and loss of status. It is essential that postdrill reviews do not take on a punitive aspect. For that reason such reviews should not be attended by managers who have direct responsibility for salary administration and promotions, because their presence tends to impede honest inquiry and discussion of performance. A postdrill review should take no more than one day. It should be facilitated by the local champion, who should prepare a brief written summary with lessons learned and comparison of all significant predrill predictions and postdrill outcomes. Each team member should receive a copy. Copies should go to a very few concerned management and high-level staff. NOTE: It is essential that recorded predrill predictions must be those on which the actual decision to drill was based.

Performance Tracking and Communications

Results of exploratory wells and of postdrill reviews are compiled, analyzed, and reported to top management and to exploration managers and geotechnical staff with the intent of identifying bias, recurring errors, and recommending remedies, and of recognizing noteworthy and objective prospect performance.

Professional Pride in Objective Estimating

Companies that benefit by effective operational risk analysis typically undergo a change in some of their organizational ethos, in which geotechnical staff recognize and accept the need for reasonable and unbiased estimates and develop professional pride in providing them. They begin to focus on adding value—making money for the firm—rather than on just drilling wells. This results in improved corporate performance and overall strength, with the stockholder being the chief beneficiary.

Persistent Problems in Implementation

Characteristic, counterproductive patterns of implementing corporate risk analysis also recur among modern oil and gas companies.

Making Risk Analysis More Important than Prospect Generation

The most important task in petroleum exploration is the generation of new prospects and plays. That is where the value is added, and it is the most creative aspect of the business. Geotechnical staff must be aware of this basic fact. After the prospect or play has been identified, geoscientists then carry out risk analysis of the proposed venture. They attempt to measure it by estimating reserves, chance, and profitability; they design appropriate bid levels, select prospects for an optimum portfolio, and examine predictions and results to improve performance. *Risk analysis will help us conduct our business more profitably and efficiently, but it does not find oil and gas. It presupposes a steady supply of good prospects, and thus of good prospectors.*

The Desire for a Cookbook

Meaningful exploration risk analysis requires that professional staff must understand and integrate (1) probability and statistics, (2) economics, finance, and bid strategy, and (3) geology, geophysics, and engineering. There are no automatic answers, there are no shortcuts, and there are no cookbooks (even though some geotechnical staff are continually looking for them). All estimates involved in prospect evaluations express informed and constrained subjective probability. The beauty of the method is that predictive performance is testable over time, so that conscientious professionals can gradually improve their performance by comparing their predictions with actual outcomes. Consistent use of software can assist in addressing these problems.

Black Boxes

Because risk analysis is readily adapted to computerized, interactive flow sheets and programs, an exploration company's risk analysis procedure may become obscure, poorly understood, and mysterious—and thus take on the status of a mistrusted black box. Successful firms have learned that productive prospectors must understand the risk analysis process if they are to trust the output. Otherwise, they will try to find ways to subvert the system in order to achieve outputs they think are more appropriate. Several policies can help avoid this problem:

1. Keep it simple; remember that risk analysis is not a precise tool—it provides approximate answers only;
2. Be sure that geotechnical staff are trained and that knowledgeable assistance is available to counsel prospectors, especially during the first year or two; and
3. Management should be sure that the risk analysis process is transparent and that it is not being used for corporate power games.

Prospect Police

The most successful corporate risk committees act as knowledgeable advisors and counselors, not as prospect police having the power to veto any given venture. The reason is simple: Exploration teams must be accountable for their professional work product. In estimating prospect parameters, what they need is *experienced counsel*, not an imposed *committee decision*. Companies that use centralized, empowered risk committees to choose the prospects for drilling may show a year or two of improved performance. After that, however, exploration performance generally drops off. *Divided accountability causes diminished accountability.* Once prospectors learn what the declared or unofficial hurdles are, motivational bias begins to creep back into their predictions.

It is also important that prospect presentations to the exploration committee are kept informal, using work maps and sketches. Preparation of formal maps and diagrams is not cost-effective for such presentations.

Hidden Hurdles

Nearly every company acknowledges the obscure presence in its prospect evaluation process of hidden hurdles. These are unofficial economic requirements whose effect is to screen out prospects deemed to be less attractive than others. Hidden hurdles are usually inserted into the process by staff who are not accountable for exploration performance but see themselves as guardians protecting the organization against irresponsible explorationists. Typical examples of hidden hurdles include:

1. arbitrary elevated discount rates;
2. overly cautious drilling-cost estimates;
3. secret minimum prospect-reserves requirements; and
4. excessively high minimum economic field-size requirements.

Ironically, most hidden hurdles have the opposite economic impact from what they were intended to do—they tend to select against long-term, large-reserve ventures, the kind that build companies.

Unconstrained Intuitive Decision Making

Some exploration managers are reluctant to embrace risk analysis. They correctly perceive that it will constrain their exercise of intuitive decision making. The problem is that for some of these managers, exploration decision making becomes involved with the inappropriate exercise of ego. Risk analysis is not a substitute for good business judgment, but it will certainly assist in making proper, well-founded exploration decisions.

Economic Naïveté among Geoscientists

One of the all-too-common characteristics of geologists and geophysicists is that many of them perceive themselves as being part of a scientific priesthood in which they deliberately avoid acquiring a working knowledge about economics, finance, and business. This is largely a self-imposed handicap and may reflect a desire to be unaccountable. It may also be one of the leading reasons why geoscientists are generally absent from corporate boardrooms. The fact is, however, that economics is an essential aspect of prospect evaluations and thus of successful prospecting. When geoscientists maintain such economic naïveté, they invite improper use and even manipulation of their professional work by others. All geoscientists employed by the company should be aware that economic understanding will empower them professionally, and that it is their individual responsibility to master such knowledge.

Appendix A

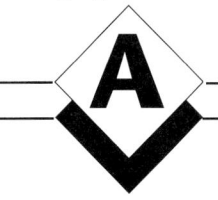

Methods for Calculating the Mean of a Lognormal Distribution

All of the following methods are based upon a distribution in which $n = 9$, and the constituent values are:

P90% = 0.6MM		
P80% = 1.25MM		
P70% = 2.1MM		
P60% = 3.3MM		
P50% = 5.0MM		
P40% = 7.6MM		
P30% = 12.1MM		
P20% = 20.0MM		
P10% = 43.0MM		
Total = 95.95MM		

KEY VALUES	NATURAL LOGS (ln)
P99% = 0.1MM	
P90% = 0.6MM	
P84% = 0.95MM	
P50% = 5.0MM	1.6094
P16% = 26.5MM	
P10% = 43.0MM	
P1% = 250.0MM	

1. *Arithmetic Mean* ($\overline{x}$)
   $\overline{x} = 95.95 \div 9 = \underline{10.66}$ MM

2. *Swanson's Mean (Msw):*
   $\qquad$ 0.3 (P90%) + 0.4 (P50%) + 0.3 (P10%)
   Msw $\quad$ 0.3 (0.6) $\quad$ + 0.4 (5.0) $\quad$ + 0.3 (43.0) =
   $\qquad\qquad\qquad\qquad\qquad\qquad\qquad\qquad$ $\underline{15.08}$ MM

3. *Statistical Mean (Mst):* assumes a continuous distribution, (i.e., $n = \infty$), with contribution from values greater than P1%
   $= e^{\mu + \sigma^2/2}$
   $= e^{ln(5.0) + ln(26.5/5.0)^2/2}$
   $= e^{ln(5.0) + ln(5.3)^2/2}$
   $= 5.0 e^{(1.6677)^2/2}$
   $= 5.0 e^{(2.7812)/2}$
   $= 5.0 e^{(1.3906)}$
   $= 5.0 \times 4.0173$
   $= \underline{20.01}$ MM

   Where $\mu = ln$ median (P50%) value
   $\sigma = ln$ standard deviation (P16% ÷ P50%)

4. *Statistical Mean, truncated above P1% (Mst [t > 1%]):*
   Mst(t > 1%) = $\underline{15.77}$ MM [Compare with item 2, Swanson's Mean (= $\underline{15.08}$ MM)].

NOTE: Upper truncation is also discussed on pages 14 and 20.

NOTE: The statistical mean is theoretically the preferred expression. However, I recommend against its general use, for the following reasons:

1. For field-size distributions, we do not ordinarily anticipate that a given trend or basin will have an infinite number of fields; instead we generally find tens to perhaps a few hundreds of fields. Accordingly, the continuous distribution, when n = ∞, seems inappropriate, and leads to an inflated mean field size.

2. For prospect parameters such as Area, Average Net Pay, Gross Rock Volume, HC-recovery in barrels per acre-foot (bbl/af) or thousand cubic feet per acre-foot (mcf/af), Prospect Reserves, Initial Production Rates, etc., the recommended probabilistic estimating connotations of P99%, P90%, P50%, P10%, and P1% treat those very large outcomes greater than P1% as practically and geologically impossible. Because the statistical mean includes contributing values larger than P1%, such untruncated means are unrealistically large. The P99% and P1% estimates then become very useful as lower and upper plausibility or credibility checks that encourage iterations leading to greatly improved estimates.

3. When such distributions are truncated at P1% and the truncated mean is calculated by incremental summing and averaging, such truncated mean values approach values obtained by using Swanson's Mean. Truncation at the small end of reserves distributions, reflecting commercial or economic thresholds, reinforces the practical utility of Swanson's Mean.

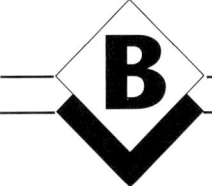

Appendix B: Graphical Method for Combining Probabilistic Distributions by Multiplication

In conjunction with their long-running AAPG School, "Managing and Evaluating Petroleum Risk," Capen, Megill, and Rose developed a graphical procedure to carry out the analytical method by which several probabilistic distributions may be combined by multiplication. This procedure gives the "ideal" results that would occur through multi-trial Monte Carlo or Latin Hypercube simulation, without any minor variations caused by random sampling. The method assumes that all distributions to be combined are lognormal, and that differences in their variances are not excessive. However, even normal distributions may be combined with satisfactory results, as long as their distributions have low variance (i.e., P10/P90 ranges are less than about 5).

I. Develop ranges for reserves parameters (Productive Area, Average Net Pay, HC-recovery Factor in bbl/af or mcf/af—see **Figure B-1**):
   A. Remember that all estimates express subjective probability judgments.
   B. Getting started
      1. Assume lognormality
      2. Make reasonable low-side and high-side estimates of the parameter, remembering the prevalent conservative bias to set predictive ranges too narrow. Plot the low-side estimate at P90% and the high-side estimate at P10% on a cumulative log probability graph. Draw a straight sloping line connecting them on the graph.
      3. What is the resulting P50% value? Is that a plausible "best guess" value?
      4. Estimating a middle value
         a. What's wrong with "most likely"?
            - Geologists don't intuitively identify it—confuse with median, mean, mode, etc.;
            - Not identifiable on cumulative curves plotted on log probability paper;
            - Useless in calculating the mean.
         b. P50—the median—proportional patterns in lognormal distributions (P10/P50 = P50/P90)
         c. Don't start the estimating process with a P50% estimate, to resist "anchoring."
   C. Iteration and Reiteration
      1. Project the sloping line downward to the P99% intersection; what is the resulting P99% value? Is it consistent with a minimum value barely sufficient to support flow into the borehole? Is it consistent with the structural and stratigraphic geometry of the prospect? *Is it consistent with existing geotechnical data?*
      2. Project the sloping line upward to the P1% intersection; what is the resulting P1% value? Is it consistent with available structural, stratigraphic, or reservoir data (i.e., is it a "high-side value so large as to be barely possible," *honoring the data?*
      3. Taking steps C1 and C2 into account, adjust the position and slope of the distribution. Work back and forth between maps, cross-sections, production data, etc., and log probability graphs, adjusting, examining implications of different cases, iterating, and reiterating until the distribution represents a best-fit to P1%, P10%, P50%, P90%, and P99% requirements.

II. Steps in combining distributions with log probability paper (*three variables*). See **Figure B-2:**
   A. Remember that multiplying the three 10th percentile values for Area, Pay, and HC-recovery will not give a 10% reserves product—as a matter of fact, it gives a product of 1.3%! Similarly, multiplying the three 90th percentile values gives a 98.7% reserves product, not 90%. However, multiplying the three 50th percentile values <u>does</u> indeed yield a 50% reserves product!

B. WE CAN USE THIS: Multiply the three P10% values for Area, Net Pay, and HC-recovery to yield a reserves product that should be plotted at 1.3%. Similarly, multiply the three P90% values for Area, Net Pay, and HC-recovery and plot the resulting reserves product at 98.7%. Also multiply the three P50% values to give reserves P50% and plot that. Draw a best-fit line through these three points: this line is the graphical reserves distribution. Pick off the P90% and P10% reserves values (and the P50% reserves value) and employ them using *Swanson's Rule*, to find mean reserves.

C. ALTERNATIVE APPROACH: What *are* the appropriate percentile values that, when multiplied, *will* generate 10% and 90% reserves values? It turns out that multiplying the three 23% values gives a 10% reserves product, and multiplying the three 77% values gives a 90% reserves product (see Ed Capen's *A Proof*—following). We can put this to work:
  1. Find the 23% values for Area, Pay, and HC-recovery from the plots you made on log probability paper. Multiply them to produce the 10% value for reserves; plot this value on log probability paper.
  2. Similarly, find the 77% values for Area, Pay, and HC-recovery from the same plots; multiply them to produce the 90% value for reserves; plot this value also.
  3. Plot a "reserves" line on your log probability paper, using the derived and plotted 10% and 90% values plus the 50% value you determined earlier.
  4. Calculate the mean of this reserves distribution using Swanson's Rule.

D. For combining two variables: multiplying two P90%'s gives P96.5%; multiplying two P10%'s gives P3.5%.

III. *Question:* Why can't I just calculate the three means of Area, Net Pay, and HC-recovery Factor, and multiply them to get the reserves mean?

Answer: You can (approximately), but you won't know anything about the *variance* (i.e., slope) of the distribution—you won't know what P90% and P10% are! And often it's important to calculate the NPV of the P90% and P10% cases using DCF analysis. Method C allows you to estimate the appropriate values for Area, Average Net Pay, and HC-recovery Factor to employ the cash-flow model used to determine the NPV of each reserves case!

A Proof

How do we know that multiplying the 77% points for area, pay, and recovery will lead to the 90% point for reserves?

$$\text{recovery} \times \text{net pay} \times \text{area} = \text{reserves}$$
$$Y_1 \times Y_2 \times Y_3 = R$$
$$X_i = \ln Y_i$$

Where X_i is normally distributed with mean μ_i and variance σ^2. All the variances are equal.

(This assumption causes no trouble. Our tests showed that we would have errors of no worse than 4% using this approximation. In oil and gas exploration, a 4% error amounts to a direct hit.)

Multiplying Ys is equivalent to adding Xs.

$$\ln R = \ln (Y_1 \times Y_2 \times Y_3)$$
$$= X_1 + X_2 + X_3$$

What is the variance of the sum of the Xs?

Assuming independence, the variance of a sum is the sum of the variances.

$$\sigma_\Sigma^2 = \text{variance of the sum} = 3\sigma^2$$
$$\text{And } \sigma_\Sigma = \sigma\sqrt{3}$$
$$\sigma = \sigma_\Sigma / \sqrt{3}$$

This says that the st. dev. of area, for example, equals the st. dev. of reserves divided by the square root of 3.

We know that the std. dev., σ, is just the scale factor for the standard normal, Z. "Standard" means zero mean and variance = 1.

So a Z_{area} would equal $Z_{reserves}/\sqrt{3}$.

Example: Say we want $Z_{reserves}$ to be at the 90% point. Z = 1.28 for 90%. Divide $1.28/\sqrt{3}$ to get 0.739. Therefore $Z_{area} = 0.739$. What cumulative probability goes with 0.739? A look at the normal probability tables shows 77%. Thus if we have three variables to multiply, by choosing their values at the 77% points, the product will be at the 90% point.

It should be clear that the $\sqrt{3}$ comes from using three factors in the product. If your system had just two variables, you would use $\sqrt{2}$ instead. Following the same logic, you can now handle any number of variables.

Ed Capen—circa 1990

Appendix B   129

AREA

600 acres

200 acres

60 acres

P10% = 600 ac   P50% = 200 ac   P90% = 60 ac

(P1 = 1500)
(P99 = 25)   Area (acres)

AVERAGE NET PAY

40'

20'

10'

P90% = 10'

P50% = 20'

P10% = 40'

(P1 = 75')
(P99 = 6')   Net Pay (ft)

HC-RECOVERY FACTOR

400 BAF = P10%
200 BAF = P50%
100 BAF = P90%

BAF = barrels per acre-foot (also baf)

(P1 = 700)
(P99 = 60)   HC-Rec (baf)

RESERVES

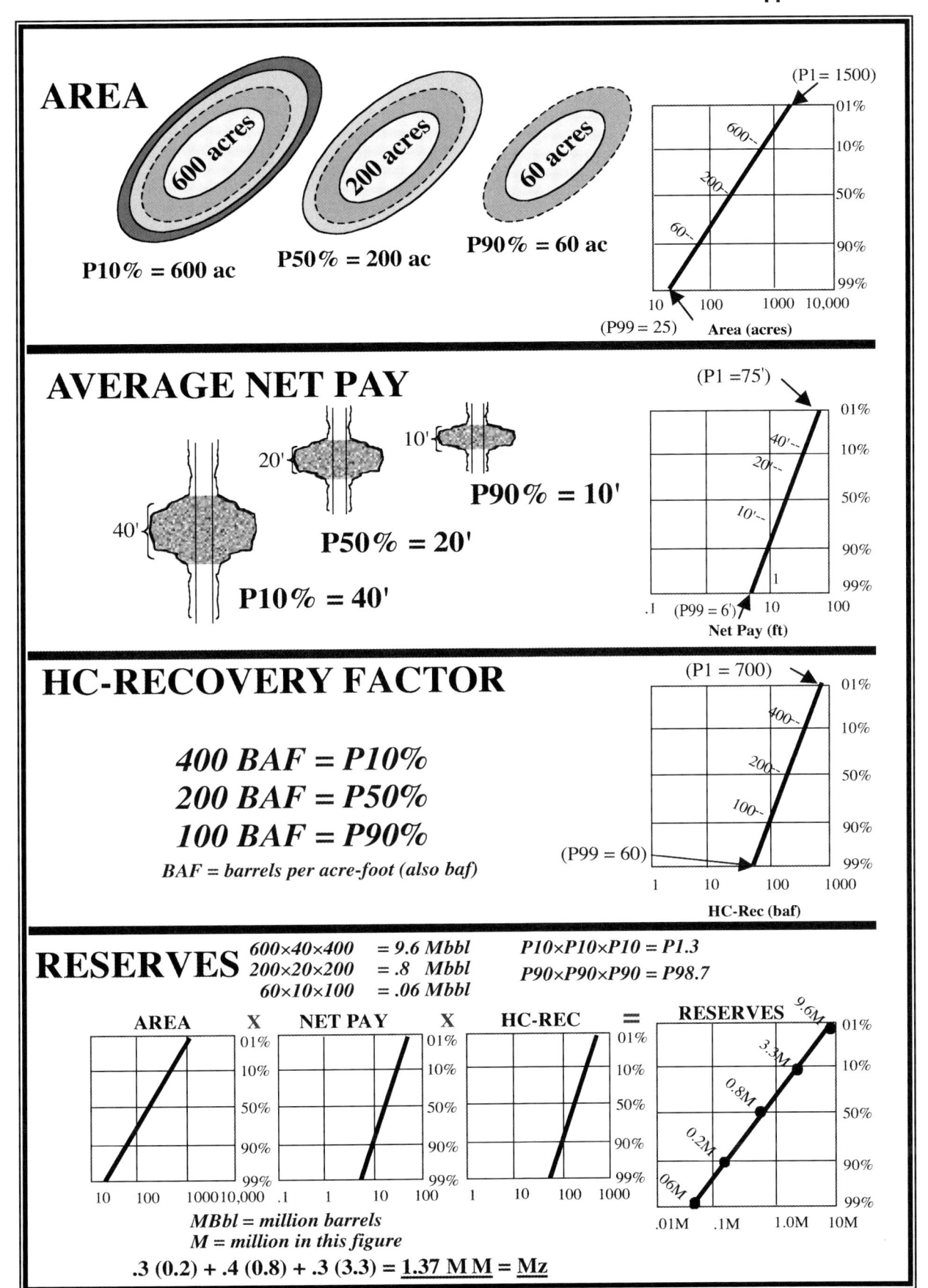

600×40×400 = 9.6 Mbbl   P10×P10×P10 = P1.3
200×20×200 = .8 Mbbl   P90×P90×P90 = P98.7
60×10×100 = .06 Mbbl

AREA X NET PAY X HC-REC = RESERVES

9.6M
3.3M
0.8M
0.2M
.06M

MBbl = million barrels
M = million in this figure

.3 (0.2) + .4 (0.8) + .3 (3.3) = <u>1.37 M M</u> = <u>Mz</u>

Figure B-1

Multiplying Three Cumulative Probability Distributions

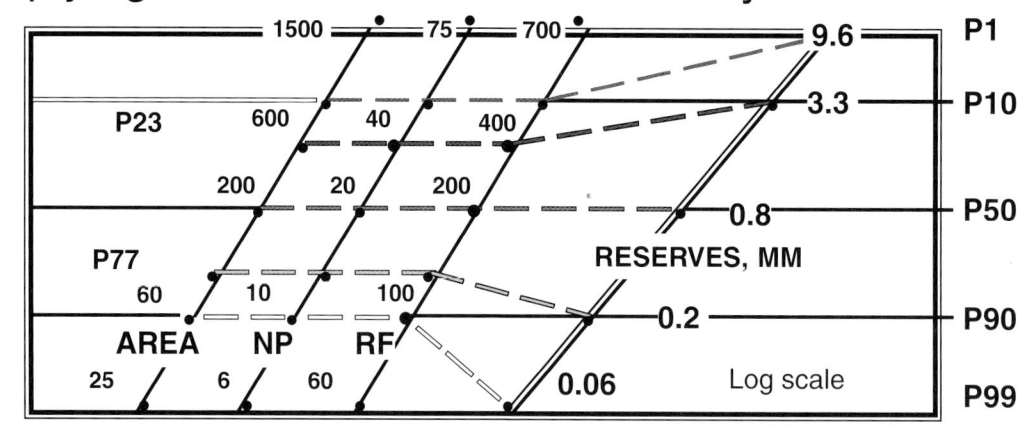

TWO METHODS FOR DERIVING THE RESERVE DISTRIBUTIONS:

	AREA		AV NET PAY		HC-REC.		RESERVES	
I.	P90	x	P90	x	P90	=	P98.7	⎫ DETERMINE
	P50	x	P50	x	P50	=	P50	⎬ P10 and P90,
	P10	x	P10	x	P10	=	P1.3	⎭ CALCULATE MEAN
II.	P77	x	P77	x	P77	=	P90	⎫
	P50	x	P50	x	P50	=	P50	⎬ CALCULATE MEAN
	P23	x	P23	x	P23	=	P10	⎭

Figure B-2

Appendix C

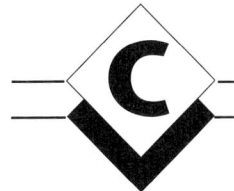

A Recurring Problem in Estimating Prospect Reserves—Determining Reasonable "Low-side" Values (P99% and P90%)

During the period 1935–1969, a field-size distribution of discoveries in the Texas Gulf Coast (**Figure C-1**) indicates that the smallest field sizes (= P99%) contained between 3,000 and 4,000 recoverable bbl. During the next 19 years (1970–1988), the P99% discovery size was only a little smaller—about 2,000 bbl (**Figure C-2**). Similarly, in the northern part of the Midland Basin/Red River Arch province, the P99% field size was about 1,000 bbl as of 1945, and about 650 bbl as of 1957. In the Silurian (Niagaran) pinnacle-reef play of northern Michigan, P99% for discovered fields was about 5,000 bbl in the period 1968–1974 (inclusive), and about 1,000 bbl for the period 1975–1988. And yet all these very small, money-losing events qualify as "discoveries"—mobile hydrocarbons were sensed, the wells were completed, and oil was produced, presumably for sale. The implications are depressing but profound: *there is always a possibility that your discovery is going to turn out to be a very small accumulation!*

Most experienced exploration risk analysts know that the most common cause of overestimation of prospect reserves is that the "low-side" estimates (P99% and P90%) are too large. But how to arrive at appropriate low-side estimates? This section addresses that problem using six different examples.

Example 1

In our short courses, we use a simple prospect exercise called the RMAG prospect (for the Rocky Mountain Association of Geologists, where it was first used). The RMAG exercise provided good examples whereby the low-side values for Area, Average Net Pay, and HC-recovery Factor were all quite low because the existing data demonstrated that such marginal values were entirely possible. Thus the P90% value for Area was about 60 acres (24 ha), and the P99% value was about 20 acres (8 ha). The P90% value for Average Net Pay thickness was about 6 feet (2 m) and P99% was 4 feet. HC-recovery Factor was given (P90% = 100 bbl/af [barrels/acre-foot]; P10% = 300 bbl/af, consequentially P99% was about 60 bbl/af, which approaches an effective reservoir minimum). The resulting reserves distribution had P90% reserves of about 96,000 bbl and P99% reserves of 27,000 bbl.

Example 2

But consider a second situation, where consistent and reliable regional log and rock data indicate that average net reservoir thickness is never less than 16 feet (5 m) and ranges systematically and regionally up to 80 feet (24 m). Even taking into account the geometric adjustment factor, P99% for Average Net Pay probably shouldn't be less than about 12 feet; P90% should be around 16 feet. Consider a prospect in this setting, where HC recoveries are consistently poor, ranging from 60 bbl/af to 150 bbl/af. Here, the productive area necessary to provide around 10,000 bbl—about the minimum amount of recoverable oil necessary to sustain flow—would of necessity be around 14 acres (5.7 ha) if Average Net Pay was 12 feet and HC-recovery was 60 bbl/af. However, only 6.5 acres would be required to contain 10,000 bbl if Average Net Pay was 16 feet and HC-recovery was 100 bbl/af.

Example 3

You must also take into account the effects of geometries consistent with the anticipated trap type. For example, suppose your prospect is a fault trap as shown in **Figure C-3**, minimum reservoir quality is projected to be 60 bbl/af (P99%), and average net pay thickness in such poor reservoir rock must be at least 40 feet (12 m).

Given that the dip-rate of the reservoir-zone is about 300 feet (90 m) per mile, this geometry imposes minimum value upon possible area of the low-side case (**Figure C-4**).

In order to arrive at the requisite 40 feet of average net pay in such trap geometry, the height of the hydrocarbon column must be about 65 feet. This forces the downdip position of the oil/water contact to be positioned about 1,000 feet south of the trapping fault,

TEXAS GULF COAST DISCOVERIES 1935–1969

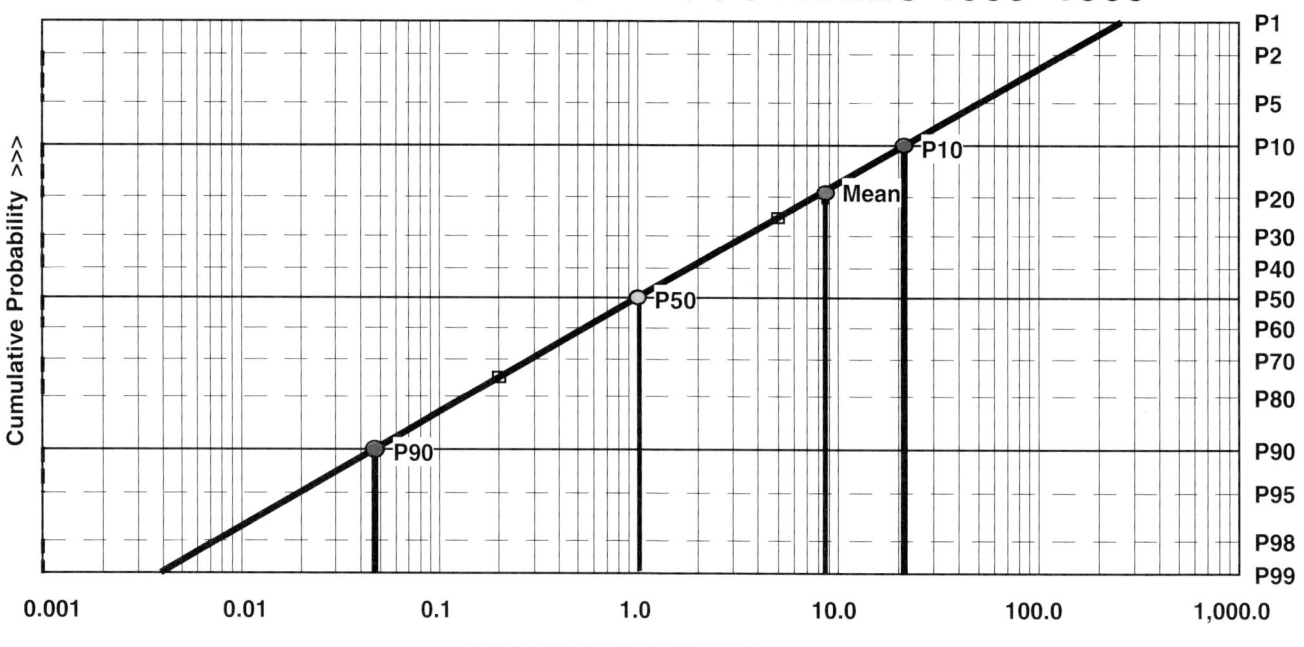

P99 = 0.004 MMBOE
P90 = 0.050 MMBOE
P50 = 1.00 MMBOE
P10 = 21.3 MMBOE
P1 = 258 MMBOE
MEAN = 8.5 MMBOE

Figure C-1

measured along the north-south axis of the structure, as shown by **Figure C-4**. Because the structural geometry requires an elongated east-west closure, the length of the minimum closure measured along the fault must be about 1.85 miles, or 9,800 feet. The area of this minimum closure (shaded in Figure C-3) is about 112 acres (9,800 ft. × 1,000 ft. ÷ 2 × 43,560 ft²/acre). The product of the three P99% values is 269,000 bbl (112 acres × 40 ft. ave. net pay × 60 bbl/af). Obviously, the corresponding P90% values for Average Net Pay, Area, and Reserves would have to be much larger.

For additional perspective, suppose that the required P99% value for average net pay is 20 feet, rather than 40 feet; still using 60 bbl/af, this places the oil/water contact 500 feet south of the fault, and reduces the minimum area (P99%) by half, to 56 acres. Additionally, prospectors must remember that the reserves P99% value is the approximate product of the P90% values for area, average net pay, and HC-recovery factor. For elongated structural traps, P99% reserves accordingly may be substantially greater than the minimum 10,000 to 50,000 bbl required to support sustained flow.

Example 4

Consider a prospect located on a large, gentle domal anticline **(Figure C-5)**, in which the reservoir dip away from the apex of the closure is very gentle, say 30 feet per mile. Further, let us suppose that regional reservoir data indicate that P90% = 120 bbl/af and P99% = 60 bbl/af are appropriate estimates for this prospect. Also, assume that appropriate estimates for net reservoir thickness are 15 feet (P90%) and 10 feet (P99%). The structural geometry leads to the following possible P99% outcome, keyed to a 10,000-bbl minimum reserves case **(Figure C-5)**:

We now adjust net reservoir thickness to obtain average net pay: P99% = 8 feet and P90% = 12 feet. Now, in order to achieve the requisite 8 feet of P99% average net pay thickness, the thickness of the oil column at the apex of the structure must be around 15 feet, which then requires a linear distance of about 1.0

TEXAS GULF COAST DISCOVERIES 1970–1988

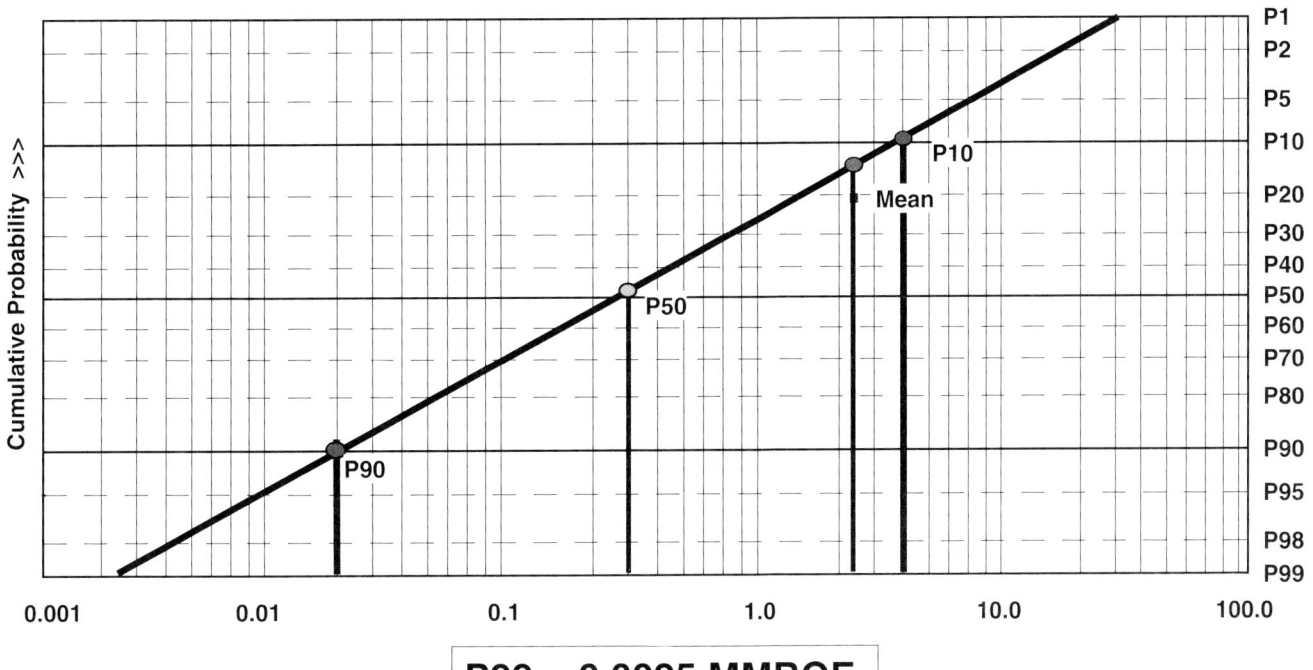

P99 = 0.0025 MMBOE
P90 = 0.02 MMBOE
P50 = 0.3 MMBOE
P10 = 4.0 MMBOE
P1 = 30 MMBOE
MEAN = 2.5 MMBOE

Figure C-2

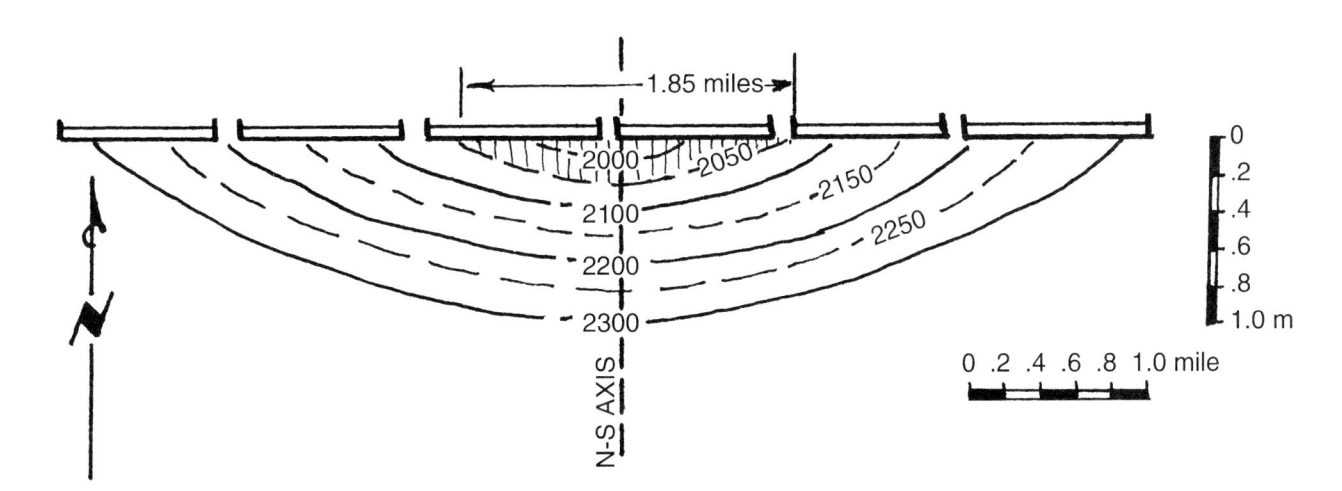

Figure C-3

mile for the length of the elongated axis of the saturated area. The corresponding area of closure is: $\pi r^2 = 3.1416 \times (2,640 \text{ ft.})^2 \div 43,560 \text{ ft.}^2/\text{acre} = \underline{503 \text{ acres}} =$ P99%. Obviously, P90% area would have to be much larger, perhaps approaching 1,000 acres.

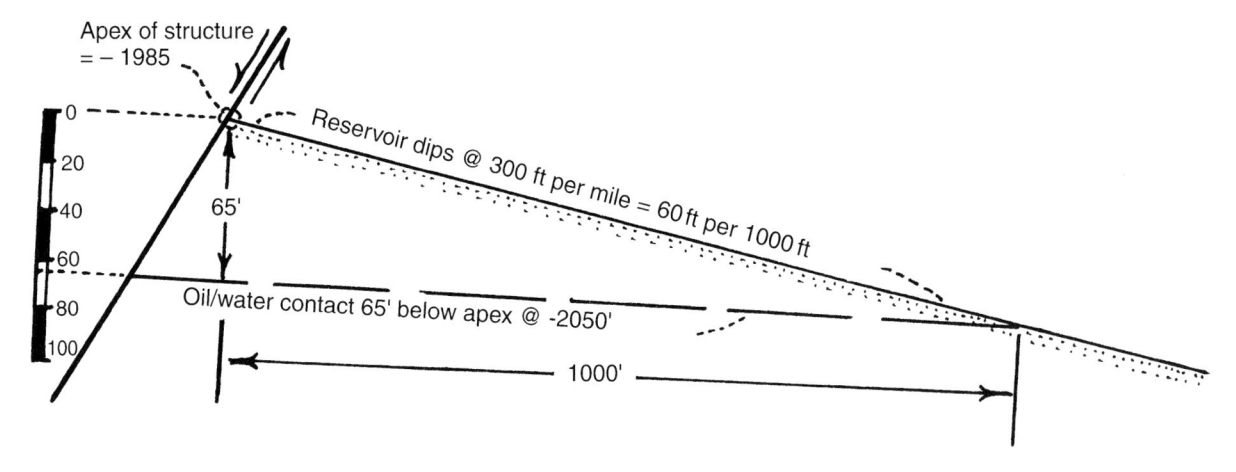

134 A Recurring Problem in Estimating Prospect Reserves

Figure C-4

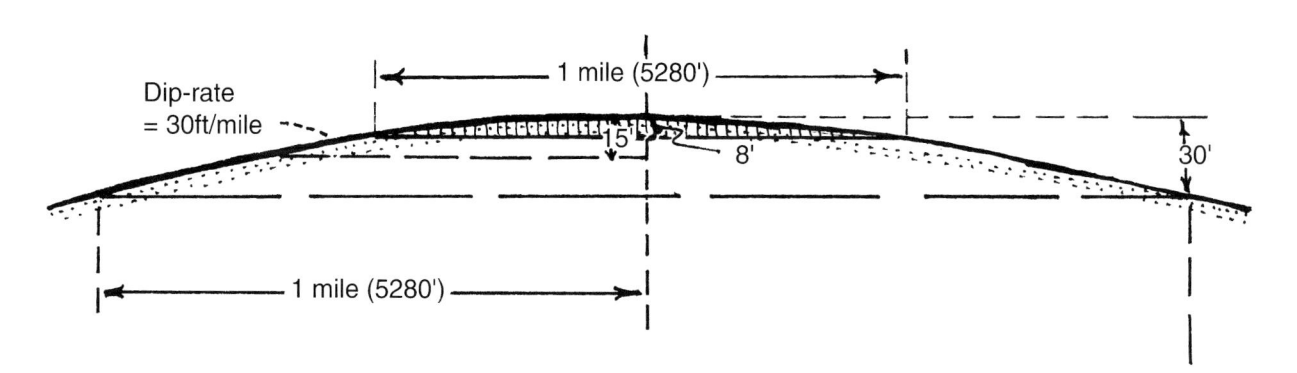

Figure C-5

Example 5

Suppose you are exploring an undrilled frontier trend containing perhaps 100 structural closures, some large, some intermediate, some small. Given the usual exploration pattern, your prospectors *can* identify closures too small to contain the 25 million barrels (MM bbl) they think is the minimum required to develop; but what your prospectors *cannot* consistently do in such a trend is to identify those large closures that contain very *small* accumulations (because of severe underfilling, or very poor reservoir quality or thickness, or because of faulty geophysical data or interpretations). In any case, if you drill only prospects you think are large enough to contain at least 25 MM bbl, your low-side areas (P99%) could well be larger than 20 or 40 acres, and P90% areas could certainly be several hundred acres or even more. As a result, P99% reserves could well be larger than 10–20,000 bbl—it could properly be 50–100,000 bbl, or maybe more. Correspondingly, P90% reserves might be from about 200,000 up to around one million barrels, or more. *But only because you are not going to drill any but the largest closures.*

Example 6

Consider a prospect in the Gulf of Mexico that features a fairly well-defined amplitude anomaly that is congruent with structural contours, and a "flat spot" that may indicate a gas-water contact, also consistent with the structural picture. Your geotechnical staff think there is ± 20% possible variation in the median Area parameter of 400 acres because of imperfect resolution. So, in this case, P90% = 320 acres and P90% = 480 acres.

What's the message? There's no "cookbook"—*you cannot blindly assign a low-side value to the reserves parameters.* You must understand the range of geologic values, the structural patterns, and the exploration maturity of the trend. Then you must integrate these considerations and ***think probabilistically***. But, in any case, it's not a bad idea to start with very small assumptions for P90% and P99% values for Area, Average Net Pay, and HC-recovery Factor—*and then adjust them upward as the geotechnical evidence justifies.*

Final admonition:—Remember that the most common field size discovered in west Texas in the 1930s and 1940s (during the "flush" period of discovery, when many very large fields were being found) was a one-well field—around 10,000 to 20,000 bbl. During all the subsequent decades, even up to the present time, the most common field size has remained about the same—the one-well field. Sure, such reserves sizes have gradually decreased, but only a little. *So, when constructing the reserves distribution for your prospect, ask yourself, "Do I really think that there's no chance of my prospect turning out to be a mediocre little one-well field?"*

Appendix D

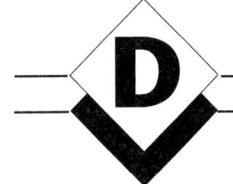

Evaluating and Combining Multiple-objective Ventures

In many prospects and proposed trends or contract areas, there may be multiple-zone, or multiple-play candidates. Some multiple ventures may be simple involving only two objectives and with clear independent and/or shared attributes. Other multiple ventures may be quite complex involving many objectives and with complex and subtle issues of partial dependencies further complicated by issues of marginal commerciality.

Sometimes a prospective contract area may contain an existing trend having some remaining exploration potential, as well as a second, deeper play, or another play in a different part of the exploration area. Some plays may be part of a single petroleum system involving partial dependencies among some or all geologic chance factors. In some prospective contract areas there may also be one or more producing fields to consider as well.

Several practical principles of multiple ventures should be emphasized:

1. As the number of objectives in any multiple venture increases arithmetically, the complexity of combination increases geometrically;
2. Monte Carlo or Latin Hypercube simulation is required for all but the simplest multiple-objective ventures;
3. Geologic dependency is common, especially involving the hydrocarbon charge and closure chance factors;
4. Many apparently complex ventures can be simplified and approximated by practical, common sense methods of consideration;
5. Analysts are well advised to focus on objectives that are "stand-alone commercial or economic" and ignore those that provide only incremental cash flows augmenting primary producing objectives; and
6. For comprehensive treatment of multiple-objective ventures, the reader is referred to James Murtha's excellent 1995 SPE paper.

Following the principle that a picture (or example) is worth a thousand words, two examples are provided herein, which should provide the careful reader with a good understanding of the concepts and procedures used in evaluating multiple-objective ventures. Part 1 describes several aspects of a two-objective multizone prospect, in which Monte Carlo simulation is avoided by basing calculation on only the mean reserves case of each objective. Part 2 describes a multiple venture involving two plays and a producing property, which employs a decision-tree analysis as well as Monte Carlo simulation.

Part 1: Multiple-zone Prospect Example: Geologic and Economic Assumptions

CASES 1 & 2:

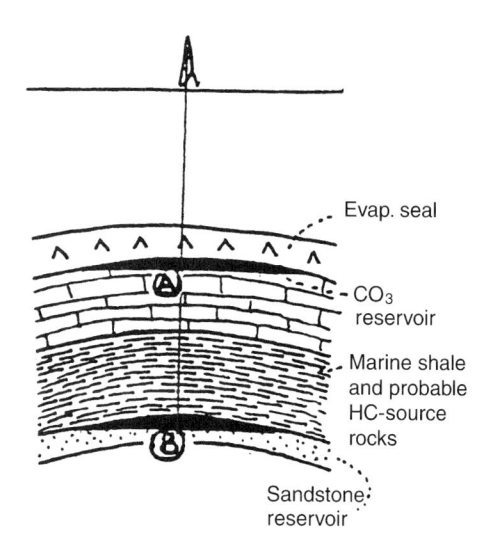

[Diagram showing well penetrating Evap. seal, CO₃ reservoir (A), Marine shale and probable HC-source rocks, Sandstone reservoir (B)]

CASE 3:

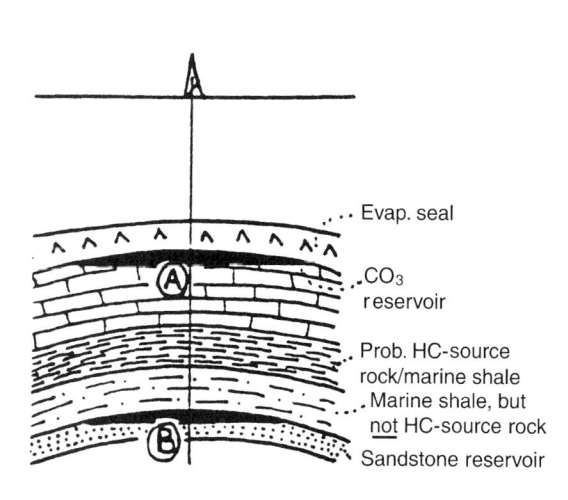

[Diagram showing well penetrating Evap. seal, CO₃ reservoir (A), Prob. HC-source rock/marine shale, Marine shale but not HC-source rock, Sandstone reservoir (B)]

Table D-1

Description Prospect with two objectives, A & B. Dry-hole cost = $1 MM. Note: In this example, only four geologic chance factors are employed. Also, geologic chance of success (Pg) = commercial chance of success (Pc).

Objective A Low-relief anticlinal closure, carbonate reservoir resting on mature (?) source rock, capped by evaporite topseal. Mean reserves estimated 2 MMBOE, equiv. PV = $10 MM.

Prob. reservoir = 0.7 (reservoir thickness, Φ, k)
Prob. structure = 0.5 (critical closure, seis resolution, low-relief structure)
Prob. HC-charge = 0.7 (adequacy, timing)
Prob. seal/trap = 0.9 (preservation of evap. cap)

Pc = .221 (Pf = .779)
EV = 0.221 ($10 MM) – 0.779 ($1.0 MM)
 = $2.21 MM – $.779MM
 = (+) $1.431 MM

Objective B Low-relief anticlinal closure, sandstone reservoir overlain by marine shale top seal, also mature (?) source rock. Mean reserves est. 10MM BOE, equiv. PV=$20MM.

Prob. reservoir = 0.4 (reservoir thickness, Φ, k)
Prob. structure = 0.5 (critical closure, seis resolution, low-relief structure)
Prob. HC-charge = 0.7 (adequacy, timing)
Prob. seal/trap = 0.7 (effectiveness of topseal)

Pc = 0.098 (Pf = 0.902)
EV = 0.098 ($20MM) – 0.902 ($1.0MM)
 = $1.96MM – $0.902MM
 = (+) $1.058MM

Similar to prospect above, except that the HC source rock is positioned in the upper half of the marine shale unit, directly beneath the carbonate reservoir (A), so that it does not rest directly upon the sandstone reservoir (B). Accordingly there may be some reduced chance of hydrocarbon emplacement in the sandstone reservoir, because of the difficulty of "downcharging" against the natural buoyancy of hydrocarbons in formation water, as well as the difficulty of oil migrating through a considerable thickness of tight shale to access the sandstone reservoir rock.

Case 1: All Geologic Chance Factors Are Independent; Dry-hole Cost = $1 MM

Productive Chance			A	B		Venture Prob.		Value	Risked Value
Both:	0.022	a) A and B both productive	.221 ×	.098 =		.022	×	(+)$30MM	= (+) $0.660MM
Only one:	0.275	b) A productive, B dry	.221 ×	.902 =		.199	×	(+)$10MM	= (+) $1.990MM
At least one:	0.287	c) A dry, B productive	.779 ×	.098 =		.076	×	(+)$20MM	= (+) $1.520MM
		d) A and B both dry	.779 ×	.902 =		.703	×	(−)$1MM	= (−) $0.703MM
						1.000			EV = (+)$3.467MM

Case 2: Dependent (Structure, HC-charge) and Independent (Reservoir, Seal/Trap) Chance Factors; Dry-hole Cost = $1 MM

Step 1:
Prospect A = Pres × Pseal = .7 × .9 = .63 = Pg (and .37 Pf) are independent factors
Prospect A = Pstr × PHC = .5 × .7 = .35 = Pg (and .65 Pf) are dependent factors
Prospect B = Pres × Pseal = .4 × .7 = .28 = Pg (and .72 Pf) are independent factors
Prospect B = Pstr × PHC = .5 × .7 = .35 = Pg (and .65 Pf) are dependent factors

Step 2:

Productive Chance			A	B	Prob.	Both A and B	Venture Prob.	Value	Risked Value
Both:	0.062	a) A and B both productive	.63 ×	.28 =	.176 .	35	.062 ×	(+)$30MM	= (+) $1.86MM
Only one:	0.195	b) A productive, B dry	.63 ×	.72 =	.454 .	35	.159 ×	(+)$10MM	= (+) $1.59MM
At least one:	0.257	c) A dry, B productive	.37 ×	.28 =	.104 .	35	.036 ×	(+)$20MM	= (+) $0.728MM
		d) A and B both dry	[1 − (.062 + .159 + .036)] = 1 − .257 = .743 × (−)$1MM = (−) $0.743MM						

EV = (+)$3.435MM

Case 3: Dependent and Independent Chance Factors, as in Case 2, but Now Including One Geologic Chance Factor with Subfactors That Are Both Dependent and Independent; Dry-hole Cost = $1 MM.

Because of the position of the HC source rock as noted in **Table D-1**, there might be some reduced chance of hydrocarbon emplacement in the sandstone reservoir.

For Prospect A, we break down the HC-charge chance factor into three subfactors:
Probability of HC-charge = 0.7
Subfactors: HC-1) adequate organic richness = 0.9
HC-2) thermal maturity = 0.9   } Product = 0.73
HC-3) migration/ emplacement efficiency = 0.9

Subfactors 1 and 2 are common to Prospect B as well as Prospect A, but subfactor 3 (migration/emplacement efficiency) is more problematical in Prospect B, and is therefore assigned a probability of 0.5. All other geologic chance factors remain as shown previously in Case 2.

Step 1:
Prospect A (Independent) = Pres × Pseal × PHC3 = .7 × .9 × .9 = .56 = Pc (and .44 Pf)
Prospect A (Dependent) = Pstr × PHC1, 2 = .5 × .8 = .40 = Pc (and .60 Pf)
Prospect B (Independent) = Pres × Pseal × PHC3 = .4 × .7 × .5 = .14 = Pc (and .86 Pf)
Prospect B (Dependent) = Pstr × PHC1, 2 = .5 × .8 = .40 = Pc (and .60 Pf)

Step 2:

Productive Chance			A	B	Prob.	Both A and B	Venture Prob.	Value	Risked Value
Both:	0.031	a) A and B both productive	.56 ×	.14 =	.078	.40	.031 ×	(+)$30MM	= (+) $.936MM
Only one:	0.218	b) A productive, B dry	.56 ×	.86 =	.482	.40	.193 ×	(+)$10MM	= (+) $1.93MM
At least one:	0.249	c) A dry, B productive	.44 ×	.14 =	.062	.40	.025 ×	(+)$20MM	= (+) $.500MM
		d) A and B both dry	[1 − (.031 + .193 + .025)] = 1 − .249 = .751 × (−)$1MM = (−) $.751MM						

EV = (+)$2.615MM

Combining Reserves Distributions

1. In this example, the reserves distributions of the two prospects have not been combined, because the P10%, P50%, and P90% values were not provided, only the means). So, for the "both A & B" productive cases, reserves were combined simply by adding the two means, which is not strictly accurate.
2. Properly, reserves distributions of the two prospects, represented by P10%, P50%, and P90% values, can be combined by Monte Carlo simulation. However, this requires combining chance-weighted distributions through *addition*, not *multiplication*, as we did graphically in Appendix B, with the three components of prospect reserves (Area, Average Net Pay, and HC-recovery Factor). Unfortunately, adding probabilistic distributions is not practical to perform graphically, so we should rely on Monte Carlo simulation to carry it out.

Part 2: Combining Multiple Types of Ventures*

This multiple-venture example illustrates the procedural steps involved in combining three objectives—a producing property, a medium-risk new play, and a high-risk new play (Section A).** It employs a probability tree for the partially dependent plays, as well as a Monte Carlo simulation. The probability tree solution (Sections B.1 and B.2) uses only mean reserves outcomes for the different cases, yielding a total expected mean outcome for reserves of 36.10 MMBOE, having a total expected net present value (ENPV) of $261.7 MM. Section C, the Monte Carlo simulation (50,000 trials), shows the probability range of possible reserves outcomes. The distribution of reserves outcomes for all possible cases is shown as a frequency distribution (or probability-density graph). The P90% outcome is 11.19 MMBOE, the P50% outcome is 35.49 MMBOE, the P10% outcome is 153.22 MMBOE, and the mean outcome is 36.72 MMBOE, which agrees well with the 36.10 MMBOE figure derived using the probability tree and mean values (Section B). Thinking about the overall venture in a simplistic way, the P90% outcome expresses a scenario in which the producing property low-side case turns out to be the only project of the three that is successful, even marginally. The P50% case (35.49 MMBOE) represents an outcome in which the producing property turns out to be the P50% to P_{MEAN} case, and one of the two plays emerges successfully, providing "mid-range" reserves (≈P50% to P_{MEAN} if Play "Beta," or P80% – P60% reserves if Play "Gamma"). The P10% outcome for the overall venture would either require all three ventures to succeed moderately, or the producing property and one of the two plays to succeed at relatively high probability levels.

Similarly, part D shows Monte Carlo simulation of probabilistic ENPV for the multiple venture outlined in part A, employing the appropriate NPV/BOE for the different subventures ("Alpha," "Beta," and "Gamma"). In other words, part D utilizes all the probabilistic outcomes of the entire venture in terms of ENPV, rather than reserves, and allows the ENPV of all possible reserves outcomes to be expressed.

---

*The assistance of Robert V. Clapp is acknowledged with gratitude; Clapp prepared the probability tree (Section B) and carried out the Monte Carlo simulations (Sections C and D). Note that the distributions were not truncated above P1% and that Clapp utilized the "P10 = small" convention.

**Chance of geologic success based upon five chance factors; also, chance of geologic success = chance of commercial success in these examples.

A. Descriptions and Assumptions

1. *Producing Field "Alpha" Prob. = 100%:*

A producing field discovered and developed several years ago. Projected additional recoveries (some to be added through additional development and more efficient technology; anticipated capital investments ($15MM) included in $7 NPV/bbl figure):

Projected Additional Recovery:
P1% =   7.4 MMBOE
P10% = 10.0 MMBOE
P50% = 14.1 MMBOE
P90% = 20.0 MMBOE
P99% = 26.5 MMBOE
Mean = 14.6 MMBOE

$\underline{\text{\$NPV of Mean Reserves Case =}}$
14.6 MMBOE × \$7 NPV/BOE = \$102.2MM

2. *New Play "Beta":*

A moderate-risk, moderate-potential, relatively shallow play having chance of play success = 0.72, chance of average economic prospect success = 0.34, four tests committed, so chance of at least one economic prospect success is $1 - (1 - .34)^4 = 0.81$, so chance of economic play success = 0.72 × 0.81 = 0.58: Cost of play failure is \$20MM.

Economic Play Reserves:
P1% =   1.0 MMBOE
P10% =   3.4 MMBOE
P50% =   14.0 MMBOE
P90% =   60.0 MMBOE
P99% = 200.0 MMBOE
Mean =   26.5 MMBOE

Geologic Chance Factors:
Shared = 0.72
   HC source rocks = .80
   HC generation/migration = 1.00
Independent = 0.34
   Reservoir = .60
   Closure = .80
   Containment = .90
   Pmefs = .70

$\underline{\text{\$NPV of Mean Reserves Case =}}$
26.5MMBOE × \$5NPV/BOE = \$132.5MM

3. *Provisional New Play "Gamma":*

A high-risk, high-potential, deeper play, having chance of play success = 0.4 or 0.8, chance of average economic prospect success = 0.17, three tests committed, so chance of at least one prospect success is $1 - (1 - 0.17)^3 = 0.42$, so chance of cumulative economic play success = 0.8 or 0.4 × .42 = 0.336 or 0.168. There is partial dependency between Play Gamma and Play Beta, involving the shared chance factor HC source rocks: if Play Beta proves that HC source rocks are present, then the chance of HC source rocks will increase for Gamma to 0.8; if HC source rocks are absent in Beta, chance of HC source rocks will decline to 0.4 at Gamma. Cost of play failure is \$30MM.

Economic Play Reserves:
P1% =   2.0 MMBOE
P10% =   8.0 MMBOE
P50% =   44.0 MMBOE
P90% =   240.0 MMBOE
P99% = 1,000.0 MMBOE
Mean =   105.0 MMBOE

Geologic Chance Factors:
Shared = 0.80
   HC source rocks = .80
   HC generation/migration = 1.00
Independent = 0.17
   Reservoir = .60
   Closure = .80
   Containment = .50
   Pmefs = .70

$\underline{\text{\$NPV of Mean Reserves Case =}}$
105 MMBOE × \$3.50 NPV/BOE = \$367.5MM

B. Combining Ventures (Nonstochastic Methods)

1. Probability Tree (see **Figure D-1**).
2. Expected Net Present Values of different play outcome combinations, based on mean reserves case only:

Possible Outcomes	Prob	$NPV(MM) of Mean Reserves Case	Risked $NPV(MM)
β and Γ both successes	.196	($132.5 + 367.5 = +$500MM)	$98.00MM
β success and Γ fails	.271 + .117 = .388	($132.5 + 30MM = +$102.5MM)	$39.77MM
β fails and Γ success	.046 + .027 + .034 = .107	($367.5 + 20MM = +$347.5MM)	$37.18MM
β and Γ both fail	.063+.027+.037+.0169+.046+.012 = .309	(–$20 + –30MM = –$50MM)	$–15.45MM

ENPV of both plays (mean reserves cases) =	$159.50MM
ENPV of mean reserves of producing field "Alpha" =	$102.20MM
Total ENPV of all ventures (mean reserves cases) =	$261.70MM

Appendix D

Probability Tree Showing All Possible Combinations for Beta and Gamma Plays

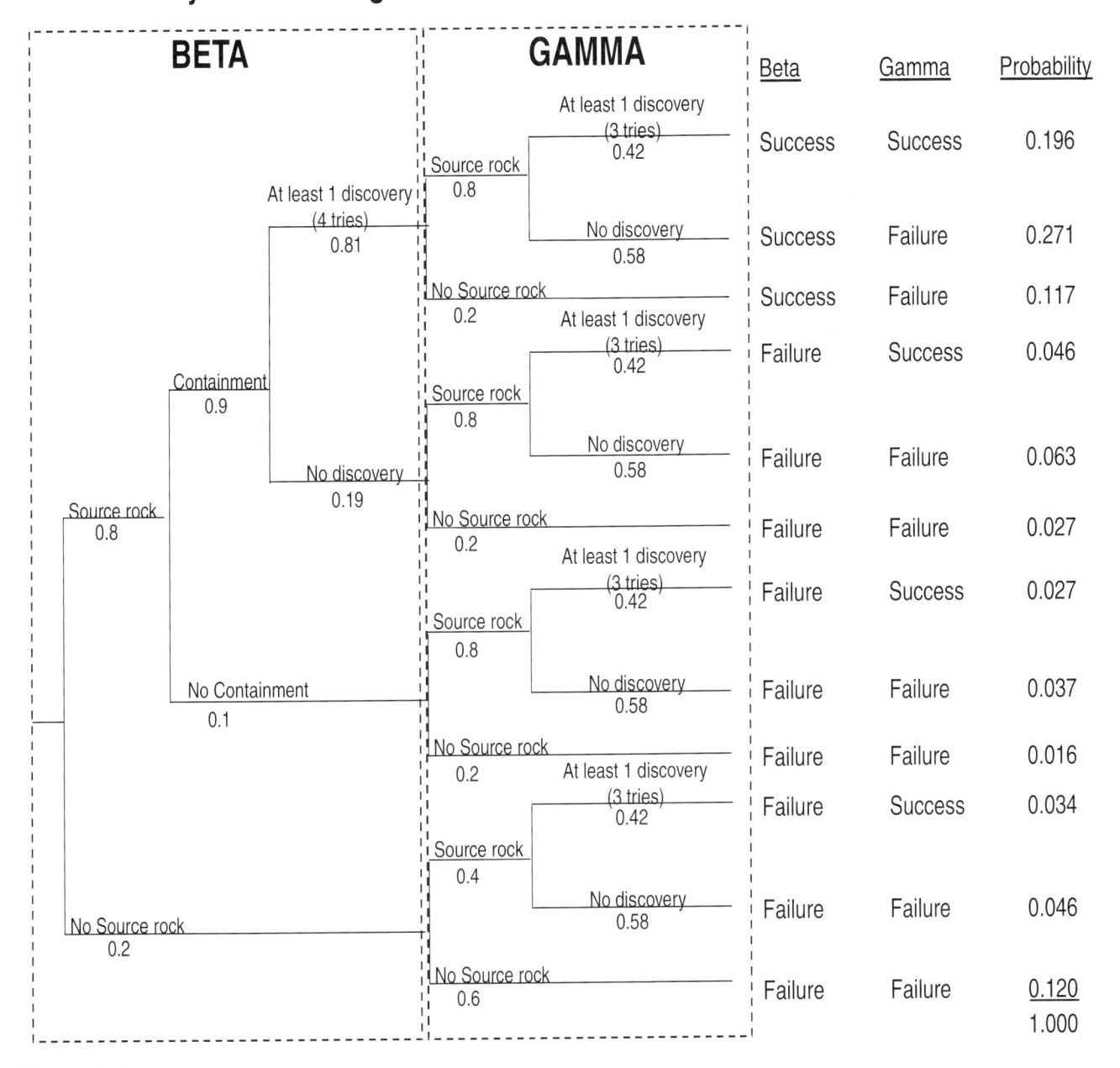

	Beta	Gamma	Probability
	Success	Success	0.196
	Success	Failure	0.271
	Success	Failure	0.117
	Failure	Success	0.046
	Failure	Failure	0.063
	Failure	Failure	0.027
	Failure	Success	0.027
	Failure	Failure	0.037
	Failure	Failure	0.016
	Failure	Success	0.034
	Failure	Failure	0.046
	Failure	Failure	0.120
			1.000

Figure D-1

C. Stochastic Method of Combining Expected Reserves of All Ventures

Probabilistic distribution of Total Reserves, employing Monte Carlo simulation of all ventures' reserves distributions, and estimated venture chances of success and failure (producing property Alpha Pg = 100%). (See **Figure D-2**; note use of "90% = small" convention.)

Forecast: Total Reserves   Cell: E14

Summary: Certainty Level is 100.00% based on Entire Range
           Certainty Range is from -∞ to ∞ MMBOE
           Display Range is from 0.00 to 150.00 MMBOE
           Entire Range is from 5.12 to 11,948.83 MMBOE
           After 50,000 Trials, the Std. Error of the Mean is 0.63

Statistics:	Display Range	Entire Range
Trials	46,014	50,000
Percent of Other	92.03	108.66
Mean	36.72	61.75
Median	24.75	(unavailable)
Mode	14.25	(unavailable)
Standard Deviation	29.92	141.61
Variance	894.98	20,052.95
Skewness	1.66	(unavailable)
Kurtosis	5.27	(unavailable)
Coeff. of Variability	81.48	229.31
Range Width	150.00	11,943.71
Range Minimum	0.00	5.12
Range Maximum	150.00	11,948.83
Mean Std. Error	0.14	0.63

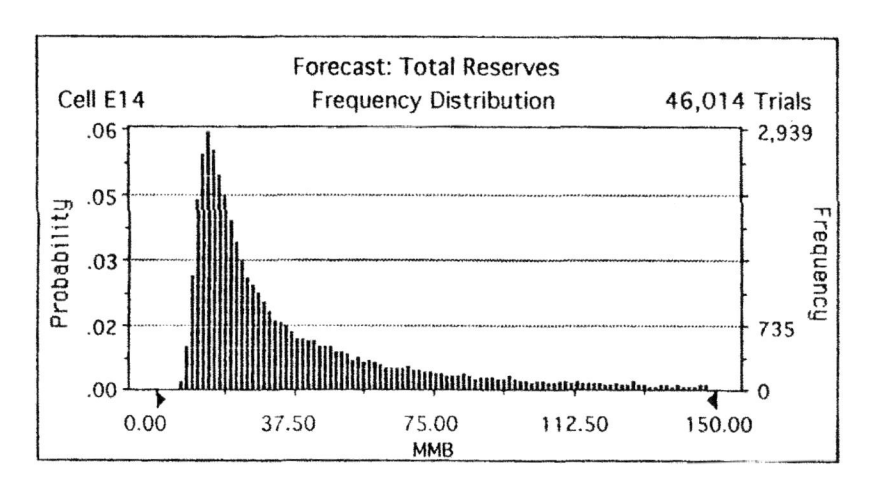

Forecast: Total Reserves (Cont'd)   Cell: E14

Percentiles for Entire Range (MMBOE):

Percentile	Total Reserves
0%	5.12
10%	11.19
20%	17.27
30%	23.34
40%	29.42
50%	35.49
60%	41.57
70%	56.09
80%	81.08
90%	153.22
100%	11,948.83

End of Forecast

Figure D-2

D. Stochastic Method of Combining ENPVs of All Ventures

Expected Net Present Value of different play-outcome combinations, employing Monte Carlo simulation of all ventures' reserves distributions, anticipated NPV/bbl for different ventures, and estimated venture chances of success and failure (producing property "Alpha" Pg = 100%). (See **Figure D-3**; note use of "P90% = small" convention.)

Forecast: Total NPV   Cell: F14

Summary: Certainty Level is 100.00% based on Entire Range
Certainty Range is from -∞ to ∞ MM$
Display Range is from 0.00 to 1,000.00 MM$
Entire Range is from -14.18 to 41,829.42 MM$
After 50,000 Trials, the Std. Error of the Mean is 2.32

Statistics:	Display Range	Entire Range
Trials	48,066	50,000
Percent of Other	96.13	104.02
Mean	193.64	261.09
Median	129.81	(unavailable)
Mode	51.67	(unavailable)
Standard Deviation	184.20	517.66
Variance	33,928.59	267,973.37
Skewness	1.83	(unavailable)
Kurtosis	6.38	(unavailable)
Coeff. of Variability	95.12	198.27
Range Width	1,000.00	41,843.60
Range Minimum	0.00	-14.18
Range Maximum	1,000.00	41,829.42
Mean Std. Error	0.84	2.32

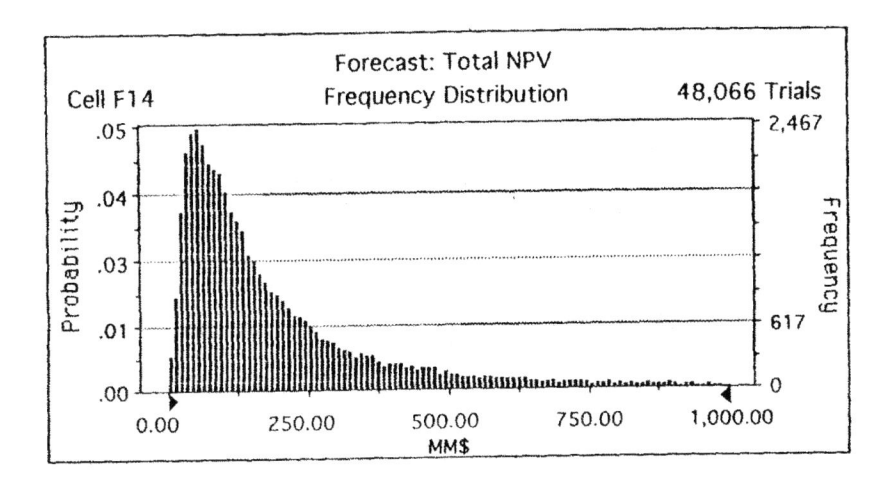

Forecast: Total NPV (Cont'd)   Cell: F14

Percentiles for Entire Range (MM$):

Percentile	Total NPV
0%	-14.18
10%	15.66
20%	45.50
30%	75.34
40%	105.18
50%	141.97
60%	193.14
70%	244.32
80%	343.80
90%	546.71
100%	41,829.42

End of Forecast

Figure D-3

Appendix E

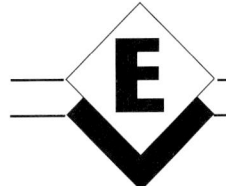

Steps in Geotechnical Procedure for Prioritizing Petroleum Prospectivity in New Exploration Areas

I. PETROLEUM GENERATION/MIGRATION (THE KITCHEN)
   A. Is the existence of a kitchen already clearly demonstrated by the documented presence of producing fields, shows, and seeps? If so, where is the kitchen? Where has generated petroleum gone? When? Through what did it migrate? Make maps showing all this.
   B. If no kitchen can be demonstrated, then:
      1. What are the stratigraphic units that contain possible source rocks (SR)?
         a. Are they from one of the seven known marine worldwide anoxic events (i.e., are they Silurian, Upper Devonian, Pennsylvanian–Lower Permian, Upper Jurassic, Aptian–Albian, Turonian, or Oligocene–Miocene)? What is the evidence?
         b. Otherwise, are there *local* marine anoxic units or lacustrine fine-grained units that could contain HC source rocks? Evidence? Localized humic-rich units?
         c. For *all* suspected SR units, make maps documenting control and dimensions/values of:
            (i) Areal extent
            (ii) Thickness
            (iii) Richness (TOC or SPI)
            (iv) HC type (oil, mixed, gas)
      2. Did they generate oil or gas (thermal history)? When (timing)? TTI evidence? Peak generation reached? Evidence (VR, coal rank, TAI, etc.)? Make maps.
      3. Where did the generated petroleum go? Evidence? Make maps.
         a. Routes
         b. Concentration
         c. Efficiency (horizontal vs. vertical migration, impedance)
         d. Compare with production and shows
      4. Critical uncertainties—What are they? Can they be resolved or reduced?
         a. Before deciding to enter area: Cost? Confidence in results? Time?
         b. Before deciding to drill: Cost? Confidence in results? Time?

II. RESERVOIR ROCKS
   A. Are some reservoir objectives already demonstrated by economic production? Where? Map their probable extent, thickness, and quality.
   B. If some or all reservoir objectives are suspected or projected:
      1. What are the stratigraphic units containing them? Evidence? Show on columnar section.
      2. For all inferred reservoir objectives, make maps showing control and dimensions/values:
         a. Areal extent
         b. Thickness
         c. Reservoir quality (sand%, net-to-gross, % porous, % permeable, etc.)
         d. Depositional environment/provenance/mineralogy; analog examples
         e. Abruptness of lateral facies changes (reservoir rocks to lateral seal)
         f. Comment: Preference should be given to reservoir units overlain by potential sealing units—essential couplet (top seal/reservoir)
      3. Critical Uncertainties—What are they? Can they be resolved or reduced?
         a. Before deciding to enter area? Cost? Confidence in results? Time?
         b. Before deciding to drill? Cost? Confidence in results? Time?

III. TRAPS (CLOSURES)
   A. Are some traps already demonstrated by economic production? What are the trap types? Where located? Size of closures? Map the fairways of occurrence.
   B. For those traps that are predicted, what are the trap types (i.e., anticlinal, fault, combination, stratigraphic, basin-centered [generational], etc.)?

1. Map trends or fairways of different trap types
2. What reservoirs would they affect?
3. Analog examples
4. Did traps (closures) form before generation/migration? Evidence?
5. Are traps favorably located with respect to migration?
6. Reliability of geological/geophysical data (show areas on maps)
   a. Repeatability—identification and delineation by independent workers
   b. Reliability of geological/geophysical data (show areas on maps)
      (i) acquisition
      (ii) time-depth conversions
      (iii) processing
      (iv) variable reliability among different trap types
      (v) map your confidence in seismic interpretation
      (vi) 2-D vs. 3-D—resolution vs. cost
7. Critical trap uncertainties—What are they? Can they be resolved or reduced? By seismic? Other geophysical methods? Geologic methods?
   a. Before deciding to enter area: Cost? Confidence in results? Time?
   b. Before deciding to drill: Cost? Confidence in results? Time?

IV. CONTAINMENT
   A. Is containment already demonstrated by economic production? What aspect of containment (top seals? fault seals? lateral permeability barriers?) Where? Map them.
   B. Where containment is not proven and must be predicted:
      1. What are potential top seals, seat seals, and lateral seals? Where are they developed? Map them.
      2. Preservation—make HC-gravity and HC-type maps
         a. Thermal—map areas of thermal immaturity, oil-prone, gas-prone, overcooked (by stratigraphic or structural level). Evidence?
         b. Flushing—salinity and piezometric maps showing ground-water movement
         c. Biodegradation—evidence? manifestations? Map.
         d. Post-accumulation structural adjustments—tilt-and-spill, breaching; locations? Evidence?
      3. Critical containment uncertainties—What are they? Can they be resolved or reduced? How?
         a. Before deciding to enter area? Cost? Confidence in results? Time?
         b. Before deciding to drill? Cost? Confidence in results? Time?

V. PROVISIONAL PLAY IDENTIFICATION, DELINEATION, GRADING
   A. List possible plays (include proven plays showing remaining prospective area of play).
   B. Overlay maps showing kitchen, reservoir, traps, and containment for each play, grade sectors of coincidence.

VI. CRITICAL PLAY UNCERTAINTIES
   A. What are they? List and map.
   B. Can they be economically investigated/resolved in time to influence decision to get into area? Cost? Confidence in resolution? Time required?
   C. Can they be economically investigated/resolved in time to influence decisions to drill? Cost? Confidence in resolution? Time required?

VII. ANALOG BASINS AND PLAYS
   A. Location, geologic succession, tectonic situation, documentation
   B. Elements that are very similar and significant
   C. Elements that are dissimilar and significant

VIII. EXPECTED FIELD-SIZE DISTRIBUTION
   A. Source of data and confidence
   B. For analog basin?
   C. For analog play?
   D. Implications for exploration success

IX. DETERMINING MINIMUM ECONOMIC FIELD SIZE (MEFS)
   A. For the proposed area, estimate the cost of exploration (drilling, seismic, other G&G, land, overhead).
   B. At your estimated $PVX% per BOE (for example, $3.50 PV12% per MMBOE), how much total oil must you find to cover the above exploration costs?
   C. What is the smallest field (MMBOE) that could be profitable on a stand-alone basis, assuming several similar producing fields exist in this area?
   D. Divide B by C—Is it reasonable to suppose that many fields exist in the area? Reiterate until you have a reasonable number of economic fields that together would provide the total oil to cover only exploration costs. The average field size is MEFS.
   E. Divide MEFS by play chance to yield operational MEFS.

Appendix F

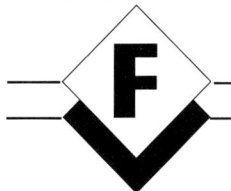

Reconstructing Parent Field-size Distributions from Offshore FSDs

Ordinarily, when one constructs a field-size distribution (FSD) for a given offshore producing trend (=play), *it has already been effectively truncated at the low end by the cost of platform construction and installation.* Smaller uncompleted accumulations—the kinds of accumulations that would routinely be completed as small fields if the trend were onshore—are simply reported as "good shows" encountered while drilling an exploratory dry hole. Ordinarily these will be indicated by positive drill-stem tests, or probable productive zones evidenced by borehole geophysical logs.

Moreover, the chance of success (Pc), defined by geologic chance factors (Pg), and multiplied by the percent of the natural distribution of accumulations of commercial size or larger, reflects this truncation.

But the parent FSD can be recreated, and the natural chance of success (defined by geologic chance factors) can be estimated, as illustrated below.

a. First, consider an FSD in a mature province such as west Texas, where you will complete any discovery well finding reserves adequate to cover completion costs, regardless of how much of the original exploratory investment (G&G, leasing, drilling, overhead) will be recovered **(Figure 38a)**. Practically, this means that any flowing discovery will be completed.

b. By comparison, suppose that exactly the same natural endowment and distribution of petroleum accumulations was present in a developing offshore trend in which 10 fields had been discovered and completed, and 14 of 40 total exploratory dry holes had reported flowing shows of oil and gas, which had been judged inadequate to support a platform **(Figure 38b)**.

Completed discoveries in
 objective reservoir zone 10
  Unsuccessful exploratory wells
   Uncompleted exploratory wells
    reporting flowing shows from
    objective 14
   Dry holes having no shows from
    objective 26
   Total failures 40
Total exploratory wells 50
Success ratio (Geologic) 24/50 = .48
Success ratio (Economic) 10/50 = .20

c. Now, let us suppose an observed offshore FSD (10 fields) as shown below:

FIELD	EUR (MMBOE)	FRACTILE CUMULATIVE %
J	5.6	90.9
I	7.4	81.8
H	9.5	72.7
G	12.8	63.6
F	17.0	54.5
E	23.5	45.5
D	35.0	36.4
C	55.0	27.3
B	100.0	18.8
A	235.0	9.1

d. The natural or parent distribution can be reconstructed as follows:
   1. Assume P99% = ≈10,000 BOE—estimated minimum reserves required to flow (i.e., to be detected);
   2. Total number of accumulations (14 shows + 10 fields) = 24= n;
   3. Incremental fractile % assigned to each accumulation = 100% ÷ (n + 1) = 25 = 4%;
   4. *Reconstructed parent distribution* **(Figure 38b)**:

FIELD	EUR (MMBOE)	FRACTILE CUMULATIVE %
14 small accumulations	~40,000 to 4.2 MMBOE	96% → 44%
J	5.6	40%
I	7.4	36%
H	9.5	32%
G	12.8	28%
F	17.0	24%
E	23.5	20%
D	35.0	16%
C	55.0	12%
B	100.0	8%
A	235.0	4%

e. *Discussion:* This reconstruction **(Figure 38b)** suggests that the effective (= commercial) threshold is currently about 5 MMBOE = P42%, so Pmefs = 42%.

If, with additional technology and infrastructure, fields down to 2 MMBOE could be produced, the reconstructed FSD suggests that perhaps four of the show-holes may represent such fields.

Also, if one estimates the likelihood of finding a field larger than, say, 100 MMBOE (given that the test well indeed makes a discovery in the first place!), using the observed offshore FSD, such an event has a chance of about 18%. However, if one employs the "correct" FSD, reflecting the natural or parent distribution, the chance of finding the same 100 MMBOE or larger accumulation is greatly reduced, to only about 8% **(Figure 38b)**.

The important things for the offshore explorationist to grasp are that:

1. Any offshore FSD has already been naturally truncated by platform costs;
2. The parent FSD can be reconstructed **(Figure 38b)**;
3. Marginally economic opportunities are represented by uncompleted show-holes whose number can be estimated;
4. Probabilities associated with larger fields will be substantially overestimated unless the reconstructed parent FSD is used, especially for economically demanding offshore ventures; and
5. The operative chances of geologic and economic success for offshore trends can be "backed out" from the results reported to date.

Appendix F 151

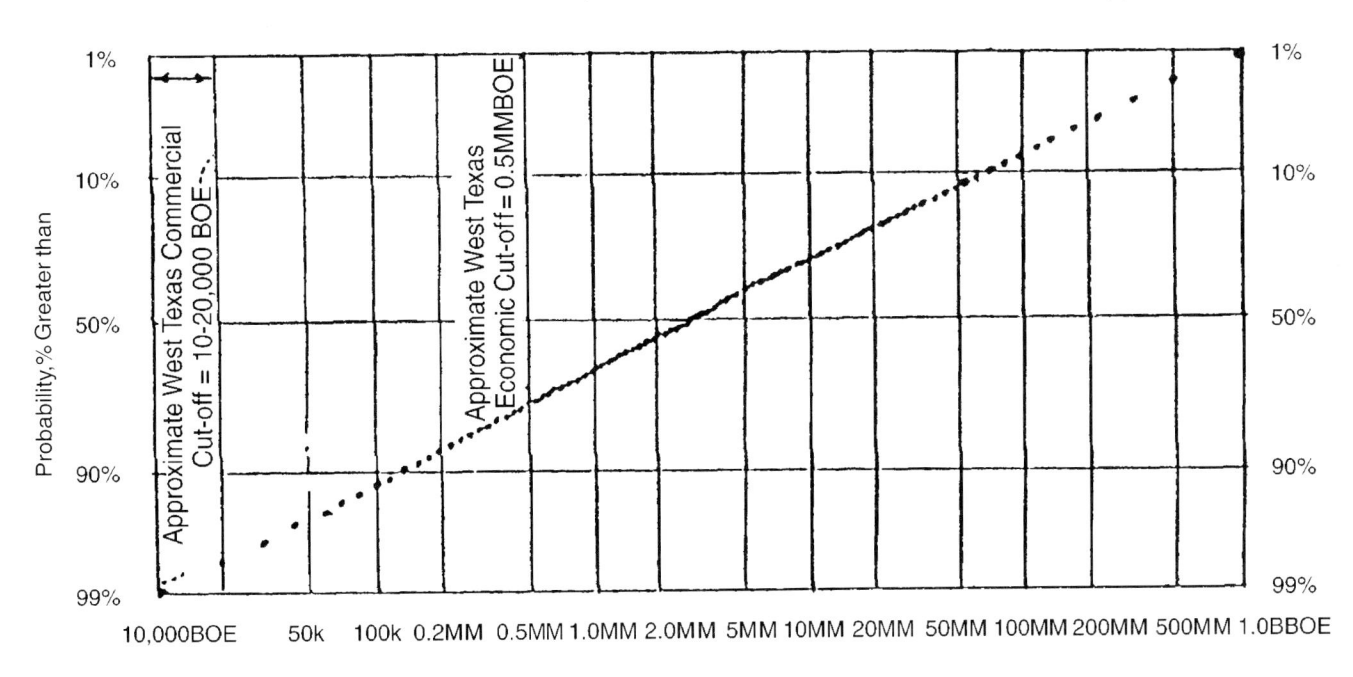

Figure 38 a

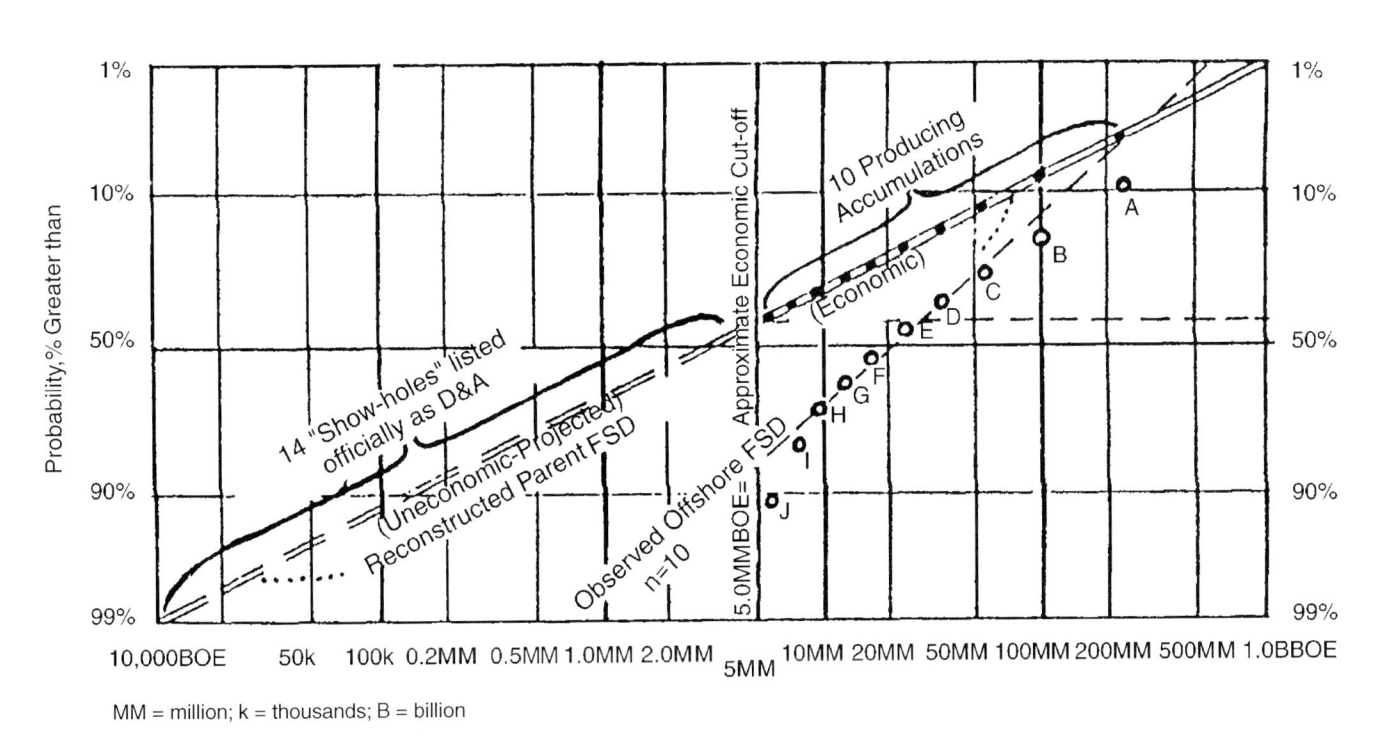

Figure 38 b

Figure 38 a, b *Offshore FSDs are truncated by platform cost.*

Appendix G

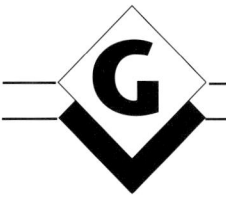

Matrix for Comparing, Ranking, and Planning New Exploration Plays

		Play Name Location, Basin, etc. Analog Plays				
Geotechnical Parameters	Working Interest	Effective WI				
	Reserves	MEFS				
		P90%				
		P50%				
		Pmean				
		P10%				
	Chance of Success	Shared Chance				
		Independent Chance				
		Pg				
		Pmefs				
		Pse				
		Critical Geo-Risks				
Economic Parameters	Unrisked NRI Value	Actual $Value (Net/Gross)				
		Present $Value (Net/Gross)				
	Costs	Explor. Failure Cost (Net/Gross)				
		Total Success Cost (Net/Gross)				
		Risked Finding Costs (Net/Gross)				
		Max. Neg. Cum. Net Cash Flow (Net/Gross)				
	Ranking Measures	EPV ($) (Net/Gross)				
		Risked Inv. Eff. At 100% WI				
		OWI (%) At Corp. Risk Tolerance				
		Risked Inv. Eff. At OWI				
	$PV, Net Economic Reserves Outcomes ($MM)	Total Failure				
		Worst Case				
		P90%				
		P50%				
		Pmean				
		P10%				
Business Criteria	Timing	Start Date				
		Max. Neg. Net Cash Flow (Date)				
		Payout Date				
		Project Life				
	Political Risks & Consequences	Primary				
		Secondary				
	Operating Risks & Consequences	Primary				
		Secondary				
	Method of Acquisition					
	Business Needs & Sensitivities	Contractual Needs				
		Contractual Concessions				
		Negotiating Strategies				
	Personnel & Service Needs	New Staff				
		Tech Services				
Comments & References						

References Cited

Alexander, J.A., and J.R. Lohr, 1998, Risk Analysis—Lessons Learned: SPE 49030: Society of Petroleum Engineers Annual Meeting, New Orleans.

Andreatta, G., and G.M. Kaufman, 1986, Estimation of Finite Population Properties when Sampling is without Replacement and Proportional to Magnitude: Journal of the American Statistical Association, Vol. 81, No. 395, p. 657–666.

Arps, J.K., and T.G. Roberts, 1958, Economics of Drilling for Cretaceous Oil and Gas on the East Flank of the Denver-Julesberg Basin: AAPG Bulletin, Vol. 42, No. 11, p. 2549–2566.

Arthur, M.A., and S.O. Schlanger, 1979, Cretaceous "Ocean Anoxic Events" as Causal Factors Development of Reef Reservoired Giant Oil Fields: AAPG Bulletin, Vol. 63, p. 870–885.

Attanasi, E.D., and D.H. Root, 1994, The Enigma of Oil and Gas Field Growth: AAPG Bulletin, Vol. 78, No. 3, p. 321–332.

Baker, R.A., 1988, When is a Prospect or Play Played Out?: Oil and Gas Journal, January 11, p. 77–80.

Baker, R.A., H.M. Gehman, W.R. James, and D.A. White, 1986, Geologic Field Number and Size Assessments of Oil and Gas Plays, in Rice, D.D., ed., Oil and Gas Assessment—Methods and Applications: AAPG Studies in Geology, No. 21, p. 25–31.

Bally, W., and S. Snelson, 1980, Realms of Subsidence, in Miall, A.D., ed., Facts and Principles of World Petroleum Occurrence: Canadian Society of Petroleum Geologists, Memoir 6, p. 9–94.

Bayes, T., 1764, An Essay Toward Solving a Problem in the Doctrine of Chances, in Bernstein, P.L., 1996, Against the Gods, the Remarkable Story of Risk: John Wiley & Sons, New York, 383 p.

Bernoulli, D., 1738, Specimen Theoriae Novae de Mensura Sortis (Exposition of a New Theory on the Measurement of Risk), in Bernstein, P.L., 1996, Against the Gods, the Remarkable Story of Risk: John Wiley & Sons, New York, 383 p.

Bernoulli, J., 1713, Ars Conjectandi, in Bernstein, P.L., 1996, Against the Gods, the Remarkable Story of Risk: John Wiley & Sons, New York, 383 p.

Bernstein, P.L., 1996, Against the Gods, the Remarkable Story of Risk: John Wiley & Sons, New York, 383 p.

Boccia, A., 1996, The Trouble with High Risk Exploration: Carlisle Associates, Cambridge, Mass., May, p. 1–4.

Brealey, R.A., and S.C. Myers, 1988, Principles of Corporate Finance: McGraw-Hill, New York, 889 p.

Brown, P.J., and P.R. Rose, 2000, The "Gray Area" between Prospects and Plays—Assessing Volumes, Value, and Chance: EAGE 62nd Conference, Glasgow, Scotland, p. A-33.

Capen, E.C., 1976, The Difficulty of Assessing Uncertainty: Journal of Petroleum Technology, August, p. 843–850.

Capen, E.C., 1984, Why Lognormal?, in Capen, E.C., R.E. Megill, and P.R. Rose, eds., Course notes for AAPG School "Managing and Evaluating Petroleum Risk": AAPG Education Dept., Tulsa, Okla., 350 p.

Capen, E.C., 1991, Rethinking Sunk Costs: SPE 22017, Hydrocarbon Economics & Evaluation Symposium: Society of Petroleum Engineers, Dallas, p. 1–6.

Capen, E.C., 1992, Dealing with Exploration Uncertainties, in Steinmetz, R., ed., The Business of Petroleum Exploration: AAPG Treatise of Petroleum Geology—Handbook of Petroleum Geology, Chapter 5, p. 29–61 (plus 4 errata pages for some printings).

Capen, E.C., 1995, A Problem with Experts: SPE Hydrocarbon Economics and Evaluation Symposium Proceedings: Society of Petroleum Engineers, Dallas, p. 255–266.

Capen, E.C., 1996, A Consistent Probabilistic Definition of Reserves: SPE Reservoir Engineering: Society of Petroleum Engineers, Dallas, p. 23–28.

Capen, E.C., R.V. Clapp, and W.M. Campbell, 1971, Competitive Bidding in High-Risk Situations: Journal of Petroleum Technology (SPE-AIME), June, p. 24–36.

Capen, E.C., R.V. Clapp, and W.W. Phelps, 1976, Growth Rate—A Rate-of-Return Measure of Investment Efficiency: Journal of Petroleum Technology, May, p. 531–543.

Cardono, G., 1545, Ars Magna, in Bernstein, P.L., 1996, Against the Gods, the Remarkable Story of Risk: John Wiley & Sons, New York, 383 p.

Chamberlin, T.C., 1931, The Method of Multiple Working Hypotheses: Journal of Geology, Vol. 39, No. 2, p. 155–165.

Chorn, L.G., 1999, Matching the Analysis Technique to the Investment Problem: Traditional DCF to Real Options: Society of Petroleum Engineers #52950, presented at the SPE Hydrocarbon Economics and Evaluation Symposium, Dallas, March 1999.

Clapp, R.V., 1995, An Alternative Concept of Investment for Improved Profitability Measures: SPE 30051, Hydrocarbon Economics & Evaluation Symposium: Society of Petroleum Engineers, Dallas, March 26–28, p. 179–185.

References Cited

Clapp, R.V., and R.D. Stibolt, 1991, Useful Measures of Exploration Performance: Journal of Petroleum Technology, October, p. 1252–1257.

Coleman, J.M., and D.B. Prior, 1982, Deltaic Environments, in Scholle, P.A., and D. Spearing, eds., Sandstone Depositional Environments: AAPG Memoir 31, p. 139–178.

Cozzolino, J.M., 1977, A New Method for Risk Analysis: Massachusetts Institute of Technology, Sloan Management Review, Vol. 20, No. 3, p. 53–66.

Cozzolino, J.M., 1978, A New Method for Measurement & Control of Exploration Risk: Society of Petroleum Engineers of AIME, SPE 6632, March, 37 p.

Cronquist, Chapman, 1997, SPE/WPC Reserves Definitions Approved: Journal of Petroleum Technology, May, p. 527–528.

David, F.N., 1962, Correspondence between Blaise Pascal and Pierre de Fermat, as reported by David, F. N., in Games, Gods, and Gambling: Hafner Publishing Co., New York, p. 229–253.

De Moivre, A., 1733, Doctrine of Chances, in Bernstein, P.L., 1996, Against the Gods, the Remarkable Story of Risk: John Wiley & Sons, New York, 383 p.

Demaison, G., 1984, The Generative Basin Concept, in Demaison, G., and R.J. Murris, eds., Petroleum Geochemistry and Basin Evaluation: AAPG Memoir 35, p. 1–14.

Demaison, G., and B.J. Huizinga, 1994, Genetic Classification of Petroleum Systems Using Three Factors: Charge, Migration, and Entrapment, in Magoon, L.B., and W.G. Dow, eds., The Petroleum System—from Source to Trap: AAPG Memoir 60, p. 73–89.

Dickinson, W.R., 1974, Plate Tectonics and Sedimentation, in Dickinson, W.R., ed., Tectonics and Sedimentation: Society of Economic Paleontologists and Mineralogists (SEPM) Special Publication 22, p. 1–27.

Dixit, A.K., and R.S. Pindyck, 1994, Investment Under Uncertainty: Princeton University Press, Princeton, N.J., 468 p.

Dott, R.H., Sr., and M.J. Reynolds, 1969, Sourcebook for Petroleum Geology: AAPG Memoir 5, 471 p.

Downey, M.W., 1992, It All Begins with People, in Steinmetz, R., ed., The Business of Petroleum Exploration: AAPG Treatise of Petroleum Geology—Handbook of Petroleum Geology, Chapter 16, p. 201-203.

Drew, L.J., 1990, Oil and Gas Forecasting, Reflections of a Petroleum Geologist: Oxford University Press, New York, Oxford, 252 p.

Edwards, W., 1982, Conservatism in Human Information Processing, in Kahnemann, D., P. Slovic, and A. Tversky, eds., Judgment Under Uncertainty: Heuristics and Biases: Cambridge University Press, New York, p. 359–369.

Fisk, H.N., 1954, Sedimentary Framework of the Modern Mississippi Delta: Journal of Sedimentary Petrology, Vol. 24, p. 76–99.

Forman, D.J., and A.L. Hinde, 1986, Examination of the Creaming Methods of Assessment Applied to the Gippsland Basin, Offshore Australia, in Rice, D.D., ed., Oil and Gas Assessment—Methods and Applications: AAPG Studies in Geology No. 21, p. 101–110.

Gehmann, H.N., 1970, Graphs to Derive Geometric Correction Factor: Exxon Training Materials (unpublished), Houston.

Graunt, J., and W. Petty, 1662, Natural and Political Observations Made upon the Bills of Mortality, in Bernstein, P.L., 1996, Against the Gods, the Remarkable Story of Risk: John Wiley & Sons, New York, 383 p.

Grayson, C.J., Jr., 1960, Decisions Under Uncertainty, Drilling Decisions by Oil and Gas Operators: Harvard University Graduate School of Business Administration, Boston, 402 p.

Halley, E., 1693, Transactions, in Bernstein, P.L., 1996, Against the Gods, the Remarkable Story of Risk: John Wiley & Sons, New York, 383 p.

Harper, F.G., 1999, BP Prediction Accuracy in Prospect Assessment: A 15-Year Retrospective: preprint of paper to be presented at AAPG International Conference, Birmingham, England.

Horner, D., 1990, On the Theory of Inevitable Disappointment, Decision Making Under Risk: Theoretical Note No. 21 (unpublished), 2 p.

Howell, J.I. III, R.N. Anderson, A. Boulanger, and B. Bentz, 1998, Managing E&P Assets from a Portfolio Perspective: Oil and Gas Journal, November 30, p. 54–57.

Hunt, J.M., M.D. Lewen, and R.J.C. Henuet, 1991, Modeling Oil Generation with Time and Temperature Index Graphs Bend on the Arrhenius Equation: AAPG Bulletin, Vol. 75, No. 4, p. 795–807.

Johns, D.R., S.G. Squire, and M.J. Ryans, 1998, Measuring Exploration Performance and Improving Exploration from Predictions—with Examples from Santos' Exploration Program: Proceedings of 1998 Australian Petroleum Producing and Exploration Association, Canberra.

Johnson, B., 1992, Polarity Management: HRD Press, Amherst, Mass.

Johnston, D., 1997a, Oil Company Financial Analysis in Nontechnical Language, 3rd printing: PennWell Books, Tulsa, Okla., 362 p.

Johnston, D., 1997b, International Petroleum Fiscal Systems and Production Sharing Contracts, 3rd printing: PennWell Books, Tulsa, Okla., 325 p.

Jones, D.R., and M. Smith, 1983, Ranking South Louisiana Trends by Probability of Economic Success: Oil and Gas Journal, October 24, p. 149–156.

Kaufman, G.M., 1962, Statistical Decision and Related Techniques in Oil and Gas Exploration: Prentice-Hall, New York, 307 p.

Kaufman, G.M., 1983, Oil and Gas—Estimation of Widespread Resources, in Adelman, et al., eds., Energy Resources in an Uncertain Future: Ballinger, Cambridge, Mass., 434 p.

Klemme, H.D., 1975, Giant Oil Fields Related to Their Geologic Setting—a Possible Guide to Exploration: Bulletin of Canadian Petroleum Geology, Vol. 23, p. 30–66.

Klemme, H.D., 1980, The Geology of Future Petroleum Provinces: Revue de l'Institute Francais de Petrole, Vol. 35, No. 2, Special issue for 25th International Geological Congress, Paris, p. 337–349.

Klemme, H.D., and G.F. Ulmishek, 1991, Effective Petroleum Source Rocks of the World: Stratigraphic Distribution and Controlling Depositional Factors: AAPG Bulletin, Vol. 75, p. 1809–1851.

Landes, K.K., 1951, Petroleum Geology, 1st edition: John Wiley & Sons, New York, 660 p.

Lehman, J., 1989, Valuing Oilfield Investments Using Option Pricing Theory: Society of Petroleum Engineers, SPE 18923, p. 125–136.

Lerche, I., and J.A. MacKay, 1999, Economic Risk in Hydrocarbon Exploration: Academic Press, 20 p.

Levorson, A.I., 1967, Geology of Petroleum: W.H. Freeman & Co., San Francisco, 724 p.

Lohrenz, J., 1988, Profitabilities on Federal Offshore Oil and Gas Leases: A Review: Journal of Petroleum Technology, June, p. 760–764.

MacKay, J.A., 1995, Utilizing Risk Tolerance to Optimize Working Interest: SPE 30043, Hydrocarbon Economics & Evaluation Symposium: Society of Petroleum Engineers, Dallas, p. 103–110.

MacKay, J.A., 1996, Risk Management in International Petroleum Ventures; Ideas from a Hedberg Conference: AAPG Bulletin, Vol. 80, No. 12, p. 1845–1849.

Magoon, L.B., 1988, The Petroleum System, A Classification Scheme for Research, Exploration and Resource Assessment, in Magoon, L.B., ed., Petroleum Systems of the United States: USGS Bulletin 1870, p. 2–15.

Magoon, L.B., and W.G. Dow, 1994, The Petroleum System, in Magoon, L.B., and W.G. Dow, eds., The Petroleum System—from Source to Trap: AAPG Memoir 60, p. 3–24.

Mann, D., G. Goobie, and L. MacMillian, 1992, Options Theory and Strategic Investment Decisions: Journal of Canadian Petroleum Technology, Vol. 31, No. 5, p. 52–55.

Markowitz, H.M., 1952, Portfolio Selection: Journal of Finance, Vol. VII, No. 1, March, p. 77–91.

McCrossan, R.G., ed., 1973, The Future Petroleum Provinces of Canada—Their Geology and Potential: Canadian Society of Petroleum Geologists, Memoir No. 1, 720 p.

McMaster, G.E., 1998, New Trends in Exploration Risk Analysis: privately printed paper for limited circulation by Amoco Corporation.

McMaster, G.E., and P.D. Carragher, 1996, Risk Assessment and Portfolio Analysis: The Key to Exploration Success: privately printed paper for limited circulation by Amoco Corporation.

Megill, R.E., 1984, 1977, An Introduction to Exploration Risk Analysis, 2nd and 1st editions: PennWell Publishing Co., Tulsa, Okla., 273 p.

Megill, R.E., 1985, Long-range Exploration Planning: PennWell Publishing Co., Tulsa, Okla., 90 p.

Megill, R.E., 1988, 1979, 1971, An Introduction to Exploration Economics, 3rd, 2nd, and 1st editions: PennWell Publishing Co., Tulsa, Okla.

Megill, R.E., 1992, Exploration Economics, in Steinmetz, R., ed., The Business of Petroleum Exploration: AAPG Treatise of Petroleum Geology—Handbook of Petroleum Geology, Chapter 10, p. 107–115.

Megill, R.E., and R.B. Wightman, 1984, The Ubiquitous Overbid: AAPG Bulletin, Vol. 78, No. 4, p. 417–425.

Miall, A.D., 1984, Principles of Sedimentary Basin Analysis: Springer-Verlag, New York, 490 p.

Miller, B.M., 1986, Resource Appraisal Methods: Choice and Outcome, in Rice, D.D., ed., Oil and Gas Assessment—Methods and Applications: AAPG Studies in Geology No. 21, p. 1–23.

Moody, J.D., J.W. Mooney, and J. Spivack, 1970, Giant Oil Fields of North America, in Halbouty, M.T., ed., Geology of Giant Petroleum Fields: AAPG Memoir 14, p. 8–18.

Moran, S., 1992, Analysis of International Oil and Gas Contracts, in Steinmetz, R., ed., The Business of Petroleum Exploration: AAPG Treatise of Petroleum Geology—Handbook of Petroleum Geology, Chapter 25, p. 307–318.

Murris, R.J., 1984, Introduction, in Demaison, G., and R.J. Murris, eds., Petroleum Geochemistry and Basin Evaluation: AAPG Memoir 35, p. x–xii.

Murtha, R.J., 1995, Estimating Reserves and Success for a Prospect with Geologically Dependent Layers: Proceedings of 1995 SPE Hydrocarbon Economics and Evaluation Symposium, Dallas, p. 73–84.

Nederlof, M.H., 1979, The Use of Habitat of Oil Models in Exploration Prospect Appraisal: Proceedings from the 10th World Petroleum Congress, Panel Discussion 1, Paper 2, p. 13–24.

Newell, N.D., J.K. Rigby, A.G. Fischer, A.J. Whiteman, J.E. Hickox, and J.S. Bradley, 1953, The Permian Reef Complex of the Guadalupe Mountains Region, Texas and New Mexico: W.H. Freeman & Co., San Francisco, 230 p.

Newendorp, P.D., 1975, Decision Analysis for Petroleum Exploration: Petroleum Publishing Company, Tulsa, Okla., 668 p.

Otis, R.M., and N. Schneidermann, 1997, A Process for Evaluating Exploration Prospects: AAPG Bulletin, Vol. 81, No. 7, p. 1087–1109.

Owen, E.W., 1975, Trek of the Oil Finders: A History of Exploration for Petroleum: AAPG Memoir 6, 1647 p.

Paddock, J.L., D.R. Siegel, and J.L. Smith, 1983, Option Valuation of Claims on Physical Assets: The Case of Offshore Petroleum Leases: MIT Working Paper No. MIT-EL 83-005WP, p. 1–40.

Pascal, B., and P. de Fermat, 1654, as reported by David, F.N., in Games, Gods, and Gambling: Hafner Publishing Co., New York, p. 229–253.

Pees, S.T., ed., 1989, History of the Petroleum Industry Symposium—Guidebook: AAPG, Tulsa, Okla., 84 p.

Pickles, E., and J.L. Smith, 1993, Petroleum Property Valuations: A Binomial Lattice Implementation of Option Pricing Theory: The Energy Journal, Vol. 14, No. 2, p. 1–26.

Pray, L.C., 1988, The Western Escarpment of the Guadalupe Mountains, Texas, and Day Two of the Field Seminar, in Tomlinson Reid, S., R.O. Bass, and P. Welch, eds., Guadalupe Mountains Revisited—Texas and New Mexico: West Texas Geological Society Publication 88-84, p. 23–31.

Rose, P.R., 1984, Checklist for a Pragmatist, in Capen, E.C., R.E. Megill, and P.R. Rose, eds., Notes for AAPG short course "Prospect Evaluation," Chapter 5: AAPG Education Dept., Tulsa, Okla., 2 p.

Rose, P.R., 1987, Dealing with Risk and Uncertainty in Exploration: How Can We Improve?: AAPG Bulletin, Vol. 71, No. 1, p. 1–16.

Rose, P.R., 1992a, Chance of Success and Its Use in Petroleum Exploration, in Steinmetz, R., ed., The Business of Petroleum Exploration: AAPG Treatise of Petroleum Geology—Handbook of Petroleum Geology, Chapter 7, p. 71–86.

Rose, P.R., 1992b, Risk Behavior in Petroleum Exploration, in Steinmetz, R., ed., The Business of Petroleum Exploration: AAPG Treatise of Petroleum Geology—Handbook of Petroleum Geology, Chapter 9, p. 95–104.

References Cited

Rose, P.R., 1994, Implementing Risk Analysis in Exploration Organizations: What Works? What Doesn't?, Program: AAPG Annual Convention Abstracts, Denver, June 12–15, p. 245–246.

Rose, P.R., 1995, Getting from Geological Chance-factors to Chance of Economic Success: What Are We Risking?: AAPG Annual Convention Abstracts, Houston, March 5–8, p. 83A.

Rose, P.R., 1996a, Exploration Plays: Risk Analysis and Economic Assessment, Course notes for AAPG short course: AAPG Education Dept., Tulsa, Okla., 400 p.

Rose, P.R., 1996b, Risk Analysis of Exploration Plays, Abstract: AAPG Bulletin, p. 1331.

Rose, P.R., 1996c, Making Better Estimates of Prospect Reserves: AAPG Annual Convention Abstracts, San Diego, May 19–22, p. 122A.

Rose, P.R., 1997, Risk Analysis of Petroleum Exploration Ventures by Modern Corporations: A Report Commissioned by Japan National Oil Corporation, March, 102 p.

Rose, P.R., 1998, Exploration Plays: Risk Analysis and Economic Assessment: A Report Commissioned by Japan National Oil Corporation, February, 103 p.

Rose, P.R., 1999, Common Methods for Acquiring Petroleum Rights: Advantages and Disadvantages: Society of Professional Earth Scientists Newsletter, May, Vol. 37, p. 1–7.

Rose, P.R., and R.S. Thompson, 1992, Economics and Risk Assessment in Development Geology, in Morton-Thompson, D., and A.H. Woods, eds., Development Geology Reference Manual: AAPG Methods in Exploration Series No. 10, p. 1–57.

Roy, K.J., 1975, Hydrocarbon Assessment Using Subjective Probability and Monte Carlo Methods, in Grenon, M., ed., Methods and Models for Assessing Energy Resources: Proceedings of the First IIASA Conference on Energy Resources: International Institute for Applied Systems Analysis, Luxemburge, Austria, p. 279–290.

Schuyler, J.R., 1989, Applying Expected Monetary Value Concept: How Many Prospects is Enough?: Oil and Gas Journal, December 11, p. 87–90.

Sloss, L.L., 1963, Sequences in the Cratonic Interior of North America: Geological Society of America Bulletin, Vol. 74, p. 93–114.

Sluijk, D., and M.H. Nederlof, 1984, Worldwide Geological Experience as a Systematic Basis for Prospect Appraisal, in Demaison, G., and R.J. Murris, eds., Petroleum Geochemistry and Basin Evaluation: AAPG Memoir 35, p. 15–26.

Sluijk, D., and J.R. Parker, 1986, Comparison of Predrilling Predictions with Postdrilling Outcomes, Using Shell's Prospect Appraisal System, in Rice, D.D., ed., Oil and Gas Assessment—Methods and Applications: AAPG Studies in Geology #21, p. 55–58.

Squire, S.G., 1996, Reservoir and Pool Parameter Distributions from the Cooper/Eromanga Basin: Society of Petroleum Engineers, SPE 37365, 9 p.

St. John, B., 1992, Managing an Exploration Program for Success, in Steinmetz, R., ed., The Business of Petroleum Exploration: AAPG Treatise of Petroleum Geology—Handbook of Petroleum Geology, Chapter 15, p. 187–199.

Steinmetz, R., ed., 1992, The Business of Petroleum Exploration: Treatise of Petroleum Geology—Handbook of Petroleum Geology: AAPG, Tulsa, Okla., 382 p.

Stermole, F.J., and J.M. Stermole, 1990, Economic Evaluation and Investment Decisions, 7th edition: Investment Evaluations Corp., Golden, CO, 587 p.

Thaler, R.H., 1992, The Winner's Curse: Paradoxes and Anomalies of Economic Life: Free Press, New York, 230 p.

Thompson, R.S., and J.D. Wright, 1985, Oil Property Evaluation, 2nd edition: Thompson-Wright Associates, Golden, Colo., 243 p.

Tversky, A., and D. Kahnemann, 1974, Judgment Under Uncertainty: Heuristics and Biases: Science, Vol. 185, p. 1124–1131.

Uman, M., W.R. James, and H.R. Tomlinson, 1979, Oil and Gas in Offshore Tracts: Before and After Drilling: Science, Vol. 205, p. 489–491.

Vail, P.R., R.M. Mitchum, Jr., and S. Thompson III, 1977a, Seismic Stratigraphy and Global Changes of Sea Level, Part Three: Relative Changes of Sea Level from Coastal Onlap, in Payton, C.E., ed., Seismic Stratigraphy—Applications to Hydrocarbon Exploration: AAPG Memoir 26, p. 63–82.

Vail, P.R., R.M. Mitchum, Jr., and S. Thompson III, 1977b, Seismic Stratigraphy and Global Changes of Sea Level, Part Four: Global Cycles of Relative Changes of Sea Level, in Payton, C.E., ed., Seismic Stratigraphy—Applications to Hydrocarbon Exploration: AAPG Memoir 26, p. 83–98.

Waples, D.W., 1980, Time and Temperature in Petroleum Formation: Applications of Lopatin's Methods to Petroleum Exploration: AAPG Bulletin, Vol. 64, p. 916–926.

Waples, D.W., 1994, Maturity Modeling: Thermal Indicators—Hydrocarbon Generation and Oil Cracking, in Magoon, L.B., and W.G. Dow, eds., The Petroleum System—From Source to Trap: AAPG Memoir 60, p. 285–306.

White, D.A., 1980, Assessing Oil and Gas Plays in Facies-cycle Wedges: AAPG Bulletin, Vol. 64, No. 8, p. 1158–1178.

White, D.A., 1988, Oil and Gas Play Maps in Exploration and Assessment: AAPG Bulletin, Vol. 72, No. 8, p. 944–949.

White, D.A., 1992, Selecting and Assessing Plays, in Steinmetz, R., ed., The Business of Petroleum Exploration: Treatise of Petroleum Geology—Handbook of Petroleum Geology, Chapter 8, p. 87–94.

White, D.A., 1993, Geologic Risking Guide for Prospects and Plays: AAPG Bulletin, Vol. 77, No. 12, p. 2048–2061.

Wood, J.E., et al., 1990, The Domestic Oil and Gas Recoverable Resource Base: Supporting Analysis for the National Energy Strategy: Energy Information Administration, Office of Oil and Gas, US Dept. of Energy, SR/NES/90-05, 56 p.

Yergin, D., 1991, The Prize, The Epic Quest for Oil, Money, and Power: Simon & Schuster, New York, 877 p.

Index

Acquisition of petroleum rights, 93–99
Amerada, 95
Analog plays, 13, 65, 67, 69, 71–77, 148
Arco/Vastar, 95
Area, 127–130, 128
    field, 11, 22, 69, 70
    productive, 17–19
Area versus depth plot, 23
Area-wide sales, 95–97
Arithmetic mean, 125
Auctions, 98
Average net pay, 127–130
Average net pay thickness, 11–12, 19, 20, 21, 22
Average prospect (=local) chance, 84–85
Average reinvestment rate, 49

Barrels of oil equivalent (BOE), 50
    estimates versus actual, 7
    field-size distributions, 11–12
    large field discoveries, 2
Bias
    conservatism, 8
    motivational, 28
    overconfidence, 8
    overoptimism, 8
    patterns of, 45–46
    predictive, 45–46, 100
    prevalent optimistic, 6, 7
    risk decisions and, 91, 92
    under uncertainty, 8–10, 28–31
Bidding. *See also* Petroleum rights acquisition
    area-wide sales, 95–96
    overbidding, 95, 97–98
    sealed bonus, 94–98
Bidding efficiency, 95, 96
Black boxes in risk analysis, 123
Black-Scholes model, 52
BOE. *See* Barrels of oil equivalent
Business and political risks, 42–43
Business strategies, 107–111

Capital
    allocation, 99–100
    cost of, 49
    risk reduction, 93

Cash-flow analysis, discounted, 6, 24, 49–50, 53–54
Cash-flow models
    decision-tree analysis, 50
    exploration, 49–50
    in exploration risk analysis, 120
    segmented, 50
Cash-flow rate of return, discounted (DCFROR), 53–54
Casino analog, 1–2
Central Limit Theorem, 9, 10–11
Champions in risk analysis implementation, 121
Chance, 84–85
Chance adequacy matrix, 38
Chance factors
    business and political risks, 42–43
    geologic. *See* Geologic chance factors
    independent versus dependent, 41–42
    location and evaluation, 42
    mechanical, 42
    multiple-objective prospects, 41–42, 137–145
Checklist for petroleum prospectivity, 3, 65, 147–148
Chevron Oil, 58, 95
Closure, 3, 35, 65, 147–148
CNCF. *See* cumulative after-tax net cash flow
Combining ventures, 137–145
Commercial success (Pc), 24–25, 32–33, 38–42
Commercial truncation, 40
Competence in play analysis, 114–115
Completion success, 24, 33
Confidence level, 37, 38
Containment, 36, 148
Contracts, 6, 57, 88–89, 98–99
    analyzing terms, 88–89
    exploration, 57
    performance, 98
    problems, 57
    production sharing, 6
    sanctity of, 99
    terms, 110
Cookbook approach, 123
Corporate acquisitions, 4, 99
Corporate reinvestment rate, 49
Corporate system
    exploration risk analysis, 120
    industry practices, 120
    prospect evaluation, 31–32

160　Index

Cost
　　capital, 49
　　dry-hole, 54, 138–139
　　exploration, 85–86, 88
　　"sunk-cost concept," 40
Creaming curves, 68–69
Crystal Ball, 50
Cumulative after-tax net cash flow (CNCF), 50
Cumulative probability, 9–11

DCFROR. *See* Discounted cash-flow rate of return
DCF. *See* Discounted cash-flow analysis
Decision-tree analysis, 50, 100, 142, 143
Dependency, geologic, 137
Depositional topography, 63–64
DHC. *See* Dry-hole cost
DHIs. *See* Direct hydrocarbon indicators
Direct hydrocarbon indicators (DHIs), 24, 26
Discounted cash-flow (DCF) analysis, 6, 14, 24, 49–50, 53–54
Discounted cash-flow rate of return (DCFROR), 53–54
Discounting, 49–51, 95
Discount rates, 49–51
Discovery, economic, 40
Discovery process modeling, 67–68
Diversification and risk reduction, 93
Drilling prospects, identification, 3
Drilling technology, 3
Dry-hole analysis, 43, 44, 88
Dry-hole cost (DHC), 54, 138–139

Economic analysis, 49–56. *See also* Play risk analysis; Risk analysis
　　Black-Scholes model, 52
　　of capital, 49
　　cumulative after-tax net cash flow (CNCF), 50
　　DCF valuation problems, 50, 52
　　discounted cash-flow analysis, 6, 24, 49–51, 53–54
　　discounted cash-flow rate of return (DCFROR), 53–54
　　discount rates, 49–51
　　dry-hole cost (DHC), 54
　　expected net present value (ENPV), 54
　　exploration cash-flow models, 49–50
　　growth rate of return (GRR), 54
　　investment efficiency (IE), 54
　　maximum negative cash flow (MNCF), 54, 55
　　net investment cash-flow stream, 50
　　net present value (NPV), 50
　　optimum working interest (OWI), 55–56
　　option pricing theory, 52–53
　　present value factors, 51
　　recommended economic measures, 53–56
　　reinvestment rate, 49
　　risk-adjusted value (RAV), 54–55
　　"sensitivity analysis," 50
　　software, 50
　　time value of money, 49
Economic discovery, 40
Economic success (Pe), 24, 25, 32–33, 38–42
Economic truncation, 12, 40, 78–80
$ENPV_{(AT)}$. *See* Expected net present value (after tax)
ENPV. *See* Expected net present value

Estimated ultimate recovery (EUR), 4
Estimates, 9–15
　　barrels of oil equivalent (BOE), 7
　　biases under uncertainty, 8
　　commercial success (Pc), 39–40
　　deterministic, 5
　　economic success (Pe), 39–40
　　estimated ultimate recovery (EUR), 4
　　field number, 69–70, 88
　　geotechnical parameters, 5
　　geotechnical uncertainty, 6–8
　　improving, 13–15
　　lognormal distributions, 9–13, 125
　　low-side, 30, 131–135
　　probability of producible reserves, 3
　　prospect chance of success, 36, 41
　　prospect and play portfolios, 100–102
　　prospect reserves, 17–31
　　risk and uncertainty and, 5–6
　　subjective probability, 36
　　uncertainty and, 6–8
EUR. *See* Estimated ultimate recovery
EV. *See* Expected value
Excel, 50
Expected net present value (after tax) ($ENPV_{(AT)}$) equation, 5–6
Expected net present value (ENPV), 54
Expected value (EV), 1, 31, 91–92
Exploration
　　acquisition strategies, 4
　　cash-flow models, 49–50, 120
　　contract problems, 57
　　drilling prospect identification, 3
　　drilling technology, 3
　　exploration trend selection, 3
　　failure and success, 32–33
　　high-risk, 47–48
　　measuring value, 3–4
　　operations, 4
　　performance assessment, 113–115
　　planning, 112–113
　　play management, 107 116
　　portfolios, 1–2, 4, 105–107
　　projects as business ventures, 4
　　reservoir technology, 3
　　staged, 93–94
　　subjective probability estimates in, 36
Exploration cost, 85–86, 88
Exploration plays. *See* Plays
Exploration risk analysis, 117–123
　　corporate process, 120
　　implementing, 121–123
　　petroleum industry practices, 117–123
　　play analysis, 120–121
　　"prospector myth" versus systematic exploration, 117–119
Exxon, 58, 95

Failure, nongeologic aspects, 42–43
Field area, 11, 22, 69, 70
Field density, 69
Field number estimates, 69–70, 88

Field reserves, 69, 70
Field size, 4
    minimum commercial field size (MCFS), 61–62
    minimum economic field size (MEFS), 61–62, 77–78, 86, 89
    net present value, 89
Field-size distributions (FSDs), 11–12, 67–70, 89, 148
    analogs in play analysis, 13, 65, 67, 69, 148
    concepts and principles, 67–69
    creaming curves, 68–69
    discovery process modeling, 67–68
    economic truncation and, 12, 40, 78–80
    global, 72
    parent, from offshore FSDs, 12, 78, 80, 149–151
    and petroleum system approach, 60
    prediction with analog trends and interpretive shifts, 71–77
    production limited, 70–71
    production not established, 71, 72
    production well established, 70
    Texas Gulf Coast, 131, 132, 133
Flowability, 33
FSDs. *See* Field-size distributions

Geochemistry, 3
Geological Survey of Canada, 58
Geologic chance factors, 34–36, 38, 80–82
    closure (traps), 3, 35, 65, 147–148
    coincidence of, 80
    containment, 36
    and dry holes, 44
    hydrocarbon source rocks, 35
    independent versus dependent, 41–42, 137
    migration, 35
    multiple-objective prospects, 41–42, 137–145
    primary, 35–36
    recommended, 34–36
    reservoir rock, 3, 35, 147
    shared versus independent, 80, 82
    virtues of, 38
Geologic play maps, 64–65
Geologic reserves, 4
Geologic success (Pg), 32–33, 38
Geometric correction factor, 22
Geometry factor adjustment graph, 22
Geophysics, 3
Geotechnical analog models, 13
Geotechnical consistency, 105
Geotechnical estimates under uncertainty, 5–15. *See also* Estimates; Uncertainty
    improving, 13–15
    lognormality, 9–11
    prospect reserves, 6–8
Geotechnology, prospect and play portfolios, 100
Global discoveries, 2, 45
Government regulations, 110
Graphical methods, 9–11
    combining lognormal distributions, 25
    combining probabilistic distributions by multiplication, 127–130
    cumulative log probability, 10, 11
    cumulative probability, 9–11
    prospect reserves distribution, 24, 25
Gross rock volume (GRV), 19, 21, 23
Growth rate of return (GRR), 54
GRR. *See* Growth rate of return
GRV. *See* Gross rock volume
Gulf Oil, 95

HC-recovery factor, 23, 24, 127–130
Hydrocarbon accumulation, 34
Hydrocarbon charge model, 65
Hydrocarbon indicators, direct (DHIs), 24, 26
Hydrocarbon-recovery factor, 23, 24, 127–130
Hydrocarbon-recovery field reserves, 11–12
Hydrocarbon source rocks, 35

IE. *See* Investment efficiency
Incremental success, 33
Industry experience, 7, 28–30, 43–48
    actual industry performance, 43–44
    estimating prospect chance of success, 43–44, 43–48
    historical changes in trend success rates, 46–47
    impact of 3-D seismic data, 44–45
    overestimation of prospect reserves, 7, 28–30
    patterns of predictive bias, 45–46
    trouble with high-risk exploration, 47–48
    using trend or basin success rates, 46–47
Industry practices in exploration risk analysis, 117–123
Investment efficiency (IE), 54

Kerr-McGee Corp., 95
Kitchens, 58, 64, 65, 66, 147

Latin Hypercube simulation, 24, 127, 137
Lognormal distributions
    area, 19
    average net pay thickness, 19, 20, 21, 22
    calculating, 12–13, 125
    combining, 25
    graphing, 9–11, 118
    gross rock volume, 19, 21, 23
    importance of, 11
    mean (average), 12–13, 125
    and portfolio performance, 100–102
Lotus with @Risk, 50
Low-side estimates, 30, 131–135
Low-side values, RMAG prospect, 131

Management of exploration projects, 91–116
    acquiring petroleum rights, 93–99
    biases affecting risk decisions, 91, 92
    criteria indicating competence, 114–115
    good play managers, 115
    inventory and portfolio, 4
    optimum working interest, 92–93
    plays, 107–116
    prospect and play portfolios, 99–107
    risk-adjusted value, 91–93
    risk mitigation, 93
    risk and risk aversion, 91–93
    risk tolerance, 92–93

sealed bonus bidding, 94–98
staged exploration, 93–94
Maps, 63, 64–65
Markets, 110
Maximum negative cash flow (MNCF), 54, 55
MCFS. *See* Minimum commercial field size
Mean
arithmetic, 125
lognormal distribution, 12–13, 125
statistical, 13, 125
Swanson's, 13, 125
MEFS. *See* Minimum economic field size
MERR. *See* Minimum economic reserves required
Midland Basin/Red River Arch province, 131
Migration, 35
Minimum commercial field size (MCFS), 61–62
Minimum economic field size (MEFS), 61–62, 77–78, 86, 89, 148
Minimum economic reserves required (MERR), 78
MNCF. *See* Maximum negative cash flow
Mobil Oil, 95
Modeling
Black-Scholes model, 52
cash-flow, 49–50, 120
decision-tree analysis, 50, 142, 143
discovery process, 67–68
exploration, 49–50
exploration risk analysis, 120
geotechnical analog, 13
hydrocarbon charge, 65
kitchen geochemical, 58, 64, 65, 66
play analysis, 64, 65, 66, 87
Monte Carlo simulation, 24, 127, 137
combining multiple types of ventures, 140, 144–145
multiple-objective ventures, 137–145
Motivational bias, 28
Multiple-objective prospects, 41–42
Multiple-objective ventures, 137–145

Nature's envelopes, 14, 122
Net investment cash-flow stream, 50
Net present value (NPV), 14, 50, 89–90
Net revenue interest (NRI), 6
NPV. *See* Net present value
NRI. *See* Net revenue interest

Obligatory wells, 105
Offshore FSDs, 12, 78, 80, 149–151
One-well fields, 134–135
Optimum working interest (OWI), 55–56, 91–93
Option pricing theory, 52–53
OWI. *See* Optimum working interest

Parent field-size distributions, 12, 78, 80, 149–151
Performance
analysis, 43, 120
assessment, 100, 113–115
exploration, 113–115
forecasting, 100
plays versus prospects, 114
Performance contracts, 98

Petroleum-generative depressions, 64
Petroleum investigations, 60, 61
Petroleum prospectivity checklist, 3, 65, 147–148
Petroleum rights acquisition, 93–99
auctions, 98
conditions of acquisition, 94
corporate acquisitions, 99
overbidding, 95, 97–98
performance contracts, 98
private treaties, 98–99
sanctity of contracts, 99
sealed bonus bidding, 94–98
staged exploration, 93–94
Winner's Curse, 94–95, 96
Petroleum systems, 58–60, 61
Play (= shared) chance, 84
Play, definition, 3, 60
Play risk analysis, 57–90, 115–116. *See also* Economic analysis; Plays; Risk analysis
analogs in, 65, 67, 148
chance of play success, 80–83
economic play success, 82–83
geologic chance factors, 34–36, 38, 41–42, 80–82
criteria indicating competence, 114–115
geologic concepts, 62–67
economic truncation, 12, 40, 78–80
field-size distributions, 67–80, 86, 89
geologic play maps, 64–65, 87
geotechnical data, 84–87
$PV per BOE of discovered reserves, 86
average prospect chance, 84–85, 85, 87–88
cost of exploration, 85–86, 88
field number, 88, 89
play chance, 84, 85, 87
primary parameters, 84–86
secondary (derived) parameters, 86–87
"global anoxic events," 64
integration, 82–83
kitchen-geochemical modeling, 58, 64, 65, 66
patterns and principles, 115–116
play concept, 57–58
play selection, 60–61
plays and petroleum systems, 58–60, 61
procedure, 87–90
contracts, 57, 88–89
dry holes, 88
economic field-size distribution, 89
economic play success, 89
expected net present value, 90
exploratory tests, 86
key economic measures, 90
lease/acquisition price, 90
mean economic play reserves, 89
net present value, 88–89
play models and maps, 87
prospects versus plays, 61–62
stratigraphic sequences, 63–64
techniques, field number estimates, 69–70, 88
total geology integration, 64
working principles, 116
worldwide versus provincial source rocks, 64

Play risk analysis checklist, 3, 65, 147–148
Plays. *See also* Play risk analysis; Risk analysis
    comparing, ranking, and planning, 3, 111, 153
    data integration, 62
    exploration contracts, 57
    exploration performance, 113–115
    exploration planning, 3, 111–113, 153
    exploration play concept, 57–58
    field number estimates, 69–70, 88
    field-size distributions (FSDs), 67–70
    history and development, 57–58
    "kitchens," 58, 64, 65, 66, 147
    managing, 107–116
    minimum commercial field size (MCFS), 61–62
    minimum economic field size (MEFS), 61–62
    and petroleum systems, 58–60, 61
    play attributes and business strategies, 107–111
    play selection importance, 60–61
    plays versus prospects, 61–62
Portfolios, 99–107
    benefits, 99–100
    estimates, 100–102
    lognormality and performance, 100–102
    management, 1–2, 4, 99–107
    model, 101
    predictability versus size, 102–104
    problems with, 105–107
    prospect, 99–107
    requirements, 99
    selection, 120
    static versus dynamic, 105–106
Postdrill reviews, 122
Potential reserves, 4
Predictive bias, 100
Predictive performance, 26–28, 43, 100. *See also* Prospect chance of success; Success
Present value (PV), 6
Prevalent optimistic bias, 6, 7
Private treaties, 98–99
Probability
    chance adequacy matrix, 38
    cumulative distributions, 9–11, 127–130
    experience in assessing, 36–38
    field number estimates, 69–70, 88
    play risk analysis, 86, 89
    producible reserves, 3
    and risk analysis, 2–3
    subjective estimates, 36
    uncertainty and, 26
Producible reserves, 3
Production sharing contracts, 6
Productive area, 17–19
Productive field area, 22
Productive field areas graph, 22
Profitability distribution, 24
Profitability of producible reserves, 3
Prospect
    definition, 57
    evaluation, 31–32, 137–145
    generation versus risk analysis, 122
    identification, 3
    multiple-objective, 41–42, 137–145
    play versus, 61–62
Prospect chance of success. *See also* Success
    commercial, 38–42
    corporate system and, 31–32
    economic, 38–42
    estimating, 41
    expected value concept, 31
    exploration risk analysis, 120
    geologic chance factors, 34–36, 38, 41–42
    geologic components, 34–36
    implementation, 36–38
    industry experience, 43–48
    monitoring and improving predictive performance, 43
    nongeologic aspects, 42–43
    patterns of predictive bias, 45–46
    predictive performance, 26–28, 43, 100
    subjective probability estimates, 36
    success rates, 32–33
Prospectivity checklist, 3, 65, 147–148
Prospectors, 2, 117–119
Prospect and play portfolios. *See* Portfolios
Prospect-reserves distribution, 24–26, 38–42
Prospect-reserves forecasting, 6
Prospect risk analysis, 4. *See also* Prospect chance of success; Prospect-reserves distribution
    average net pay thickness, 19, 20, 21, 22
    distribution, 24–26
    estimating reserves, 6–8, 17–31, 131–135
        gross rock volume, 19, 21, 23
        hydrocarbon-recovery factor, 23, 24
        industry experience, 28–31
        "low-side" values, 131–135
        monitoring and improving predictive performance, 26–28
        multiple-objective ventures, 41–42, 137–145
        overestimation, 7, 28, 29, 30
        parameters, 17–24
        productive area, 17–19, 20, 21, 22
        structural geometry, 131–132, 133, 134
    geometric correction factor, 19, 22
    gross rock volume, 19, 21, 23
    hydrocarbon recovery factor, 23, 24
    industry experience, 28–31
    monitoring and improving predictive performance, 26–28
    productive area, 17–19
PV. *See* Present value

RAV. *See* Risk-adjusted value
Reality checks, 120
    improving estimates, 14
    probability ranges of ventures with varying uncertainties, 26
    prospect reserves estimates, 20
Record keeping, 43
Regional mapping, 63
Reinvestment rate, 49
Reserves, 4
    calculating, 127–130
    economic play, 87, 89
Reservoir rock, 3, 35, 147

Reservoir technology, 3
Risk, 5–6, 42–43
Risk-adjusted value (RAV), 54–55, 91
Risk analysis, 2–4, 121–123. *See also* Economic analysis; Play risk analysis; Prospect risk analysis
   background and history, 2–3
   corporate process for, 120
   estimated geotechnical parameters, 5
   expected value (EV) concept, 91–92
   exploration, 117–123
   field number estimation, 69–70, 88
   field-size distributions (FSDs), 67–70
   geotechnical uncertainty, 6–8
   implementation, 121–123
   optimum working interest (OWI), 91–93
   and petroleum exploration, 3–4
   plays versus prospects, 61–62
   risk-adjusted value (RAV), 54–55, 91
   risk and risk aversion, 91–93
   risk tolerance (RT), 91–92
   risk and uncertainty, 5–6
Risk analysis software, 120
Risk reduction, 93
Rocky Mountain Association of Geologists (RMAG) prospect, 131

Scheduling, 100
Sealed bonus bidding, 94–98
Sea-level stands, 64
Sedimentary basin analysis, 58
"Sensitivity analysis," 50
Shell Oil, 58, 95
Shows, 33
Silurian (Niagaran), 131
Single-value forecasts, 5
Software
   Basin-Mod, 64
   Excel with Crystal Ball, 50
   Lotus with @Risk, 50
   risk analysis, 120
   Statistical mean, 13, 125
Statistics
   bell-shaped curve, 9
   Central Limit Theorem, 9, 10–11
   cumulative log probability distributions, 11
   cumulative probability distribution, 9–10
   "equal to or less than" versus "equal to or greater than," 9
   graphical methods, 9–11
   improving estimates with, 14
   lognormal distributions, 9–13, 25, 100–102, 125
   mean of lognormal distributions, 12–13, 125
   in risk analysis, 2–3
Stratigraphy, 3, 63–64
Subjective probability estimates, 36
Success. *See also* Prospect chance of success
   business and political risks, 42–43
   commercial, 32–33, 38–42, 82
   completion, 33
   economic, 25, 32–33, 38–42
   economic play, 80–83, 86, 89
   geologic, 32–33, 38–42
   incremental, 33
   nongeologic aspects, 42–43
   technical and mechanical effects, 42
Success rates
   basin, 46–47
   by well class, 45
   predicted versus actual, 43
   technology and, 42
   trend, 46–47
   wildcat, 45, 46
"Sunk-cost concept," 40
Swanson's Mean, 13, 125
Swanson's Rule, 128

Technology and success rates, 42
Tenneco, 95
Texaco, 95
Texas Bureau of Economic Geology, 58
"Theory of Inevitable Disappointment," 106–107
Three-dimensional (3-D) seismic data, 24, 26
   and exploration performance, 44–45
Time value of money, 49
Traps (closure), 35, 147–148
   type, 131–132, 133, 134
Truncation, 12, 40, 78–80

Ubiquitous Overbid, 95, 97–98
Uncertainty. *See also* Risk
   biases affecting judgment under, 8–9, 28–31
   estimating risk and, 5–6
   expressing, 6–8
   geotechnical, 6–8
   magnitude of, 6
   reducing, 30–31
   risk and, 5
   substantial, 6
Universal prospect risking scheme, 43
Unocal, 95
U.S. Geological Survey, 58
U.S. Minerals Management Services, 58
Utility theory, 2–3

Value measurement, 3, 3–4
Volumetric reserves, 4

Wells
   field-size distributions and, 70
   obligatory, 105
   success rates by well class, 45
"Wildcat chance," 45, 46
Wildcat success rates, 45, 46, 117–119
Winner's Curse, 94–95, 96